THE ADVENTURE OF WEAK THEOLOGY

SUNY series in Theology and Continental Thought
Douglas L. Donkel, editor

THE ADVENTURE OF WEAK THEOLOGY

READING THE WORK OF JOHN D. CAPUTO THROUGH BIOGRAPHIES AND EVENTS

ŠTEFAN ŠTOFANÍK

Cover image, Autumn, by Sarah Mina C.

Published by State University of New York Press, Albany

Printed in the United States of America

For information, contact State University of New York Press, Albany, NY
www.sunypress.edu

Library of Congress Cataloging-in-Publication Data

Names: Stofanik, Stefan, author. | Schrijvers, Joeri, editor.
Title: The adventure of weak theology : reading the work of John D. Caputo through biographies and events / Stefan Stofanik ; edited by Joeri Schrijvers.
Description: Albany : State University of New York, 2018. | Series: SUNY series in theology and Continental thought | Includes bibliographical references and index.
Identifiers: LCCN 2017058940| ISBN 9781438471952 (hardcover : alk. paper) | ISBN 9781438471976 (e-book)
Subjects: LCSH: Caputo, John D. | Postmodernism—Religious aspects—Christianity. | Philosophical theology.
Classification: LCC B945.C144 S76 2018 | DDC 191—dc23 LC record available at https://lccn.loc.gov/2017058940

10 9 8 7 6 5 4 3 2 1

For Riba

Contents

FOREWORD ix
Lieven Boeve

EDITOR'S INTRODUCTION: Rain without Rain—Štefan Štofaník's *The Adventure of Weak Theology* xiii
Joeri Schrijvers

PREFACE xix

Introduction 1

1 Adventure 19

2 Call 27

3 Brother Paul 33

4 Transgression 39

5 Two Loves 49

6 Freedom 67

7 Interlude (More than One) 75

8 Freedom Again 91

9 Between Heidegger and Derrida 111

10 Dancing in the Void 155

11 The Advent of Weak Theology 173

12 Kingdom (In Place of a Conclusion) 183

Epilogue: How? 197

AFTERWORD: AN EAR FOR MY VOICE 231
John D. Caputo

NOTES 239

BIBLIOGRAPHY 271

INDEX 283

Foreword

There are two good reasons for this book to be published. First of all, of course, because it is a fine academic work on a contemporary continental philosopher who has a lot to say and about whom there is a lot to say. The second reason is that its author was never able to publish this book himself, having died in a car accident in May 2014. It should be clear, though, that the first reason is the one that is most important for publishing and reading this book.

The author, Štefan Štofaník, born in Košice (then still in Czechoslovakia) in 1976, arrived in Leuven in 2005 at the age of twenty-nine to study theology. As a young man of eighteen or nineteen years old, he spent a few years in what he characterized as a very traditional seminary in Slovakia, Spišska Kapitula-Spišske Pohradi, affiliated with the Faculty of Theology at the University of Bratislava, in order to become a priest. His grades were excellent, as we learn from the transcripts, and this allowed him to continue his studies in the St. Mary's Seminary and University in Baltimore, Maryland (USA). However, before being ordained, he left the seminary and came to the Katholieke Universiteit Leuven, initially in 2000, in order to enroll in the master's in European studies program, a degree he obtained magna cum laude in 2001. He then returned to Slovakia and started working as a journalist. In the meantime, he had married and became the father of two children. When the magazine for which he wrote collapsed in 2004, and with the European labor market now open, he decided to leave for the UK, in order to earn more money for his family. He worked there first as a waiter and after a few months as an office manager of a construction company. But the call of theology sounded and resounded, until he finally gave in. He applied to Leuven again, this time for the theology and religious studies program, which eventually gave him access to the doctoral program. At the same time, due to his excellent results, he was able to acquire a research fellowship at KU Leuven. Under my supervision, he was promoted to a doctorate in theology in 2013 with a dissertation on John D. Caputo and his work. And it is this doctoral research that constitutes the basis for this current book.

Over all these years, I came to know Štefan as very creative and determined but also at times a very shy and unsure scholar. In him, I would even dare to say, I sensed at least a bit of the depth of what might be called (if you will excuse the cliché) the "Slavonic soul," characterized on the one hand by deep melancholia and being burdened by the weight of time and history, and, on the other, by exuberant attempts to free oneself, at least temporarily, of this fate, in feasting, laughter, and event.

These biographical details are important for understanding Štefan Štofaník's book. To shed light on the work and achievement of John Caputo, it was not only Caputo's biography and writings that served Štefan in writing this work, and not only the biographically inspired writing of Antoine de Saint-Exupéry, whom he cites, but also his own biography, coming from a very rural and traditional Catholic atmosphere, and being challenged by the many ideas and events found outside that atmosphere. He wanted to do something significant with his life, and he did so by following the call of theology wherever it might lead him—and then assumed the task of making sense of religion and Christian faith today by entering into a deep dialogue with John Caputo. Indeed, in a very personal but consistent way, our author analyzes the work of one of the most prominent North American philosophers of religion and also deals with the turn to religion in contemporary continental philosophy, in particular its reception in phenomenology and deconstruction. Štofaník's study is a very daring and creative enterprise, which now and then seems to take the shape of a "study without study," and in this regard echoes the style of an author under scrutiny himself. Benevolent readers, however, will be charmed by the surprising and engaging way that the author leads them through his work. Less benevolent readers might let themselves be challenged by the methodological introduction and conclusion, which make an argument *pro domo* on behalf of our author and the way he chose to write this book.

Our author creatively employs several techniques that serve his cause but at the same time flirt with the limits of high academic formal writing. He follows a bio-bibliographical method, with the intention of showing how it came to pass that Caputo has developed the particular philosophical-theological career that he did, thus bearing witness to Johann Baptist Metz's adage that theology is always also biography. At the same time Štofaník engages in a conceptual archeology in relation to his biographical account, in which the internal development of some of the main concepts of Caputo's "weak theology" are displayed and commented upon. While doing so, Štofaník is not afraid to develop his own narrative line within the book, which leaves readers sometimes with the impression that they are reading a novel rather than an academic study. He very consistently and very aptly illustrates his analysis with excepts from the work of Saint-Exupéry, which for Štofaník not only makes the link to his own biography but also helps the reader to see more clearly the points made in the exposition in the chapters.

The way in which Štofaník proceeds makes reading this book an event: an event about an event; an event to try to understand an event, the event of the theology of the event. It leaves readers sometimes a bit puzzled, because this way of proceeding takes them by the hand, so to speak, that they become part of the story in the same way that the author himself has become part of it. A quite strange experience it must be for readers, then, and I would be very keen to know what this experience has meant for them.

Apart from this, however, there can hardly be any doubt that the argument of the book is consistent, both at the level of contents and of method. The author makes this clear along the road, and yet again in the chapter "Kingdom." As a matter of fact, in this book our author not only presents us with a creatively written analysis of Caputo's career, but also with a candid criticism and a proposal to think with, against, and at the same time beyond Caputo. At times, one might have wished that the author was even more critical of Caputo, but from the book itself it becomes clear why this is not so. In the end, despite all criticism, Caputo remains Štefan's hero.

In sum: both the analysis and the criticism are insightful and present the reader with a very nuanced picture of Caputo, the development of his work, and the "weak theology" he has come to argue for today. This book was definitely not meant to be the end of the trajectory, as it has no proper end. But it leads us to understand why a theology of the event, and its specific features, speaks to so many contemporaries who want to make sense of religion today and fear being encapsulated in closed narratives and rigid institutions. This book therefore offers an important and challenging lesson for all those who intend, from within the narrative and institution, to work on a theology that allows for the freedom to open oneself up for the event of God, and to bear witness to this event in the praxis of everyday life.

—Lieven Boeve

Editor's Introduction

Rain without Rain: Štefan Štofaník's *The Adventure of Weak Theology*

Štefan Štofaník. Friend. Colleague. Former seminarian. Father of two. These things don't even begin to describe him. Stef was a bit of a "character," as they say. I remember the days (and nights) we spent as members of the research group Theology in a Postmodern Context fondly.

The book lying before you is, in a way, Stef's intellectual testament. *The Adventure of Weak Theology*, first submitted as a doctoral dissertation and now turned into a book, seems like the best homage and honor one can do to Štefan. The book itself is remarkable. Presenting a sort of genealogy of Caputo's weak theology, it demands the reader be attentive and patient: even if at times Štofaník seems to lose track, he always reemerges with an inspiring point that sticks—only late in the book, for instance, will he tell us why Saint-Exupéry communicates for him the impossibility of inhabiting a (religious) tradition ironically, "without religion" that is (14).

My hope, sometimes, is that some of his points have inspired Caputo to write the intellectual autobiography *Hoping Against Hope: Confessions of a Postmodern Pilgrim* (2015). There has been very little contact between Caputo and Štofaník. I remember telling him, very, very often, to get in touch with Jack and exchange ideas, even to go and meet him or at least to try to get him on the jury of the dissertation. But, for one reason or other, Stef always was reluctant to do so—even if, occasionally, *yes, yes*, I will do so. The reason for this, one finds within this precious book, is that he wanted to have it published before getting in touch with his "object of study"—though he would have detested this term. He'd rather sit "in a rocking chair by the fire" (225), having a sip of some Redbreast and a smoke, before sending emails to "verify or falsify the hypothesis" of the present book.

Štefan had character. As a matter of fact, I am pretty sure he only contacted Caputo once his work was completed. Caputo then wrote to Štefan that he was "positively startled" that there was a chapter called "Brother Paul." Very few of us readers of Caputo would know of this episode in Caputo's life then, and Caputo was right in saying "that I would say is very perspicacious of you." As usual, Štefan downplayed Jack's high esteem of his work—the evidence is right there in this old Facebook conversation I had with Štefan, or: how even digital presences can spook.

Of course, Stef too had been in a seminary and had grown to love Caputo's ways in life, as they were particularly close to his own. Stef, too, had been accustomed to this "strong theology" that Caputo, sometimes desperately, seeks to expel. Stef, too, had had his troubles with the authoritarian manners of his teachers; left the seminary (but not until reading Saint-Exupéry's *Citadelle* under the covers, with a flashlight!); went to Bournemouth, England; came to Leuven; and then left the academy. Stef wanted to be a writer rather than a scholar—the quips at contemporary academia are never far off in this book, and perhaps are a bit all too sarcastic in the last chapter.

He was in Slovenia, with Polona, his girlfriend, I believe, when he finally emailed the manuscript to Caputo. I am not sure how much of the book Caputo had read then, but I can imagine his surprise. Here was a complete genealogy of his weak theology, traced back especially to his *Against Ethics*, that at times even ridicules Caputo's "coming out of the closet as a theologian." I think Caputo immediately recognized that here, in Štefan's book, was an intense personal involvement with this thought, and I think, too, that Štefan—a theologian without theology—pretty much saw Caputo for what he had always been, a theologian, but then one that is one of a kind and with the sort of personality of which Stef could say: "I particularly like this fellow."

That was the only motivation he had to write this book—he didn't want to be a scholar, nor a professor, nor did he care for a PhD all that much. Stef wanted to write. And write he did. I imagine, back in 2013, that this book was a bit of a surprise for Caputo, an event even. All of a sudden, this unknown guy from Leuven, Belgium, writing to him with what was clearly not a Belgian name, writing on "Brother Paul" no less! Štefan insisted that the form of this book should be something of an "imaginary talk" between friends by a bonfire, but it is really my hope that something in Stef's manuscript prompted Caputo to ponder the muteness of the universe a bit more thoroughly. It was only after the imaginary talk turned real, at least virtual—through a very brief email conversation—that Lyotard's concept of the "inhuman" (and the smile on the surface of an otherwise mute matter) makes an appearance in Caputo's work.

In the chapter "Dancing in the Void," Štofaník argues without really arguing—he tells a story rather—that Caputo puts all sorts of abysses on a par. Štefan had a feel for Nietzsche as much as he had a taste for the impossible. He seems to have regretted that Caputo's weak theology has a strong "orientation" (187) and that Caputo forgot that the desert about which we talk, experience, and write is in effect "more than one":

Nietzsche's dancers dance to a different song than weak theologians. It is an odd chapter, to be sure, and Štefan does not really seem to speak his mind. Again, one will have to wait and pay attention before Štofaník tells us the real point of all these digressions toward Saint-Exupéry. Perhaps one should reread or read more carefully even.

If anything, Štofaník shows us how to read in his book. He gives us long quotes, some of which we already know, but then focuses on a turn of phrase that we have always read passed. It is a remarkably modest "deconstruction of weak theology" (78) that he sets out to do—especially in the first parts of the book; later on the desire to deconstruct seems to disappear. There are two concurring trends in the book. At first, he tries to critique and deconstruct Caputo's version of weak theology, stating that this particular version too is but one name: there might be "more than one" weak theology. Then, in a second phase, Štefan falls victim, I think, to his own modesty and is spellbound by the "logic of the without," as perhaps we all have been and Caputo, for sure, too. At this juncture, Štofaník gets lost because of the fact that every deconstruction ends up with more things to deconstruct, so that all that is left is deconstructions over deconstructions over deconstructions . . . You can almost feel Stef wondering: What if what I write here is, in effect, one more deconstruction, one more story to tell? In this second phase, then, you'll see a sort of eulogy of the story, of the narrative he's composing—later on he will compare it to an opera, although he clearly preferred the sonata. I think he did get stuck here and should have contacted Caputo, not to verify or falsify the hypothesis—*à quoi bon?*—but to have a chat, light a fire, and think. Štefan acknowledges two tendencies in Caputo. Again, this is long before weak theology appeared on the scene: on the one hand, one should "demythologize Heidegger" and put the "question of being" on a diet, so to say, without the grand story of new beginnings and old, bygone, epochs—"the story is too big and easy to debunk" (139) (although we're still trying to debunk it). On the other hand, once weak theology arrives on the scene, Štefan notes, it is possible and even desirable for us to tell stories, to dream and imagine things differently, to perhaps sit by bonfires and listen to good ol' storytelling. Like many of us (and Caputo, too, I believe), Štefan got tired of deconstructing.

He wanted something of an affirmation but was not yet ready, I think, for the *viens, viens, oui, oui* he singles out in Caputo's *The Weakness of God*. I am not implying he will ever have been, nor that he should have done so. I only regret his not being around for telling stories about it now, especially after Caputo's *Hoping Against Hope*. There *is* an affirmation in *The Adventure of Weak Theology*, though, and there is no doubt that Štofaník took the entire project of weak theology seriously, very seriously even, that is, as something real. He believed, like many of us, that the "strong theologies" coming to us through seminaries, through Brothers Paul, through an abundance of Mass, is too strong and forgets about the fragile human condition that does not always "believe" and walks around with sticks like blind men and women. Štefan felt for the latter and had "faith" in them, more than he trusted the men of strong theology (are there any women here?). "Nobody trusts theology": these are the first words Caputo spoke here in Leuven, and Štefan and I were present. It made a big impression on me, and I was unaware that it did on Stef, too. Yet, being educated in Leuven, we both grew wary of anything that would be without anything and, considering the "end of metaphysics," of anything that would "underlie" anything too.[1] We were "dancing in the void" to be sure. Stef and I were therefore troubled by the very concept of a "religion without religion." Once I entered a classroom, where I had to teach about Caputo's religion without religion, soaking wet and dripping rain (it does rain a lot in Belgium, you know), and said: "The only thing you need to know about religion without religion is that it is just about as real as rain without rain." I should have skipped the class, perhaps. Stef had pretty much the same idea: there was a lot of reverence toward the tradition—how could there not be, being stamped with it as a former seminarian—and a lot of respect for Caputo's religion as well. This respect is obvious from the numerous times Štefan, in his second phase, tries, wants, and is willing to diverge from Caputo's viewpoints but nonetheless solicits his author's approval by mentioning that he had used the same methodological strategy earlier. This second phase, then, is a bit of "diverging without diverging," if you will.

The Adventure of Weak Theology, even though written in 2012–2013, will stand its ground. It maps Caputo's path to his weak theology better than anyone has done before and does not shy away from several (quite) amazing features in Caputo's career: his early dismissal of Derrida (anyone?), his break from the "system of Heidegger" (let's call it what it is), his quasi-privileging the tragic views of things (forgetting about a certain desert), only to opt for theology later on—you will have heard it here first.

Of particular importance is the chapter "Between Heidegger and Derrida," in which Štofaník traces Caputo's way from Heidegger to Derrida and mentions some awkward statements about Derrida on Caputo's part. Were it not for Caputo (and the De Man affair), we would perhaps still be dancing in the void, reveling in this aestheticism of endless interpretations and deconstructions. But, for us, mediocre fellows and scholars, it is good to know, too, that Caputo is not all about Derrida, not just one more "Derridean," that more than one thing is going on in this name. And, for one thing, Štefan Štofaník tells a pretty good story!

It is not just a story, though, and Štefan would be one of the first to state that this is a very serious matter—smiling all the while though. Weak theology is serious business and Štefan took it really seriously, hoping that, in some way or another, he could be a part of it. I hope, here, with this book, his name will become inscribed in the adventure of weak theology and this book will be a further inscription in the spaces carved out by Caputo.

I dread concluding this introduction, for although it might be the first thing you read, it is probably the last thing I tell to Štefan (except for certain prayers, and tears, which I won't tell you about). I learned from Štefan not to take things too seriously. He once told me, late at night, about the typewritten letter Caputo received from Heidegger. I remember my amazement—as I was probably reading Heidegger's *Parmenides* at the moment—and regret to only have later realized that it was Stef's way of telling me not to take it too seriously. Academic business, well, is still a business. Stef and I never really talked about academic issues. As good friends, we obviously had more important things to discuss than philosophy, let alone theology.

To conclude—I do not want to conclude. Stef felt it, I feel it, and Stef communicates it, even though he wants to break free of the spell. What attracted Štefan is that Caputo's "speech," his voice (you will learn how important the voice is for Štofaník), is outside of rigid confessional boundaries. The unwarned reader, too, will notice that Stef speaks to the believer and the seeker more so than to professional theologians and academics. Qua writing, I feel that there are very few books that can compete with this.

Be that as it may. There certainly are a few flaws to be noticed in the book. However, it is not because he didn't notice or had the chance to notice Caputo's magnificent *The Insistence of God* or noted the importance of this theology, perhaps; it is, rather, that Štefan didn't notice the depth (If any—I am serious. And awaiting Stef's response.) of Caputo's yes—of Caputo's affirmation.

First of all, Štefan was wrong when he says that there are no saints in weak theology. He is, struck by "strong theology," adhering to the canon of saints of the traditions, and blind to those saints that don't get the light of (a rainy) day—Štefan forgot that there is light, even on a rainy day. Caputo is keen in *Hoping Against Hope* to tell us the story of these little souls and little saints, who insist that God exists through their very own practices. There's a bunch of them, Stef, and more than you knew. Second, I think Stef was oblivious to the breadth, and there is one, of Caputo's affirmation, of the *yes*. For Caputo, one needs the rainy days in order to tell what a sunny day is: after all, we only know that it is life that is important through the very possibility of death. Without the latter, the former would be but a life of an object, of little or no importance. It is finitude that makes the days of our lives, rainy or sunny, important and meaningful. It is because of this *peras*, these limits, that all of our dreams are limitless. You need to say yes, my friend. There are rainy days, there are sunny days, and even if you can't have both at the same time, you can't have the one without the other. So, when Caputo says things like: "what I am getting at [. . .] under the name of the rose [under the name, Stef, there's a place under the sun for everyone], of the religion of the rose is a certain uncertain religion, whereas 'beliefs' are more likely movable furniture. Life is more like jogging than driving to work; the joy is in the journeying, not getting to the terminal destination," I just wish Štefan had taken it a bit more seriously, read more carefully—it is the first thing we should realize, admit to, the first yes.[2]

Even if "weak theology" or "religion without religion" is but a dream, I think Štefan, somehow, may have forgotten this: it is better to dream and not to forget, than to forget how to dream.

My dear friend Štefan, Stef, let me address you in the fraternal moment you touch late in your book (because you like "that fellow"): I salute you and smile at you, wherever you are, and conclude with the song you once sang to me in the middle of an abandoned parking lot somewhere in Czechia, on your way home: *Shine on, you crazy diamond.*

—Joeri Schrijvers

Preface

I like to imagine that whoever turns to these pages will understand one hundred percent the tremendous sense of relief that I feel as I am about to hand this work in for evaluation. I have been looking forward to this moment for so long—indeed, I fear I might have dawdled more time away daydreaming about it than I spent working on bringing it about—but now, at last, the day has come. I have done my due. How on earth did I ever end up here? Par quel miracle?

"That which is read first is written last," wrote in the preface to *Prodigal Sons* Alexander Bloom. "The author knows—or thinks he knows—what awaits the reader. The reader may have expectations but ventures into unknown territory."[1] When it comes to a book, the reverse is also true. As I am putting these last lines on paper, I know much less about what awaits me than do those who will read them. Upon submission of their writings, most authors indeed venture into unknown territory and they are overwhelmed with contradictory sentiments.

But never mind that now. Wonders never cease; and although I did not just sail right through it all, here I am at long last, rustling with pages in my hands. I feel excited, like having reached first base—a good start that, so the story goes, is half the race. With all travails forgotten, I am enjoying the moment while it lasts. As I duly should, according to Sandra Pyke. For the "science game now shifts to a new ground with new rules. Your rating first depends on getting some articles out; then, once you've demonstrated that you can publish, your rating depends on whether you are publishing in respectable journals; then your rating depends on whether you have a good book out; and then . . ."[2]

Then can wait until it comes. But that I got through it all and with a sane mind could never have happened without all the fantastic people around me, especially those from the research group Theology in a Postmodern Context. The discussions we had, even the places we frequented to have them, joys and sorrows we shared, scholarly and otherwise—I am convinced they are all written in golden letters in the "book of lives." Friends, we have made it, thanks for all the fun along the way.

My promoter Prof. Dr. Lieven Boeve allowed me to be the melancholic Easterner that he thinks I am, and he was the most patient supporter of, if not a coconspirator in, the way I write. It is thanks to him that I did not have to wait till I was forty-four to find my own voice.

—RAKOVA STEZA,
SLOVENIA, FEBRUARY 2013

Introduction

> It is well that the road you follow, your direction, should appear to you an end, for otherwise you would weary of faring towards something that can never be attained. Well do I know it, the ordeal of a journey through the desert, which at first seems hopelessly impracticable. And then I picture a lonely sand dune, far ahead, as being an ideal halting place, grateful as a promised land. But when I reach it, lo, all the magic has gone out of it! Then I tell myself that a certain notch on the horizon is surely the ideal halting place; but here, too, when I reach it, the glamor is departed. Then I select another target, and thus, from target to target, I make my way out of the wilderness.
>
> —Antoine de Saint-Exupéry,
> *The Wisdom of the Sands* (Citadelle)

"Although the Universe is under no obligation to make sense, students in pursuit of the PhD are," declaimed Robert Kirshner during a public lecture at the University of Durham.[1] The same goes for a book like this. So Professor Kirshner's quirky counsel is perhaps quite befitting after all and I, for my part, will stick by it. I pledge to fall over backward to make sense.

This raises the question how best to proceed. I suppose one useful strategy would be to ratchet the scope of the foregoing metaphor up a notch and then yes, to bend, lean, and fall backward in time so as to retrieve what has come to pass. To account for the invention of sense by going back whence it came upon (*invenīre*) me. On top of that, this better be a controlled fall, lest everything break into pieces; it is enough that the following chapters are bestrewn with orphaned ideas. Therefore, in order to walk through this introduction in one piece—walking, I hear, has also been described as controlled falling, although usually forward—I have resolved to follow the fail-safe guide of the five W's: *Who? What? Where? When? Why?*

But hang on for a moment. Does this guide not contain also an H—*How?* Of course it does, and my original plan was, indeed, to include it in this introduction. After I wrote it, however, it became clear to me that having such an extensive, heavy methodological discussion right at the beginning would very likely be counterproductive. For this reason I moved it to the very end and it now stands separately, as an epilogue.

After charting out the methods, motives, and the backstory of the work at hand, I shall also provide a sketchy map of its subdivisions.

Who?

The Adventure of Weak Theology is first and foremost about John D. Caputo, an American author who spent nearly all of his career teaching philosophy at Villanova University and then the last few years prior to his retirement lecturing in religion at Syracuse University. Since the publication of his first article more than four decades ago, Caputo has written prolifically on a variety of topics, exploring links between medieval mysticism and the philosophy of Martin Heidegger, arguing tirelessly the case for radical hermeneutics, examining religion through the prism of deconstruction, and waging an all-out war against theology's love affair with power.

While Caputo's ideas and allegiances developed, indeed even reversed over time, his work "has not been void of certain tenacious consistencies," as Keith Putt has put it.[2] "Caputo has always manifested personally and professionally an implicit obligation to deal with religion, with what he considers to be the mystery that lies inherent in the flux."[3] Even when, in view of his career as a professional philosopher, he considered it prudent to conceal the passion "for God, for the religious, and for the mystical" that was driving him,[4] he admits that he has "always been reflecting on philosophical questions by exposing them to theological and religious resources."[5] A peculiar constancy, for it essentially meant that it made no difference which direction Caputo took; he has at all times treaded the spaces between, has always been a little lost, and as he made his way through no philosopher's land, what had at first been only an indistinct feeling, a vague call, had gradually turned for him into a calling, a conviction that "for the true anchorites [. . .] the desert was a medium through which they must pass on the way to redemption."[6] For "[y]ou must first lose your self if you would save yourself according to the ancient economy."[7]

As it happened, the wilderness did not swallow Caputo; instead, he mapped it out. It is to a large extent thanks to him that continental philosophy of religion thrives in American universities like never before. And by braving the philosophical frontier, in time Caputo also found himself—or, as he relates it, he found his voice. This is another constancy in Caputo's work, albeit an incessantly developing constancy, if there is such a thing: I am speaking about his literary voice, which Michael Zimmerman described as possessed of "generous portions of vitality, irony, and humor, all of which enable it to speak in tones unburdened by the spirit of gravity that afflicts the voices of so many American commentators on Heidegger's thought."[8] That afflicts the voices of so many academicians, some would say, period. At first, one hears very little in the desert. Nothing except one's heartbeat and breathing counterpointed by the wind whistling in the dark. Silence like that can be truly disturbing. When one finally dares to speak out, the surrounding stillness magnifies even the quietest words into "the voice of one crying out in the desert." Duly was it in the wilderness that John became a prophet, hence also Zimmerman's confidence that "Caputo would have been an outstanding preacher, had he pursued his interests in the priesthood."[9] In the desert, Caputo learned how to laugh.

That said, a small but critical concession is now in order: No one ever journeys across such vast stretches of space and time truly unaccompanied. Even in the desert there is no question of pure soliloquy, just like one's voice is never quite one's own. We are, to avoid needless esotericism, always already in dialogue, philosophers and theologians maybe even more so than anybody else. Thus, reminisces Caputo, "I passed my intellectual youth consorting with saints and mystics and medieval masters who told me spellbinding tales and opened my eyes to an altogether new and astonishing world."[10] Thomas Aquinas, the father of Thomism, and Meister Eckhart, nicknamed the father of German thought, were the magi and masters Caputo talked with and talked about, followed later by Angelus Silesius and even more recently by Jacques Maritain and Pierre Rousselot. These all also play an important role in *The Adventure of Weak Theology*. But the most "spellbinding tales" Caputo ever heard were probably told by Heidegger, so much so that the spell had to be eventually broken for him by Derrida.[11] It was he, the Parisian father of deconstruction, who helped Caputo find his voice,[12] while it is fair to say that Caputo, in turn, gave voice to Heidegger and Derrida in the English-speaking academia: "If, today, reference to, say, Heidegger, or even Derrida, is no longer considered as exotic (and questionable) as it once was," wrote Mark Dooley, "this is in no small part due to Caputo's multiform effort."[13]

By the way, the two paradoxical statements uttered here thus far—the one about the incessantly developing constancy and the other about one's voice not being entirely one's own—are well founded in Caputo's case. For while it is true that Derrida helped Caputo find his own voice (Caputo speaks about it often; he was then forty-four), what this really meant was that Derrida, by his own example, encouraged Caputo not only to break free from the confines of academic literary sobriety, and therefore to write more personally, but also to write more like Søren Kierkegaard. Caputo found his own voice when he allowed himself to write like Kierkegaard. This is no charge of a lack of originality; on the contrary. Anyone who has read the Danish master of pen and of the human soul will undoubtedly agree that to be compared with Kierkegaard is a compliment and quite possibly every philosopher-writer's secret ambition. It was, in any case, Caputo's dream. Ever since he first discovered Kierkegaard at the age of eighteen, Caputo never stopped regarding him as his personal hero.[14] The father of existentialism from the Paris of the North has been the "most consistent influence" on Caputo,[15] even if this direction became obvious in Caputo's work only gradually.

Here, indeed, I talk about the consistency of direction, namely the one pointing backward toward one's cradle in time. Not so much to one's Bethlehem, though, as to one's Nazareth—that is, to our late teen years or so, by which time we had already come to ponder the Universe and it still ungrudgingly made sense to us. When we later began to wander about the deserts of Palestine or, for that matter, of philosophy, we kept unrolling Ariadne's thread without as much as being aware of it and, in fact, often quite contrary to our intentions. Books get ever more difficult to write because the thread grew longer, but if we were lucky, it was still there. Unbroken.[16] The umbilical cord through which we remained forever connected with our homes because home is what sense really signifies. Caputo, I believe, is a "Heideggerian," or even a "Derridean," only inasmuch as he has always been an admirer of Kierkegaard. And of Saint Thomas. It could be that Caputo wished to choose between the two, but to no avail. The twine just would not break. Having more than one home, one is also a little lost . . .

In addition to all the characters mentioned already, this work also alludes to Emmanuel Levinas and Gilles Deleuze, a prophet and a maverick, whom Caputo consulted regularly on matters of alterity and event, respectively. They, too, were at home in Paris and at home with more than just one discipline. We should not be surprised: After all, it has been suggested that Parisians trace the origin of their name back to the Gallic root for doing things; they are the "working people."[17]

Finally, the book you are holding is also about me. It cannot be otherwise. Conventions of academic writing may require depersonalized objectivity, but they virtually never demand that we do not sign our own texts (temporary nondisclosure of authorship for the purposes of blind review obviously does not count). Why not? Well, precisely because the texts in question are our own. But are they therefore automatically about us? I believe so. At least implicitly, to be sure, whereas sometimes the most efficient way to communicate one's findings is to be boldly autobiographical. Again, the personal dimension in academic writing is probably more readily discernible in the works of philosophers and theologians than anywhere else, except for maybe literary scholars. They are also the most likely to appreciate both the importance of and inescapability from personal experience in scientific research and writing. Caputo for one believes that "there would be no passion, no creation, without personal involvement, and so there will always be an autobiographical element in the process of creation."[18] On top of that, I dare say we cannot make sense without reference to our place within it. Sense is our home; in sense we dwell and the Universe, or a book, only makes sense insofar as they are places to dwell.

Unless I live within my book, it is senseless . . . This conviction is my way of countersigning Matthew (6:21): "For where your treasure is, there also will your heart be." I too do not believe in work that one can simply put aside at the end of the day and then sleep peacefully. I care for no less than true *Sorge*. So I brought my treasure here with me. I also carry a slew of string that links me with my own home and that runs, like a thread, throughout this entire work. As a matter of fact, it also points to Paris, though not always, to a man who was both saint and magus, although only with a deck of cards. He was no father of anything or anyone, save for the fatherless child who once felt so alone in the Universe that he moved his chair repeatedly to watch the sunset fort y-four times. That child was a (little lost) prince, *The Little Prince*, and the father was a saint, Saint-Exupéry. Ever since I discovered him when I was still a young student, he has been my hero as a writer. Unbroken. *And he knew all too well the ordeal of a journey through the desert, which at first seems hopelessly impracticable.* What better companion could I wish for myself on this endless journey through this book, this piece of writing? The book itself is not about Saint-Exupéry, but I wrote it with him, because it was he who helped me find my own voice.

What?

I am always ready to insist, when one seeks to fully understand the workings of a system of ideas, on the importance of talking about the involved people and why they said what they said. *The Adventure of Weak Theology*, however, is not merely a chronicle of Caputo's intellectual journey. That too, and admittedly more so than I originally intended; but inasmuch as I am no historian but a student of theology, by way of telling a story I was, in fact, trying to elucidate the principles. At times, this quasi-journalistic style of mine might be needlessly getting in the way—I have been told so and shall probably hear it again—therefore the present caveat. This book is, or it is meant to be, about weak theology.

For the greater part of his career Caputo profiled himself as a philosopher. He occupied the David R. Cook chair of Philosophy (at Villanova) and he also fell over backward to make sense in the realm of pure thinking while, as we have seen, keeping his love for theology to himself. But who are we kidding? We all know that doing one's best refers to an attitude, but nine times out of ten the actual results follow their own mysterious patterns of causation. Particularly so when this proverbial "falling over backward" contradicts our deepest instincts. Trying is praiseworthy, but knowing when to stop is wise. Eventually, Caputo also gave in:

> I confess I have a weakness for theology. Against the sound advice of my attorneys, my investment counselors, and my confessor, and after holding out for as long as possible against my inner *daimōn*, I have finally succumbed to the siren call of this name. I do not know how to avoid speaking of theology. So be it. I am prepared to face the consequences. *Hier stehe ich.*[19]

Strictly speaking, the birth of weak theology coincides with the publication in 2006 of these words in the introduction to *The Weakness of God: A Theology of the Event.* That is when the rest of us first heard about weak theology from Caputo. "Strictly speaking," however, is yet another rhetorical overstatement that has to do more with the intentions of the one who uses it—like doing one's best to gloss over the divergent facts—than with the reality itself. Here the reality is that Caputo's *best* had never been good enough; before *The Weakness of God* or after it, his philosophy was always marked by theological thinking, even as his theology remains strongly philosophical.

There is, however, no need to hammer away at the same point over and over. Except now to define the scope of the present work. First of all, I switch freely between speaking about weak theology and a theology of the event. Both refer to the same project in the context of Caputo's oeuvre. And second, inasmuch as the boundaries between philosophy and theology appear porous in Caputo's work, I make no special point of respecting them either. Where Caputo claims something ostensibly as a philosopher, but the examples he uses or the implications he makes are theological, I treat his words as a (crypto-)theology. Stated otherwise, I do not speak about weak theology strictly. Rather than taking as my starting point *The Weakness of God* and then following anything explicitly theological after it, I trace Caputo's theology wherever and whenever it bursts through the surface, discussing its origins even as far as before Caputo published anything at all. In this respect, *The Adventure of Weak Theology* is a work of genealogy.

So what is this weak theology anyway? "A way of thinking about God which is not held captive by a determinate confessional boundary," explains Caputo.[20] "It's also weaker in the sense that it's less sure of itself, less certain, and less determinate."[21] Caputo wants us to think of his project as a "'theology without theology' that accompanies what Derrida calls a 'religion without religion,' as a 'weak theology' that accompanies [Gianni] Vattimo's 'weak thought,' or perhaps even as the weak messianic theology that should accompany [Walter] Benjamin's 'weak messianic force.'"[22]

How does Caputo wind up in such company? By differentiating between the *name* of God and the *event* that is astir in that name, hence a theology of the event. Caputo understands the word "God"—the name of God—to refer to a specific event, one which we experience as a call from afar, a call for justice, forgiveness, hospitality—simply the call that is "calling upon what is best in us"[23]—and theology is our human way of interpreting this call.

However, this is only a partial answer, because, according to Caputo, "any theology, weak or strong, is the explication of the event that is implicit in the name of God."[24] The difference between strong and weak theology, and hence also the specificity of Caputo's theological project, depends on the way one approaches this call. We are called to do justice—it is, according to Caputo, something like a primordial human experience. But this call cannot be traced back to an identifiable entity that is calling us. All we can fairly say about this call is that it is an event. And because events are inherently undecidable, Caputo believes that all attempts to speak about the ontological identity of the one who calls us are destined to fail:

> Is it *really* God who calls, or is it some hidden power in my own mind? Is it *really* the call of conscience, of some Socratic *daimon*, or of a Cosmic Spirit? How am I to say? Who has authorized me to preside over that debate, to decide that undecidable? I do not know the name or address of this address. To pursue that question is to treat the call like a strong force with a definite place on the plane of being or power, not a weak one that solicits me from afar. [. . .] The name of God is a name of an event, of I know not what, of a bottomless provocation, like the name of love or of justice, and I am in no position to stop the endless chain of substitutions in which it is caught up.[25]

This, in a nutshell, is the starting point for everything else Caputo claims qua theologian, and to those who "do not have the least idea of what that means," he gives free advice to stop reading him and "check the stock market page to see how their portfolios are doing."[26] A rather cheeky way to acknowledge a *differend*—"Beware of strong theology!"[27] and "Blessed are the weak theologians, for they admit they have not seen God"[28]—but well, meet a Kierkegaardian speaking. Not only that; the rift goes deeper. Weak theology, we are compelled to believe, is not really a theology after all. Let us ponder upon this for a moment.

As I argued elsewhere, it is quite possible to perceive weak theology as having no interest in *Theos* at all. Instead of saying that God calls us, according to a theology of the event, it would be more precise to say that the Kingdom of God that is *called for* is also the Kingdom of God that *calls*, where the Kingdom of God does not stand for the kingdom of an identifiable entity but simply for our way of being in the world.[29] Weak theology would be ipso facto a kind of "basileology" were it not for Caputo ridding himself also of the second part of the word. As he puts it, a theology of the event "re-describes the work of theology not as the analysis (-ology) of 'God' ('strong theology') but of the 'event' that is harbored in the name of God, which is where things get even riskier, more novel, and less orthodox ('weak theology')."[30] "In the place of what I call 'strong theology,' I offer a certain 'poetics' of the human condition, not a theo-logic but a 'theo-poetics.'"[31] In the final analysis, weak theology is a poetics of the Kingdom.

What else it is depends largely on who asks or, alternatively, whom Caputo addresses and why, when explaining his point of view. Thus, for example, in a somewhat fiery reaction against what he took as a "perfect misunderstanding" of his own work,[32] Caputo puts Martin Hägglund in the picture by describing weak theology as the second stage in his "devilish mix[ing] of faith and atheism" rather than an unjust theologization of his "coconspirator" Derrida.[33] Ultimately, just like any theory out there, weak theology is subject to diachronic evolution and synchronic inner tensions alike. With respect to the latter, *The Adventure of Weak Theology* is a work of archaeology.

Where?

I do not want to go overboard with the five W's, at least not where doing so would result in a hollow text. I picked the method to guide me, not to enslave me. Concerning the *Where?* of the work at hand, I only have one (twin) place to introduce, in addition to those mentioned already. To recapitulate, I began with the Universe and that, in fact, should say it all if Paris did not compete for the title. Perhaps a less equally matched couple that we talked about were the two shores of the philosophical continent (many believe America, not Europe, carries the present day); Philadelphia's veneration of the nineteenth-century Copenhagen set the tone for everything that follows; and the desert, those spaces between philosophy and theology, is where everything came to pass.

But with the desert there is more. Before we watch the adventure of weak theology unfold, it will be useful to get acquainted with the Universe's dark side, the only other true contender for the dictionary entry as a synonym for everything. Consider the abyss, that silent void of which we can conceive no greater—and yet we conceive of more than one, for such is the power of faith.

On the one hand, the abyss refers to what Levinas described as the "anonymous rustling [also translated as rumbling] of the *there is*, the uncontrollable stirring of the elemental."[34] It also denotes the "realm of great cosmic stupidity," as Nietzsche remarked, where chance falls down carelessly upon us "like a slate from a roof striking down some beautiful purpose of ours."[35] The abyss is the name we have for the Universe without sense, for the anonymous existence in an utterly indifferent Universe that neither knows nor cares whether we are here or not. This is the monstrous abyss gazing back at us if we look into it but for a moment too long.[36]

On the other hand, when faith looks into the abyss, instead of the cold gaze it is met there by the loving eyes. We believe, we trust that it cares for us, but an abyss it is nevertheless—"the mystical abyss of the Godhead beyond God," as Caputo puts it, following great mystics.[37] This abyss, to be sure, is also dark and still, but it is a silent night, Saint-Exupéry's

> silence of God, like a shepherd's sleep than which no sleep is softer, though threatened seem the lambs and ewes; when both flock and shepherd cease to be, for who can tell one from the other in the starry night, when all is at rest, and a wan glimmer of sleep-bound wool . . .[38]

Faith really is the keyword here, because on any other accounting the two renderings of the Universe seem indistinguishable. "If we stick to the phenomenal facts," argues Caputo, "the borders between the negative infinite of the formless *apeiron* and the positive infinity of *aliquid quo major nequit*, between the formless *tohu wa bohu* of *il y a* and infinite givenness, tend to blur."[39]

This might be as good a technical explanation of what Caputo means by undecidability as we are likely to get, but Caputo is also a great poet of the abyss: "I will describe a shadowy, formless penumbra that hovers over us, a demi-being or shade that haunts us and disturbs our sleep . . ."[40] Caputo knows what he is talking about, for the abyss has cost him many sleepless nights as well:

> I have more and more been taken by the thought of the anonymous, of the impersonal horizon by which we are everywhere surrounded, by the ring of impersonality that closes in all around us. I wonder now if what I once called the divine, the dark night and bottomless abyss of the Godhead, is not simply the anonymity of a nameless night, a darkness pure and simple, rather the veil [*sic*] of a deeper, more divine dimension. I wonder if we do not all speak a lost language, a language that will have been lost when once [*sic*] the earth drops back into the sun and turns to ash.[41]

Although some particularly evocative images of the abyss got a few of his friends worried, Caputo never thought that the specter of being completely forgotten in the Universe was an unequivocally bad thing. Faith is genuine only when there is no other way, when there is no proof to support it, so Nietzsche's great cosmic stupidity is, in fact, a necessary condition for faith (or hope, or love) to occur:

> The anonymous has a productive role to play. The thought, the suspicion, the anxiety, the unnerving premonition that overtakes us as we lay awake at nights, or as we wend our way down a long and empty highway, that behind it all there is nothing behind it all, nothing to prop up the beliefs and practices we most cherish, nothing that underwrites them, nothing we know of—that is the condition of the faith.[42]

In other words, "abyss" may well translate a bottomless pit, but it is as well a well of bottomless possibilities. God's silence, not noisy miracles, produces saints, as the extraordinary life of Mother Teresa testifies. God's silence, for "had your prayer availed, and had you discovered God, you would have merged yourself in Him, having fulfilled yourself, and then what need were there for you to grow in stature, so as to become?"—says a saint (Exupéry). Because "faith makes its way in the dark, seeing through a glass darkly, and it is genuine only to the extent that it acknowledges the abyss in which we are all situated, the undecidability and ambiguity which engulfs us all," says Caputo.[43]

The abyss, which barely earned its place in my grand scheme of the five W's, happens to be, after all, Caputo's point of departure[44] and the *locus theologicus* of weak theology:

> Is the event [of the call] a breeze blowing out of paradise, the wind that swept across the darkness of the deep (the *ruach Elohim*), or is it only the anonymous rumbling of I know not what? God only knows![45]

When?

Time is of the essence. My makeshift concordance ranks time as the twenty-ninth most frequently used word in all of Caputo's texts and the fourth most common noun, outranked only by God, Derrida, and Heidegger (poor Kierkegaard used too many pseudonyms to stand a chance).[46] There is not a single chapter in *The Weakness of God* where time would not be mentioned, and chapters 8, 9, and 10 are entitled "Quotidianism: Every Day, or Keeping Time Holy," "Back to the Future: Peter Damian on the Remission of Sin and Changing the Past," and

"Forgiven Time: The Pharisee and the Tax Collector," respectively. On top of that, one of the most pleasant discoveries I made in the past half a year or so was that Caputo entertains himself with reading about the meaning of time in astrophysics,[47] and he even refers to it in his texts.[48] And yes, *The Adventure of Weak Theology* is about the past, present, and future of Caputo's theological thinking. At this point, however, I would only like to say a few words about the *When?* of the present work in the practical sense.

I first heard about John D. Caputo seven years ago in the office of my promoter. I already was significantly older than most of the undergraduate students at our faculty, so my ignorance about one of the "big names" in the field would seem inexcusable, but I guess Caputo is not the kind of author you come across easily if you are not a professional systematic (and even philosophical) theologian. About this unfortunate fact—that to my nontheologian family or friends, for example, I could just as well talk about some godforsaken Spanish village[49]—I shall have a thing or two to say in a minute. I will also tell you more about how or why I got to know about Caputo in the first place, but for now suffice it to say that I did end up writing my master's thesis ("Deconstruction in Theology: Kevin Hart and John D. Caputo") and my advanced master's thesis ("The Weak Theology of John D. Caputo: A Critical Analysis and Evaluation") about his work. After that, the original plan for the doctoral dissertation that was to become this book was to expand on the previous work by bringing on board Richard Kearney and to explore how the particularity of religious traditions (attested to in the earlier works of the research group Theology in a Postmodern Context) related to the essential particularity of religious truth.

With hindsight, I think this was quite an ambitious research project, and in any case I did not carry it through. I find some solace in the words of Marston Bates, who thought of research as the "process of going up alleys to see if they are blind."[50] Or perhaps more to the point, I think of Francis Crick, who once said that "in research the front line is almost always in a fog."[51] And since one needs, supposedly, three to make the cut, I also include Caputo:

> As I started to write what turned out to be *Prayers and Tears*, I decided that I had to start with Derrida and situate this problematic in terms of Derrida by showing how to put deconstruction to work in the service of religious faith. So, I thought, I will need a couple of chapters at the beginning on Derrida and religion—and that was a hole from which I never reemerged.[52]

Similarly, I never got beyond what I at first intended to be just an extensive chapter on Caputo's theology of the event. Unlike Caputo, however, I had not made a name for myself by works comparable to *Radical Hermeneutics* or *Against Ethics* prior to my own version of "The Prayers and Tears of Jack Caputo." With regard to *The Adventure of Weak Theology*, any unlikely exercise in genealogy would be therefore completely superfluous—the paths I took, the things I learned only gradually, they are all there in plain sight. Had I made a better use of my time, I would have tried to cover the tracks. Instead, I take this as a reminder that as an aspiring writer I still have very far to go.

Why?

Now having said that, I am not trying to sell this work short. Straying from the original plan need not always be a bad thing, especially not when doing so opens the door for surprises. My other (and thus far unacknowledged) hero author recalls how writing the *Hitchhiker's Guide to the Galaxy*

> episodically meant that when I finished one episode I had no idea about what the next one would contain. When, in the twists and turns of the plot, some event suddenly seemed to illuminate things that had gone before, I was as surprised as anyone else;[53]

and yet no one could ever go back after having seen the world the way Douglas Adams did.[54] So on the one hand, there is the sobering experience of getting stuck midway through the project, the realization that doing one's best really is not enough. But to allow research to follow its own path, even when that means losing oneself in reading, also has a positive side—it makes new events possible. Perfectly planned and executed research is the best strategy we know of for the verification of our hypotheses, but the paradigm shifts are often brought about by stray thinkers.

In the last few days I read about Göbekli Tepe, perhaps the most significant archaeological discovery in centuries. The human origin of this "fat hill," this settlement therefore, in southeastern Turkey has been recognized at least since 1964, but at that time the limestone blocks scattered all around were mistaken for Byzantine grave stones and the site was abandoned as uninteresting. Then in 1994, "standing under a lone tree on a windswept hilltop," Klaus Schmidt of the German Archaeological Institute of Istanbul thought to himself: "This place is a supernova. [. . .] Within a minute of first seeing it I knew I had two choices: go away and tell nobody, or spend the rest of my life working here."[55] And he was right. The place, which for three decades archaeologists dismissed as the same old story, turned out to be an eleven-thousand-year-old religious temple built by hunters and gatherers who knew nothing of farming, pottery, writing, or even a wheel . . .

Caputo's work may not be ancient (nor is it finished, as he is currently working on *A Theology of the Event, II*), but it spans a long enough period, both in real time and in its reference, for us to be easily misled into thinking that we have heard it all. Now imagine the loss if Göbekli Tepe had remained ignored. Likewise, passing over "yet another deconstructionist," thinking that he has little to offer besides Parisian graves, can mean the difference between remaining forever stuck with the same old story on the one hand, and making an important discovery on the other. David Gelernter, I think, identified the potentially dangerous attitude well when he complained that "scientists nowadays rarely know how to read seriously. They are accustomed to strip-mining a paper to get the facts out and then moving on, not to mollycoddling the thing in search of nuances."[56] Derrida, on the other hand, got famous for reading differently. In a 2002 biographical movie about him, Derrida was asked: "Have you read all the books in here?" "Why no," Derrida replied, "only four of them. But I read these very, very carefully."[57] Because ultimately nothing, as Derrida has demonstrated, nothing ever is the same old story.

Here, then, is my first answer to the question regarding the purpose of my book: It is the result of my close reading of Caputo. *The Adventure of Weak Theology* makes no pretense to novelty and does not really come up with surprising new discoveries, although some amusing facts that I uncovered are generally little known. But it does cover the development of Caputo's theology in a way that, to my knowledge, is unprecedented both in scope and in idiom. It is my hope that this work will be particularly useful to people who would otherwise dismiss weak theology all too easily.

Second, as I promised, I need to say a few words about the meeting I had with my promoter seven years ago. The road toward this book began there and so it is to this meeting that I must look for the ultimate answer to the question *Why?* Why Caputo, indeed?

I had no idea which author or topic I should write about, and very little to go by to even choose the general direction, as I knocked on Professor Doctor Lieven Boeve's door. All I could tell him was that I wished to work on a project that I would be able to regard as personal; to write on something that I could easily relate to my own concerns. I wanted to be intrigued but, as I said, I did not really know where to look. I was also anxious to stay away from dogmatism and I believed this narrowed the field of search down to philosophical theology or philosophy of religion, but that was about it. It was not my first meeting with Professor Boeve. Two had taken place before and I had checked out two authors; I thought they were okay but no more than that. And then I mentioned Kierkegaard as an example of the kind of existentialist thought I felt attracted to. "Well, if you like Kierkegaard, then perhaps you should consider Caputo," said Lieven. "Caputo . . . ? Is he Italian?," I asked wondering to what extent that meant Rome (what a simplistic vision of the world I had). "Actually no, he's American," replied Lieven as he walked out of the office to look for a book in the library shelves. "Here, I think we can start with this," he said when he returned, handing me *Religion With/out Religion: The Prayers and Tears of John D. Caputo.*[58] "There is an interview at the end, sometimes that's the best way to start making sense of an author. If you like it, you can write about him." And so I, a former journalist, first learned about Caputo by reading "What Do I Love When I Love My God? An Interview with John D. Caputo,"[59] and this time I was convinced. What won me over, I think, was Caputo's emphasis on the mystery that surrounds us, on not knowing who we are and, in fact, being exactly that, "the ones who do not know who we are, who are a question for themselves."[60] I was also intrigued by what I perceived as the mystique associated with deconstruction, the baffling invasion of philosophy's *enfant terrible* into theology. I was curious and lured by the prospect of playing in that fringe field, so when I met with Professor Boeve again, I said yes and the rest is history.

As a matter of fact, *The Adventure of Weak Theology* is in at least one important aspect significantly more defiant than it is deferential. What if, for example, I were to say to you now that my third and final reason why I wrote about Caputo's theology is because I really like that fellow? I would be going against the sound advice of Caputo, who thinks one should not risk writing "in a style that gives scandal to academic protocol"[61] (like he does) before one gets "tenure and promotion,"[62] as well as against that of my promoter, who suggested that I stay cool and hold myself back from such literary escapades at least in the introduction and conclusion.

I know for sure that this was the most valuable, perhaps indeed critical advice, and yet I must say it: To tell the truth, my second reason why I wrote about Caputo's theology is that I really like that fellow. It's personal. Just like I always wished my project would be, like on that afternoon in Professor Boeve's office. But if I now feel compelled to defy his well-intended advice, it is only because I have some important methodological points to make. So it is not an act of senseless defiance, after all. Quite the reverse. I am, in fact, setting the stage for the final act of deference to the standards of academic writing. This time, at least, I intend to stick to the plan and to make good on my promise to make sense . . .

*Nevertheless, for the reasons that I already mentioned, the section on methodology—*How?*—is now itself "deferred." I pray for the reader's patience, for it will be only at the very end that I shall try to explain why I chose to write the way I write.

* * *

For easier orientation, I also promised to provide a kind of "map," so here it comes:

"Adventure" (chapter 1) introduces Caputo's method of radical hermeneutics as his proposed antidote to the situation where "a good many theologians adopt the same high handed, unilateral and imperial tones as sovereign states, which reserve the right to make an exemption of themselves." The second half of the chapter discusses why summaries, such as "radical hermeneutics is what Caputo's theology is all about," are inadequate in describing a theory. What is required is a story—in this case the narrative of the adventure of weak theology.

"Call" (chapter 2) complements the previous chapter, arguing that if left on its own, a historical narrative would also fall short of describing Caputo's theology. A theology of the event, as it is officially recognized, is itself also an event. That is to say, something is going on in "what happened" that does not exactly coincide with the story, or rather transcends that story. The sense of what happened changes as the event unfolds. The concept of the call, on which Caputo's theology is built, is introduced.

"Brother Paul" (chapter 3) follows young Caputo in the novitiate of the Brothers of the Christian Schools. The two conflicting loves of the young student—Saint Thomas and Kierkegaard—are brought to the fore. The chapter ends at the point where Caputo left the formation in order to pursue the path of an academic philosopher.

"Transgression" (chapter 4) gets its title from Caputo's defiance of monastic boundaries to run after his dreams, but several other meanings of transgression are also analyzed. In particular, I deal with Caputo's desire to cross over the limits imposed on us by pure reason and with his plea for the transgression of the narrowly defined boundaries of our intellectual and religious traditions. A short discussion of Caputo's attitude to radical orthodoxy is also included. Caputo's theology, I conclude, is in an important sense a function of the answers for which he has been able to come up with the question: Transgression whereto?

"Two Loves" (chapter 5) follows Caputo's struggle to reconcile his two great loves mentioned previously. This endeavor leads him from Jacques Maritain and Pierre Rousselot to his discovery of Heidegger, whom he credits with helping him break the grip of dogmatic Catholicism. The path then continues via Angelus Silesius and Meister Eckhart and eventually returns to Aquinas. These are the orthodox years of Caputo's academic career. The important concept of *Gelassenheit* is introduced.

Chapters 6, 7, and 8—"Freedom, "Interlude," and "Freedom Again," respectively—form one large whole as they were initially conceived as one chapter. The backbone of the chapters is the story of Bark, a Senegalese slave immortalized in Antoine de Saint-Exupéry's *Terre des hommes* (*Wind, Sand and Stars*).

In "Freedom" Bark's story is intertwined and interrupted with the peculiar connections between freedom, proper names, and the force of gravity. The chapter itself is cut short just after I have indicated that there might be much more to Caputo's theory (and personal history) of freedom than his overtly Levinassian attitudes might indicate.

"Interlude" picks up where "Freedom" left off, arguing that deconstruction implies that everybody is more than one. Caputo as well as anybody else. The underlying theme of this interlude is the possibility of more than one weak theology. Admittedly, an inordinate amount of space is taken by demonstrating how Caputo necessarily contradicts himself at times, which, however, is not regarded as a fallacy but rather as an opportunity to recontextualize and develop his work.

"Freedom Again" begins again with Bark's journey home; this time we find him lost in Agadir. Bark's "madness of freedom without direction" is then compared to Caputo's concept of religion without religion. As promised, I also discuss other, mostly suppressed, versions of Caputo's freedom. I argue that the freedom from particular religion, as advocated by Caputo, poses a triple problem: Because this freedom lacks a concrete sense of orientation, it results in a sterile dreaming; because Caputo's thinking precludes any concrete sense of mission, he cuts himself off from an important strand of cultural dreaming; and because weak theology of this particular kind requires a dismissal of the complex question of the source, it eventually turns against Caputo and proves him self-contradictory.

"Between Heidegger and Derrida" (chapter 9) itself actually begins like some series with the discussion of "love at first sight" and "hindsight bias," which is then linked to the historical if largely unknown fact that Derrida was anything but Caputo's hero in the beginning. The entire section is dedicated to the analysis of Caputo's articles published in the early 1980s in which he takes a Heideggerian stance against Derrida. The story then continues with Caputo gradually turning against Heidegger and discovering how much he has in common with Derrida—the *Kehre* that significantly changed the character of Caputo's thinking and eventually also his theology. I drop the story where Caputo publishes his *Prayers and Tears of Jacques Derrida*.

"Dancing in the Void" (chapter 10) is the penultimate series chapter that could be subtitled "How to Read Caputo?" Dance is a metaphor for style (in this case, the style of writing) but also an image of series of approaches and withdrawals. Void is just another term for the abyss, which Caputo said had been haunting him forever, and which I kept encountering across the entire book but now will revisit through Caputo's character named Felix Sineculpa.

"The Advent of Weak Theology" (chapter 11) concludes the historiographical part of my book with a very brief discussion of Caputo's first expressly theological work, *The Weakness of God*, published in 2006. In addition, I explore two paths in this chapter, one looking back and another looking forward, toward the promise of weak theology.

"Kingdom" (chapter 12) is the final of the series and it also stands "in place of a conclusion."

1

Adventure

"There is a good reason that nobody trusts theology. Nobody outside the confessional religions trusts theology and with good reason."[1] These words reverberated through one of the (almost) countless classrooms of the Catholic University of Leuven on a cool spring morning a couple of years ago, and at that point Professor John D. Caputo could be certain that he had just bought for himself the full attention of the entire audience for at least the coming few minutes. It was like an opening line of a great book: The vast majority of best-selling novels begin in such a way, with some sort of a provocation, with a hook—or bait—that catches the readers off guard, intrigues them so that they really want, nay, need to know what happens next. Caputo's lecture, of course, was not a novel. But addressing those words to theologians, to the teachers and students of theology for whom theology is a mission and/or a source of living, inevitably caused quite some disturbance of which the most telling sign was the sudden silence. You could hear a pin drop: What? Did we just hear him say that nobody trusts what we are doing? Surely, we wanted to know why. Or, to say the least, we were eager to hear why the celebrated philosopher of religion and lately also a theologian thinks that this is the case.

For sure, nobody in the classroom expected to hear a rehearsal of the Vatican-style critique of the ongoing de-Christianization of the Western society. Nor was such a rehearsal offered. Instead, Caputo pointed the finger at theology itself, blaming it for its unwillingness to "present itself and understand itself except as sovereign theology, imperial theology."[2] If nobody outside religions—and, in fact, not too many people inside religions either[3]—trust theology today, it is because, we were told by Caputo, "a good many theologians adopt the same high handed, unilateral and imperial tones as sovereign states, which reserve the right to make an exemption of themselves."[4] Whatever else we heard from Professor Caputo on that spring morning and, in fact, whatever else he has had to say at least since he wrote his *Radical Hermeneutics*, has been the function of precisely this diagnosis: Theology suffers the lack of credibility because of its misguided belief that it is somehow exempted from the "mess" of our earthly life, that it is above the uncertainties that haunt human existence and above the "flux" in general. If no one trusts theology, it is because theologians tend to "agree that everybody is human, every one subject to the human condition, save themselves, who are themselves saved, having been in one way or another exempted from this condition and hard-wired up to God."[5] And so, according to the same logic, theology can only hope to become credible again if and when it assumes a radically hermeneutical position. That is, one which is not above but within the flux.

Now, this was a considerable spoiler, such as when somebody reads the conclusion of a book beforehand in order not to be scared of whatever unfortunate events will befall the hero character in the preceding chapters. Likewise, I should have perhaps warned the readers to skip over the previous paragraph lest their fun with this work be lost. For the fact is that radical hermeneutics is what John Caputo's work, including his theology of the event, is all about. No suspense left! In principle, anyone who gets easily bored by long and arduous deciphering of theoretical details could as well skip over most of what follows without thereby risking overlooking my basic point, which is to show what Caputo's theology of the event tries to say. That's how we often read anyway, no? The *TOC*, the *introduction*, and the *conclusion*, and if these seem interesting enough, we skim through the rest and hope for a happy accident, believing that it belongs to the nature of a true scholar to be serendipitous. And of course, considering the amount of texts that contemporary savants need to cope with, often the happy accident means finding somewhere within the text its concise summary.

But regardless of the unprecedented proliferation of academic writing, with which no mortal can keep pace anymore, I wonder whether this truly is the best way to proceed. Is Caputo's theology, or anyone's theology, or any theory whatsoever satisfactorily reducible to even a *perfect* summary of its theses? If this indeed were the case, if summaries were enough, then you are *already* wasting your time because much of what follows will provide you with little more than a repetitive demonstration that I have meticulously studied the subject at hand. At times, perhaps, you will find my text amusing, but so long as summaries meet one's ends, all has been said already and there is nothing new here to find. Indeed, should things be so simple, I would only continue filling the pages because one just does not write a book on Caputo's theology by merely stating that it is (attempting to be) radical hermeneutics all the way down—even if this is true!

Simplicity is seldom the mark of our theories. Maybe the world really is marvelously simple; that would be the very mark of its perfection. Our interpretations of the world, however, are decidedly imperfect, multilayered, nonlinear, and above all temporal, that is, marked by the passing time and themselves subject to the flux. Our theories are nothing more and nothing less than stories . . .

I like to think here of Antoine de Saint-Exupéry's favorite image of the mountain, which one can only "understand" after one climbs it because the meaning of the scenery that offers itself to the climber at the mountaintop cannot be transferred by words:

> When I speak of "the mountain" I signify the mountain to him alone who has torn himself on its thorns, scrambled up its crags, sweated upon its rocks, picked its flowers, and then drunk deep of the wind that sweeps the summit. I signify—but I *grasp* nothing. And when I say "mountain" to a fat huckster, the word takes no purchase on his heart . . .[6]

Saint-Exupéry also believes the same is true about poetry,

> for even as the scene glimpsed from the mountain-top lacks power to enchant the heart, and has meaning only if it is the meed of the climber's weariness, built up as it were by his effort [. . .] even so is it with the poem that is not begotten of your effort. For though the poem may be another's work, yet the joy it bestows is the fruit of your labours, of your soul's ascent . . .[7]

and I would like to venture here a hypothesis that the same be true about all fruits of human effort and creativity, which therefore do not easily lend themselves to simple summarization. Hence, when somebody commenting upon Caputo's work (and this also includes Caputo himself) says that a theology of the event is an instance of radical hermeneutics, or at least that radical hermeneutics is what Caputo is getting at, this is all true but only inasmuch as it is also true when Saint-Exupéry tells someone that the mountain of which he speaks is high. True, but in a reduced, lifeless way, because

> having given much heed to men's converse and their disputations, I know well the perils of the intellect, whose dogma is that words can *grasp*. It is not by way of language that I shall transmit what is within me; for it is inexpressible in words. I can but *signify* this in so far as you may understand it through other channels than the spoken word. [. . .] Else, I have to drag it out, laboriously—that sunken world within me. And thus, as my clumsiness avails, I display this aspect or that alone—as in the case of my mountain, of which I may say merely that it is high. But it is far more than that, and behind those weak words I have in mind the far-flung glory of the night when one stands on the heights, alone and shivering, amongst the stars.[8]

But how else, one could conceivably wonder, do I propose to introduce Caputo's theology of the event if not by summarizing it or even—good heavens—without words? However, such question, while definitely understandable, would only bear witness to the well-known difficulty inherent to the usage of analogy, namely, that every analogy limps. In a certain sense, the task of understanding a theology of the event does resemble Saint-Exupéry's ascent of the mountain. But, of course, that does not necessarily mean that the truth of Caputo's theology is fully comprehensible only to Caputo himself, since he alone climbed up its slopes and is unable to express the meaning of his journey in words. Such a conjecture is not unheard of—but I think it should be left to people who have nothing better to do anyway!

Rather than the ultimate impossibility of communication, I meant to illustrate by Exupéry's parable that a theology of the event is indeed like a journey, or like a story if you like. Caputo's theology of the event has itself an eventful character, its own history of dreams once dreamed, of goals once set, of obstacles met and overcome along the way, and the whole set of other obstacles it will have to grapple with as it heads toward the future. Not unlike a novel, a theology of the event has an intricate plot that is essential to it but that a simple summary—"it is radical hermeneutics all the way down"—more or less overlooks. For sure, no one would say that by knowing that it is a "story about the adventures of the wandering sailor Ishmael and his voyage on the whale ship *Pequod*, commanded by a one-legged Captain Ahab who is obsessed with a huge whale" actually *gets* Herman Melville's *Moby-Dick*. Similarly, it would be rather naïve to think that one gets Caputo's theology on the basis of knowing what it is all about. To understand a theology of the event, one must trace its steps.

Perhaps this line of argument can be criticized as effectively confounding popular novels and serious academic work. Just as well, however, one could point out that what has been said here is, after all, nothing revolutionary. At least not if we can fairly assume that every work of theology is *also* autobiographical. For if we indeed can, then to *trace* a certain theology instead of just *summarizing* it simply means to apply this assumption in practice.

Needless to say, to think of every work of theology as partly autobiographical is a serious and far-reaching assumption. Hermeneutical theologians tend to accept it as an axiom, and it is easy to see what they mean when one reads Saint Augustine's *Confessiones*. On the other hand, it is significantly more difficult if not plain impossible to identify autobiographical moments in, for example, the *Summa Theologica* of Saint Thomas Aquinas. In fact, the great majority of theological literature, classical as well as contemporary, prefers the cool "scholastic" style over the passionate confession of one's life and faith.

But does this automatically mean that, in principle, the work of an author can be completely uninfluenced by his or her life? Certainly not! Picking up again on the case of Doctor Angelicus, the apparent lack of autobiographical references gives us no right to read his magnum opus as if it was delivered to us from on high by an angel without personal history. For one thing, the risk involved with such reading is that we shall misunderstand Thomas, just like some philosophers—among others, Immanuel Kant—arguably never quite understood Saint Anselm of Canterbury. They read and criticized his *ontological argument* for the existence of God, but they never really did justice to it because they failed to acknowledge one simple autobiographical fact—namely, that the famous proof was written in a Benedictine monastery by a Benedictine monk; it was conceived in a place of prayer and by a man of prayer. Or, as William Desmond puts it, that "when Anselm first formulate[d] the proof, very clearly it [was] situated in an ethos of religious meditation"—so when we fail to take this ethos into account, "we are only juggling abstractions."[9] A noncontextual reading of Saint Thomas, especially when coupled with some magisterial backup, can easily lead us to the point where his theology ends up on the altar as a binding *theologia perennis*, in which case it becomes difficult to imagine why, after Thomas, we should theologize at all.

Hence, to assume that every theology is autobiographically loaded means, at the very least, to take on the hermeneutical position vis-à-vis works of theology, that is, to take seriously their original context. Understood in these terms, I think this is a fair assumption.

Yet, in the case of Caputo we can go further still, for he has been known for his preference of Augustine over Aquinas, the passionate seeker of God—*quid ergo amo, cum deum meum amo?*—over the calm genius of scholastic knowing—the *quinque viae*. More precisely, Caputo has been known for his *shift* from Aquinas to Augustine (as in Heidegger's *Kehre* or Kant's awakening from his *dogmatic slumber*) and above all for his shift from writing in a serious, dry, scholastic style to discovering his own personal voice.

This shift, allegedly brought about by encounters with Derrida—"I gratefully acknowledge the help of Jacques Derrida in loosening my tongue"[10]—is critical for our understanding of Caputo and his theology of the event, and I will treat it with due respect later in the text. At this point I merely wish to stress again that a simple summary of a theology of the event would necessarily miss this eminently biographical point and it would miss it even if it was a perfect summary. *Perfect* in a sense that it would omit nothing, not even a reference to that shift. By its very nature, even a point-by-point, careful, and all-inclusive summary of Caputo's theology will necessarily miss the shift and its significance because, in its disinterested academic seriousness, such summary (résumé) does not function as a *biography* but rather like a *curriculum vitae*. In other words, the distinction between biography and a curriculum vitae closely mirrors the difference between tracing a certain theology and merely summarizing it. The important point here is that just like in the case of an ordinary CV, summary lacks the plot. However, it is only from the plot that autobiographical elements, such as Caputo's *Kehre*, receive their meaning and their significance.

It is on these grounds that I believe that a fair introduction to Caputo's theology can justifiably resemble a novel. Or, in any event, such exposé should allow for a style that does not rule out event, adventure, and emplotment. It should provide an opportunity for the ascent of the mountain.

Conveniently enough (although this is, admittedly, a precalculated convenience), what I am getting at here ties in rather nicely with what Caputo realized in his shift—with the *what* of his shift, so to say: I am talking about the question of style, about the way we write.

Unfortunately, it seems that in academia we have somehow learned to disregard this question as banal, to say the least, perhaps even downright detrimental to the standards of academic rigor. And yet, it is quite possible that the "high handed, unilateral and imperial attitude" of theology Caputo criticized in Leuven is at least as closely related to the way we write as it has to do with the "exemptions we make of ourselves." Whatever other exemptions Caputo had in mind, it may well be that very few people trust theology today simply because only very few people actually understand it. It is as if professional theologians have exempted themselves from the need to be understood. Way too many theological texts, especially in the fields of philosophical and systematic theology, are so technical that they make sense only to a very limited circle of specialists and to no one else.

To be sure, it would be singularly unfair to expect from academic theologians that they do away completely with their technical language. Not only unfair, but also counterproductive, since many of the technical terms we use are, in fact, shorthand for the traditional concepts and well thought-through ideas. Without such terms we would basically have to reinvent the wheel every time we wanted to say something.

Even so, the usage of academic jargon in theology does become increasingly problematic as our true mission—to promote a better understanding of our faith—gets subordinated to the unavoidable need to earn money, to ensure the availability of resources so as to be able to do any research at all. Regrettably, this is a scenario to which the current academic climate seems particularly conducive. So when it happens, as it time and again does, that we find ourselves captive to the requirements of academic prestige (because acclaimed authors get the funds), we cut back on writing for the faithful and we write increasingly only for each other. What once started as a genuine lack of time and energy on our part to ensure that people outside our "royal academic palace" actually understand us very quickly devolves into our near-total inability to make ourselves comprehensible. And then comes Dan Brown—mind you, a novelist—with his *Da Vinci Code* and he brings about more theological misinformation than all Catholic theologians will be able to rectify in a lifetime. That is, unless the preferences of a readership change inexplicably overnight. Chances are, however, that such a miracle will never happen.

Caputo, although he writes mostly in a fairly readable way—"as clearly as he can in American English,"[11] as he likes to say—is well aware and critical of this problem. On that cool spring morning in Leuven we also heard him complain that "it is only very occasionally that confessional theologians rise above these limits [the inner circles of academic theology] and gain a wider audience, and when they do, how they did it and what was going on there repays careful study."[12]

Curious as we were, we would have loved to hear some examples, but Caputo gave us none. Only later, in his interview with Carl Raschke, I came across some concrete names: One of the people named was Thomas Kuhn about whose *Structure of Scientific Revolutions* Caputo says, "it is hard to imagine a book that has been more widely assimilated into the general culture," since "all sorts of people speak of 'paradigm shifts' without even knowing where this phrase comes from."[13] Another favorite of Caputo is William James, "who wrote a lucid, witty, scintillating American English that made the language dance and became a public figure of considerable importance."[14] Søren Kierkegaard wrote just like that, but in Danish, and to give a more recent example too, Caputo thinks highly of Richard Rorty.[15] Finally, Caputo also praises the "Jesus Seminar" people who "write in a traditional style but they have very good marketing skills and they have gone a long way to alerting a wider public to the radical results of historical Jesus research."[16]

You're right! With the possible exception of Kierkegaard and the Jesus Seminar fellows, these are not even theologians. The question is whether such conspicuous lack of theologians on Caputo's list of admirable writers is symptomatic of the current unattractiveness of theology, or just a matter of Caputo's personal preference, or whether it indicates both perhaps. Is it really impossible today to find a notable theologian who can compete with Kuhn? Whatever the answer to this question may be, we cannot deny that theology does not fare particularly well in contemporary society. Most of our work remains confined within our small academic ghetto and has minimal impact even on the other equally "technical" academic disciplines, let alone the everyday life.

Now, in order to change this, we do not need to aim at selling eighty million copies worldwide, or maybe even more, so as to beat Dan Brown at his own game. Even if we had such wild ambitions, we would need marketing skills light years beyond those of the Jesus Seminar magi. But while it is true that marketing skills are vital for reaching the audience on any scale, it remains improbable that even the best of advertising would turn boring texts into bestsellers. Put differently, the first and probably also the best thing we can do in order to increase the public relevance of theology is to improve our style. Caputo somewhat refines this point, saying:

> My hypothesis would be that we do not need to write in an avant-garde style. But we do need to cross over disciplinary barriers and to write in a way that can be understood—unlike the way we train our doctoral students to write, in analytic or continental programs—and in a way that can in fact make the language dance![17]

We can, but we do not necessarily need to, experiment much, but we should at least try to make ourselves comprehensible. My present task in this respect is somewhat different, however, as Caputo already does try to write so that nonspecialists can also understand him, and he does it well. It would be pointless to undertake a translation of Caputo's theology into colloquial English when in fact Caputo did so before he even set pen to paper. I cannot advance Caputo's style, but I can offer a unique perspective on what he says—my individual reading of weak theology. And so in the following pages I have took it upon myself to *show* how it is that Caputo's theology of the event is, at its core, an attempt at radical hermeneutics. In so doing, I have repeatedly crossed the barriers between the scholarly description and storytelling. For this is not a mere summary of weak theology. We are about to follow the adventurous story of weak theology.

2

Call

He thought: "I know no other truth. I only know the structures which are more or less convenient for me to speak about the world. But . . ."

This time he paused for a while and I did not dare to interrupt him.

"Although it seemed to me at times as if they resembled something . . ."

"What do you mean?"

"When I seek I have already found because the spirit desires only what it already has. To find is to see. And how would I look for something that doesn't even have any meaning for me? As I told you, the regret for love is still love. No one suffers from the desire for that which has not been conceived. And yet, there seemed to be longing in me for something that did not yet have a meaning. Why else would I have walked in the direction of truths which I could not conceive?"

[. . .]

"It was a face that illuminated one side of me, and not the other, for it made me turn toward it. But I still don't know it . . ."

—Antoine de Saint-Exupéry, *Citadelle**

*My translation of: "Il réfléchit: 'Je ne connais point d'autre vérité. Je ne connais que des structures qui plus ou moins me sont commodes pour dire le monde. Mais . . .' Il se tut longtemps cette fois et je n'osai point l'interrompre: 'Cependant il m'est apparu quelquefois qu'elles ressemblaient à quelque chose . . .' 'Que veux-tu dire?' 'Si je cherche j'ai trouvé car l'esprit ne désire que ce qu'il possède. Trouver c'est voir. Et comment chercherais-je ce qui pour moi n'a point de sens encore? Je te l'ai dit, le regret de l'amour c'est l'amour. Et nul ne souffre du désir de ce qui n'est pas conçu. Et cependant j'ai eu comme le regret de choses qui n'avaient point encore de sens. Sinon pourquoi aurais-je marché dans la direction de vérités que je ne pouvais concevoir?' [. . .] 'Il était pour moi un visage qui m'éclairait d'un côté et non de l'autre puisqu'il me faisait tourner vers lui. Mais je ne le connais point encore . . .'"

Call it a recollection, if this passage from Saint-Exupéry's *Citadelle* reminds you of Plato and of his explanation of how we arrive at truth. As for the setting, "he" in the dialogue is "the only true geometrician"[1] in the vast desert empire of which the narrator—the point-of-view character—is the sovereign king. The only true geometrician, unlike the ten thousand exegetes, was a humble man well aware of his human limitations. In fact, rather than talking big about his knowledge, he regarded himself as a "man who sometimes dreams of geometry, when more urgent matters, such as sleep, hunger or love, no longer govern him."[2] "The truth has never revealed itself to me,"[3] he used to say. For sure, he always hoped to touch it, to unveil it, but in the end, he was only able to find himself.[4] And yet, the desert king held him in high esteem precisely because of such unpretentious humility. The geometrician was invited to the king's table every day. And in turn the king, when he could not sleep, would often visit his friend the geometrician in his tent, taking off his shoes politely, drinking tea, and enjoying his wisdom.[5]

It was indeed on one of those occasions that the geometrician talked about the face toward which he constantly had to turn because it shone on him from the one side but not from the other. So if you were reminded of Plato, you could picture him sitting there as well, listening to the geometrician and drinking his tea. And you could imagine what his response would be: "You are speaking from my heart, dear friend. You were saying that it sometimes appeared to you as if those structures that you were discovering resembled something. Could it possibly be that you were recalling them because your immortal soul contemplated them in eternity long before you were even born?"

Thus, to be sure, you could call it a recollection, but you could also call it—a call! They are not the same: Remembering directs us toward the past, whereas a call directs us toward the future—even if, in this particular case, they both seem to point to eternity. Still, I prefer to think of the preceding passage as the geometrician's meditation on the call. "That may well be," he could respond to Plato, "and I'm not in the position to tell what my soul saw in eternity or even if it existed before I was born or not. But when I think about it now, it did not feel exactly like recalling something. See, when I recall something that I once knew but I forgot about it, then I think to myself: But of course, silly me, I knew this all along and how could I have forgotten? There is no attraction involved; no gut feeling that I should search in this direction and not in the other. When there is, it is because I am aware that I should already know what I am trying to recall, like when I can't come up with someone's name although it's on the tip of my tongue, which I find most annoying. But there was this face, for want of a better word, which I did not know and which I don't even know today, as I've already told you. Now, I do not think this face ever caused me any annoyance and it certainly wouldn't show itself to me suddenly like that forgotten name often does, whenever I stop trying to recall it. No, in fact I was never able to stop trying. It didn't annoy me, but it made me long for it. It called me, and it called me from the one side but not from the other."

All of this is, of course, only a fiction—I mean a fiction about Saint-Exupéry's fiction. The only true geometrician of the fictional desert empire never spoke these words, but he never explicitly endorsed Plato's ideas either; hence, this was a plausible or at least not an inconsistent account of events. In any case, I like this fictional possibility because, thus described, the "face" figures as the source of the call, or even better—the face in Saint-Exupéry's text is a metaphor for the event of the call.

But why event? What happened? Did something particular happen to the geometrician that he told his friend about while they were drinking tea, but about which he did not care to tell us? Well, lots of things happened in fact, such as that recurring feeling that the structures he was discovering resembled something. Or think of the face that would illuminate him from the one side but not from the other. However, you probably would not regard these as events worthy of the name, and honestly, neither would I. For in order to speak about events—at least in the sense in which this term will be used in the present work—it will be wrong to conflate events with what is happening. Here we already touch upon one of the crucial premises of a theology of the event: a basic Deleuzean distinction that Caputo repeats, the difference between events and simple occurrences. Event is not what happens but that which is going on *in* what happens.

Accordingly, as a matter of fact, many things must have happened in the life of our geometrician, although Saint-Exupéry seems intent on telling us only about the king's visits. The ruler loved to watch his wise man preparing the tea, and he was "touched at seeing him so intent on the tea [. . .] that during these meditative minutes, he was more absorbed in the tea than in a problem of geometry."[6]

> "So you, who know so much, do not despise the humbler joys of life?" I said.
>
> For a while he kept silent. Only when he was quite satisfied with the tea did he make answer.
>
> "I who know so much—what has that to do with it? Why should a guitar player despise the ceremonial of tea merely because he knows something about the relations between the notes of music?"
>
> [. . .]
>
> After a pause he added: "I wonder now! I doubt if my triangles can enlighten me as to the pleasure given me by the tea. Yet it may well be that this pleasure can throw a little light on my triangles."

> "What do you mean by that, my friend?"
>
> "When I experience an emotion, a need comes on me to describe. Thus when I love a woman, I will talk to you of her hair, her eyelashes, her lips, her gestures which are music for the heart. Would I talk of her gestures, lips and hair and eyelashes, were there not the face I have discerned behind these things? I can describe the elements of beauty in her smile; nevertheless the smile came first."[7]

These were the things that happened—the tea and the things about which the geometrician could talk and which he could describe. But the smile came first! But the love came first, which is why it is foolish to try to give reasons for love. Reasons and descriptions only come after the event and whatever happens, for which one can find words, derives its sense from that event. Hence the longing and the sense of orientation came first and only because of them could the geometrician scramble for words and come up with the "face" toward which he constantly had to turn because it shone on him from the one side but not from the other. The sense of it all—the event within what happened—was the call, that strange attraction toward something that he did not know and yet he could not ignore.

Indeed, as Deleuze would say, events are about the sense—and not about the meaning—of what is happening. Since this sense/meaning dichotomy lies at the heart of the distinction between what happens and what is going on in what happens, it will come as no surprise that this distinction is also crucial for our understanding of Caputo's theology. In fact, Caputo even explicitly says that his hitherto most theological work, *The Weakness of God: A Theology of the Event*, was inspired by Deleuze's *The Logic of Sense* and is "very much a contribution to a '(theo)logic of sense.'"[9] Bear this in mind as we go on and there will be more about it later, but for now I am more interested in the call, in the event of the call.

Here is one of those summaries against which I argued previously, but it is still a good summary: Everything in Caputo's theology of the event stands and falls on the event of the call. When Caputo speaks about the call, of course, he does exactly the same thing as Saint-Exupéry's geometrician, namely giving a name to an event in order to be able to talk about it. The face—the call. From this moment on, the event that is "transpiring" in a theology of the event will be referred to as "the call" and it is all well and fine, for as long as we do not forget that beyond or rather beneath all this talk (inside the names) there is an event—the event of the call. In other words, there is something alive within a theology of the event, except that it is a *no-thing*, less than something, it is an event. And yet, without this event a theology of the event would have/make no sense.

This is also very important for the following methodological reason: We have already begun to follow the adventure of weak theology—a name Caputo uses as a synonym for his theology of the event—and there is a real risk, as we go on, that we will confuse this adventure with the adventurous story of John D. Caputo. Naturally, such confusion is for the most part unavoidable and undesirable. Why, in fact, should we want things otherwise? Is this not the story of *Caputo's* theology? It surely is! And, as previously argued, Caputo's theology is autobiographically charged; whence the inescapability of a certain undecidability between the adventure of weak theology and the journey of its founding father.

However, so long as our main interest is a theology of the event, we should not allow the intellectual journey of Professor Caputo to outshine his own work. What is needed here is a delicate balance between, on the one hand, the exposition of the event that animates a theology of the event and, on the other hand, the narration of the story of this event's current avatar—Caputo's weak theology. Subtle indeed as it is, we can easily see that this balance is but another way of distinguishing between what happens and what is going on in what happens. It is also the same as admitting (in agreement with the arguments given earlier) that in order to understand Caputo's theology we must 1) trace its development, that is, we must see what happened; *while at the same time* we must 2) remember that the *sense* of a theology of the event derives from the event of the call that is as different from what happened as it is inextricably linked with it.

Now here lies the complication: In order to do justice to Caputo's theology of the event, both 1) and 2) are equally important and, indeed, they need to be kept in a well-balanced tension. Unfortunately, however, these two sides of the same story cannot be handled in the same way. As for what happened, the suitable method offers itself rather obviously and I have discussed it already, hence only a reminder: I am talking about the biographical narrative. This is relatively simple. For the one thing, everything that happens does so in history, in time. This is why a "diachronic" narrative usually works best when we need to tell what happened. Also, and this is particularly important, on the level of what happens, time flows only in one direction—from the past through the present and on into the future. So it is quite easy to plan a chapter on the actual developments in Caputo's theology: It all started with the doctorate and later Caputo met Derrida and he loosened his tongue, and so on and so forth.

However, with respect to the second point, when it comes to the event of a theology of the event, things become more difficult. It may seem counterintuitive, but events—and especially sense—belong to the sphere where time can flow in all directions. Deleuze calls this time *aion* as opposed to *chronos* (which is the time of what happens) and the idea about time flowing in all directions becomes somewhat less surreal when you substitute the word "significance" for sense. This is certainly not a bad approximation of sense and it does help to see how sense—in this case significance—can operate retrospectively. For example, how the significance of the serious, dry academic style of Caputo's first two books changes with Caputo's shift in style to which I referred in the introduction. The obvious complication comes from the fact that with respect to the sense of weak theology the planning of the chapters cannot be as straightforward as with respect to biography. What comes where and when? There is no simple answer to this question because there is no simple sequence—and yet there can be no question of omitting the sections on sense if we want more than just Caputo's story, interesting as it may be.

In order to deal with this difficulty as best as I can, I have decided to alternate between the biographical, chronologically organized sections and the sections entitled "series," such as the present one. It is actually a modest attempt to imitate Deleuze's style of *The Logic of Sense*, which itself consists of thirty-four series. Once again, while on the surface just a matter of style, it is also much more than that. Prominent Deleuze commentator James Williams offers such an unbeatably lucid explanation of what is at stake here that I could not resist quoting it at length:

> The use of series as opposed to chapters in *Logic of Sense* is significant. In most books, the order of the chapters is important and resistant to jumbling or to skipping. This is not the case for series, since these are designed to operate in different orders and as independent blocks or connected chains. Though the series follow on from one another in some key ways, and though in some sense all the series are connected, they also operate independently of the order they are presented in. The connections between series are not order-dependent.[9]

Thus, besides the fact that *The Logic of Sense* served as an important source of inspiration for Caputo's thus far most important theological work, it also seems fruitful to follow Deleuze's masterpiece on the level of style. I would not go as far as saying that it does not really matter where one starts reading the "series" in my work, but they are indeed meant to "bleed into one another" even to the extent of a certain repetition. If they should not be read totally at random, it is only because of the subsequent editing, whereby a kind of "learning spiral" was introduced, so that the latter series build upon the former. In any case, as I have said, for the adventure of a theology of the event these series are equally as important as the story about what happened. Equally important—not more! Let us therefore move now on to the biography.

3
Brother Paul

On the preexistence of souls, I have an even more radically negative opinion than Saint-Exupéry's geometrician. Therefore, I think the best place to start is southwest Philadelphia on that sunny October Saturday, 1940, when the future Professor Caputo was born. Christened John D., he was raised in a Catholic family of second-generation Italian immigrants and answered to the nickname *Jackie* until religious sisters in grade school reminded him of his proper name.[1] For Caputo, this was to become a matter of quite some significance in his relation to Jacques Derrida—a point to which we shall return later—but it seems that even then the issue of names mattered to the young pupil, and Caputo learned to distinguish between the people who know him and call him Jack, and those who do not know him all that well and call him John, which reminds him of nuns:[2]

> I think of being a small child in grade school, terrified of those black-and-white figures that hovered over me, like angels of terror, delegates of heaven and hell, of dark powers and vast cosmic forces. I'm sure they were unselfish and very good women, but some of them, I think, were teaching grade school because they loved God, not us. At any rate, they scared the daylight out of me—and they called me "John," where everyone else, my family and my friends, called me "Jack." So my world divided between John/Jack, the outside hostile "world"/the familial and familiar. All my life everything "official" and impersonal went under the name of "John." When I began to publish, I used "John D.," which was meant to build a wall as high as possible around that scared little boy back in grade school that I am (was/will always be).[3]

Little can be reconstructed from this period on the basis of existing interviews. Still, if the basic traits of a person's character show themselves already in childhood, we can think of young Jackie/Jack as somewhat similar to who the older John D./Professor Caputo came to be: A child and a man of two worlds, still European and already American, a child and a man of double voice and double nature or, as he once said in response to Cleo McNelly Kearns, "at once Kierkegaardian and Philadelphian, melancholy and upbeat, religious and aesthetic."[4]

It must take no less than such character, we can imagine, to make a decision—in one's teens and in post–World War II America—to enter a religious order. Today it may come as a bit of a surprise that Caputo, an author known for his vivid humor and who does not shy away from scorching irony, once spent fifteen months in the novitiate of the Brothers of the Christian Schools. Picturing Caputo as a member of the order founded by Saint Jean-Baptiste de La Salle—a man "whose 'normalizing' teaching methods Foucault singles out for abuse in *Discipline and Punish*," as Caputo himself pointed out[5]—is . . . well, rather amusing. And yet it happened. It is a simple and irrefutable fact bearing heavily on the story of weak theology. Young Brother Paul (just one more name to add to the list next to John/D./Jack/Jackie)[6] spent those fifteen months mostly in silence, allowed to speak only for three hours on Thursdays and Sundays. "It was very difficult, but it transformed me," Caputo tells us, and he says it with gratitude: "I'm eternally in the debt of that training. It plucked me from the streets of southwest Philadelphia and made me into someone else."[7]

It was at this time that Brother Paul met his first love. This is not about Caputo's family life, obviously, since he was still in the novitiate then. No, here I am talking about the "Melancholy Dane," Søren Kierkegaard. *Stará láska nehrdzavie*, they say in Slovakia—old love does not rust—and Caputo definitely confirms this wise saying with regard to Kierkegaard: "From the time I was eighteen years old, when I first discovered him, Kierkegaard has been my hero. Unbroken. All the time I was studying Saint Thomas and, later on, Heidegger and then Derrida—at no matter what point in my life—Kierkegaard has always been my hero as a writer."[8] Indeed, Kierkegaard's influence on Caputo's style surpasses even that of Derrida, which is quite a thing to say considering that Derrida loosened Caputo's tongue. Derrida helped Caputo see that even in an academic work it is possible to write with one's own voice; he helped him to "let it all out" and to "write what Jack is thinking."[9] But when that happened, the stylistic turn Caputo's writing took was decidedly Kierkegaardian, not Derridean.

Once again, however, more is at stake here than just a question of style. Old love does not rust, and the way in which we are affected throughout our lives by the loves of our late teens and early twenties, when we really begin discovering the world, should not be underestimated. Caputo brings up the same point with respect to Carl Braig and the influence his book *Vom Sein* had on young Heidegger:

> I think that his book had the kind of influence upon Heidegger which one is subject to at twenty years of age, when one's world is

> only beginning to take shape. It is an age of high excitement and deep impressions, when a teacher can exercise a lasting but not easily analyzable impulse upon the directions of one's path. Decisive influences are ineffable, indeterminate, obscure. Braig's book is full of motives and themes which are so thoroughly transmuted in Heidegger's mature writings that their original form is no longer recognizable.[10]

Ineffable, indeterminate, and obscure—sometimes not to be found in the indices of names at the end of our works at all. But even if commentators every so often overlook them, our early loves are often the secret reason behind what, how, and also why we write.

Hence, the (not so) secret ingredient of Caputo's theology is Kierkegaard, but there are more! We are told that young Brother Paul would read Kierkegaard "secretly at night, after the lights went out, with a flashlight"[11] (we are also told that the flashlight is a joke), while "during the day and with all due decorum" he studied Saint Thomas Aquinas. He, too, was a hero of Caputo's young age, as well as Jacques (another Jack!) Maritain and Martin Heidegger, Meister Eckhart and Angelus (another angel!) Silesius.

It is true, as I have said before, that Caputo has been known for his preference of Augustine over Aquinas, but for a second time, early loves should never be taken too lightly. Even today, Caputo prefers to say "Saint Thomas" rather than "Aquinas" and when asked why, he answers:

> It has to do with the fact that when I first opened my intellectual eyes there was Saint Thomas, his angelic hand (if that is not an oxymoron) outstretched to lead the way, and I have always, always been unable to repudiate that beginning, even after I had strayed off to different and stranger sites and very heterodox opinions.[12]

Not only did Saint Thomas occupy Brother Paul's mind at the same time (well, almost—during the day and during the night) as Kierkegaard, but they actually competed for the young novice's heart. The legacy of Caputo's double voice and double nature: Kierkegaard and Aquinas,

> two conflicting loves, the great philosophical reconciler of nature and grace, faith and reason, the author of several nimble and much anthologized proofs of God's existence, along with the great champion of the leap of faith who made merciless mockery of every such proof.[13]

In terms of Caputo's style, however, this inner "conflict of loves" becomes only noticeable in hindsight. For whatever author Caputo is today, he was nothing like that in the past. Saint Thomas, in fact, held

Caputo under his spell for quite some time. We probably would not know about this if Caputo himself had not pointed it out, but even long after he had parted with the Brothers of the Christian Schools, already as a professor at Villanova University, Caputo wrote an article on Thomas's ontological proof of God's existence and Kant's refutation thereof.[14] What is interesting in that article, aside from the argument itself, is the fact that Caputo employed in it proper symbolic logic. So when you then find him later teasing Richard Swinburne for thinking that the arguments for the existence of God can be formulated in the language of symbolic logic,[15] you not only get the point but also the joke.

It was, however, the later Saint Thomas—Saint Thomas after his own *Kehre*, Saint Thomas auto-deconstructed—who seems to have left the most lasting impact on Caputo's work. Caputo would later refer to the Doctor Angelicus on many occasions, but with the regularity typical for what one considers very important, he would not forget to mention the mystical experience Saint Thomas had on December 6, 1273. We can find the most extensive description of what happened on that fateful morning in Caputo's *Heidegger and Aquinas*,[16] but the story is quite well known, so I shall just say that after this experience Saint Thomas stopped writing altogether (his *Summa* unfinished) and when pressed to explain why, he answered: "Everything which I have written seems like straw to me compared to what I have seen and what has been revealed to me."[17]

Even as recently as a decade ago, honorable superiors in Catholic seminaries in Slovakia regarded a reference to this *totaliter aliter* experience of Saint Thomas as rebellious. It was, indeed, often pulled out by students to say: "Ha! We have it on the authority of Saint Thomas himself that this *theologia perennis* is nothing but straw!" For young Brother Paul as well as for the later Professor Caputo, however, this never was a question of a simple refusal of metaphysical thinking or of rational thinking in general. Being so closely linked with Derrida and postmodernism, Caputo is nowadays often subject to being perceived through stereotypes, despite his emphasizing all the time that he is not postmodern in the sense of being antimodern, just as he is not anti-Enlightenment but rather tries to be enlightened about the Enlightenment. Similarly, it would be wrong to assume that Caputo thinks that Saint Thomas's mystical experience resolved it all in favor of mysticism and against rational knowledge. True, Caputo thinks this was the best "last" thing for Saint Thomas to live through, after which the most natural course of things for Thomas was to meet the Lord (Saint Thomas died three months after his mystical experience), but he does not think that Saint Thomas should not have written what he wrote at all. On this point, I think, Caputo is in agreement with

W. Norris Clarke who, respectable Thomist scholar that he is, points out that Saint Thomas never claimed that

> well-made straw cottages, sculptures, and signposts are not helpful, even necessary along the journey, nor that he had put an end to all Western metaphysics and its usefulness for everybody else along the journey, as a propaedeutic for the mystical and final heavenly vision.[18]

To put this differently, rather than refuting the scholastic rationality of Saint Thomas *tout court*, by pointing to the mystical experience of Saint Thomas Caputo intends to show that even the author of *Summa Theologica* knew that his rational account of things was necessarily limited. What is at stake here is the delimitation and transgression of reason, not its complete uselessness.

Seen from this perspective, Kierkegaard and Saint Thomas—the two conflicting loves of the young novice—do not even need to be entirely irreconcilable. Perhaps one can indeed find a certain parallel between Kierkegaard's leap of faith and Saint Thomas's mystical experience and subsequent silence. In any case, even if linking Caputo's two early heroes in such a way seems a bit awkward, it still is a particularly fruitful strategy because the tension involved in this unlikely union actually defines the entire corpus of Caputo's later work (and therefore weak theology, too).

Here we have another overarching and therefore potentially misleading summary, but this time we have it on the authority of Caputo himself. "The question of the limits of what can be discursively, demonstratively established by rational argument and what lies beyond or eludes those limits has always provoked me,"[19] he tells us in one of the interviews; and when he says always, he really means right from the start, as the question of "how to think about reason and what lies outside or beyond reason" was the very first question with which Caputo dealt in a serious academic way, and which eventually led to his dissertation and his first book, *The Mystical Element in Heidegger's Thought*.[20] Later the problem of the delimitation of reason and of the transgression of reason's limits gave birth to a more general interest on Caputo's part in the space between philosophy and religion,[21] which is one constant thread running through all Caputo's work and which is why nowadays Caputo is quite deservedly praised (and sometimes blamed) for practically establishing the field of continental philosophy of religion on the American academic scene.

Well, it all started there, in the novitiate, with Kierkegaard and with Saint Thomas, and with all the other names mentioned, about which I shall say more in due time. But before young Brother Paul could get this far, he had to transgress his own limits. More precisely, he had to break through the limits imposed on him by his religious community. For it is one thing to read Kierkegaard secretly at night. Often, we only have evenings and nights left for doing what we like doing after we have spent the days doing what we need to do. Such is the unfortunate but banal way of life. How difficult or unbearable this becomes depends on how big the distance is between what one likes doing and what one has to do—this gap is directly proportional to the desire to change the course of things. "In graduate school, I felt I had to prove to my professors that I knew the modernist map, that I could fill a blackboard reproducing its boundary lines," Caputo tells us about his studies at La Salle University. "But my most abiding desire, my most hidden simmering instinct was to twist free of all that . . ."[22] Now, we may never succeed entirely in following our most abiding desires, but it would be foolish not to try if there is a chance. Young Brother Paul saw such chance in postgraduate studies. So we find him, at the end of this period, meeting with the provincial of the Brothers of the Christian Schools to discuss his ambitions:

> "[And I said] I think I've figured out what I want to do, I want to teach philosophy. I want you to send me to Fordham University in New York City, it's a good Catholic university, and I'll come back and teach philosophy at La Salle for the rest of my life, and I promise I'll be good at it."
>
> And the Brother Provincial said: "Well, maybe. But maybe we'll send you to work in the orphanage and you'll spend the rest of your life serving in the orphanage, because what's important to you is the will of God as it's expressed by your superiors."
>
> "Well, actually, no. I want to teach philosophy." And we could not reconcile those differences.[23]

Were it not for this transgression, perhaps we would have never known that there once was one Brother Paul.

4
Transgression

Once there were discovered traces of a man who, having left his tent at dawn to head toward the sea, walked up to the cliffs and fell down, because the cliffs were steep. There were logicians there who studied the signs and learned the truth about what had happened, for there was no link missing from the chain of events. The steps followed one after the other and each step was made possible by the previous one. And so they followed the steps backward from consequence to cause and they brought the dead man back to his tent. And they went forward from cause to consequence and they returned him to death.

"We have understood everything," exclaimed the logicians and they congratulated themselves.

And I felt that to understand would mean to know, as I did, about a smile more fragile than still water because it could be tarnished by a single thought, a smile which perhaps at that moment did not even exist because it belonged to a sleeping face, and which was not even from here but from the tent of a stranger a hundred days of walking away.

—Antoine de Saint-Exupéry, *Citadelle**

---

*My translation of: "On découvrit une fois les traces d'un homme qui, ayant à l'aube quitté sa tente en direction de la mer, marcha jusqu'à la falaise qui était verticale et se laissa choir. Il était là des logiciens qui se penchèrent sur les signes et connurent la vérité. Car aucun chaînon ne manquait à la chaîne des événements. Les pas se succédaient les uns aux autres, il n'en était aucun que lé précédent n'autorisât. En remontant les pas de conséquence à cause on ramenait le mort vers sa tente. En descendant les pas de cause à conséquence on le reforçait dans sa mort."

"Nous avons tout compris," s'écrièrent les logiciens qui, les uns les autres, se congratulèrent.

"Et moi j'estimais que comprendre c'eût été connaître, comme il se trouvait que je connuse, un certain sourire plus fragile qu'une eau dormante puisqu'il eût suffi d'une simple pensée pour le ternir, et qui peut-être en cet instant n'existait point puisque d'un visage endormi, et qui justement n'était point d'ici mais de la tente d'un étranger située à cent jours de marche."

Our acquaintance, the desert king, indeed knew what the traces in the sand could not reveal: The dead man had for long been tormented by an impossible love until that morning when he could no longer bear the blaze of that fire and so he extinguished it in the cold sea. A man in love left footprints in the sand, but love evaporated from its own trace, leaving behind but a thread of signs stretching from the tent to the cliffs. Logicians studied those signs and explained them without ever grasping the sense of what happened, for indeed—as we learned from Blaise Pascal—the heart has its reasons, which reason does not know.[1] Had they really wanted to understand what happened, the logicians would have had to transgress the strict boundaries of their science and look for the answer in a tent a hundred days of walking away. Such possibility, however—that there could be something invisible at play—did not even cross their minds. Why should it? Was not the chain of steps written in the sand unbroken? Why then, they would ask with William Occam, complicate the story with a detour of hundreds of miles? Why tie themselves up in unnecessary knots?

Still, we may suspect that the logicians would have remained oblivious to the role that the "smile more fragile than still water" played in this tragedy even if the "detour" had not been necessary because the femme fatale lived right there, in the very same tent. For the logicians, something as evanescent as a smile could not be of any consequence, certainly not in competition against the hard facts written in the sand.

This explains why logic—the well-structured reasoning—every now and then produces simultaneously the most elegant (*pace* Occam) yet the most useless (*pace* Pascal) solutions to some of our most pressing questions. Very little seems logical in love and war, in prayers and tears, in happiness and suffering. Perhaps even nothing logical by definition. Hence, there have always been voices calling for a prison break, insisting that in order to understand who we are—and to understand the sense of what is really happening to us—we ought to allow for the transgression of the limits imposed on us by pure reason. That we should get beyond this or that within the limits of reason alone and bring in religion and poetry, desire, play, and chance—simply all those unruly things that "reasonable" people view with suspicion for their ability to lead us into chaos. Over thirty thousand square days of the desert to wade through without direction instead of a single path connecting the tent with the sea. A land or a mountain "that I will show you" against the fatherland and one's own kin. Forty years in the desert, hungry and homeless but free. Well then, screw freedom together with all this beyond-the-reasonable complexity of life, the logicians will say. This is madness begetting still more madness:

> We protest, they said, in the name of reason. We are the priests of the truth. Your laws are laws of a god that is less reliable than ours. You have your armed men and with this weight of muscles you can crush us. But we will have reason against you even in the basement of your jails. [. . .] You must make us your ministers, because we are the ones who know.[2]

The Grand Inquisitor could not agree more. Not so the king, however! Far from granting them their wish, after hearing out what the logicians had to say, the king sincerely began wondering about the limits of stupidity. He would have, without the slightest hesitation, taken the only true geometrician as his advisor, had his old friend ever wished for it. Whereas the logicians, in their arrogant certainty, in their unwillingness to see beyond the straight line of their thinking, irritated the king like no one else: "How pretentious you are, he told them, following the dance of shadows on the walls and thinking that you know . . ."[3]

Shadows on the walls. Could this be again an allusion to Plato, his legendary Allegory of the Cave? That would be interesting, would it not, considering that Plato supported the rule of those who know? The idea of a philosopher-king is originally his; philosophers that are kings or kings that have become philosophers are the guardians of Plato's ideal city, the Kallipolis. But just as Plato would not pick leaders from among the cave prisoners who were only aware of the shadows on the wall, but would single them out from among those few who transgressed the boundaries of the cave, saw the Sun, and "are able to grasp the eternal and unchangeable," so also Saint-Exupéry's desert king would gladly take advice from the only true geometrician because he was somehow able to follow the signs that were not there to be seen, arriving safely at truths without any perceptible traces to tag along. For the king, the true knowledge meant much more than the deductive and inductive art of reasoning.

So why this parable? And what's more, why use this parable when it actually seems to be leaving us a bit perplexed as to who is right here? It is not *that* easy to rebut the arguments of the logicians; they might indeed be right even when in prison. Well, that is precisely why. Our history, at least the history of what we call the Western world, is littered with the proposals to let those "who know" lead us, but somehow we have never been able to agree conclusively on what counts as true knowledge. The sober, well-structured, and evidence-based reasoning of the logicians or the almost mystical and therefore unrepeatable but so much more holistic wanderings of the geometrician? Aquinas or Eckhart? Occam or Pascal? Pascal the scientist or Pascal the tormented author of the *Pensées*? Hegel or Kierkegaard? On and on, the opposing camps entrench themselves and the debate continues right up to our own times, say between the analytic and continental philosophers—the latter considering the former heartless (too much like Saint-Exupéry's logicians), while the former disregard the latter as true philosophers altogether (all this whining isn't really philosophy, it's merely literature). Or speaking more generally, ours is the period—*has been* the period for some time now—of the clash between modernity, between the Enlightenment as the age of reason on the one hand, and whatever postmodernity means on the other. However one looks at it, across the ages it is becoming ever more evident that the one thing that those who claim "to know" actually do not seem to know is what it means to know. Nevertheless, epistemology continues to fascinate us like few other things, and maybe precisely because the fundamental nature of knowledge keeps evading us. The quest for what can we know and how can we know it cuts across all scientific disciplines, and it keeps theologians busy just as surely as it occupies philosophers.

It will not come as a surprise, therefore, that Caputo, too, is a partaker in this quest; and inasmuch as this quest has always also been a struggle, an intellectual war, Caputo's philosophical and theological work is like a battlefield on which the competing interpretations clash. Not unlike Saint-Exupéry's desert king, Caputo has time and again expressed impatience with too much certainty resulting from the lack of willingness and/or ability to look beyond one's straight line of thinking and beliefs. And inasmuch as knowledge has always also been coupled with power—the synchronized "deployment of force and the establishment of truth" in Foucault's terms[4]—Caputo, again not unlike the king, has been suspicious of the rule of those "who know" and of the powers that be in general.

By way of example, Caputo got extremely frustrated when some of his colleagues (read: philosophers) refused to transgress the narrow boundaries of their own academic tradition during the infamous Cambridge-Derrida affair. As Caputo recalls these events, "in the spring of 1992 Derrida was nominated to receive an honorary degree from Cambridge University. On May 9, 1992, a letter was published in the London *Times* urging the faculty of Cambridge to vote against awarding this degree to Derrida."[5] For the nineteen signatories, who self-proclaimed themselves as those "working in leading departments of philosophy throughout the world," Derrida's work did not meet the "accepted standards of clarity and rigor."[6] They went even as far as suggesting that Derrida simply made his career out of "translating into the academic sphere tricks and gimmicks similar to those of the Dadaists or of the concrete poets."[8] No one at Cambridge University, for that matter, had asked the undersigned for their advice on the issue; to those angered by the incident it must have appeared as if the signatories were saying: "You, Cambridge University, must make us your ministers, because we know!" Caputo went ballistic. Reacting to what had happened even some years later in his *Deconstruction in a Nutshell*, he ridiculed the signatories for "trying very hard to make themselves look international" while in fact being "for the most part intensely narrow 'analytic' philosophers."[8] Defending not only his friend Derrida, but also what he regarded as the right to do philosophy otherwise, Caputo lashed Derrida's deriders for "appointing themselves Defenders of the Good and the True,"[9] and some of them for "maintaining the dominance of a narrow and culturally irrelevant style of philosophizing in the American Philosophical Association and Ivy League departments of philosophy [. . .] with the result that philosophy today tends to be of almost no importance whatsoever in the United States and in most of its major universities."[10]

By academic standards, this was one formidable display of indignation, not that dissimilar from what the middle finger means in street parlance. A fitting example, I think, of just how fierce the battle for what counts as true knowledge can get; it was, indeed, not for nothing that the logicians feared that they may end up with their truth in jail.

On most other occasions, however, Caputo chose to be a little more reserved, simply stating, for example, that philosophers annoy him "when they try to insulate themselves against the biblical tradition, when they are dismissive and even contemptuous of it."[11] In this particular case, Caputo's relative reservedness may be due to the fact that he, too, once was somewhat guilty of a similar lack of courage to cross through the firmly established borders. Speaking of the role that religion has played in his work, Caputo in an interview with Keith Putt once confessed that "[a]t first it [religion] was a strictly personal issue for me. I was a philosopher and philosophers are antagonistic to it, allergic to it; they do not want to hear it or talk about it."[12] Only gradually did Caputo shift from a purely philosophical work in the fields of hermeneutics and deconstruction to a more general and interdisciplinary interest in continental philosophy and religion. And, eventually, also to theology.

As Caputo became party to a theological quest, of course, the parameters of his quest for knowledge also altered. Theologians are by no means spared from the obligation to ask what can be known and how. Only knowing in theology is much more conspicuously intertwined with believing, and there is one extra source of knowing to ponder on—revelation. But the tussle between the logicians and the geometrician continues with an undiminished intensity. It cannot be otherwise; theology will not do without a quarrel: Not only are the stakes potentially much higher (such as the eternal bliss or damnation) and probably many more souls involved, but theology as we know it practically does not exist without philosophy. The epistemological battle thus merely spills over into it. In theology, Caputo seems to suggest, the clash that parallels the epistemological battle occurs between religious fundamentalism and weak theology, or even between (radical) orthodoxy and (radical) heterodoxy.

As one may expect, Caputo sides in this quarrel with the geometrician and the king. He is highly critical of too much confidence typically displayed by the fundamentalists and opposed to any straightforward unshakable knowledge of how things *really* are in general. That is, as we have seen and shall see again and again, the main thrust of Caputo's radically hermeneutical position and of his theology of the event, too: "to deny that the God's-eye point of view makes sense, to deny that there is some overarching and unitary right view at all, that there is some right way if only we could figure it out."[13] For the same reason Caputo believes that "serious philosophy and theology involve a work of ceaseless critique of our capacity to deceive ourselves," constantly reminding us that "nobody is hardwired up to the Secret."[14] So with regard to religious fundamentalism, Caputo seems almost dumbstruck—"Fundamentalism is very difficult for me to understand because it really does seem to me to be perfectly crazy. [*Laughter*] You have to wonder how people can let things like that get inside their heads."[15] And even more lost for words regarding the prevalence of fundamentalism in the United States: "If you've come to me for an explanation of that, you've come to the wrong person."[16]

What is wrong with fundamentalism, according to Caputo, is that it "attempts to close down the open-ended question 'what do I love when I love my God?' with a fixed Answer [*sic*], to trap the passion for God within literal formulations."[17] A logicization of the passion for God, so to speak—"one more case of Aaron and the golden calf, one more confusion of the raft with the ocean."[18] In words of the king of Saint-Exupéry:

> How pretentious you are, he told them, following the dance of shadows on the walls and thinking that you know . . . do not come near me, you slaves, armed with your hammer and nails, pretending that you have built and launched the ship.[19]

For the ship is, in the first place, born out of the desire for the sea. It is that desire that launches the ship—an event that pulls together all the material and workers, wood planks, nails, ropes, and sails, but that none of these elements can capture. This sailing ship is but one of the many possible incarnations of the desire for the sea, but it cannot contain this desire. Because, as the king explains, creation (just as well as an event) is of a different nature than the created object (that which is happening); creation

> escapes from the traces that it leaves behind and it cannot be read in any signs. You will always discover these marks, these traces, and these signs, which are arising from each other. For the shadow of all creation on the wall of reality is pure logic. But such obvious discovery will not prevent you from being stupid.[20]

These words of Saint-Exupéry's king, I think, describe nicely not only the correlation, in Caputo's theology, between the event that animates religion and the particular religious incarnations thereof, but consequently they also explain why Caputo has such a problem with religious fundamentalism. To really know—to arrive at the final, overarching, and unitary right view—one would have to transgress beyond the realm of marks, traces, and signs and capture the uncapturable, contain what cannot be contained. That, according to Caputo, is impossible. We are but slaves armed with hammer and nails, this is our hermeneutical situation, and, as Caputo likes to say following Heidegger, this is the difficulty of life. Nobody is hardwired up to the secret. We should learn to live with it.

When you think about it, from this perspective transgression looks a whole lot different from what we began with; now it is a transgression halted, an impossible transgression pointing us toward where one cannot go. I would like to save this important observation for the next series, however, and return for one more moment to the battlefield where Caputo wages war with (radical) orthodoxy.

Orthodoxy, while praiseworthy for preserving a "considerable and undeniable treasure" of "venerable memories," also deserves deconstruction because, according to Caputo, not quite unlike fundamentalism, it is "inordinately attached to itself and inordinately given to closing itself up into a well-rounded circle, in which contingent human constructions are draped in the garments of divinity, in which human beings confuse themselves with God."[21] But in addition to what he regards as confusing the raft with the ocean, Caputo finds orthodoxy questionable for its propensity to link itself with (often violent) power:

> Orthodoxy, like history, is written by the winners. Orthodoxy *is* the history written by the winners. The unorthodox have very often been excommunicated, exiled, or simply killed so that their point of view

> has been extinguished in order to let the prevailing view look like God's point of view. One could of course attribute the victory of the orthodox to the Holy Spirit, but if so the Holy Spirit got considerable help from a lot of killing.[22]

In the face of what has indeed been a very bloody history, Caputo pleads for what he calls "weak theology," arguing that "the very idea of orthodoxy—and this goes *a fortiori* for anything called radical orthodoxy—should make us wonder how much fear and anxiety, how much repression and authoritarianism, how much exclusionary and ex-communicatory will-to-power simmers beneath its surface."[23]

There you have it. Radical orthodoxy. A certain intellectual bad blood between this movement and Caputo is difficult to overlook. In fact, when on that cool spring morning in Leuven Professor Caputo criticized the "imperial theologians who get themselves mixed up with God" for ruining the credibility of theology, it was rather clear to us that among them he also included the sharks of radical orthodoxy. Compare this:

> They [the imperial theologians] agree that everybody is human, every one subject to the human condition, save themselves, who are themselves saved, having been in one way or another exempted from this condition and hard-wired up to God.[24]

And this:

> Milbank and the school of radical orthodoxy confess that we are all historically situated, all the offspring of a language and the complex nest of linguistic, cultural and social conditions, that we all have our own inherited narratives to which we cling because they make sense to us, which they even concede is largely for aesthetic reasons. [. . .] Nonetheless, Christian theology must make an exception of itself because its story is the only one that happens to make sense, the only one that supplies genuine religious transcendence, while everyone's story is nihilistic. [. . .] Everything else is *nihil* and nugatory, violent and degraded—except for a little patch of being, truth and beauty that is Cambridge.[25]

Not that far from the passion with which Caputo snapped at the defamers of Derrida! It is, moreover, almost amusing to see the innocent University of Cambridge involved in such diatribe once again. It is, of course, radical orthodoxy that has been the thorn in Caputo's side; and so as to remove all possible doubts about it, Caputo also once said that he is "even considering starting up a movement entitled 'radical heterodoxy,' with its own Web site and perhaps programmatic statement," and that he will tolerate no dissent from the movement's principles.[26]

So what of the transgression? From all that has been said here, can we form a general idea about what transgression means in Caputo's thought and specifically in a theology of the event?

We have seen the properly directed transgression that meant crossing over the limits imposed on us by pure reason. There was a plea for the transgression of the narrowly defined boundaries of our intellectual and religious traditions. We have also come across the directionless transgression—the aimless drifting in the flux of our existence, which is but a transgression halted right after it has delivered us from our self-deceptions: You won't get further than our hermeneutical situation! And there is at least one more sense in which transgression operates in Caputo's thought, one that comes, in fact, closest to what transgression means in everyday talk but that was not mentioned here: Transgression as in the transgression committed by the Prodigal Son.

Hence the answer is negative—and why should it surprise us when making sense of Caputo? If by the general idea we mean a simple and overarching abstraction, then the meaning of transgression in Caputo's thought defies such generalization. Like an event, because it *is* an event, transgression in the work of Caputo engenders multiple solutions. The heart of the matter here is that transgression is a vector. It is defined by its direction, so transgression always implies the question: Whereto? Whereto shall we cross over and where shall we end up? If in our theological quest we transgress the limits imposed by reason, do we cross them toward the mystical union with God? Or do we instead risk ending up in the dark night of the soul like Saint John of the Cross, Saint Paul of the Cross (John and Paul!), Saint Thérèse of Lisieux, Mother Teresa, and countless others? And if we transgress the borders of our religious traditions, will our dwelling place inevitably be the desert-like religion without religion? Or shall we instead learn how to "inhabit a construction, understanding that it's a construction?"[27] This is, for Caputo, probably the most tormenting of all questions: "Can you inhabit a tradition with ironic distance?"[28]

> [H]ow can someone be ironically committed? How can someone "witness," even "unto death," how can someone be on fire with love, with the cold breath of irony breathing down their neck? Is not an "ironic witness" a form of iron wood, a square circle, like that mediocre fellow Climacus warns us against, a half-hearted lover who keeps his finger crossed behind his back even as he takes the marriage vows?[29]

As a matter of fact, for Caputo this question signifies an ongoing quest. An expression of longing for some home, too, but above all an unanswered question—a reflection of a certain lostness, or of destinerrance, to use the expression Caputo borrows from Derrida. But if Caputo feels a little lost—something that he admits readily while admonishing us all to recognize the same wanderers in ourselves—it is, I think, in the wake of the event of transgression. Caputo's transgression, so to speak, took over the reins and he would never be quite able to keep up with it, never quite in a position to control where it goes. Caputo's theology is thus in an important sense a function of the answers he has been able to come up with to the question: Whereto? A theology of the event is the history of the event of transgression. The adventurous history to which we shall turn now.

5
Two Loves

For many young Catholic intellectuals of John Caputo's generation, Jacques Maritain was an admired hero, and the young Caputo was no exception. Well, not too much of an exception, to say the least. For there is no knowing without asking him directly how much he was on the whole fascinated by Maritain's version of Thomism. Be that as it may, on several occasions in his writings Caputo does look back on how as a graduate student he cherished Maritain's book *Les degrés du savoir* (*The Degrees of Knowledge*).[1] As he tells us, this was the book in which he read with the excitement of a young student "how the various strata of reason, faith, and mystical union are layered, how the gears mesh, how all things work unto one in a culminating, fulminating vision of God."[2] As a matter of fact, *The Degrees of Knowledge* awoke Caputo's interest in mysticism, which he then further developed in what he now regards as the first phase of his work—a period that is the subject matter of this chapter. But there was more to Caputo's interest in Maritain than just his popularity. Confirming, in a sense, what we said previously about the autobiographical loading of theology, the first impulse that drove Caputo to Maritain was deeply personal. And thereby—will that surprise us?—hangs a tale.

We have already seen how in the course of his religious formation young Brother Paul spent his study days followed by sleepless nights (armed with a flashlight) oscillating between his two conflicting loves, Saint Thomas and Kierkegaard. It has been also said that as a graduate student Caputo felt torn between the need to appease his professors with the theoretical understanding of modernity and the desire to pull himself free from all that. Needless to say, one can hardly, if at all, be at peace with oneself when split like this. Surely, a serious thinker will make an effort to pull the different strands together into one harmonious whole. Likewise, Caputo's two inner conflicts (or was it perhaps only one conflict represented in two different ways?) called for a solution. And as it happened, it was the book of Maritain that marked the first step on Caputo's "personal intellectual journey between the medieval synthesis of Aquinas and the ironic nominalism of Kierkegaard."[3]

At first glance, the chasm between Saint Thomas and Kierkegaard must have appeared to young Caputo somewhat akin to that between Exupéry's logicians and the geometrician—which in turn has many of the hallmarks of the fissure between the Enlightenment and its discontents. Now this is not to imply that Saint Thomas was a forefather of modernity, but it is an interesting parallel worth noting *en passant* because it was precisely through the struggle to reconcile his two conflicting loves that Caputo came upon a passage leading beyond the confines of modernity.

In any case, whatever became of Caputo's thought in the years to come had its origins in his curious double allegiance to the Doctor Angelicus and to the Melancholy Dane. Could they be more different? *The* logician and *the* geometrician. The master of structured ratiocination whom no one could defeat in scholastic disputations, and the sickly scribbler of unscientific postscripts who in his own time seemed to be losing against everyone. The one venturing to prove that God exists, while the other laughing at every such proof. The one endorsing faith supported by reason, while the other trembling before the irrational faith of Abraham. And not least of all, we can imagine that for Caputo Saint Thomas and Kierkegaard also stood for the conflict between the gravity and the wings, epitomizing the tension between the weight of Caputo's traditional upbringing, onerous but sensible, and the (unbearable?) lightness of the call to explore the unknown lands.

So how exactly was Maritain involved in this to all appearances impossible equation? First of all, this problem was only rationally impossible, that is, there seemed to be no way out of it within the horizon of simple logic—but it clearly was not impossible for Caputo to experience his double love in real life. The impossible was, in fact, very real, and I would love to imagine that Caputo also found some consolation in Saint-Exupéry's dismissal of pure logic:

> Misled by reasoning run wild, these numskulls believed that contraries exist. Whereas life is a network of relations so complex that if you destroy one of your two seeming contraries, you die. For bear this well in mind: the only contrary of anything whatsoever is, and is but, death.[4]

Brother Paul, on the other hand, was young and very much alive and it was only natural that he would have wanted to see how other people coped with their own contradictions. That being so, maybe Maritain was an obvious choice. Because the story goes that he was legendary for the talent to blend in his own life what appeared like incompatible opposites. Plus: he was one really passionate scholar. Now when the logicians in our little tale failed to grasp the true meaning of the traces in the sand, it was to a large extent because they disregarded the role of the heart. Young Caputo was not going to make the same mistake:

> That is why, as a tormented youngster, I turned to French Thomists for help, for in Paris Thomism had a heart. Maritain, a French Thomist who managed to combine a love of the theory of intentionality of John and of Saint Thomas with a passion for art and mysticism (a feat which paled in comparison with his managing to combine marriage with celibacy), was clearly a man even more conflicted and tormented than I.[5]

Conflicted and tormented Maritain might have been, but as we have just seen that was precisely the type of a person that could offer Caputo a helping hand. And the young Caputo was not going to be let down by Maritain, even if what he found in *The Degrees of Knowledge* was perhaps not entirely what he was looking for. One fortunate stroke of serendipity, one could say. True, Kierkegaard had to wait for the moment, but in stark opposition to the principles of modernity Caputo found oppressive, Maritain pushed the door ajar for him toward an understanding wherein transgression of the limits imposed on us by reason no longer meant an intellectual sin but rather a commendable ascent. Together with yet "another passionate French Thomist" whom Caputo studied at that time, Pierre Rousselot, they portrayed this "crossing of the borders from reason to its beyond as a movement into a deeper, higher, truer, simpler region, an ascent to a more intuitive union or unitative vision, to a kind of hyper-presential contact with God."[6] "My young heart," Caputo tells us, "skipped a beat."[7]

Allowing for crossing beyond the limits of reason surely played well with the young Caputo's desire to twist free from the grips of modernity. When today Caputo professes to be a postmodern thinker, it is first and foremost because he "absolutely resist[s] the idea that reason is what Kant and the Enlightenment said it is, which makes everything look programmable and makes folks with religious faith look a little tipsy."[8] Put differently, Caputo refuses to accept the modern abyss between faith and reason[9]—just the abyss that Maritain and Rousselot tried to bridge with their accounts of epistemological and spiritual ascent. So for being the first to help him see that it is, in fact, perfectly conceivable to look on faith and reason not as static opposites, even adversaries, but as the dynamically connected aspects of the same process, Caputo will forever remain in Maritain's and Rousselot's debt.

But in the long run neither of them (and especially not Maritain with his oft-quoted traditionalist motto: "*Vae mihi si non Thomistizavero*—Woe to me if I do not Thomistize") could hold young Caputo's attention for too long. They were still too traditional, too Thomist, and too un-Kierkegaardian so to say. What Maritain and Rousselot offered was without doubt a gladly received relief but by no means a lifelong cure for Caputo's divided heart. When both your truths are obvious but absolutely contradictory, there is nothing you can do but change your language.[10] For this reason Caputo needed more than just a French extension of Saint Thomas—he needed a new language. However, in those preconciliar days, finding a new voice among the thinkers approved by the Magisterium was not very easy, to say the least. So in order to arrive at a better balance between Saint Thomas and Kierkegaard, Caputo would have needed courage to break free from the gravitational pull of his traditional Catholic upbringing. For Kierkegaard was neither Catholic nor Thomist. Neither Maritain nor Rousselot could facilitate that. That was a feat reserved for Martin Heidegger.

The author of *Der Satz vom Grund* (*The Principle of Reason*), Caputo relates, "came to occupy a place in my young intellectual life that was once occupied by Jacques Maritain,"[11] and the book itself "eventually became for me a better way of doing the work that once was done for me by *Les Degrés du Savoir*."[12] How or why precisely Caputo turned from Maritain to Heidegger and what he learned from him is really a story in its own right, albeit the basic motivation behind it is again not entirely new to us. For one thing, Heidegger's genealogy of reason seems to have resonated better with Caputo's scholarly instincts than the rationalization of Thomists, which, by and large, lacked a historical perspective. But, even more importantly I think, through his captivating ability to charm his readers—to cast a spell over them[13]—Heidegger supplied Caputo with enough psychological energy to undertake the sought-after transgression of his own.

Like what is known as rebound in matters of love: The old relationship is going downhill, but one hesitates to abandon it, often up to the time when something—somebody—new and, more often than not, someone maddeningly fascinating arrives on the scene with what appears like a promise of perfect contentment. Just what the doctor ordered. *Appears*, however, is the operative word here. For after they fulfill their raison d'être, these rebounds tend to fail just as well and at times even more miserably than the relationships that preceded them. In time, rebounds almost always forsake us, but they leave us free even if a little lost—perhaps older and scarred, but free indeed to start anew.

In a sense, one could say that Heidegger was someone like that for young Caputo. A sort of rebound although a fairly long-lasting one, for that matter, since he held Caputo "captive for fifteen years or more."[14] As a matter of fact, even after Heidegger's "spell" was broken by Derrida, Caputo continued to work on Heidegger for at least another five years, presumably squaring accounts.[15] Nevertheless, it was, indeed, Heidegger whom Caputo credits with helping him to "break the grip of dogmatic Catholicism" and leading him "into the contemporary philosophical world."[16] Thanks to Heidegger Caputo finally got his wings. And only when he later felt ready to speak in his own voice did Caputo free himself from Heidegger—determinedly but not without gratitude for having been first freed by him some twenty years before.

And, boy, was Caputo fascinated! This was, without doubt, largely due to the fact that with Heidegger the scattered pieces of Caputo's puzzle suddenly began falling into place. In order to appreciate this observation, it is important to understand that Heidegger would never have been able to achieve for young Caputo what he did had he come to him straightforwardly saying: "Here. Forget about everything that you've learned so far. I have a better alternative that will set you free." Caputo simply valued (as I believe he still does, to avoid possible misunderstanding) his Catholic tradition too much for such a brazen advance to work, and in fact he later often criticized Heidegger for disregarding his Catholic and Scholastic roots too uncritically. No. The lure of Heidegger lay precisely in his ability to offer Caputo numerous points of contact with what he had previously learned, points that served as good omens, reassuring the young student that he was still on the right way even as he was finally getting somewhere. Heidegger had a new language on offer, no doubt about that, but it was a new language built upon the old words.

It will not come as a surprise, therefore, that it was from within his Catholic intellectual lifeworld that Caputo first found Heidegger worth his attention. This was in the mid-sixties when Caputo started graduate school,[17] and he recalls:

> When I first read what Heidegger said about 'being-in-the-world' and how the question of whether there is a world makes no sense for beings whose Being is being-in-the-world that struck a chord that resonated deeply with the 'realism' of my Catholic philosophical upbringing. We were all realists, afraid it seemed that someone was going to steal the world out from under us if we so much as took our eye off it. [. . .] Then Heidegger came along and said that the project of proving or establishing the existence of the world, or realism, or certainty, the need for a proof to back up whatever knowledge we have managed to acquire, was already too late. For as soon as Dasein comes to be it is already in the world and in the truth, and the very being of Dasein has already laid skepticism to rest.[18]

Click! The first piece of Caputo's puzzle snapped into its place, for what else was Heidegger delivering if not the long-overdue good news that contemporary philosophy owed to Catholic theology? At long last Catholic philosophers and theologians could avail themselves of a truly relevant antidote against modernity, which they needed like air because, as Caputo observes on behalf of Catholics:

> After all, try as we might, and much as we wanted to be, we never really were moderns. [. . .] We just could not embrace the modernist worldview, the whole idea of rigid territorial distinctions between faith and reason, sacred and secular, private and public, fact and value, subject and object, mind and body.[19]

As we can see, at first Caputo's fascination with Heidegger was primarily a function of his desire to break free from the constraints of modernity. But Heidegger had more to offer than just a powerful and up-to-date critique of the modern worldview. Or rather, that critique was indeed what to Caputo and to many of his Catholic contemporaries mattered most, but what *really* fascinated them was *how* this critique was executed. A new language built upon the venerable archives. As if in some peculiar intellectual dance, where withdrawals are interlocked with approaches in one coherent movement, Heidegger both departed from and yet again returned to the traditional sources with which Catholic intellectuals could and indeed felt obliged to identify. Thus, for example,

> when Heidegger offered a critique of what he called "onto-theo-logic," when he said that an atheism about the God of metaphysics, about the *causa sui*, was closer to the truly divine God, we knew instantly what he was talking about. We had all been dragged through the pits of onto-theo-logic by the Neo-Scholastic manuals and we had had enough of it.[20]

A much welcome departure therefore from onto-theo-logic of the Neo-Scholastic textbooks, but not so much a departure from the tradition that gave rise to Neo-Scholasticism. Quite the opposite. Because Caputo also tells us that his generation was at the same time inspired by what they perceived as a new phenomenon in continental philosophy—"a substantive convergence of our most treasured medievalist convictions with the latest philosophical work"[21]—a phenomenon that, as we shall see, was in no small degree attributable also to Heidegger.

Heidegger's appeal to the medieval sources in support of his critique of modernity was indeed what particularly endeared him to young Caputo, whose prior education, as we know, had been strongly influenced by a close reading of Saint Thomas.[22] And it was not only because Caputo could in this way relate to Heidegger's thought more easily that he instantly knew what Heidegger was talking about. That too of course, but equally importantly, Heidegger helped Caputo discover for himself authors that he had previously more or less overlooked, most notably Meister Eckhart of Hochheim, a great medieval mystic whom Caputo has held in high esteem ever since.

This, incidentally, was another fortuitous discovery on Caputo's part because by means of Meister Eckhart Caputo was eventually able to return back to Saint Thomas. A rather unexpected stroke of good fortune, right? For if at the end of the day Caputo returned to Saint Thomas, one may wonder if his "transgression" was in fact anything more than just an unnecessary roundtrip. Yet, I think that to dismiss roundtrips as unworthy of serious consideration would be mistaken. Perhaps all of our journeys are more or less circular (". . . and unto dust you shall return") and it does not matter so much where we get but who we become along the way. Likewise, Caputo's journey certainly was not trivial and it was not in vain, for upon his return Caputo found a different Saint Thomas even as he, too, had changed. Now let us take these developments step by step.

Johannes Scheffler is a good person to begin with. Scheffler was born in 1624 in Silesia at Breslau and was raised up as a Lutheran. On that account, obviously, Scheffler by no accepted standards belonged to the medieval period. Nevertheless, he did have a strong connection to the traditions of Middle Ages by virtue of his admiration for the great medieval Christian mystics. In fact, Scheffler also wrote mystical poetry himself and is much better known by his pen name, which he adopted in 1653 after his conversion to Catholicism: Angelus Silesius—the author, among other collections, of the celebrated *Cherubinische Wandersmann* (*The Cherubinic Wanderer*). One of the poems from this collection, entitled "Ohne Warum" (Without Why), plays an important role in our little tale:

> The rose is without why; it blooms because it blooms;
> It cares not for itself; asks not if it's seen.[23]

While deceptively naïve and short like nearly all Angelus Silesius's poems, as he composed his pieces chiefly in the classical form of Alexandrine couplets, this poem has been vastly influential. So much so that Jorge Luis Borges does not hesitate to suggest that these few words summarize poetry in its entirety.[24] As for Heidegger, he was no less impressed when he wrote:

> The entire fragment is so astoundingly clear and neatly constructed that one is inclined to get the idea that the most extreme sharpness and depth of thought belongs to the genuine and great mystics. This is also true. Meister Eckhart proves it.[25]

And Heidegger did not just leave it at praise of the great depth of Angelus Silesius's thought. Over and above that, he made use of "Without Why" in *The Principle of Reason*—the very book that had such profound impact on the young Caputo's intellectual development. *The Principle of Reason* comprises thirteen lectures of an influential course Heidegger gave in 1955–1956 and in the course of which he set himself the task of demonstrating how what we call reason is really an offspring of modernity and as such needs to be stripped of its pretense to rule over everything. In pursuing his goal, Heidegger focused specifically on the *principle of sufficient reason* of Gottfried Leibniz, which, according to Heidegger, lies at the very heart of modernity. It is here that Angelus Silesius's poem comes in. For Heidegger presents "Without Why" as the counterexample to the seemingly all-embracing principle of Leibniz, pointing to a way of being wherein reasons are not given because questions are not asked. The rose is without why. Perhaps not without because, as indeed the botanists would be quick to point out—it blooms because it blooms—but without why, that is, without questions.

Heidegger is, of course, conscious of the possibility that his reference to Angelus Silesius's poem will be misunderstood; that his critics may argue that by pointing to the "rose which is without why" he only proves the obvious, that is, that roses (unlike human beings) are incapable of asking questions. Against such accusation Heidegger defends himself with an argument that need not concern us here in its entirety, but which ends with the words:

> What is unsaid in the fragment—and everything depends on this—instead says that humans, in the concealed grounds of their essential being, first truly are when in their own way they are like the rose—without why. We cannot pursue this thought any further here.[26]

We will pursue this further later on. But, note that in Caputo's judgment, Heidegger's take on the contrast between Leibniz's principle and Angelus Silesius's mystical poem was no less than brilliant.[27] According to Caputo's interpretation,

> Heidegger exposes the rule of the principle of reason to its other, to the thinking which has the boldness and the audacity not to demand reasons—rather the way one learns to float only by surrendering every attempt to swim and by remaining perfectly still. That takes practice and a bit of courage; it is simple but hard. Poetic thinking is like that. It achieves a relationship with the world which is more simple and primordial than reason; it is in touch with things long before the demand for reason arises and, indeed, is so deeply tuned to things that the need for reasons never arises.[28]

And even long after he first came across *The Principle of Reason*, in fact at the time when he was already becoming increasingly irritated by "later" Heidegger, Caputo was still of the opinion that such a powerful critique of modernity and its guiding principle, as the one conjured by Heidegger, was simply unprecedented:

> Now I daresay there is no more radical or wonderful delimitation of the principle of reason than that. Another stunning postcard from Freiburg. And I mean that seriously.[29]

Let us pause here for a moment and consider what effect (if any) had this "powerful Heideggerian tale"[30] on Caputo's theology of the event. One of the concepts that are basic to Caputo's theology (and to any Christian theology, for that matter) is the concept of the kingdom of God, particularly as it was proclaimed by Jesus. Since Caputo's interpretation of the attributes of the kingdom of God is a subject matter of a dedicated series later in this work, let us for now content ourselves with the understanding that in Caputo's theology the kingdom of God stands against the world. While, for example, "the kingdom of God is a kingdom of base, ill-born, powerless, despised outsiders who are null and void in the eyes of the world,"[31] the world itself represents "the order of power and privilege and self-interest, of the business as usual of those who would prevent the event"[32]—the very event of the *call* for justice that, as we know, lies at the heart of a theology of the event. Hence, "the kingdom comes to contradict the world and contest the world's ways," asserts Caputo, "and it always looks like foolishness to the world's good sense."[33]

Now there are a number of "foolish" ways in which the kingdom contradicts the shrewd world, one of which Caputo refers to as quotidianism—the trustful everydayness that is so wonderfully exemplified by God's lowliest creatures, such as the lilies of the field or the birds of the air, who neither sow nor reap.[34] That such trustful attitude, when undertaken by humans, amounts to foolishness in the eyes of the world is clear: "Nothing is more certain in this post-Edenic quid pro quo world of ours than that we must sow in order to reap, that there is no free lunch."[35] In fact, as Caputo has just pointed out, it is plain impossible for us to live like the lilies and birds. Nevertheless, quotidianism that is characteristic of life in the kingdom of God does not really entail dismissal of the necessity to earn our living. It is an attitude of trust, not of indolence. But just as "trusting" is a near-synonym of "unquestioning," so also quotidianism comes close, even overlaps with living without why. Like the rose. And sure enough, Caputo states explicitly that "Angelus Silesius's mystical rose should be added to the botany of the kingdom, along with the lilies of the field."[36]

To live like the rose, without why—Heidegger also believed that this was the implicit lesson of Angelus Silesius's poem. However, he only touched upon this line of thought in passing and decided not to pursue it any further. At first, Caputo regretted this omission on Heidegger's part and decided to follow up on it "on Heidegger's behalf" by demonstrating "the elaborate analogy that exists between the relationship of the soul to God in German mysticism, and the relationship of Dasein to Being in Heidegger's later writings."[37]

At that time, when he was writing *The Mystical Element in Heidegger's Thought*, Caputo was still willing to give Heidegger the benefit of the doubt as to why he chose not to think through the implications of "living like the rose" and what his conclusions would have been. Bear in mind that Heidegger truly was a wizard at winning people over and the links between *The Principle of Reason*, works of medieval mystics, and the attitude of quotidianism appeared nothing less than self-evident. Well they were, but only for Caputo, not for Heidegger. Heidegger's recourse to medieval Christian authors did not tally with his worldview, which turned out to be decidedly pagan. For this reason, twenty years later, in *The Weakness of God*, Caputo had to admit that

> unfortunately, Heidegger does not follow the mystical poet all the way through. For when Heidegger tells us to be like the rose, he is not telling us to trust God's loving care, which is what Angelus Silesius was saying, the way the lilies of the field do, which is what Jesus said, but to trust ourselves to physis and to the child-play of aion. Physis is the worlding of the world, the world's own energy and life, not God's.[38]

Not that such disillusioned appraisal of Heidegger's thought on Caputo's part came out of the blue. Already when he was working on *Radical Hermeneutics*, Caputo realized that the halcyon days of his fascination with Heidegger were over and that perhaps he no longer could speak on Heidegger's behalf. For when making a plea for letting "earth and sky and the gods" be so that we, humans, can also be what we truly are, mortals[39]—which, too, was a corollary of "living without why'"—Heidegger seemed to consistently ignore the obvious ethical implications of his own thinking. Caputo simply could not fathom why Heidegger

> tends to be a little more interested in letting jugs and bridges be and to let it go at that, and he never quite gets around to letting others be, to our being-with others as mortals, to the fellowship or community of mortals.[40]

"I do not think there is anything in what he says which excludes his doing this," argued Caputo. "He just never does."[41] But why not, if it was as plain as the nose on his face that this was the way to go? If truth be told, Heidegger was bound to dumbfound his followers by revelations against which his inattention to ethics looked banal, to say the least. Here I am hinting at Heidegger's complicity with Nazism, but when Victor Farias, followed by Hugo Ott, brought this incomprehensible association to public attention Caputo's *Radical Hermeneutics* had already been in print. So despite his growing reservations about Heidegger's thought, even his early criticism thereof, Caputo ventured to think *for* Heidegger, to stretch his thought in the direction where Heidegger himself did not wish to go, when for all he knew discussing ethics on Heidegger's behalf seemed no longer feasible. If for whatever reason Heidegger failed to see what to Caputo appeared obvious, Caputo decided to

> do it for him and, by doing so, restore to *Gelassenheit* its ethical context. For remember that in Eckhart, to whom we owe this idea, *Gelassenheit*, letting-be, meant love, *caritas*.[42]

Thus far, I only glossed over the concept of *Gelassenheit* (rendered into English as letting-be), claiming that it, too, is a corollary of living without why. This is, indeed, so, but perhaps a little more detailed explanation is in order here; besides, it will serve as a convenient link to the point where we departed from the timeline that is proper to our narration of Caputo's story.

Speaking of timeline, time—the sense of temporality peculiar to the life in the kingdom of God—is also what Caputo means when he brings the concept of *Gelassenheit* into a theology of the event. It has been said that, according to Caputo, what sets life in the kingdom of God apart from the life of the world is the attitude of trust that Caputo calls quotidianism. But now we can also see that everydayness, which is what quotidianism means, obviously has a temporal dimension—that is, inasmuch as "day" relates to our experience of time.

In a few words, quotidianism is an attitude of trust, but just as everything else that we feel, do, and profess, this trust takes place *in* time and therefore concerns *time*: To trust in time also means to trust the time itself. So when we are beseeched not to worry about tomorrow, for tomorrow will care for itself (Matt. 6:34), we are really asked to *let* tomorrow *be* tomorrow so that we can live today as today. And that is precisely what *Gelassenheit* means, at least in its temporal sense in which Caputo explicitly brings it to the fore in *The Weakness of God*:

> In the kingdom time can be experienced authentically only by taking time as God's gift and trusting ourselves to time's granting, which is God's giving. We trust what time gives because God gives time. [. . .] By letting go of our own self-possession, by opening ourselves to God's rule, we release the day from its chains. The temporality that is opposed to the kingdom is a bound time, a time in which today is dragged back into the past by recrimination or wrenched forward into the future by worry, planning, and calculation. The temporality of the kingdom, on the other hand, is free, open, unbound, unchained, a day or time that is savored one day at a time, experienced, lived for itself, in its own upsurge, instant by instant, day by day. *Then* and only then we will be able to work.[43]

Letting tomorrow be tomorrow (and, for that matter, letting yesterday be yesterday), so as not to let pass the only time we have at our disposal, clearly already is an ethical maxim. But as we have seen, when Caputo promised to "restore to *Gelassenheit* its ethical context," he had in mind more than just trust, he also meant love, (and) caritas. The parenthesized "and" here simply indicates the double orientation of love, as in love for God and love for God's creatures. Thus, according to Caputo, who in this respect follows Meister Eckhart, *Gelassenheit* in the context of our love for God

> means seeking nothing exterior or outside—or, better, not seeking at all—but simply letting God's life well up in us and flow through us as an inner principle of life. We should love God as we love life, Eckhart said, for Himself, not as we love our cow, that is, for its milk.[44]

In other words, in a theology of the event *Gelassenheit* keeps us away from the worldly quid pro quo attitude toward God. Letting-be as love stands in direct opposition to our viewing of God as a *means* to achieve our own goals, even when these goals are as noble as eternal life. And finally, by extending this refusal to treat God as a means, so that it covers God's entire creation, we get at what Caputo means by a generalized *Gelassenheit*

> which lets be, which releases gods and mortals, earth and sky—and let us expand this Greco-Germanic catalogue to include male and female, Greek and Jew, East and West, weak and strong, healthy and sick, animal and human (and whatever else we have been inclined to subordinate, hierarchize, marginalize). In this generalized *Gelassenheit*, the task is to let all things be what and how they are. And that is what we mean by an ethics of *Gelassenheit*—which is all at once an ethics of liberation, toleration, and solidarity.[45]

Now that the concepts of *quotidianism* and *Gelassenheit* have been at least partly clarified, it is time to tie up loose ends and resume the story of Caputo and his theology where we left off. We wanted to know whether Heidegger's delimitation of reason, particularly as it was based upon his reading of Angelus Silesius's poem, eventually found its way into Caputo's theology of the event. As we have seen, the answer really is yes and no.

On the one hand, Caputo's early hopes to be able to call on Heidegger's support when reflecting on the ethical implications of "living without why" came to naught. Heidegger's progressively mythologizing way of thinking, as well as his more or less deliberate failure to assign to "human others" the kind of moral significance they deserved, eventually resulted in Caputo's theology taking a decidedly opposite direction.

On the other hand, however, we must give credit where credit is due, which in this particular case means recognizing that Caputo first learned about the concept of *Gelassenheit*—for which, as he says, he has considerable affection[46]—from Heidegger. Indeed, I think it is fair to say that young Caputo (after all the skips forward, we are following young Caputo again) got his Eckhart from Heidegger:

> I had not studied the medieval mystic Meister Eckhart in particular before I encountered his sermons in Heidegger, but I knew at once where Eckhart was coming from. I recognized immediately what Heidegger was talking about when he began to refer to Meister Eckhart.[47]

But hold your horses—so did Caputo learn about Meister Eckhart from Heidegger or did he not? True, the liberty with which Caputo uses phrases like "I knew at once" and "I recognized immediately" might get a little bewildering. So to be precise, Caputo was not entirely unfamiliar with Meister Eckhart when he stumbled upon his sermons in Heidegger's work, but it looks as though he only knew just enough for those chancy encounters to pique his interest: "I mean, Heidegger *and* Eckhart? Now *that's* an interesting combination and a line of thought to pursue! And if Heidegger and Eckhart, then why not, for that matter, also Heidegger *and* Aquinas?"

Of course, Heidegger's involvement in Caputo's (re-)discovery of Meister Eckhart is not entirely new to us, but up to this point I only mentioned it tangentially. Now I hope to fill this gap, and I will begin with turning to—well, again Angelus Silesius. After all, it was his mystical poem that first gave rise to Heidegger's and Caputo's interest in the idea of *Gelassenheit*. The rose is without why; it is what it is and it is just like that without asking for reasons. That, to be sure, is the poetic rendering of the sum and substance of *Gelassenheit*, except that Angelus Silesius was not the first thinker to either coin the term or to describe its underlying concept. If truth be told, present-day scholars are not even sure if Angelus Silesius was a mystic in the proper sense, that is, whether or not his poems originated from his own mystical experience. A bone of contention here is that if Angelus Silesius indeed had visions of mystical nature, then one is compelled to wonder why they were so unoriginal when it came to their theological import. For Angelus Silesius's verses seem to provide no new ideas—one only finds in his poems insights that were already present in the works of Eckhart, Tauler, Spanish Carmelite mystics, the Theologia Deutsch, and others.[48]

Even so, Angelus Silesius's genius should not be underestimated, for he really brought mystical poetry to perfection. Maybe the ideas conveyed in his poems were not originally his own, but he understood them nonetheless and, what is more, he understood them so deeply that he was able to pass them on in a form that was simultaneously uplifting and instructive. In the words of Grover Zinn, Angelus Silesius contributed to the mystical tradition with something that was at least as important as the original accounts of mystical experience: "a moving, persuasive, and potentially transforming restatement of key mystical themes in epigrammatic verses that strike with heat and light, affection and intellection."[49] Another example of how writers (before I was only talking about novelists, but the same goes for poets and even scriptwriters) often get the better of us, academic theologians, when it comes to making ideas clear and publicly recognized.

Hence it is little wonder that Heidegger spoke so highly about Angelus Silesius. On the other hand, however, we should not leave unnoticed the fact that when Heidegger praises Angelus Silesius's "Without Why," he in the same breath refers to Meister Eckhart. That is because Heidegger knew where the ideas so wonderfully versified by Angelus Silesius originally came from—or, at the very least, Caputo believed that this was indeed the case.[50] Moreover, even if this was actually the only time in *The Principle of Reason* that Heidegger mentioned Meister Eckhart, young Caputo found the link between the medieval mystic and Angelus Silesius so intriguing that he decided to trace it on his own and later went to great lengths in *The Mystical Element in Heidegger's Thought* to substantiate it both historically and textually.[51]

And here our little tale—the story of the young Caputo's journey—has come full circle, even if only until we follow it further. For after Caputo successfully established the link between Meister Eckhart and Angelus Silesius (and therefore also Heidegger), he believed nothing kept him from extending this connection even further so as to include in it also his first teacher: Saint Thomas. Another "Click!" and another piece of his puzzle safely in place. Caputo's journey to the unknown lands bore fruit; the transgression paid off: If Saint Thomas could be allied with such "renegade" mystics and poets, and if he indeed could be meaningfully linked to Heidegger, then he perhaps was not necessarily as metaphysical and as onto-theo-logical as he had appeared. Here's Caputo's summary:

> When I discovered that Heidegger's history led up to a brilliant contrast "The Rose Is Without Why," and when I learned that Silesius was to a great extent versifying Meister Eckhart of Hochheim, and when I then found that Eckhart was a Dominican who pushed to a mystical extreme what he learned from "brother Thomas" (Saint Thomas), that *deus est suum esse*, well, then, eureka, my heart was afire and skipped another beat.[52]

For the sake of academic accuracy I should perhaps add that not all scholars thought that the connection between Meister Eckhart and Saint Thomas was as straightforward as Caputo seemed to suggest. W. Norris Clarke, for example, fears that "Caputo's attempted move from Thomas through Eckhart towards Heidegger is more obscuring than illuminating,"[53] and he suggests that Meister Eckhart, "although declaring himself (perhaps quite sincerely) to be a follower of Brother Thomas, is really following the call of an older, and not a Christian, master [presumably Plotinus]."[54] Now this may be a valid argument, but from the perspective of our recount of the story of weak theology it does not make much difference. For young Caputo really believed that "Eckhart waved the wand of mysticism over the metaphysics of St. Thomas, which later took the form of the mystical poetry of Angelus Silesius, who became a touchstone for Heidegger's task of 'overcoming metaphysics,' of the delimitation of 'onto-theo-logic,'"[55] and around this belief he constructed not only his doctoral dissertation but also his first two books (*Heidegger and Aquinas* and *The Mystical Element in Heidegger's Thought*).[56]

Before we move on to the next series, I would like to make some final remarks about what "kind" of Caputo we have at the end of this period. For those familiar with his later work (after he found his voice and started writing about how we really do not know who we are) it may come as a surprise that Caputo was once a firm believer in a deep mystical union with God that was characterized by anything but lostness. True, even in his early years there was a certain "negativity" involved in his interest in mysticism, but this negativity, as we have seen, had only to do with the critique of the limits imposed on us by reason. Caputo's interest in the mystical was "rooted in the fact that it positions itself at the limits of metaphysical reason."[57] No lostness, no *destinerrance*—not yet—only transgression. And a transgression that was not negative at all but that represented "a kind of crowning perfection that superseded rationality," even as "mystical union crowns what metaphysical theology seeks."[58]

> —[I]n my more orthodox Catholic youth, I would have said that in mystical experience we are touched by . . .
>
> —Revelation?
>
> —Yes, and even beyond revelation—by God, directly immediately, wordlessly, whereas Revelation is always given in words. Whereas now I stress that we are touched by something I know not what.[59]

What a contrast between the young and the older Caputo—or let us from now on say early and later Caputo, since he prefers it that way "given the inevitable implications of 'young' for my present sorry state"[60]—found in Caputo's response to Carlson.

Many scholars have commented upon the affirmative character of the early Caputo's writings as well. Thomas A. Carlson, just to stick to one example, shows how early Caputo took Meister Eckhart's side, not Heidegger's, in the discussion of *Gelassenheit*. Both authors were in favor of letting-be, but while for Meister Eckhart this meant giving ourselves "over to God's loving care," what Heidegger meant was that we need to "release ourselves to an inscrutable world-play."[61] At least that is how Caputo read them, and Carlson points out:

> While the young Caputo admits that we cannot meaningfully argue that one call or the other is actually the right one, he does want to warn that without something like the care-full and loving assurance found in Eckhart's religious matrix, the negativity of *Gelassenheit* will prove to be too severe, too secular and worldly, too austere and impersonal—in short, too dangerous and barely, if at all, viable.[62]

Indeed, as Carlson did not fail to notice, in *The Mystical Element in Heidegger's Thought* Caputo argues that "there can be—if anything—only a 'finite hope' in Heidegger, a hope which is never insulated from despair, a waiting which acknowledges the possibility of a final disappointment," and that the "comparison with a religious thinker such as Meister Eckhart thus underlines something distinctive about Heidegger's thought, the danger in Heidegger's thought."[63] The danger into which, so it seems, Caputo later slipped himself. Quoting Carlson one more time:

> If the youthful Caputo can seem to agree that hope requires assurance, and if he can argue that such assurance is to be found especially in the religious matrix that gives determinate content to *Gelassenheit*, grounding our human hope in the "radically personal relationship" of a father and son who are bound by dispositions of "love and trust" (ME, 249), the later, more deconstructive Caputo will seem to suggest something quite different, if not the reverse: namely, that hope is required—and indeed that hope is even possible—only when such assurance is lacking.[64]

Now the question that will guide us through the following parts of this book is how this change (the *turn*, the *kehre*) came about. Indeed, why? Even on the shallowest of all shallow levels this change in direction could appear somewhat enigmatic. For one could say (superficially, I repeat) that the early Caputo had everything, he was a star:

> Insofar as my work with continental philosophy had to do with the intersection of continental philosophy with Aquinas and Eckhart, with the medieval metaphysical and mystical traditions, it evoked a favorable response among my fellow catholics. It was on the basis of that work that I was elected president of the American catholic Philosophical Association back in the 1980s.[65]

So why venture into the unknown lands again? Caputo admits that he has a "hard time keeping these peregrinations straight [him]self . . ."[66] Inasmuch as this is possible based on the fragments of the story present in Caputo's writings, I shall try to follow the path with him. Do not worry, in the process we shall be also able to figure out what on earth happened to Kierkegaard. But not before we ponder over the question of freedom. For when one responds to a call by transgressing the limits, when one breaks free—one ends being precisely that: free. Whatever that means!

6
Freedom

"Good-by, old Bark. Be a man!"

The plane quivered, ready to take off. Bark took his last look at the immense desolation of Cape Juby. Round the plane two hundred Moors were finding out what a slave looked like when he stood on the threshold of life. They would make no bones about snatching him back again if a little later the ship happened to be forced down.

We stood about our fifty-year-old, new-born babe, worried a little at having launched him forth on the stream of life.

"Good-by, Bark!"

"NO!"

"What do you mean?"

"No. I am Mohammed ben Lhaoussin."

—Antoine de Saint-Exupéry, *Wind, Sand and Stars*

Bark's journey home after four years of slavery took place sometime in the spring of 1928, when Saint-Exupéry was stationed in Cape Juby, also known as the Tarfaya Strip—an isolated outpost on the edge of the Saharan desert on the western coast of Morocco. Saint-Exupéry told Bark's story twelve years later in his celebrated *Terre des hommes* (*Wind, Sand and Stars*), but the role he played in this epic tale of freedom lost and regained in fact far exceeded that of an uninvolved narrator.

In order to situate Bark's story in the wider context, we turn to the period following the end of the First World War.[1] The wartime heroes of the skies must have felt somewhat like "the lost generation" for there was not much for them to do. Prior to the Great War, flying was considered little more than a crazy adventure—something well suited for those who were ready to live strong and die young, but with practically no viable peacetime application. Fortunately for the veterans, however, a few business visionaries (often former fighter pilots themselves) thought differently, and so the 1920s and '30s turned out to be the pioneering years of commercial aviation.

Aéropostale—the company for which Saint-Ex worked at that time and whose feats he immortalized in his books—was to be the first to establish a regular airmail connection across the Atlantic. As of 1928, however, Aéropostale was "only" operating a three-thousand-mile-long line between Toulouse and Dakar. Greatly enhancing France's control over its colonial interests in Senegal, this enterprise was as important as it was extraordinary: Most, if not all, of the company's pilots were already alive when the Wright Flyer made its maiden flight of a few hundred meters; and even though the Breguet 14s in the service of Aéropostale were technologically much more advanced than the Wrights, they still needed to refuel at least eight times along the way, not to mention that on average they broke down every fifteen thousand miles or so.[2] That being so, the company set up a system of refueling stations, which also served as rescue bases. Of all these bases, Cape Juby was doubtlessly the most isolated.

Now to give Didier Daurat, the famous operations director of Aéropostale, even a greater headache, the Juby airfield was actually situated on Spanish territory (then the Spanish colony called Río de Oro) and surrounded by the nomadic Moorish tribes who were in perpetual revolt. While the formal agreements with the Spanish authorities had been signed, behind the scenes the Spaniards had no scruples about making things difficult for the company, whenever opportunities arose. The Moors, for their part, would shoot at the overflying mail planes, and when a plane was forced to land in the desert (usually due to mechanical failure, not because of shooting) they would kidnap the pilots and demanded a huge ransom.

Several solutions to this problem were tried out, with little success, before Daurat decided to send to Cape Juby his only pilot with an aristocratic background. Reputedly, the Spaniards had an even greater weakness for the *grand names* than the French, and (Antoine Marie Jean-Baptiste Roger, comte de) Saint-Exupéry certainly was such a name. On top of that, the future author of the *Little Prince* possessed a childlike charm and, apparently, almost a naïve lack of fear of strangers. And so he went to Juby. In the words of Schiff, "his mission was simple: to revive relations with the Spanish authorities and 'to set off to the rescue of any aviator in danger, at any hour, anywhere in the desert.' He was to be a little bit the Saint Bernard of the Sahara."[3]

As a chief of the Juby airfield, Saint-Ex (that's where he earned this nickname) more than proved his worth. During his stay of thirteen months, he rescued at least fourteen aviators;[4] and what is even more fascinating, on several occasions he did so with help from the Moors. Indeed, he made friends with some of them, drank tea in their tents, and they dubbed him "Captain of the Birds."[5]

Having developed the tea-making ritual to perfection, our friend the old geometrician always made tea for the king with his own hands, but the Bedouin chieftains around Cape Juby had black slaves to do the work. Saint-Exupéry met many of them:

> They would come in as soon as the chief had taken out the little stove, the kettle, and the glasses from his treasure chest. [. . .] Then the mute slave would cram the stove with twigs, blow on the embers, fill the kettle with water, and in this service that a child could perform, set into motion a play of muscles able to uproot a tree.[6]

What struck the writer-aviator most about these slaves was that they did not seem unhappy. Deprived of their freedom, they resigned themselves to the "cycle of desert life" and were contented with the comforts of the day. They served their masters faithfully—as if their past free lives had never happened:

> In this sluggish captive hulk, memories have ceased to swarm. Even the moment when he was carried off is faint in his mind—the blows, the shouts, the arms of men that brought him down into his present night. And since that hour he has sunk deeper and deeper into a queer slumber, divested like a blind man of his Senegalese rivers or his white Moroccan towns, like a deaf man of the sound of familiar voices.[7]

Perhaps it would be too much to say that the slaves around Cape Juby were happy, but they were not unhappy either. There was a certain peace about them even as they were finally "set free": When age or sickness made them too weak to be of any use, their Moorish masters released them from service, stopped feeding them, and left them to die alone in the desert. Yet, Saint-Ex never saw those discarded old men complaining. Indeed, the slaves were contented. Save for one of them, that is. Because Bark was different!

Bark was a Senegalese from Marrakech, where he had a wife and three children and where he had earned his living as a drover; between the snow-capped peaks of the Atlas Mountains in the north and the barren Saharan desert in the south he used to drive herds of cattle across the steppes. Very much like another famous if fictional herdsman—a boy called Santiago, the leading character of Paulo Coelho's *Alchemist*—Bark also felt, and with the pride of a king at that, that "he and no other held sway over the nation of ewes," because "nobody but him could say where lay the promised land towards which he led his flock."[8]

> And at night while they slept, Bark, physician and prophet and king, standing in wool to the knees and swollen with tenderness for so much feeble ignorance, would pray for his people.[9]

Saint-Ex soon realized that Bark was a walking treasure chest of living memories. And it was precisely in this sense that our Bark, indeed *this particular* Bark—because, importantly, *all slaves were called Bark*[10]—was different from all the other slaves who served tea to the "Captain of the Birds" during his visits in the Moorish tents. Not because he once had a life as a free man; others did as well. But because Bark told stories about it. Unlike all the other "Barks," who in time grew mute and resigned to their fate, this Bark had never forgotten who he once was, and that before he was kidnapped and sold into slavery people had addressed him by his proper name: "I was a drover, and my name was Mohammed!"[11]

"Before I met Bark," Saint-Exupéry wrote later, "I had never met a slave who offered the least resistance."[12] Bark, on the other hand, resisted his fate to the point of being a pain in the neck. He was no Spartacus, to be sure. He was too careful to engage in openly rebellious activities that would put him in harm's way. Except for the repeated protests at the end of each month, when his master came to collect wages Bark had earned as a part-time waiter at the airfield shack,[13] he behaved as an obedient slave. But, as Schiff points out, "probably no one knew the schedule of the northern mail better than he."[14] And with the tenacity of a gambling man—hoping that the day would come when fortune will favor him as well—Bark would secretly plead with Saint-Ex: "Hide me in the Marrakech plane!"[15]

Bark had his geography right: Any northbound mail plane could take him home or at least as far as Agadir, from where he could get easily to Marrakech by bus. But, of course, the fact that the French were regularly flying in the direction of Bark's home was not the point, simply because Bark did not have the luxury of hitchhiking. Saint-Exupéry's mission at Cape Juby was to make things easier, not to further complicate them. Rescuing (which in the eyes of the Juby nomads would amount to *stealing*) a slave would insult the Moors and jeopardize everything that the chief of the Juby airfield had been working for. "God knows," Saint-Ex wrote later, "what massacre the Moors would have done among us that very day to avenge the insult of this theft."[16] Mesmerized by the possibility of returning home, however, good old Bark could not care less. As he saw it, his interest was greater than that of Aéropostale and so, sure enough, time and again

> Bark would smile, would whisper to me how it could be done—for of course I should not have thought of this dodge: "The mails leave tomorrow. You stow me away in the Marrakech plane."[17]

"Ask, and it will be given you, knock, and it will be opened for you . . ." In the end, Bark's perseverance paid off, except that he did not really need to sneak away. Instead of flying off with Bark, Saint-Ex chose to rescue him the "proper" way. He kept sending letters to France pleading for help and when at last some charitable organizations complied, he proposed to buy Bark his freedom.

Needless to say, negotiations with Bark's master were arduous and they dragged on for months—Come on, really? A *European* buying a slave? Let's rip him off!—but in the end the "Captain of the Birds" prevailed and Bark was finally a free man again. On the day of his departure Bark climbed into the back seat of a Breguet 14 destined for Agadir and, as he was taking his last look at the place that not even an eternity spent there could turn into his home, Bark uttered those memorable words: "[I am not Bark anymore] I am Mohammed ben Lhaoussin."

Now, there are a few lessons to be drawn from Bark's story, which are in one way or another pertinent to the question of freedom. Let us begin with the most noticeable point, namely the link which seems to exist between an individual's freedom and his or her proper name. For as long as Bark was a slave, he was only one of many Barks around. As a 'placeholder name,' Bark really meant nothing more than a vocative for a slave, any slave, something like "Hey, you!" Still, because he was deprived of his freedom, Bark was exactly that—a walking and talking tool; in the eyes of the Moors, he was no less replaceable than an axe—and Bark knew it. Bark instinctively understood that proper names are the prerogative of free individuals, which is why he

> never said, "I am Mohammed ben Lhaoussin"; he said, "My name was Mohammed," dreaming of the day when that obliterated figure would again live within him in all its glory and by the power of its resuscitation would drive out the ghost of the slave.[18]

We could imagine that Bark unwittingly figured out what contemporary democratic societies take for granted, namely the relation that exists between freedom and responsibility. Freedom gives birth to responsibility and there is no responsibility without freedom, or so we believe. Admittedly, matters become more intricate when we distinguish moral responsibility from political responsibility, individual responsibility from collective responsibility, and so forth; nevertheless, in principle we agree that only the individuals acting of their own free will can be held responsible for their acts.

But could it also be that freedom is associated with proper names precisely by virtue of responsibility? For one thing, names do presuppose a response on the part of those who are named. When someone calls out my name, it is I who am responsible for answering—I and no one else. I am startled, even offended, when somebody else answers in my stead. My name therefore establishes a responsibility that is unique to me. But what if we reversed and broadened this equation? Then personal responsibility, which stems from my freedom, would in fact be the sine qua non (or at least a very good ground) for having a unique name.[19] No freedom to act on my own behalf—no responsibility, and therefore no need to respond. For as long as it was the free will and responsibility of Bark's master that counted, "Hey, you!" or "Hey, Bark!" really was enough; Bark could not act in his own name and therefore did not need a proper name at all . . .

As a quick caveat aimed at the "Sartreans," I must point out that it is, of course, entirely possible that from the existential point of view Bark remained free even as a slave. That, however, is a deeper discussion into which I do not intend to delve at this point. While readily admitting that, deep inside, even the lowliest of all slaves remains essentially free and therefore every bit as worthy of a proper name as his master, I am rather interested in the transformation that *becoming free* brings about in us. What is the effect of breaking free from one's constraints, where "breaking free" stands for a deliberately vague concept indicating any increase in freedom and responsibility, not just an essential leap from unfree to free?

For all practical purposes, I am thinking here of a certain fuzzy logic of freedom that permits taking advantage of the boundary existential concepts, such as dread (angst), in analyzing real-life situations where, unless dead, one is rarely absolutely free and, indeed, never absolutely constrained. I am therefore interested in something like a process of individualization rather than the essential link between individuality and freedom.

Existentially speaking, Bark never ceased being Mohammed ben Lhaoussin. That said and acknowledged, he was only willing to bear his name—his crown as much as his cross—when he could build freely upon that name. Freedom mattered to Bark because it made it possible for him to matter. Perhaps *this* is what having a unique name truly means then: To be able to be of any consequence, to matter.

Interestingly enough, however, as soon as we agree to interpret Bark's story in this way, the question is raised whether all of this is ultimately about freedom at all; and if it is, then what exactly do we mean when we talk about freedom? Why such a sudden reversal? Well, *to matter* is nothing else but *matter* turned into a verb, right? Now that's interesting, because physics tells us that all matter in the universe possesses rest mass and is, therefore, decidedly unfree—unfree from the force of gravity. We say that somebody is free as a bird precisely because birds seem to defy the universal pull of gravity. *Matter* is what weighs and *to matter* is to bring one's own weight to bear upon the world. Except that, of course, there would be no weight without the unfreedom of gravity in the first place. So if to have a unique name means to be able to matter and to matter means to weigh, then the freedom that we talk about—Bark's freedom—is a very special kind of freedom indeed. Seen from this perspective, Bark's freedom is in fact a freedom to be unfree.

But surely this was but a mere play on words, not an argument? That is true; but then again, there is more to Bark's story than what we have heard so far, and things looked slightly different after he landed in Agadir.

Before we follow him on his journey home, however, let us first bring Caputo to the table. Out of the blue. If you asked Caputo, out of the blue (like in the course of an unprepared interview), what he thinks of freedom, the chances are he would not really take your breath away. Most likely he would tell you, in the spirit of Levinas, that

> autonomy and freedom belong to the most classical assumptions of Greco-philosophical ethics, of onto-theo-logical ethical theory [whereas] in an anarchic an-ethics of alterity, I worry that my freedom and autonomy pose a danger to the other, to those who are defenseless; for it is my freedom that keeps them out, that keeps them down, that threatens to kill them.[20]

"Of course, viewed on the spectrum of popular politics in America today, I am, like most academics, a 'liberal,'"[21] Caputo would hurry to add in this fictional interview, lest he be misinterpreted as an antiliberal. If anything, he would rather be regarded as a postliberal, *as in* postmodern, so long as this does not mean an out-and-out rejection of liberalism but rather a dream of a better, improved liberalism. I may rightly pass for a liberal, Caputo would probably say, but the truth is that "I have come around to thinking that liberalism is not enough."[22] It is just too much linked to the ideas of the old Enlightenment for my liking. Now again, I beg your patience and understanding, for I do believe that the old Enlightenment "means more than one thing."[23] To be sure, I have now for decades argued against the rationalistic reductionism of *Aufklärers*, but that's not the entire story. At the very minimum, we have to concede that "by asserting the spurious autonomy of subjectivity [. . .] the Enlightenment also discovered the legitimate aspirations of the individual, of every individual, to be included in the common good."[24] The old Enlightenment brought about the levels of social emancipation that were hitherto unknown. It gave rise to the kind of egalitarianism of which I am very fond. That's why I always stress that the old Enlightenment wasn't all bad, far from that! The hierarchized world of old "deserved the undoing it received at the hands of the Enlightenment—and does not deserve to be revisited."[25] But that said, we still need to move beyond the old Enlightenment and foster something like a "new Enlightenment," which "puts responsibility (to the other) before rights (of the self), heteronomy before autonomy, patience before agency."[26] Likewise, we need to move beyond the old liberalism and affirm something like a new liberalism. A kind of new liberalism that respects the other—in short, a kind of liberalism in which,

> if I were to write a constitution, the "bill of rights" would come second, after the "bill" or better the "confession of responsibilities," and my declaration of independence would come right after the declaration of dependence, for rights are rooted in responsibility.[27]

This is how Caputo would probably respond if asked to say something about freedom off the cuff. We need to put heteronomy before autonomy and, as already the prophets of old demanded, we need "to let justice flow like water over the land, to let justice rule . . ."[28] So if anyone has been looking for the sum and substance of the political position advocated in Caputo's weak theology, this would pretty much be it. Plus, a strong commitment to a democracy that is always to come, to use a somewhat dreamy deconstructive formula that nevertheless says it all. In any case, this is a strong if not entirely surprising position to hold, considering the influence on Caputo of such "prophetic" thinkers as Levinas and Derrida. A very respectable if not original thing to believe and say, considering that Amos indeed preached likewise some twenty-seven centuries ago. Great but, all in all, *nihil sub sole novum*. So what's next? Shall we just conclude this chapter and move on to explore some other, preferably more interesting aspects of weak theology?

Well, perhaps that would be a little premature. Even if we were no longer interested in following Bark in Agadir, there is still this ongoing issue with summaries that can be as useful as they can be misleading. Hence, once again, I may like to think that my semi-fictional interview with Caputo was, in fact, a good summary of what he believes, but I am still obliged—on my own reasoning—to suspect that there is more to Caputo's account of freedom than that.

7
Interlude (More than One)

Toward the end of his life Derrida said that he had "always believed that everyone has more than one age" and that we carry these ages within ourselves.[1] Caputo agreed and for a good reason. For indeed, what Derrida meant was not just a capricious sentiment of an aging philosopher but a perfectly reasonable effect of deconstruction and, for that matter, also a very good epitome of Caputo's radical hermeneutics. On Caputo's interpretation, "we do not know who we are or what is to come, and we are more than one,"[2] which is to say that

> we are not who we are, and we are not necessarily who we say or think we are; we are not self-identical, not identical with ourselves, not if we are honest.[3]

Honest. That is what Derrida is, Caputo insists against critics who accuse his controversial friend of endorsing a noncommittal "anything goes" relativism or a politically useless ambivalence. There is a world of difference between undecidability and indecisiveness, so when Derrida takes undecidability seriously, he is merely honest, not indecisive. Despite appearances to the contrary, Derrida is closer to a Kierkegaardian hero of faith than to an aesthete when he says, "I quite rightly pass for an atheist,"[4] instead of simply saying that he is one. Caputo reminds us, in this respect, that

> it should not pass unnoticed that, on the other side, Johannes Climacus took every precaution to avoid saying that he is a Christian, remaining content to say that he was trying to become one, trying to rightly pass for one. That is because Derrida is convinced of the multiplicity of the self, of all the motives of belief that disturb his atheism from within, even as the believer should also, should at most "rightly pass" for a Christian (or a Muslim, etc.), being equally deeply convinced of the multiplicity of the self, of all the motives of disbelief that disturb his or her faith.[5]

But if what we like to simplify as "the self" is in fact multiple, then also any given project of a single-yet-multiple author is likely more than one. Here, then, is what I hope to be a productive summary (since I somehow cannot avoid summarizing) of what we have seen so far: The old Enlightenment means more than one thing. We are more than one. Caputo is also more than one.[6] In sum, we cannot easily summarize.

If you approached Caputo today, in his seventies, and if you ventured to ask this respectable scholar, out of the blue, what he thinks of freedom, he would most likely tell you that he takes "rights [such as freedom] to mean the right to respond to a call by which one has been visited, to answer whenever one has been addressed."[7] But Caputo has more than one age. In fact, the preceding quotation can mean more than one thing, depending on what or who is calling. Is the call by which I have been visited the call of the *other person*, for example, or is it the call of the *other in me*?

A theology of the event is more than one.

Were I able to write in chiastic structures like the literary masters, the entire edifice of this book would be built around this simple sentence, enveloping it as the central point that I am trying to make. The keystone, so to speak, of what I have been building around the event of weak theology would be the testimony to the internal multiplicity of Caputo's project. "The secret is, there is no Secret," Caputo likes to say, "none that we know of."[8] This could not be truer about his own project. There is no secret to weak theology—or, to be more precise, there is no single unifying Secret to it. Rather, Caputo's theology, like any other text for that matter, harbors multiple secrets and is thus structurally open-ended. A theology of the event, too, never quite is what it claims to be; it is never quite self-identical.

Now, if a theology of the event has its downsides, as it surely does, I would say that this open-endedness can but does not necessarily need to be among them. On the contrary, this could well be weak theology's strongest point. It enables weak theology to make itself available for fruitful reading in a vast array of contexts. Such flexibility seems to be the benchmark of a good postmodern theory.

But hold on! Did we not just a moment ago establish that internal multiplicity or structural open-endedness is the attribute of every text? Yes, we did—briefly perhaps, but this is indeed the main lesson that we have learned from deconstruction. What sense, then, does it make to commend weak theology for something that is, in fact, true of any theological text we can imagine? What sets weak theology apart?

The answer is: critical consciousness. Weak theology is built upon the awareness of the plurality that is all around us and multiplicity that disturbs everything from within. Of course, it is not *the only* critically conscious theology on the market (I must know that, having been raised on the "theology of interruption" of Lieven Boeve)—but of all theologies that I know, Caputo's theology of the event is still the one most sensitive to the flux, with which it is trying to cope precisely by means of an *intentional* open-endedness. Weak theology is deliberately weak. That is its strongest point—even as it is, potentially, its most fatal flaw.

The paradox at issue here is this: The main strength of a theology of the event is its weakness, but this strength easily turns into weakness, pure and simple, the moment it is insisted upon strongly. The idea behind this tongue-twister is quite simple: Weak theology is in constant danger of becoming too dogmatic about its weakness, too convinced of its logic of doing "without" strong claims—as is the case with its often-criticized concept of religion "without" religion. Caputo rightly rails against what he calls strong theologies for being way too certain about how things *are*; this is, as I said, weak theology's strongest point. But when he, in an overenthusiastic opposition to strong theologies, asserts how things *are not*, he is a bit like that proverbial thief who's demanding that the (other) thief be caught. One can easily slip into dogmatism about being nondogmatic; and that, conversely, is weak theology's greatest risk.

To mitigate the danger of a closet dogmatism—one that only values "pure" or demythologized and generalized structures of religiosity—weak theology has to be ready to accept the full thrust of its own deconstructive critique. It, too, needs to be open to whatever it would perhaps rather suppress, anxious that this "whatever" could turn out to be too strong, that it would put its self-proclaimed weakness into jeopardy.

Weak theology, if it is to be true to its own principles, cannot put limits on the nature of the event it purports to interpret. The event of the call is greater than weak theology precisely because it is an event, uncontainable and incalculable, structurally always more than *what is*, undecidable on all sides, even with respect to its strength or weakness. The event of the call is free to take any form, weak or strong. It can be the silent call of conscience, or indeed the powerful call that sent Jonah overboard and into the belly of a whale, only because he paid no heed. The God of a theology of the event can be *deus incognitus* just as well as the very identifiable God of Abraham, Isaac, and Jacob. Weak theology is not in the position to decide this—which it knows, that's its strength—but neither can it decide that for the sake of weakness one should refrain from making a choice. *That* would be the indecision of a Kierkegaardian aesthete. For as Caputo explains on behalf of Kierkegaard, "the whole idea in 'aestheticism' is to station oneself decisively in the field of indecision and freedom from choice."[9]

It would be quite ironic, would it not, if weak theology were found guilty of such decidedly strong indecision? Even more ironic since, as we shall see later on, Caputo once criticized Derrida for being just that—an indecisive aesthete.

I really do not think that such a fate of Caputo's theology is inevitable, though. The danger is irreducible, to be sure, since it is essential to weak theology's positive open-endedness. But in order to live up to its potential, weak theology must allow for its own transgression. It is not and cannot wish to be the last word, not even its own last word, as in: Here I stand. I cannot do otherwise. Not if it harbors an event. It is good that weak theology is more than one.

That said, I am quite convinced that Caputo would not disapprove of this deconstructive reading of his own project anyway. For one thing, he would only deserve such reading after he did exactly the same to Derrida in *Prayers and Tears*. But beyond the acceptance of this "karmic" justice, Caputo also knows that he cannot seriously frown upon a different take on his theology without thereby utterly contradicting his views on the nature of events. For, as he says, events are "infinite in the sense of being capable of endless linkings and endlessly productive dissemination."[10] Consequently, a theology of the event would be endlessly rereadable or recontextualizable with or without Caputo's consent (I think *with*) simply because the event that animates Caputo's theology can—and sooner or later also will—link itself with other names and other stories. The author of weak theology is completely powerless against it.

Finally, weak theology, like any other text, can only benefit from a deconstructive reading: Its internal multiplicity will not disappear if one turns a blind eye to it; it will only turn into a Trojan horse. Nothing good can come out of that. But when one musters enough courage to let the *other within* speak freely, it is like opening Pandora's box. Potentially still a lot of trouble, that's true, but also hope. And again, this is not only something that Caputo himself understands; this is the very soul of his work.

We may, therefore, feel quite free, even encouraged, to open the jar of weak theology and dip into its inner secrets. That being the case, there are at least two ways to pursue this goal, both of which are already reflected in the structure of the present work.

First, we can trace the story of Caputo's theology. This is perhaps the most obvious way, because when we understand how things happened, when we follow the twisting path that has led to what today passes for a coherent theory, we also have a unique chance to spot along the way all the secrets weak theology does not tell us. Historians, according to Caputo, "should be numbered among our greatest deconstructors."[11] Of course, he had historians of traditional theology in mind when he said that, scholars who study developments in the "strong" dogmatic traditions, but there is no reason why the same should not be true about the historians of weak theology. My chapters on "what happened" thus make even more sense.

It is important, however, that we understand the function of this "genealogical method" properly. At least within the scope of this work, it is meant to open texts up, not to ridicule them. Tracing the story of weak theology can indeed be very useful, but we should not think of it as of a detective work aimed at uncovering some kind of Caputan conspiracy. There is nothing *necessarily* sinister about nontelling, nothing inevitably dishonorable about secrecy. More than anything else, secrecy on the part of any author, not just Caputo, is a simple necessity. It only becomes treacherous when the author in question starts fantasizing about being exempt from it: Authors can easily trick themselves into believing that with regard to their subject they have succeeded in "saying it all"—unambiguously and, at least in principle, leaving out nothing unaccounted for. Some, like Hegel or Wittgenstein, go as far as believing that they have covered the entire history and philosophy. Others, careful not to bite off more than they can chew, content themselves with limited, highly specialized topics. But the fantasy of a self-contained coherence is universal. It is omnipresent because—and this is my point here—because we really depend on this delusion. We should not be blind to it, but we need it nevertheless. Every text, no matter how big or small, is built upon secrets, upon repression, upon denied multiplicity. Something must always drop out. Choices must be made, choices that are structurally unjust and ex post facto better forgotten, otherwise we would have no texts at all. Such is the condition of writing. Hence, internal coherence of texts may indeed be an illusion, but it is an illusion without which we would not be able to create. Coherence is of the same species as the *self*.

Therefore, and I would like to emphasize this, nothing of what we have heard so far or will hear next is intended as a simple refusal of Caputo's theology—just because it is internally split, just because it is more than one. Not at all! Every text is more than one. Neither Caputo, nor anybody else, can be a writer without keeping secrets. But again, after this has been made clear, we need to understand that one should under no circumstances risk putting pen to paper without being ready to accept that, sooner or later, some irreverent deconstructor will jump out from behind a corner with a maddening "Gotcha!" It will happen! And when it happens, an unassuming author will be able to revel in hopeful expectation, knowing that deconstruction is, in fact, a very reverent kind of irreverence. It is an expression of confidence, of having no fear (*i-re-vereri*) *of* but also *for* the text, having no fear that the exposition of secrets will undo the text in question or make it irrelevant.

Readers who fear you not actually trust you most. In the long run, nothing but such irreverent trust can keep the texts in question alive.

This trust does not need to take the form of genealogy, though. As I said before, tracing the steps of weak theology, looking back on how it has developed dialectically over the course of decades, is perhaps the most obvious but certainly not the only way to read Caputo deconstructively. Indeed, it better not be, because storytelling, while useful, is not without risks of its own. Most importantly, historical retelling of an event is not really concerned with the event itself but with the more or less chronologically ordered facts, with what happened. But that is exactly what historians should be doing, no? Certainly. Where, then, is the problem? Right there: Precisely by being what it should be, history is blind to everything that did not happen. And for this very reason, historiography makes the past seem completed, unalterable, and therefore essentially unimportant.

My former compatriot, Milan Kundera, discusses this somewhat counterintuitive point on the first pages of his most famous novel, *The Unbearable Lightness of Being*. Vouching for Nietzsche's idea of eternal recurrence, Kundera argues that

> a life which disappears once and for all, which does not return, is like a shadow, without weight, dead in advance, and whether it was horrible, beautiful, or sublime, its horror, sublimity, and beauty mean nothing. We need take no more note of it than of a war between two African kingdoms in the fourteenth century, a war that altered nothing in the destiny of the world, even if a hundred thousand blacks perished in excruciating torment.[12]

Tell that to the descendants of the victims of that pointless war! And why not, for that matter, tell the world that the Holocaust is nothing? That it *was* horrific but *is* nothing, because *it happened* and so, as the fact of the past, the Holocaust is gone and absolutely irreversible. No one can go where (or rather *when*) it will remain locked up for good. Those terrible years cannot be relived differently. We can do nothing about it, nothing that would bring in (*im-portare*) any difference into what has happened. Forget it, let go of the past, for it is un-im-portant.

Now, if only things were so easy, but they never are. I bet we all know, or at least we felt at some point in our lives, that this is not a question of letting go of the past; it is a question of being released from it. We have no power over what happened, but what happened surely has power over us. Does this mean then that the past is *not* nothing? That depends on what we mean by the past.

If the past is merely what happened, then Kundera is right. One would be wrong to say that the Holocaust is nothing, as anybody with a bit of *sense* would quickly point out, and such a daredevil would also likely end up locked up for good. But all along, the danger of such an outrageous statement would not reside in the statement itself, but in what that statement failed to say: That the past *is* nothing but it *means* a lot, perhaps it means everything. As what happened, the past is gone, over and done with, dead and buried. But as for its significance, the sense of what happened, the past is eternal. Not eternal like the God of philosophers, the unmovable and unchangeable God of metaphysics, but eternal as in *aion*, the time of events, always present. In its facticity, the past was once real but now it is gone, whereas in its eventfulness understood in terms of the sense of what happened, the past is hyperreal and very much present. Even more than that! In its significance, the past is infinitely revisable.

Thus it is the sense of what happened that holds sway over us, not the past itself, because, unlike what happened, the sense of the past does not perish, even if it is continuously subject to change. Without such temporality, one that makes the past available and revisable at any time, the past itself is unimportant. Kundera rightly understands that for the past to be of any significance, it has to be more than what happened. Except that he finds the solution to the extension of the past in Nietzsche's myth of eternal return. It is in this sense that he speaks of

> the profound moral perversity of a world that rests essentially on the nonexistence of return, for in this world everything is pardoned in advance and therefore everything cynically permitted.[13]

It is, in other words, either a concept of continuously flowing time, which, when flowing for long (very, very long) enough will, by simple chance, recombine all the elements of the Universe so that what happened will happen again, and then again and again, and thus will give the past its due weight—the eternal return *pace* Nietzsche—or it is, *pace* Deleuze, the two concepts of time "which are not reducible to one another, yet which are incomplete without one another and which give different perspectives on their shared relations."[14]

It could be, of course, argued that the past is present through memories, which are recorded well enough by the historical science. Why, then, should we introduce new concepts, why multiply explanations when one is sufficient? (And why, for that matter, complicate my work with all these digressions, when I could simply follow the story of weak theology?) Why, indeed? Because the concept of memory is not as simple as this question would suggest. Memories cannot be reduced to objective records of what happened, into the chronologically structured database of the whole historical kit and caboodle. Any machine, let's say a security camera, can record what has happened. My computer, too, has a memory and even a folder entitled "history"—but its memory is inert, it contains facts and nothing but facts, mere records of what happened. Records are not synonymous with memories, even if, quite ironically, what I mean by memory is exactly what *to record* means etymologically: to commit what happened to one's heart (*cor*).[15] Memories are more than facts; they are the truths of the heart.

Understood thus, memories can indeed explain the continuing presence of the past sufficiently, because, as truths of the heart, they are alive and they make sense. At the same time, however, memories are not identical with historical facts; they go far beyond what happened. Memories are alive not as artifacts stored in our archives, but as images of historical facts we relive over and over again. Memories are like reenactments: Even if they were word for word, fact by fact, identical with what happened, they would never be the same.

This point finds an amusing expression in a short story by Jorge Luis Borges entitled "Pierre Menard, Author of *Don Quixote*." The story takes the form of a literary review of a monumental, if virtually unknown, project of a fictional twentieth-century French writer who resolved to reproduce *Don Quixote*. Not mechanically copy it but write it again; and not a new *Don Quixote* but *the Don Quixote*. Menard's "admirable ambition was to produce pages which would coincide—word for word and line for line—with those of Miguel de Cervantes."[16] "My undertaking is not essentially difficult," he confessed in a fictional letter to the narrator/literary critic, "I would only have to be immortal in order to carry it out."[17] Even so, within the time that he had left after arriving at his decision, Menard succeeded in recreating, word for word indeed, the "the ninth and thirty-eighth chapters of Part One of *Don Quixote* and a fragment of the twenty-second chapter."[18] And now comes the interesting part: After reading these chapters, the critic feels compelled to admit that, despite all the difficulties involved, "the fragmentary *Don Quixote* of Menard is more subtle than that of Cervantes."[19]

> The text of Cervantes and that of Menard are verbally identical, but the second is almost infinitely richer. (More ambiguous, his detractors will say; but ambiguity is a richness.) It is a revelation to compare the *Don Quixote* of Menard with that of Cervantes. The latter, for instance, wrote (*Don Quixote*, Part One, Chapter Nine):
>
> *. . . la verdad, cuya madre es la historia, émula del tiempo, depósito de las acciones, testigo de lo pasado, ejemplo y aviso de lo presente, advertencia de lo por venir.*
>
> [. . . truth, whose mother is history, who is the rival of time, depository of deeds, witness of the past, example and lesson to the present, and warning to the future.]

> Written in the seventeenth century, written by the "ingenious layman" Cervantes, this enumeration is a mere rhetorical eulogy of history. Menard, on the other hand, writes:
>
> *. . . la verdad, cuya madre es la historia, émula del tiempo, depósito de las acciones, testigo de lo pasado, ejemplo y aviso de lo presente, advertencia de lo por venir.*
>
> [. . . truth, whose mother is history, who is the rival of time, depository of deeds, witness of the past, example and lesson to the present, and warning to the future.]
>
> History, *mother* of truth; the idea is astounding. Menard, a contemporary of William James, does not define history as an investigation of reality, but as its origin. Historical truth, for him, is not what took place; it is what we think took place. The final clauses—*example and lesson to the present, and warning to the future*—are shamelessly pragmatic.
>
> Equally vivid is the contrast in styles. The archaic style of Menard—in the last analysis, a foreigner—suffers from a certain affectation. Not so that of his precursor, who handles easily the ordinary Spanish of his time.[20]

Memories are as different from the historical facts as is Menard's *Don Quixote* from that of Miguel de Cervantes. Memories are infinitely richer with sense, with which they also change over time: "It is not in vain that three hundred years have passed, charged with the most complex happenings,"[21] writes Menard about the arduousness of his endeavor to the storyteller, whose subsequent review of Menard's text is essentially a reflection upon this point. Menard's *Don Quixote* is not and cannot be the same as the text of Cervantes, even if it is verbally identical with it. The sense of the text, its significance, has changed dramatically over the intervening three hundred years that separate Menard and Cervantes.

Memories have their origin in what happened, but they are never identical with what happened because memories are continuously altered by the ever-shifting sense of the past. Memories, unlike simple historical facts, participate in the event that gave rise to them. And it is precisely due to their affinity with events that memories matter. Historical facts may be unimportant, but not so our memories of what happened. Far from unimportant, memories can actually turn out to be quite dangerous, such as the dangerous memory of the sacrifice of Jesus, "the memory of an event that we now see provoked a transformation of our heart, or at least of our laws, our institutions, and hence of our society," as Caputo said not so long ago.[22]

Incidentally, the idea of dangerous memory seems to be particularly dear to Caputo because it expresses the kind of weak force that lies at the heart of weak theology. Compared to historical facts, as we have seen, memories are significant, but their significance wields only a weak force. Unlike what we mean by, for example, *fate* or *God's providence*, dangerous memory has no power over our actions, no means to make us act in a particular way. But, as the sense of what happened, it constitutes kind of a reference point that defies our every attempt to erase it. Dangerous memories are urging us, they are possessed of a certain nagging power, a bit like the incessant pleading of Bark: "Hide me in the Marrakech plane!"; or like the persistent appeal of the importunate widow to the unjust judge: "Grant me justice against my adversary" (Luke 18:1–8). At heart, all memories are dangerous, endowed with a "power or sway of a lord"—which is apparently what "danger" originally meant[23]—even if their power is, according to the standards of "the world" at least, weak.

To sum up, the past may indeed be nothing, but it surely means a lot, perhaps it means everything. The past conceived as the memory of what happened is crucial to who we are. We are not who we were, but we are what the memory of our past means to us. Historical truth, according to Menard, is not what took place; it is what we think took place. Put differently and with reference to the topic at hand, rather than simply the factual consequence of the past decisions made by Caputo, his theology is the product of the shifting sense of those choices. A theology of the event is its own memory, not just a by-product of what happened.

And *that* is exactly something that tracing developments in Caputo's theology cannot quite grasp. Because, as I try to emulate the kind of objectivity proper to historical science (by referring to all available evidence, even that which Caputo would rather forget, but never going beyond that evidence), my chapters on what happened are ipso facto bound to facts and therefore blind to the event. Following the (hi)story of weak theology will by all means tell us more than a simple academic summary, that we have already established. Nevertheless, left to its own devices, a genealogical reading cannot fully explain all the characteristic strategies and, especially, the sentiments of weak theology.

A Little Scenario for Illustration

Suppose that I am indeed a chronicler of weak theology. Or, at least, that I could have become one, had I not so recklessly forfeited the fame of a respectable historian in order to become an irreverent deconstructor. So, today, I use my expertise to expose what in my opinion are curious spots in the history of weak theology: things Caputo said that seem at odds with the general gist of his theory.

Generally speaking, a detective job such as this one normally requires copious amounts of patience and it is rarely appreciated. For, let us be honest, who really likes the whistle-blowers? Isn't pointing out foul play shunned by many as the foulest play of them all? Maybe. Except that the whistle-blowing part of a deconstructor's job does not really consist in picking up on the inconsistencies. That would be rather redundant, even supremely silly, given that the internal multiplicity of texts is universal. Whistles would have to sound continuously everywhere and what good would that be? For our fear of double-talk, we would never hear a single word.

No. Contrary to popular belief, serious deconstructors are seldom guilty of disrespect for the texts they read. If they are serious, they take their subjects seriously—that is why they carefully study those texts in the first place (for they probably wouldn't if they didn't believe that those texts matter). So when deconstructors actually do end up blowing whistles, it is usually because somebody is indeed playing foul. Not by being more than one, of course, but by denying it vehemently. And if you still hear a lot of whistling around, this is probably because for a very long time authorial hubris has been the norm.

I must in all fairness say, however, that Caputo hasn't been making my job particularly difficult. He is a passionate deconstructor himself, after all, and his Kierkegaardian background only reinforces his wariness of texts that claim to shelter the System incarnate. I did not have to raise the alarm a single time, nor do I think I ever will.

But there is this one problem: If anyone were to try to dissect Caputo's texts to prove that his theology is more than one, Caputo would, I fear, constitute a relatively easy target. He just does not seem to care very much about being careful. I understand, of course, that this carelessness is to a great extent attributable to his deconstructive dislike of pretense. Caputo has a reputation of being "impatient with obscurantism,"[24] and he himself claims to be "opposed to the impenetrable, imponderable, unreadable, unhearable, unbearable cant of 'continentalese.'"[25] Mind you, this happens to be a scholar who has dedicated most of his career to reading Heidegger and Derrida—possibly the most "unreadable" philosophers the Continent has produced so far.

> Time and again I have succumbed to the temptation to make myself clear, which is, as someone once warned me, a very dangerous business. For nothing offers a philosopher better protection and a surer escape than an enveloping cloud of continentalist obscurity.[26]

So Caputo's carelessness is deliberate! It is by design that, instead of putting his words to paper craftily like some foxy lawyer, Caputo sticks to his guns about "seeing if a sublime matter can insinuate itself into a colloquial manner."[27] Insofar as he can pull this off successfully, I have nothing but admiration for him. Writing colloquially about matters of ultimate concern requires more ingeniousness than most people ever realize. In fact, there would be very little need for concern if only Caputo also showed a little bit more appreciation for the safety rules that are pertinent to everyday talk.

It is, for example, generally recommended to avoid saying "never" unless one really has to. But does Caputo ever care? Never! As a professional deconstructor of his texts, I can prove to you that he uses this word, one which implies closure, about ten times more frequently than the word "openness." Truth to be told, however, Caputo usually trespasses the opposite rule, namely, the one that warns us against the excessive usage of "always." Only one in four "when-s" in his texts doesn't have an "always" to pair with, even if they aren't necessarily always paired in the actual fact.[28]

But that's just mere statistics, you might say, and I would have to concur. Statistics can be an important indicator but, left to itself, it remains blind. A little like an uninterpreted history, if there is such thing, statistics provide an ensemble of raw facts that can mean everything: You've heard it, the glass is always half empty when it is half full . . .

Still, facts should matter, no? Where shall we end up if we disregard what really happened? Caputo recounts somewhere how shortly after his *Against Ethics* was published, he received a letter from a former student who, "having absorbed its last chapter on suicide and worms inching their way to silent graves," was moved to ask him "whether something had gone dreadfully wrong" in his life.[29]

> Not to worry, I said. I have always been fascinated—or hounded—by the abyss, an abyss, some abyss, from the *Abgrund* of the Godhead in Meister Eckhart, the abyss of Being in Heidegger, the *il y a* in Levinas, to Derrida's *khora*, abyss calling to abyss (Psy. 42:7), as the psalmist says, ceaselessly it seems, wherever I turned.[30]

Well, if that's true—if what Caputo says about himself had really always been the case—then why was the author of the letter worried? It's not like he had never heard Caputo in the lecture room, right? He was his former student. He should have been familiar with Caputo's way of thinking or, at the very least, one would imagine that the student must have had some clue about what has always "fascinated or hounded" his teacher.

Unless, of course, Caputo's answer to the letter didn't represent the actual facts. As I see it, it did not. Factually speaking, Caputo's "always" amounted to a very cavalier overstatement.

—Fascinated or hounded?

—Yes.

—Always?

—Indeed, always.

—By an abyss?

—Yes. But only by some abyss, and therein lies the problem. For there are many different abysses, just like being fascinated doesn't mean the same thing as being hounded. One means bewitched, another means persecuted. One is too much light, another too much darkness. You will end up blind in either case, but there is still an abyss of a difference between, say, the *Abgrund* of the Godhead in Meister Eckhart and Derrida's *khora*.

Caputo, of course, will argue the exact opposite. He'll point out the irreducible undecidability between the "cold" abyss of an indifferent Universe and the "warm," even womb-like, abyss of the world created and continuously recreated by God. This undecidability, which puts all abysses on a par, is fundamental to Caputo's thinking, so perhaps the caring student wasn't really listening to Caputo's lectures carefully. Or conversely, as I have already suggested, Caputo's thinking has altered over time and he wasn't always saying this. "Always" is, in any case, too strong a qualifier, especially when used to describe human existence, which, if anything, is perpetual change. We truly are "always" only one thing: always in motion.

To cut the long story short, Caputo used to see things differently and so his student didn't freak out for nothing; he had indeed a good reason to be concerned. There was a time when Caputo preferred one abyss over the other, when he defended Meister Eckhart's interpretation against that of Heidegger, as was already pointed out in one of the preceding chapters. Later, Caputo defended Heidegger's abyss against that of Derrida—that phase of weak theology's adventure also belongs outside the scope of the present illustration and I will discuss it in due course.

But for now, after I have so mercilessly deconstructed Caputo, I need to sweep in front of my own door. And the question is, what is it that I have proven? My argument was that Caputo was about as correct when he said that he had always been "fascinated or hounded by some abyss" as he would be if he said that he has always been awake or asleep. Judged against what really happened, Caputo's response to his former student represented certainly a clever generalization but ultimately also rather useless tautology. He could just as well have written back: "Not to worry. I have always been Caputo," while secretly knowing that the only thing about him that has not changed over the years was his name, and even there remains quite some room for discussion. I compared historical facts with Caputo's careless "always" and proved him wrong, because that is my job as a historian-deconstructor. However, did I by doing so really tell you everything? I'm afraid not! For I never asked why Caputo, an intelligent and honest author that he is, would tell such a blatant "lie." I never inquired about the sense of his response to the worried student. In fact, I missed it completely just a moment ago, when I somewhat deprecatingly suggested that Caputo could have written back that he had always been Caputo. Was I right in pointing out that saying such a thing would constitute no more than a pointless truism?

Historically maybe, because history only cares for what happened and so it will treat any claim of the sort: "I have always been this . . ." as a straightforward school task whereby one needs to prove the factual (in-)validity of such a claim. I have always been fascinated or hounded by some abyss: Nice way to put it, Professor, but very inaccurate nevertheless! Different abysses should have different names unless, of course, you have been exclusively Eckhartian or Nietzschean right from your birth. Which you obviously have not, there really is too much discontinuity, so please don't say such things.

Why not, though? Is what we say always—that is, exclusively—based on facts? And if we don't simply talk facts, why is it that we don't? Because, as Pierre Menard suggested in his *Don Quixote*, historical truth is not what took place; it is what we think took place. Proving Caputo wrong may be an important deconstructive gesture, but the import of such genealogy is limited to the facts while blind to the event. Far from rejecting Caputo's "lie" altogether, it tells us about weak theology just as much as we can learn from the ascertainable history.

In fact, memories—because that's what evaluative statements about one's past are—can be and often are historically inaccurate, but that gives historians no inevitable right to reject such statements as simple lies. I too, therefore, must humbly take back what I said previously about Caputo's response to his former student: I cannot ever tell if it was a lie, not without risking to completely miss the point of what Caputo said. For where the sense of what happened is involved, historical science cannot be the sole judge. There is much more in memories than what meets the historian's eye. Historical truth as the truth of the heart contains elements that are irreducible to what happened. Take regret, for example, or nostalgia. Take the paralyzing sense of trespass and guilt, think of the liberating sense of forgiveness and redemption.

If I stick stubbornly to my role as a historian, if I insist on the facts, then I might as well tell you: What happened, happened. Live with it! Why mull over what is done, let alone regret something that never happened? Right? Of course not! Because what does it matter that what I wish had happened in fact never did, when this absurd wish still controls my entire life—even to the point where I am totally incapable of living in the present? Aren't countless individuals out there living just like that? Correction: Aren't we all living just like that, mourning the loss of the past that never happened, not in the recordable history anyway? The sense of the past, that past we invent for ourselves, exerts such a power over us that even the past itself cannot compete with it.

Therefore, when Caputo says that he has always been fascinated or hounded by some abyss, he may very well be right—right in a sense, if not in fact. It's just that I, as a historian, won't be able to see how, because the significance of what happened is Caputo's ultimate secret, something that only he understands and only he can tell. In other words, my inability to relate everything that he says to verifiable facts does not automatically make him wrong.

So, the last question that I have to ask myself is about the true purpose of my job. Why should I spend my days, indeed waste my time, hunting for factual inconsistencies in Caputo's texts, when in the end my work appears equally pointless as searching for inaccuracies in a novel?

Thus far I have not even spoken here about the right to change one's mind: How could one become a true scholar without growing up? Hence, when I point out that Caputo used to say something very different from what he is saying now, do I prove him inconsistent with himself? Yes, I do. But by doing so, I merely demonstrate that his thinking has developed, and develop it should . . . This way, I could prove "inconsistent" everyone on the planet, but such exercise would indeed be pointless because we would no longer talk about someone's fallacy but about the human condition. "Being wrong" has a very, very different meaning when it applies to everyone.

But then, of course, there are those situations when Caputo, with hindsight, says things that are demonstrably inconsistent with what actually happened. "I have always been fascinated or hounded by some abyss . . ." Is this where the genealogical deconstruction comes in?

Well, let's put it this way: Do I, as a bookkeeper of the facts, stand any chance against Caputo's sense of his own past? No, I don't. He'll be right even where I blow a whistle. I cannot but accept that historical facts are nothing unless they are facts interpreted, imagined, and yes, even invented (and thus no longer pure facts). There is no pure historical truth, only the truth of the heart, the truth of memories. History, in other words, isn't a simple sequence of facts but a story.

So, finally, how do I, a "positivist" historian, feel about this? A bit like Dr. Ellie Arroway, I'd say. Ellie is a SETI scientist and the main protagonist of a 1997 science fiction drama film, *Contact*, based on a novel by the late Carl Sagan. After she discovers a signal of extraterrestrial origin, which carries detailed plans for building a device for interstellar travel, Ellie is chosen to be the first human to undertake the journey and meet the originators of the transmission. Ellie is hurtled through what appears to be a network of wormholes, but the capsule stops from time to time to allow her to see the wonders of the universe. On one such occasion, shortly before she passes out, Ellie finds herself lost for words:

> "Some kind of celestial event. No—no words. No words to describe it. Poetry! They should have sent a poet. So beautiful. So beautiful . . . I had no idea."

Interestingly enough, this must have been quite a revelation for Ellie, because she had always been a staunch defender of the exact science, expressly unwilling to take seriously anything that could not be (if only in principle) supported by factual evidence. When queried on what basis governments should choose a candidate to represent humanity, she answered without hesitation that it "should be somebody fluent in the language the message was given in—science, in this case." Ellie would clearly choose mathematics over poetry until, that is, until she witnessed something that she felt she should not even try to describe scientifically. "They should have sent a poet."

Now, it's entirely up to you whether or not you think of Caputo's theology as a breathtaking celestial event, for the point remains valid either way: Whoever sets out to speak about weak theology must be prepared to go way beyond historical science understood in a narrow sense. Which, as I've said already, leaves me wondering about the purpose of my job. If now any literate—poet, novelist, or maybe even a hagiographer—is better equipped to understand Caputo than myself, a historian, because they are more or less free from the imperative to stick to the facts, then why should we need custodians of facts at all? I think the answer is both yes and no, for these are two quite different questions, after all. Whether a novelist unrestricted by what really happened can tell a better story of weak theology than I? Most likely yes. But unrestricted definitely does not mean unaffected or uninterested. Maybe memories aren't the facts, but it is equally true that without facts there would be no memories. My job as a historian of Caputo's theology, therefore, isn't irrelevant, but it's a part of a larger whole. Self-sufficient? No. The sooner I get over this legacy of modernity that was spectacularly obsessed with differentiation, the better. But neither unimportant. To trace the adventure of weak theology, the chapters on what happened and the chapters on series are equally needed . . .

8
Freedom Again

The last news we had of him was brought back to us by Abdullah who at our request had looked after Bark at Agadir. The plane reached Agadir in the morning, but the bus did not leave until evening. This was how Bark spent his day.

He began by wandering through the town and remaining silent so long that his restlessness upset Abdullah.

"Anything the matter?"

"No."

This freedom had come too suddenly: Bark was finding it hard to orient himself. There was a vague happiness in him, but with this exception there was scarcely any difference between the Bark of yesterday and the Bark of today. Yet he had as much right to the sun, henceforth, as other men; as much right as they to sit in the shade of an Arab café.

He sat down and ordered tea for Abdullah and himself. This was his first lordly gesture, a manifestation of a power that ought to have transfigured him in other men's eyes. But the waiter poured his tea quite without surprise, quite unaware that in this gesture he was doing homage to a free man.

—Antoine de Saint-Exupéry, *Wind, Sand and Stars*

Ordering a cup of tea, rather than being ordered to prepare one, should have awakened the free man inside Bark, but it did not. Something was missing, so he decided to try elsewhere, this time in the red quarter of the town.[1] "The little Berber prostitutes," relates Saint-Ex, were "so kind and tame that here Bark felt he might be coming alive." Bark relished their love, he told them his story, and "to make the wonder more wonderful he added, 'I am Mohammed ben Lhaoussin.'" But again, although friendly, the girls were not impressed: "All men have names, and so many return from afar!" They would have been just as kind to any other man, and they, like the waiter who had served him the tea, had no need of Bark.

> He was free, but too infinitely free; not striding upon the earth but floating above it. He felt the lack in him of that weight of human relations that trammels a man's progress; tears, farewells, reproaches, joys—all those things that a man caresses or rips apart each time he sketches a gesture; those thousand ties that bind him to others and lend density to his being.

But then something happened. Bark was wandering aimlessly, when a child came up and Bark casually stroked its cheek. No plan, just a spontaneous old man's act of kindness, but the child smiled and, in that flash, "awoke something in Bark" as he now "felt himself more important on earth because of the sickly child whose smile was his due." At last, Bark knew what to do, although Abdullah was certain that he must have lost his mind—"gone mad with joy." Bark walked around until he found a group of children, then strode off into the nearest shop and returned with "toys, bangles, and gold-sewn slippers," handing gifts to every child nearby. "Fool, throwing away your money," complained Abdullah as the news spread and more and more children came running to Bark. Those were the one thousand francs that the Juby mechanics Laubergue, Marchal, and Abgrall had put together from their wages to "see Bark through till he found work," but before the day was over, Bark had nothing left. Nevertheless, Saint-Ex did not think Bark had gone crazy. He was now free and he could earn his living; but "what good was this money" that he had for starting, "when the thing for which he was famished was to be a man in the family of men, bound by ties to other men?"

> And so the reign of Bark began in the glory of the sun setting over Agadir, in that evening coolness that so long had been for him the single sweetness, the unique stall in which he could take his rest. And as the hour of leaving approached, Bark went forward lapped in this tide of children as once in his sea of ewes, ploughing his first furrow in the world. He would go back next day to the poverty of his family, to responsibility for more lives than perhaps his old arms would be able to sustain, but already, among these children, he felt the pull of his true weight. Like an archangel too airy to live the life of man, but who had cheated, had sewn lead into his girdle, Bark dragged himself forward, pulling against the pull of a thousand children who had such great need of golden slippers.

Madness of a man with a proper name, but without ties to the world that would have given that name its due weight; it is true, in Agadir, unlike in Cape Juby, all men had names and many of them came from afar. Thanks to Saint-Ex, Bark was resurrected as Mohammed ben Lhaoussin. We could even say the "Captain of the Birds" helped Bark find his own voice again, but Bark was lost for words. "Anything the matter," Abdullah had asked. "No." "What are you looking for?" Abdullah asked later. "Nothing." No, nothing is the matter (it is I who do not seem to matter). And what I am looking for is nothing, no-thing. In Agadir, Bark would have been as free as a bird, if only had his flight been a true flight—that avian overcoming of the force of gravity by the power of wings, not an aimless floating.

A powerful sense of alienation drove Bark all around the town; he was evidently disoriented. "Let us go somewhere else," he told Abdullah while still sitting in the café, only to also leave Kasbah with the tender girls soon after that. Surely, Bark's lack of direction was just temporary, if one can say so about the day the Earth stood still. Bark had wished for the freedom to be unfree, to obey the call not of the wild but of home, but the layover in Agadir stopped him in his tracks. One day in Agadir was like eternity in limbo, like the seven years of Odysseus on the island of Calypso. There, Bark was not free, he was lost. Freedom had cost Bark his pied-à-terre, literally; all of a sudden, he was out of place: "He idled in front of the Jewish shops, stared at the sea, repeated to himself that he could walk as he pleased in any direction, that he was free," but he had nowhere to go.

What is personal freedom worth for people who have lost their bearings in the desert? Caravans, too, are free to go as they please; yet they always follow one celestial body and not another, sometimes a newborn star at its rising.[2] Coelho's Santiago, the shepherd I mentioned previously, was captured by Bedouin warriors on his way to the pyramids. They did not bother to put him in chains. By depriving Santiago of his horse, the Bedouins made every direction equal—for without a transport, none of the oases around could be reached—and thus they transformed the desert, which, one can read, "only moments ago was endless and free," into an "impenetrable wall." Where all paths are the same, choosing becomes impossible and Buridan's ass starves to death. For Bark, a single day in Agadir, a day of freedom pure and simple, turned out to be the worst of all prisons—like an invisible "wall enclosing a fortress," which is what the word *agadir* actually means . . .

Turning to Berber etymology, however, may be a little counter-productive, when I am, in fact, making a case for walls. "All men dwell, and life's meaning changes for them with the meaning of the home,"[3] says the desert king, as he recalls—not without nostalgia—the greatness of the palace his father had built:

> Vast was my father's palace, with one wing set apart for the women and a secret inner garden where a fountain sang. (And I ordain that every house shall have just such a heart within it, where a man may draw near to something and whereto he may retreat from something.

> A focal place of goings out and of comings in. Else, a man is nowhere. And there is no freedom in not-being.)[4]

A fountain in the heart of the house; life-giving water in the midst of a desert; a well which, though hidden, makes the desert beautiful; which draws nickers out of Bedouin horses from miles away; and which breaks the light of the blazing midday sun, projecting a rainbow on the one side of the geometrician's face, but not on the other. This singular image could fill a book, but there were also other rooms in the palace. "There were barns and cattle sheds," the king tells us, and sometimes they were empty, but the father

> forbade that either barn or shed should serve the other's purpose; for, said he, the function of the barn is to serve as a barn, and when you cease to know your way about a house, you are no longer dwelling in it. Thereto he added: "Little matters it if the one use or the other be the more productive or expedient. Man is not livestock for fattening, and love, for him, counts more than the use to which this place or that is put. You cannot love a house which has no visage, and where footsteps have no meaning."[5]

There, too, was a hall of audience, the hall where justice was administered, the hall where the dead were laid,

> and there was an empty room, whose use none knew—and which perchance truly served no purpose but to teach men that there are things secret, that never may they reach the core of knowledge.[6]

Every step was either a step closer to, or a step away from, the fountain, which, albeit secret, charged the palace with a field of weak force. Its invisible lines trailed the contours of walls, passed through doors, descended and ascended flights of stairs, which in turn restricted their smooth flow. One was free not to seek the fountain. In seeking it, however, one had to pass through those doors and climb up those stairs.

Not all people in the palace were content with the arrangement. "Once there came to me a fool," the king relates, "and said: 'Do but free us from your constraints, and then we shall wax great,'" proposing "to lay low the walls of my father's palace, wherein every footstep had a meaning, so that they might roam at greater ease within it."[7]

> See how much space is wasted here, what wealth left unexploited, what conveniences lost through inadvertence! Far better were it to lay low those useless walls and level out those short flights of steps, which merely hinder progress. Then men will be free.

> But I make answer: Then men will become like cattle in the marketplace and to beguile the tedium of their days they will invent new, foolish pastimes, which likewise will be hedged about with rules, but they will be rules devoid of grandeur. For the palace may give birth to poems, but what poem could be made about such pastimes as their games of dice?[8]

Without those walls, according to our royal friend, even though they put restrictions on the freedom of movement, the people were bound to lose "firstly, a visage they had come to know; and then, in ceasing to love it, their understanding of themselves."[9] They would be equally lost without rites that—so the king believed—were in time what dwelling places were in space:

> For it is well that the years should not seem to wear us away and disperse us like a handful of sand; rather they should fulfill us. It is meet that Time should be a building-up. Thus I go from one feast day to another, from anniversary to anniversary, from harvesttide to harvesttide[10]

. . . and from Christmas to Christmas. If "religion without religion" makes little sense, this is why. For such a tradition-free and dogma-free religion, the "messianic without messianism," is like a cathedral without walls, a temple transformed into *agora*, into a marketplace, in the name of the battle against enclosure.

Pulling down walls, however, is not the same as allowing for different paths to the fountain, not even the same as exploiting cracks in and digging tunnels through those walls. Iconoclasm could not win against idolatry, because it mistakenly targeted icons in lieu of idols. Likewise, taking religion out of religiosity cannot stop Christianity from closing upon itself, for such strategy unwittingly confuses bonds of relation with chains. The love of home should not be automatically diagnosed as agoraphobia. We build our homes, and we defend them, because we cannot truly dwell in the marketplace. What poem will one write about the game of dice? What silence will one find among the noisy, competing merchants? What, for that matter, will happen to Christmas without the Messiah, and what will happen to a year without Christmas?

Religion without religion is like the desert (*khora* is allegedly its name); you are free to go wherever you please, but you will never find water, because it is everywhere. It is true that people will not kill each other for the vapor in the wind, but they will die of thirst all the same and be dispersed like a handful of sand. "Truth strikes deep, like a well,"[11] and a well is what those desert pilgrims required.

We can also draw an analogy between religion without religion and Bark's day in Agadir. The sense of alienation may give rise to noble (and a little mad) deeds, and, in the same way as Bark, Caputo's "an-khora-ites," the "anchorites *sans* anchor," can be magnanimous. Justice is their watchword, madness of generosity beyond justice their professed ideal. They, too, call for an expenditure without return. There is this crucial difference, however: Mohammed ben Lhaoussin never intended to stay in Agadir. As heartwarming as his kindness toward the street children was, it was only a poem written in the marketplace. While it already bespoke more than the soul of a slave, it did not reach as far as the deepest core of a family man. What Bark did was a projection; inasmuch as he was seeking to regain his footing in the world, those golden slippers were a secret communication with his three children in Marrakech. He yearned for home, he meant to return. Had he been forced to remain in Agadir, only then would he have gone truly mad.

But where will Caputo's poets of the impossible go? Wherever will they return to at nightfall? And are they perchance also secretly communicating with someone, when they respond to the call for justice?

Let us consider the last question first. Here, the advocates of religion without religion claim to have no definitive answer:

> I answer the call of the child, not knowing whether the call issues from infinite depths, whether the face of the child is a trace of the Infinite or just a little blip of energy in a great cosmic dance of forces. I do not know whether there is anything infinite at all. I answer, perhaps from some obscure unconscious compulsion, perhaps from some blind instinct, perhaps from a bit of undigested beef, perhaps in response to the voice of God who calls out whenever the least of Her children is laid low.[12]

What is more, in religion without religion as well as in weak theology, being at a loss about the source of the call is not considered as an embarrassing ignorance that we must try to overcome. On the contrary, Caputo criticizes such a "search for the name" as a characteristic trait of strong theologies:

> To pursue that question is to treat the call like a strong force with a definite place on the plane of being or power, not a weak one that solicits me from afar. Indeed, to pursue that question is a way to change the subject when the only subject is the calling of and for the kingdom, rather the way someone who has been caught cheating might respond by asking, "How did you find that out?"—which is, of course, not the point.[13]

Why talk about religion without religion at this point in the book? Because, for Caputo, this is also a question of freedom. First a quick and somewhat overdue caveat, however: I do not mean to conflate Caputo's weak theology indiscriminately with what is essentially Derrida's notion of religion without religion. While it is arguable that the two are very difficult to tell apart, closer examination will be necessary in order to do justice to Caputo's theological project (more in the following chapters). Having said that, it is on Caputo's own request that we should read his theology "in the spirit of what Derrida calls a 'non-dogmatic doublet of dogma,'" and that we should "think of it as a 'theology without theology' that accompanies what Derrida calls a 'religion without religion.'"[14]

Now, if religion without religion is one of the keys to weak theology provided by Caputo in the introduction to *The Weakness of God*, the final chapter of the book, entitled "A Concluding Prayer," offers a summary of "this entire undertaking," namely, "to liberate ourselves from the anxious and obsessive search for the name and thereby to win a certain version of the freedom of the children of God."[15] This freedom, according to Caputo, is both the "freedom to do the truth [. . .] free from any anxiety about knowing the name,"[16] and the freedom from religious violence, for

> as long as the event that is desired with a desire beyond desire is contracted to the specific terms of a Proper Name, there will be wars of private property, battles over the copyright, over who owns that name, or who gets to speak authoritatively, with all the authority of the Name.[17]

One would be hard-pressed to challenge Caputo in his conviction that "these wars over the name of God" that we witness today arise "from reducing an event to a name," even if one did not accept Caputo's conclusion that this is precisely "what happens in a strong theology."[18] In fact, also the disagreement over the latter would, on the surface, seem easily resolvable, if we simply took it as a matter of definition: "From this point onwards, we shall describe theologies that reduce an event to a name as strong." Unfortunately, such a strategy would be of little use because the real question is whether every theology that is not weak in Caputo's sense of the term—that has not undergone reduction to a theology without theology—ipso facto reduces an event to a name and is, therefore, strong. Caputo would have to be out of his deconstructive senses to seriously attempt to show this to be true. Not only is it far from certain that any practicable weak theology must be modeled on Derrida's religion without religion, but deconstruction calls into question even the very dichotomy between strong and weak theologies.

Now, the bad news is that Caputo, at least when he writes as a theologian, indeed seems to pay no heed to the alarm bells sounded by deconstruction. The contrast that he draws between his weak theology and strong theologies could hardly be starker, and it sure looks as though he is following the logic of Matthew—whoever is not with me is against me[19]—rather than that of Mark—whoever is not against us is for us.[20] On the other hand, if we presume that weak theology really is possible, the good news, which we already discussed in the previous chapter, is that there are at least two of them (more than one). It is on the account of such a hitherto unknown or unrecognized "other" weak theology that I have over the last few pages concerned myself with what could be interpreted as a *cost analysis* of Caputo's project. For although I am averse to an offhand critique, a *cold analysis*, we do need to understand where Caputo's work might fall short of the promise of theology for the twenty-first century, if we are to continue his dream.

The stated promise of Caputo's weak theology is, as we have seen, "a certain version of the freedom of the children of God." The price that he expects us to pay for this freedom, however, is that from now on we shall only pray "to an Unknown God," as the last chapter of *The Weakness of God* advocates.[21] There is a certain irony in the fact that Caputo, who once "freely chose the name Brother Paul" so that when "someone said, 'Paul!,' [he] would have said *me voici*,"[22] should today blatantly ignore Apostle Paul's speech in Areopagus, and yet at the same time call him to witness about the weakness of God. For if belief in an "Unknown God" is enough, why would Paul have bothered to preach to Athenians at all?[23] But "freedom of the children of God" does not come for free, according to Caputo. To earn it, we must accept the fate of orphans who do not know their heavenly father, or even if they have any heavenly father at all—which, needless to say, is yet another moment of irony. Freedom in this sense really means the freedom from God, as in Meister Eckhart's prayer, which Caputo likes to invoke: "I pray God to rid me of God."[24]

Further considerations along these lines make one wonder what future lies in wait for the concept of religion without religion. The future is, of course, always a risky business, and Caputo is well aware of that: "Every promise is also a threat," he says, "and the event to come can be either for better or for worse."[25] However, the potential shortcoming of Caputo's version of weak theology that I am referring to does not arise from the fundamental uncertainty that besets the time to come. Should the future confirm my hypothesis that religion without religion is less than viable, it will almost certainly be due to the lack of adequate respect for the past. Caputo routinely assumes the role of a rebel hoping to scandalize everyone, especially when it comes to the expectations that both secular and religious thinkers have regarding Derrida and deconstruction.[26] "Of course I particularly enjoy the insouciance, the impudence, the downright scandal,"[27] confesses Caputo in the interview with Raschke—an attitude that is no less discernible in his later, theological writings:

> I am not theologizing philosophy but deconstructing Christianity, causing a scandal to the pious and a stumbling block to the theologians, re-imagining, reinventing "God," which is why my radical theology is considered radical atheism and a "death of God" by my evangelical friends.[28]

To the extent that Caputo's theology is the work of an "ever-suspicious sacred anarchist,"[29] I am sympathetic to it, but Caputo is willing to go way beyond commendable wariness; his religion without religion strikes me as prophetic zeal gone berserk, the product of destruction rather than deconstruction. In any case, it seems imprudent to completely write off traditional religion simply because it can give some people crazy ideas. Surely, traditional religion can be dangerous, but anything can. More importantly, what substitute does Caputo offer? Where, we must ask again, does he imagine that we should go, after the house has been torn down? Remain in the desert? I would say only a few can bear such a fate, if I seriously believed anyone could. To borrow a line from Lawrence M. Krauss, "nothing is unstable,"[30] and so is perhaps religion without religion. I suspect that sooner or later, religion without religion always gives way to another religion:

> Thus men destroy their best possession, the meaning of things: on feast days they pride themselves on standing out against old customs, and betraying their traditions, and toasting their enemy. True, they may feel some qualms as they go about their deeds of sacrilege. So long as there is sacrilege. So long as there still is something against which they revolt. Thus for a while they continue trading on the fact that their foe still breathes, and the ghostly presence of the laws still hampers them enough for them to feel like outlaws. But presently the very ghost dissolves into thin air, and then the rapture of revolt is gone, even the zest of victory forgotten. And now they yawn. On the ruins of the palace they have laid out a public square; but once the pleasure of trampling its stones with upstart arrogance has lost its zest, they begin to wonder what they are doing here, on this noisy fairground. And now, lo and behold, they fall to picturing, dimly as yet, a great house with a thousand doors, with curtains that billow on your shoulders and slumbrous anterooms. Perchance they dream even

> of a secret room, whose secrecy pervades the whole vast dwelling. Thus, though they know it not, they are pining for my father's palace where every footstep had a meaning.[31]

"Let him who fails to learn and mark three thousand years still stay," Goethe once wrote, "void of experience, in the dark, and live from day to day."[32] *Quotidianism*, characteristic of life in the Kingdom, I am afraid, was not what Goethe had in mind; and in any case, in order to forestall the bleak scenario portrayed by the desert king, Caputo will have to take questions of tradition and legacy more seriously.

There is no denying that the same forces that bind us also form us and make us grow. All life can be regarded as a prison, if entropy translates as freedom, but that is no argument against life. Nietzsche must have meant something along these lines, I think, when he said that "slavery, in both the crude and refined senses of the term, seems to be the indispensable means of disciplining and breeding even the spirit."[33] Needless to say, Nietzsche would be the last one to condone slavery, but when we think about it, Bark probably knew more about what he desired and who he was while he was still in Cape Juby than he did in Agadir. Mohammed ben Lhaoussin was temporarily afflicted by the worst of all human maladies, boredom, which deprives time of all rhythm and direction. Forces, on the other hand, are vectors; it is only thanks to the force of gravity that we can tell the difference between up and down. Birds may be free, but they are not directionless, as they must constantly fight against the pull of the entire planet beneath them. So perhaps not so much birds, but rather the wind, as Elias Canetti wrote somewhere, is the only thing in civilization to enjoy freedom.

This is a curious metaphor and I am going to play with it for a while, as it has the potential to make our discussion of another baffling aspect of Caputo's theology more engaging. I refer to weak theology's insistence on the hiddenness of the source of the call. As we have seen, Caputo washes his hands of any knowledge about who it is that calls: "I answer, perhaps from some obscure unconscious compulsion, perhaps from some blind instinct, perhaps from a bit of undigested beef, perhaps in response to the voice of God . . ."[34] Where else, other than in Caputo's theology, can one come across such statements? If uttered in a courtroom, they would cause an instant outrage. Now I do not mean to say that Caputo is wrong. Perhaps we really cannot know who or what calls us, but I think Caputo goes too far when he says we should abandon all attempts to find out. At the very least, it seems dangerously irresponsible not to seek the answer, when one of the possibilities is "some obscure unconscious compulsion." You do not just brush aside the unconscious; doing so will not make life safer or less complex. The intricacy of life, personal as well as that of a culture or tradition, is actually one of my points here: Little can be gained by the Enlightenment-style simplification and demystification. The "winding" path of weak theology proves that nothing ever is as simple as we are led to believe.

Let us take up Nietzsche again, as he is important in this story and deserves a more relevant (and perhaps less disquieting) citation:

> I will say it again: what seems to be essential "in heaven and on earth" is that there be obedience in one direction for a long time. In the long term, this always brings and has brought about something that makes life on earth worth living—for instance: virtue, art, music, dance, reason, intellect—something that transfigures, something refined, fantastic, and divine.[35]

Nietzsche is also repeatedly quoted as putting freedom side by side with promising. The paradoxical task that nature has set itself in the case of humans, Nietzsche argued, was to breed an animal with the right to make promises.[36] It is a "rare freedom" and an "extraordinary privilege of responsibility," that an "emancipated individual" can promise.[37] To promise, in turn, means to send forward (*pro-mittere*); and how, indeed, could anyone promise anything without the sense of direction? Or without there being anything to send? That was the source of Bark's madness: He was Mohammed ben Lhaoussin and his name was meant to carry within itself a promise, but his desire to send it forth was met with indifference. The girls just did not care. All men have names. So besides my disagreement with Caputo on the benefits of religion without religion, I also often wonder what kinds of promises were involved when he found his own voice. And why or how would your own voice matter in a desert? Ultimately, I would like to understand to what end Caputo strives to deny himself and his readers the joy of dreaming. But first things first, and I promised to talk about the wind.

Which wind?—one may ask, and rightly so. For "the wind blows where it wills," we read in the Gospel of John, "and you can hear the sound it makes, but you do not know where it comes from or where it goes."[38] Jesus, however, said nothing about the strength of that wind. Does that mean that we can equally well think of freedom as a gentle breeze that caressed Elijah, or as a terrible storm that blew away the black ship and cost Odysseus ten years of his life? Which of the two best describes Caputo's freedom?

Other aeolian ways to look at freedom now come to mind as well. For example, this is how Levinas sees it:

> The freedom of the subject that posits itself is not like the freedom of a being free as the wind. It implies responsibility—which should surprise, nothing being more opposed to freedom than the non-freedom of responsibility. The coinciding of freedom with responsibility constitutes the I, doubled with itself, encumbered with itself.[39]

So far so good, nothing surprising here—this is how Caputo talks. But what about a little more creative image of the wind rustling in the leaves, or rumbling in one's belly? This is clearly a far-fetched association with the *il y a*; the question is, how far? For Levinas, that rustling is anonymous, without a proper name or own voice; that rumbling is neutral, without a charge, responsive to no force fields at all. Like a free rein of the elements, like Nietzsche's picture of the Universe at liberty to draw another breath (wind) and move on without the least regard for the clever animals who had invented truth: this, too, is one face of freedom, the face of the abyss. And a very Nietzschean storm.

Levinas and Nietzsche—can the two even live under the same roof?[40] My point: Levinas and Nietzsche *do* share quarters under Caputo's roof. Maybe they do not talk to one another often, but they are *both* there. Heteronomy *and* autonomy. Go figure! Nor do we need to examine Caputo's heteronomical position on liberty again, except to give substance to the previous claim and to add a little weight to my imagery:

> There is no squinting here [in "heteronomism"] over obligation, no anxiety about gravity and heavy weights, no hand-wringing about being tied down. [. . .] Freedom is frightened not by the weight of responsibility but by the murderousness of its own aggressive forces, which love to dominate others. [. . .] The weight of the other, the ponderousness of what comes *ab extra* is precisely what swings against the same, shattering freedom and decentering the subject.[41]

Thus spoke Caputo in *Against Ethics*, contrasting his Levinasian position with the "heteromorphism" of Deleuze and Nietzsche—actually, Deleuze via Nietzsche—who, in turn, concern themselves with the free discharge of creative forces. Their forces are jealously autonomous. They "do not obey anything," complains Caputo, they "do not re-act, do not act *ab extra*. What they do is their own doing, their own being, their own willing, their own fate."[42] Whereas Caputo is a staunch defender of the force of gravity, *a fortiori* so after deconstruction was accused of taking it too lightly: "Alas, that Derrida should live to hear his name used as a sign of nonsense and resistance to gravity! Alas, that something as serious as 'deconstruction' would come to do service for such silliness,"[43] Caputo could barely control the outburst of his anger. "Deconstruction is gravity itself . . ."[44]—it is the weight of the other.

Now, enter the storm. Caputo's option for the law of the other notwithstanding—and yes, what follows is also to be found in *Against Ethics*, that is, *sub eodem tecto*—he is dissatisfied with Deleuze's "sweetened, veiled, attenuated, and blunted" reading of Nietzsche.

> This Nietzsche, Deleuze's Nietzsche, is very beautiful and I love him very much. I have learned a great deal from him. [. . .] Still, I am troubled by this Deleuzian Nietzsche. The question he provokes in me is whether Deleuze's Dionysiac has not lost his nerve.[45]

Another curious metaphor—"has (not) lost his nerve." Here, permit me to flag it for those readers who might wish to entertain themselves in the future: All you need to do is keep an eye out for the word "nerve" and whenever it pops up, read it literally. Actually, the effect will be significantly enhanced by an etymological reading, to wit, as a "tendon," "sinew," or even a "bowstring." Then imagine the confusion brought about by this peculiar, if linguistically fairly recent, connection between ties and courage.[46] For example, "a husband is what is left of a lover, after the nerve has been extracted," wrote Helen Rowland in her *Guide to Men*.[47] But does a lover turn into a husband when he loses his passionate courage, or is it rather when all the links with the beloved one are severed?

Back to our story. Has Deleuze lost his nerve? As per my neural version of *pharmakon*, by rendering Nietzsche gentler, a little more connected, did Deleuze actually lose his connection? Caputo certainly seems to think so. He says his Nietzsche is different:

> For Nietzsche, my Nietzsche, ventures on most dangerous seas, on waters tossed by fierce winds, on a deep inhabited by the darkest monsters. Nietzsche is a bold searcher and researcher who "embarks with cunning sails on terrible seas." [. . .] For the Nietzsche that most interests me [. . .] is a tremendous wind, a cataclysmic, disastrous storm that sweeps over us, a merciless burst of what Nietzsche calls his "truthfulness," which frightens me—I speak for myself—half to death.[48]

But only half to death. In the same way as a glass of the *Hitchhiker's* Pan Galactic Gargle Blaster was said to feel like "having your brains smashed out by a slice of lemon, wrapped 'round a large gold brick," Nietzsche does far more to Caputo than just make him gasp for breath.

And yet, "I like to take my Nietzsche straight up, not on the rocks," Caputo confesses in one interview.[49] No wussy drink diluting required here, thank you very much.

These are not just fancy tropes: Believe it or not, in a tie between the two Nietzsche triumphed even over Kierkegaard, when none other than Caputo was the umpire. That same Nietzsche, who wrote in *Ecce Homo* that he was "no Jack the Dreamer" but rather a warrior "dangerously quick at the draw."[50] It all happened when Caputo was reading Johannes de Silentio's "Eulogy on Abraham." Using imagery a bit like mine, Silentio wrote:

> If a human being did not have an eternal consciousness, if underlying everything there were only a wild, fermenting power that writhing in dark passions produced everything, be it significant or insignificant, if a vast, never appeased emptiness hid beneath everything, what would life be then but despair? If such were the situation, if there were no sacred bond that knit humankind together, if one generation emerged after another like forest foliage, if one generation succeeded another like the singing of birds in the forest, if a generation passed through the world as a ship through the sea, as wind through the desert, an unthinking and unproductive performance, if an eternal oblivion, perpetually hungry, lurked for its prey and there were no power strong enough to wrench that away from it—how empty and devoid of consolation life would be![51]

It is difficult to imagine how excited Caputo was, when he for the first time read these words. Finally, someone was going to provide an answer to Nietzsche, whose picture of the indifferent Universe had been haunting Caputo for some time. And not just someone, but his beloved hero Kierkegaard. Indeed, as he was reading, Caputo's "hopes soared" and he made a note in the margin of his book: "Nietzsche!"[52] But he was in for a shock:

> I looked eagerly for the resolution Johannes would offer to this terrible spectre, but his response came to me with the thud of a still more terrible disappointment: But precisely for that reason it is not so.[53]

"But precisely for that reason it is not so"—that was, indeed, Silentio's answer.[54] The Universe just cannot be so cruel, it can not. "Now though I love Johannes de Silentio dearly, though he is an author whom I would dearly love to imitate had I the nerve [!] and the wit," Caputo wrote, "I have to say that this is one of his most disappointing moments" and "Nietzsche has, at this point at least, silenced" him.[55] "And so I must confess that my impiety is Nietzschean."[56]

Shall we, therefore, conclude that Caputo's freedom is, in fact, a storm and Caputo is a hero venturing on most dangerous seas and fearlessly facing the abyss? Such interpretation would seem inevitable, but Caputo tells us otherwise:

> I cannot muster the lionhearted, macho courage required by Nietzsche's cold cosmic truthfulness. I am neither a Knight of the Infinite Abyss, ready to hurl myself into the Void, nor a Knight of l'Infini, the Infinite One who hovers over all. I am not a knight at all. I distrust favors from the Crown.[57]

This is odd. After taking Deleuze and Kierkegaard to task for either diluting Nietzsche or offering a useless counterargument from happiness, respectively, Caputo has "no heart for a battle with the abyss."[58] Are we still talking about the same Caputo who, starting with *Radical Hermeneutics* (when he also found his voice) "tried to take a colder, more deconstructed look at things, to face up to the 'difficulty of life' [. . .] without the support of metaphysical foundations, on the one hand, or of the consolations of religion, on the other?"[59] "Distrusting favors from the Crown" can be explained by Caputo's American sensibilities, but what about his ostensible rejection of courage required by Nietzsche? For what purpose?

I suggest that Caputo has no other choice, at least not if he insists on the hiddenness of the source of the call. Both attitudes are closely related, for indeed there can be no knighthood without a queen or king. As a matter of fact, on the question of "heroism" Caputo stands against nearly everyone important to him:

> For Heidegger and Kierkegaard, the kingdom is full of manly Christian warriors and knights of faith. They were both taken with the militant Pauline figure that forges ahead, pressing toward the goal, free for the future in fear and trembling. In Paul and Luther, Augustine and Pascal, Kierkegaard and Heidegger, the existential individual looks into the abyss of freedom and possibility and swoons with anxiety. The structure of Christian "factical life" is toiling and troubling, *Bekümmerung* and *Sorge*, worrying about one's daily bread (*sorgen um das 'tägliche Brot'*), fighting the good fight for bread and faith—in short, the very Pauline-Augustinian claim that the Being of Dasein is *Sorge*, dodging the bullets and boulders (*molestias*) of existence.[60]

This is not how Caputo imagines things; for him, quotidianism means something very different than Augustine's *bellum quotidianum*. It cannot be otherwise, because Caputo builds his entire theology on the claim that there is nothing and nobody identifiable to fight for, only a call from afar. That call is no less real, to be sure, it is hyperreal, as Caputo likes to say.[61] Nevertheless, it is precisely because Caputo places the origin of the call beyond (hyper) the realm of being that the call only allows for a "desire beyond desire," which is not the type of desire one can act upon, not in the usual sense anyway.

Hence Caputo is compelled to protest, this time together with Johannes Climacus, against ascription of any recognizable mission: "I have no mission,"[62] "like Johannes Climacus, I assume that one is better off if one is not convinced one has a mission,"[63] and again, "I have been given no epochal mission or commission and I can offer the reader no special information about what is going on in the History of Being, or the History of the Spirit, or History itself . . ."[64] Stated three times, Caputo got to believe this to be true. Understanding that such an attitude bespeaks lack of identity does not seem to elude him either: "It is very embarrassing to lack identity like this, but I will try my best to make a case for such undecidability, to assume at least the appearance of respectability," Caputo writes on behalf of his model nonhero, a "Dionysian rabbi," who "moves back and forth" between Athens and Jerusalem "as the seasons and his moods dictate."[65] Upon hearing Caputo speaking like this, Nietzsche would probably raise his eyebrows:

> "You should obey someone, anyone, and for a long time: or else you will deteriorate and lose all respect for yourself"—this seems to me to be the moral imperative of nature, which is clearly neither "categorical," as the old Kant demanded it to be (hence the "or else"—), nor directed to the individual (what does nature care about the individual!), but rather to peoples, races, ages, classes, and above all to the whole "human" animal, to the human.[66]

To recapitulate and clarify the last few pages, I would say that the freedom from a particular religion, as advocated by Caputo, poses a triple problem: Because this freedom lacks a concrete sense of orientation, it results in a sterile dreaming; because Caputo's thinking precludes any concrete sense of mission, he cuts himself off from an important strand of cultural dreaming; and because weak theology of this particular kind requires an offhand dismissal of the complex question of the source, it eventually turns against Caputo and proves him self-contradictory.

The first problem was best characterized by Gary Brent Madison, who thinks that the "ultimate issue here is that of reality versus fantasy."[67] Referring to Caputo's concept of a passion for the impossible, Madison writes:

> Maybe that's what the deconstructive ethics of the Wholly Other and the Absolute Future actually is when all is said and done—a dreamland. Myself, I think dreaming is a great thing, and I try to arrange for as much time for it as the exigencies of life permit. But while there are a lot of things one can pleasantly dream about, one nonetheless ought not confuse dreams with reality or dreaming with acting. That would be ethically irresponsible.
>
> That having been said, I must admit that I'll take Caputo/Derrida's fantasy world of eschatological, messianic justice any day over the all-too-real and immanent danger of religio-political fundamentalism. There's not much that Caputo/Derrida's religious-inspired, noble plea for perfect justice can do to make this imperfect world a somewhat better place—as is indeed generally the case with any such ethic of charity and benevolence—but, on the other hand, by reason of its very impracticality, and because it is "a messianicity without messianism," without determinable content, perhaps when all is said and done it can't do all that much positive harm either. So I say to you, Jack: Go ahead, my friend, dream on! *Après tout, pourquoi pas?*[68]

The second problem may look as though it contradicts the first, as I now suggest that Caputo breaks away from the way most human beings dream. But although I bring this point up only tentatively, for I myself only started thinking about it recently, I do not think there really is any contradiction. It may be possible, nay, it surely is possible to dream about the impossible. The fact that such dreaming is practically sterile was already pointed out by Madison, but here I have a different kind of dream in mind. Specifically, I am thinking about what Joseph Campbell called a *monomyth*, or if you prefer *the hero's journey*, which is discernible in narratives from around the world, but which is unimaginable without the sense of a mission. Put differently, the hero sets off for an adventure after receiving a call, but this is always a concrete call. Seen from this perspective and despite all of its benefits and great potential, Caputo's theology of the event is sadly unimaginative. Perhaps this also explains Caputo's preference for the "wisdom sayings" and parables of Jesus, when he wishes to back his hypotheses, while there is a conspicuous dearth of reference to Jesus's story, or for that matter the entire history of salvation.

Finally, by dismissing the question of the source of the call and thus effectively ruling out the hero's journey, Caputo who himself is also only human makes it too easy for discrepancies to creep into his texts. At its worst, such strategy resembles the popular myth about an ostrich sticking its head in the sand—yet another curious metaphor, by the way, especially because I know for sure that Caputo does not shy away from danger. At any rate, an ostrich behaving in this way will sooner or later get eaten, and Caputo will be proven to be "more than one."

Take his Levinasian stance regarding freedom, for example. According to Caputo, widows and orphans should take priority over one's wishes, while Deleuze's and Nietzsche's creative forces that "do not obey anything" represent the

> freedom from inhibition and blockage, freedom from the weight of being, from the weight of values thousands of years old, from the old God, from Being and Truth, from everything that weighs the will down and makes it heavy, grave, from everything that holds it in check and makes it obey, everything that prevents it from dancing. But in heteronomic [that is, Levinasian] difference, freedom is suspect, suspended, held in question, because it is aggressive, self-accumulative, and eventually, finally, murderous. Heteronomism wants to let the other be free while one is oneself held hostage.[69]

We have been through this many times across the last three chapters, but I want you to recall chapter 4 and juxtapose the previous paragraph with the account of the discussion that young Brother Paul had with the provincial of the Brothers of the Christian Schools:

> "[And I said] I think I've figured out what I want to do, I want to teach philosophy. I want you to send me to Fordham University in New York City, it's a good Catholic university, and I'll come back and teach philosophy at La Salle for the rest of my life, and I promise I'll be good at it."
>
> And the Brother Provincial said: "Well, maybe. But maybe we'll send you to work in the orphanage and you'll spend the rest of your life serving in the orphanage, because what's important to you is the will of God as it's expressed by your superiors."
>
> "Well, actually, no. I want to teach philosophy." And we could not reconcile those differences.[70]

This, by the way, is the reason why I said that Caputo's implication that the freedom of the children of God really means orphanhood was a moment of irony. Mark Dooley actually picked up on this point:

> Mark Dooley: Now what would Jesus have done in that situation? Would he have taken the road to the lofty heights of academe, or would he have gone to the orphanage?
>
> John Caputo: That's a telling question. You might say—in retrospect—the Brother Provincial was making a Levinasian point, about

> serving the widows and the orphans. But on that occasion, the model of Jesus I adopted is Jesus driving the money-changers out of the temple and doing what he thought he must do. In radical hermeneutics everything is interpretation.[71]

I wonder how radical hermeneutics, or for that matter weak theology, would interpret Jesus's stunt in the temple today, without any recourse to his sense of the mission. Note, too, what Caputo actually said to the Brother Provincial: Set me free and I promise that I will be good at it. A promise! In fact, a promise made before Brother Paul even had any right to make promises . . .

Incidentally, for someone claiming to be entirely devoid of any mission, Caputo seems unusually eager to make promises. Twenty pages into his *Against Ethics*, he acknowledges that he "had been promising for some time to write an Ethics";[72] thirty thousand feet above the earth, he promised to himself to write a book about Derrida's religion;[73] further down the line, after he retired, Caputo planned to "write a treatise entitled 'critique of pure piety'"[74] (I wonder if anyone should remind him now); and later he even considered "writing a pseudonymous 'Letter of St Paul to the Spaniards.'"[75]

Anyway, Brother Paul's discussion with the Brother Provincial took place long before the advent of weak theology, I grant you that, but the hero's journey of Caputo, his relentless chase after a very concrete and ambitious dream, did not end there, in his early twenties. Eventually, Caputo did become a respected academician. Much later, Jeffrey Robbins asked Caputo whether he had chosen to question his worldview, or it simply happened to him. Caputo answered:

> Choosing to be an intellectual means that you set a course in a certain direction that is going to be risky and dangerous. You set a course that will make things questionable and it would have been more comfortable simply not to worry about those things. But intellectuals worry about everything; that's their business. They trouble themselves about presuppositions. Especially us. Especially people who are working in philosophy and religion. And there is a certain loss and there is something unnerving about it. But I think that then there's a kind of second level of joy or affirmation in which you recognize what you affirm and love, which is not finally reducible to these determinate finite structures. What I affirm survives the death of any given construction and has a more radical irreducibility.[76]

Campbell would say yes, that's the hero's journey, but of course, Caputo perceives himself only as a "simple clerk" without any mission.[77]

At least, *pace* Madison, he won't do much harm. And then there comes the Hurricane Isabel, the worst kind of storm doing more than enough harm, and it finally seems to break Caputo:

> I have learned something about the transcendence of nature. And I have learned to never again speak in praise of the unprogrammable disruption, the interruption, the incoming of the wholly other or the unforeseeable event. From here on in, I plan to advocate uninterrupted continuity and the absolutely programmable! Kierkegaard has Johannes Climacus say somewhere that the idea of contingency among the philosophers is such an abstract and empty term for them that the only thing that would make them understand it is an earthquake—to which I would add a hurricane.[78]

Caputo actually held on to his freedom and never stopped speaking in praise of the unprogrammable disruption, and I must say that I admire him for not giving up on his mission. For, as Nietzsche has it:

> It is no small advantage to live under a hundred swords of Damocles: that way one learns to dance, one attains "freedom of movement."[79]

9
Between Heidegger and Derrida

Do you believe in love at first sight? Not just a transient, biochemically induced infatuation, but true love at first sight? That depends on who is asking and when, right? Well, let us suppose that I am, and I am asking at this very moment. Hence the question is not raised within a context of a date and we are not, I presume, romantically involved. Besides, anyone venturing an opinion here will not be really answering to me but to my text—while I as an author, so they say, am for all practical purposes dead. That should play the question down more than enough. Now then, what say you? Do you believe in love at first sight?

Not so easy to answer straightaway, is it? How so? Why, in the midst of our conversation about Caputo this inquiry seems so patently out of place that one instinctively suspects the presence of a concealed agenda. This young author must be playing some kind of a trick here. Surely, there ought to be a sufficient, even if hidden, reason for such an unrelated query. Either that, either there is some kind of a scheme, or else this text is utter nonsense.

Although most writers would find such a benefit of doubt granted by their readers flattering, reasoning along these lines also betrays a sense of uneasiness that we all feel upon encountering things that seem out of place. Indeed, we are like fish out of water when we sense incongruities: let's hope this author knows what he is doing; let somebody or something, somewhere, know what is happening. Not that we hate surprises as such, but we become irritated when no revelation follows, when we are robbed of the amusement of a final understanding. Please spare us your jokes without a punchline!

Not to worry, though, I am not playing ducks and drakes with you. We are going to talk about how Caputo became friends with Derrida, although before we get there I will want you to jump with me through some hoops. The point is, this is a fascinating story that, to my knowledge, has never been consistently told—not least because the path that came to a close when *Jacques* signed his farewell letter to *Jack* as *Jackie* was by no means straight. So much the better for both of them (and for their readers) that it was not: Here is a truly fruitful relationship, one marked by anything but witless parroting. But it was no *coup de cœur*.

Back to our lovers talk, then. Suppose, for starters, that you do answer and your answer is yes. By no means companionless, you will find yourself in league with Aristophanes, Shakespeare, and especially with Shakespeare's contemporary Christopher Marlowe who was a firm believer in love at first sight: "Who ever loved, that loved not at first sight?"—he asks famously in *Hero and Leander*.[1] However, and this is worth our notice, something larger is going on here than romantic love: "It lies not in our power to love, or hate, for will in us is overruled by fate." Love at first sight, according to Marlowe, not only exists but is, in fact, universal because we are all ruled by fate. To believe in love at first sight means to believe that "pairs of star-crossed lovers" walk through their lives separately, but when they finally bump into one another they instantly understand what has just happened. Somewhere a soul mate was born just for you and you can live in confidence that when the two of you meet, the realization will strike you, both of you, with the force of epiphany. You won't fail to notice the critical moment, so to say.

Let fate not throw us off the scent here, however. This could happen all too easily; yet, no matter how much one argues against it or how eagerly self-help gurus try to convince us that we are the masters of our fate, it just will not go away. How, indeed, could one contest such a mystery? Who will ever count the paths of all "star-crossed lovers" that have never crossed? What is the number of soul mates who never met? Impossible to tell. Of course, they must meet if we are to regard them as such. Conversely, what about the soul mates whose paths actually did join to become one? On what grounds could we deny that they were always destined to meet, that they were born for one another?

The concept of fate is unassailable because it is unverifiable. Now, for science and perhaps for life coaches this may sound like a crucial fallacy. To those unencumbered by narrow positivism, however, belief in fate can offer an important assurance that they will not accidentally waste their lives. There are people out there for whom confidence in fate is the best way to cope with life, come what (or who) may.

And this is important, this is the trail we are following. So although I personally do not put my trust in destiny, nor for that matter do I think much of love at first sight, what is going on in and around these notions interests me a lot. Noticed the language of events? Correct. One way to consider "fate" and "love at first sight" is indeed as constructs emerging from our instinctive drive to come to grips with events. These are, of course, most radical strategies, not to everybody's taste. If you fancy yourself a matter-of-fact person, then you will probably prefer much more down-to-earth explanations found in the origin stories or movie prequels. Still another breed of people are the thrill-seekers who could not care less about fate or facts and they amuse themselves with alternative realities. But in all these cases the denominator is common and we have heard it already: Let us or, at the very least, let somebody or something, somewhere, know what is happening. Arrest the flux, tame the chaos, eliminate the nonsense.

Returning to the special case of significant encounters, numerous widely known and even a greater number of untold meetings of consequence took place throughout history and they continue cropping up today—precipitated by . . . well, perhaps by fate, or by divine providence, or else by purest chance.

> Frankly, we do not really *know* why certain people do more than just cross our paths, why they also bend them, tweak them, transform them, changing our lives more or less completely. More importantly, we are quite clueless about who will revolutionize our lives next and often we do not even see the revolution happening. Not at first, at least. Now, if this does not make one's head spin, nothing will! Things happen, people come and go—and the outcome is me, or for that matter, Caputo!
>
> Consider the fact that for 3.8 billion years, a period of time older than the Earth's mountains and rivers and oceans, every one of your forebears on both sides has been attractive enough to find a mate, healthy enough to reproduce, and sufficiently blessed by fate and circumstances to live long enough to do so. Not one of your pertinent ancestors was squashed, devoured, drowned, starved, stranded, stuck fast, untimely wounded, or otherwise deflected from its life's quest of delivering a tiny charge of genetic material to the right partner at the right moment in order to perpetuate the only possible sequence of hereditary combinations that could result—eventually, astoundingly, and all too briefly—in you.[2]

I feel a bit tipsy every time I read this passage. Never mind that Bill Bryson reaches here way beyond the scope of our talk, for every individual is a microcosm and thus truly an infinitely complex tapestry woven from threads that—and this is the bottom line—appear all too random. Caputo is right: We do not know who we are and why, not if we are honest. In saying so, however, he seems to have already cut his coat according to the cloth. Most of us do not so easily reconcile ourselves to the flux and, if truth be told, I do not believe Caputo does either. Not really, not if *he* is honest. For it is one thing to push for the appreciation of the flux as a great antidote against closure; quite another thing is to dwell in chaos, to live meaningfully despite being mere playthings of events. To paraphrase on a felicitous line from the *Hitchhiker's Guide to the Galaxy*: If sentient life is going to exist in a universe ruled by events, then the one thing it cannot afford to have is a true sense of contingency.[3] Flux is strictly for the birds, we require jokes we can understand. If not us, then somebody or something, somewhere, needs to supply the punchline . . .

This is what we have stories for. They are our best means of making sense out of chaos. If we cannot tell why, we at least have a go at telling when, where, and how. We talk a whole lot about what matters to us, our lives are tales through and through—tales, which frequently include significant encounters with others.

Who among us, by way of illustration, has never wanted to hear anecdotes about how our parents met? Which one of us has never in life recounted the origins of a lasting friendship or for that matter, antipathy? When studying a particular author, scholars instinctively cast around for sources, for the predecessors declared and concealed alike. The point is that we are thoroughly social beings, so even if we do not really know who we are, we are quite certain that the answer lies chiefly with whom we have met. Accordingly, most of our narratives involve moments of significant meetings and we always prick up our ears when, in the course of a story, such moments come to pass. As though the key to what happened, our proverbial punchline, must have been bestowed on us there, right at the outset.

I briefly spoke of Didier Daurat before, the operations director of Aéropostale who sent Saint-Exupéry to Cape Juby. Now, aside from spending the rest of his later life attempting to "detach himself from the fictional alter ego" created by his scribbling pilot, it is also alleged that Monsieur Daurat "was quizzed about no moment of his distinguished life more often than about his first meeting with Saint-Exupéry."[4] A similar impulse brings us to watching Walt Disney's *Pocahontas* to see how she met John Smith; and which *Star Trek* film could possibly entertain us more than the latest one, for there we finally get to know all about how Kirk met Spock, McCoy, and the rest of the original *Enterprise* crew?

But imagine that someone succeeds in building a time machine. Theologians would rush back in time to get a kick out of seeing Paul knocked off his horse, while philosophers would make sure not to miss out on Aristotle's first day in Plato's Academy. Romantic souls would want to eavesdrop on Josephine's first tête-à-tête with Napoleon, unless they were by profession theologians or philosophers, in which case they would probably prefer Héloïse and Abelard, or perhaps Regina and Kierkegaard. Witnessing everything firsthand, would that not be great?

I dare say it would not. For the most part, I think, time travel would dash our hopes. For even if we were somehow able to go back and be present at the inaugural moments of great relationships, there would be very little extraordinary to see. Except if, that is, we were prepared to view as extraordinary also the idiosyncrasies of everyday life.

Picture Paul, heretofore Saul: *Bang, swoosh, thud. . . "By Caiaphas' beard, this heathen pony! What is going on here and where's my sword . . . ?"* No *jeez*, yet. No fingers *crossed* for the best outcome. What, do you reckon, did Saul know? *". . . and I will show him what he will have to suffer for my name."*[5] Seriously, besides leaving bystanders in no doubt about having his heart in his mouth, is it possible that the unhorsed Saul also showed some evidence of anticipating the tremendous changes that were just set in motion? Could the onlooking time-travelers tell that he had just seen the light? Was the event visible?

Unless you are a firm believer in love at first sight, a positive answer to any of the foregoing questions will probably strike you as a little far-fetched. I am of the same mind. While there may be a certain appeal to believing that things will be crystal clear at least where God has spoken or fate has ruled, a good deal of examples suggest quite the contrary. We seem to be remarkably blind, indeed many a time nothing short of obtuse, when it comes to events. Even with occasional gut feelings at our disposal, despite all the pseudo-scientific hype about ESP—still comically dumb: *"Were not our hearts burning while he spoke to us on the way and opened the scriptures to us?"*[6] You have to love these wisenheimers: *"I knew it, I always knew this was happening!"* Everybody is clairvoyant in the wake of an event, just like the disciples after they returned from Emmaus. *"Then the two recounted what had taken place on the way and how he was made known to them in the breaking of the bread."*

* * *

So where does Caputo stand? Regarding how he met Derrida, does Caputo fall prey to his own hindsight bias? Decades after what turned out to be perhaps the single most fateful event for the future of Caputo's weak theology, do his memories now tell a different story? I shall leave it to the reader to decide, for it is not my place to make any conclusions, especially when what I have to offer is also "only" that, a story.

"I got to know Jacques Derrida in the most commonplace of ways—the way we academics meet almost everyone we know outside our own institutions—by rubbing elbows with him at academic conferences,"[7] Caputo said on one occasion, suggesting a levelheaded view that nothing indicated the future significance of those encounters then, nor does he see anything like that now, in retrospect. On the other hand, Caputo often does make it sound as if Derrida appeared on his radar screen just in time to save him from Heidegger casting spells: "One of the things that happened in the 1980s, when I really encountered Derrida, was that I reached my limit with Heidegger and I found it necessary, as Levinas put it, to leave the climate of his philosophy."[8] Perhaps this is true, but as I have already suggested and as we shall soon see, Derrida was not Caputo's love at first sight. Quite the contrary: for several years Caputo actually criticized Derrida, respectfully to be sure, from within the Heideggerian camp. When Keith Putt brought up these early writings, reminding Caputo that "his life and thought are not exempt from existential motility,"[9] Caputo said:

> Everyone should have a reader like Keith Putt, who has read everything and remembered everything, including a couple of early pieces I did years ago on Derrida that, to be honest, I would thank him to forget.[10]

What follows is little more than an attempt to prevent such forgetting from happening, lest a theology of the event grow cold and stiff, no longer a passionate journey but a lifeless theory.

In order to get us back on track, let me recall that in chapter 6 I decided to trace the early years of Caputo's career as a story of two loves, Saint Thomas and Kierkegaard. This strategy led us from Jacques Maritain through Caputo's discovery of Heidegger and, via Silesius and Eckhart, eventually back to Aquinas. Caputo's first two major works, *The Mystical Element in Heidegger's Thought* and *Heidegger and Aquinas: An Essay on Overcoming Metaphysics*, date back to this period. Despite all the previous hype about Caputo's inner contradiction, however, one could have easily wondered at the end of that chapter if Caputo had after all lost his interest in Kierkegaard and satisfied himself with studying the German-Italian duo. Well, nothing could be further from the truth. Kierkegaard continued to play a crucial role in Caputo's intellectual journey and, in fact, Caputo tried from fairly early on to uncover the presence of his Danish hero in Heidegger.

One particular instance where this is clearly visible is in the article entitled "Hermeneutics as the Recovery of Man."[11] Caputo had it published in *Man and World* in 1982, the same year as *Heidegger and Aquinas*, and for several reasons the article itself provides a great opportunity to take the story up again. Caputo wrote:

> Now it has been our contention all along that the relationship of Heidegger to Kierkegaard is much more intimate than either Heidegger himself or his commentators have been prepared to admit. In

> our view, the genius of Kierkegaard, the academic renegade and tormented "exception," is amplified by the genius of Heidegger, the German professor, a species about whom Kierkegaard had not a few things to say.[12]

Life (or should I say fate?) has its mysterious ways. When Caputo wrote this essay, he said it was "part of a larger project."[13] Had he but known . . . He was never going to publish anything under the title "Hermeneutics as the Recovery of Man" again, but there was indeed a larger project underway, in fact an entire book, that he had originally considered a suitable candidate for the name:

> In earlier drafts I thought of entitling this book "Hermeneutics as the Recovery of Man," but I soon abandoned that, for "recovery" suggests "recollection" and "man" suggests both sexism and humanism. But I never gave up on the word "hermeneutics," which ever since Heidegger has meant a critique of the hollow assurances and tranquilizing powers of the metaphysics of presence and which by that fact "restores" the difficulty of things.[14]

The book in question was *Radical Hermeneutics: Repetition, Deconstruction, and the Hermeneutic Project*, published five years after the essay. But whereas in 1982 Caputo played Heidegger and Kierkegaard against Derrida, in 1987 they are all brothers in arms in their multilingual struggle against metaphysics:

> [D]ifférance exploits a peculiarity of the French language which suggests the protowriting that Derrida is after. Other natural languages must find their own ways, exploit their own peculiarities. Kierkegaard appears to have made considerable progress beyond metaphysics with Danish. And Heidegger does it all the time with German. One of the things that make Kierkegaard, Heidegger, and Derrida stand out is their ability to do this sort of thing with their own languages, instead of just talking about it, as do the rest of us.[15]

Except that this time Caputo had to "demythologize Heidegger," rather than refute Derrida, for the entire thing to work.[16] But let us not run ahead of schedule; it will pay off to follow these developments one step at a time.

Generally speaking, in the first half of 1980s—the period between his two "recoveries of man"—Caputo respected Derrida as an unquestionably brilliant commentator of Husserl,[17] and a refreshingly unconventional reader of Heidegger, "far remove[d] from the epigonism and bad repetitions of the Heidegger literati who talk like Heidegger talks, who repeat what Heidegger says, and who regard every criticism of Heidegger as a misunderstanding."[18] Brilliant and unconventional but also, at least in matters of importance to Caputo, misguided.

Incidentally, Derrida had his "annus mirabilis" a decade and a half prior to Caputo's essay under discussion. This was 1967, when he published *Writing and Difference*, *Speech and Phenomena*, and *Of Grammatology* and actually began to use the term "deconstruction." Thus, by the 1980s, Derrida was already an intellectual heavyweight, and Caputo thought it prudent to remind his own readers that he was neither "pretending to know what Derrida in the long run wants to say," nor was he unaware of the risk that he "may be deconstructed on the spot."[19] Even so, because Derrida had, in "The Ends of Man,"[20] demonstrated that regardless of Heidegger's outspoken critique of humanism, his thought "nevertheless remains a thought *of* man,"[21] Caputo reckoned that he had to intervene. *So what?*—we can imagine Caputo thinking—*How is this supposed to be a problem?*

> I stand with Heidegger's *Letter on Humanism*, and I believe that Derrida is right to say that Heidegger's treatise remains in a sense still a species of humanism, albeit of a higher sort. Derrida is right, I think, but I do not take that to be a criticism of Heidegger. I am worried more by the "end of man" than by remaining within a humanism of a higher sort.[22]

Clearly, Caputo's stance on humanism was going to change radically by the time he completed writing *Radical Hermeneutics*; as we have seen, that was one of the reasons why he decided against entitling it *Hermeneutics as the Recovery of Man*. The homonymous article of 1982, however, did not stop at questioning Derrida's putative antihumanism. At that time, Caputo was actually more concerned with "recovery" than with "man." He wanted to show, in opposition to Derrida, that

> [a]fter Heidegger, hermeneutics means a recovery of origins, a return to the more primordial, which has nothing to do with the "nostalgia for presence" but on the contrary everything to do with what Kierkegaard calls the "courage" for repetition.[23]

Considering how much ground we still need to cover in this chapter, I will have to dispense with the detailed account of Caputo's argument. In a nutshell, Caputo maintained that there are two different types of

> recovery or retrieval which feed into the hermeneutic strategy of [Heidegger's] *Being and Time*—the Kierkegaardian notion of existential "repetition" and the phenomenological return to beginnings in Husserl.[24]

While it may be correct to say, Caputo held, that Husserl's return to the beginnings "remains under the spell of the metaphysics of presence,"[25] Kierkegaard's repetition and, by extension, Heidegger's *Wiederholung*—"Dasein's recovery of itself, its self-retrieval"[26]—"has made a breach with the metaphysics of presence."[27] "Far from being a being of nearness," Caputo argued against Derrida, "Dasein is precisely a being of distance."[28] Now, as Robert Cumming had quipped a year before, "any comparison of Derrida with Heidegger may seem to be elucidating the *obscurum per obscurius*."[29] But if the foregoing citations suggest that he was right, this is a false impression. Beneath the surface of Caputo's philosophical jargon hide concerns with which we are, in fact, already familiar. The keywords are freedom and the abyss. Caputo took it upon himself to explain, with the help of Kierkegaard, that the origin that Heidegger's hermeneutics retrieves is the primordial experience of "finitude and absence,"[30] and the movement of return

> means having the courage to face up to the nothingness which inhabits Being and the thought of Being. It is not nostalgia but courage for the hard and inhospitable. It is the acknowledgment of our finitude, fallibility and mortality. It is a recovery of man; for man, *homo*, means *humus*. This recovery is the call to remember, man, what you are: *memento homo, cineris est et in cinerem reverteris*. It is the recovery of the memento mori.[31]

It is also the recovery of the abyss.[32] You do not get anything back by following this path, except for the freedom to become what you have always been; here, as well as in Kierkegaard, the recovery/repetition means

> the initiation of something new, a retrieval in which Dasein discovers (uncovers, recovers) what it is capable of, what it has all along been "sent" to do. We must hear the *schicken* in Heidegger's use of the words *Schicksal* and *Geschick* in *Being and Time*. These words have nothing to do with fate and determinism, but with sending, *mittere*, mission.[33]

And that is what, according to Caputo, Derrida got wrong. He has been "misled by his critique of Husserl,"[34] and thus failed to appreciate the true import of Kierkegaard's concept of repetition:

> Derrida thinks that repetition means you get the girl back. But he has not taken adequately into account the Kierkegaardian element in repetition. He gets no further in the understanding of repetition

> than Constantine Constantius, who has an aesthetic theory, and not as far as the anxiety of Job and Abraham.[35]

Caputo was convinced that it was precisely due to Derrida's misunderstanding of Kierkegaard that his "critique of presence tends to pass over surreptitiously into a critique of retrieval itself."[36] Had Derrida got further in the understanding of repetition, he would have known that the only thing that gets "repeated" is "an innermost potentiality, the latent possibility to be or become oneself, which we have neglected, overlooked, 'forgotten.'"[37] That is no nostalgia for the paradise lost, nor is it any metaphysical presence, only a newly recovered openness to the mystery—the primordial abyss at the core of human experience. Hence, Caputo's first "message" that he had ever sent to Derrida was:

> If retrieval means the recovery of the abyss, of the mystery, of the absence which inhabits human experience, that is also what I take hermeneutics to be. Hermeneutics thinks—contrary to Derrida (and Rorty)—that there is something deeper to be sought, something more primal. Hermeneutics turns on this commitment to the primordial. The movement of its circle is always circling back on something more essential. Hermeneutic violence is always practiced in the service of retrieval. If recovery is the life of hermeneutics, then deconstruction is but a moment through which it passes. And that is why I reject the disjunction which Derrida proposes[38]

. . . and also the reason why Caputo disagreed with what he perceived as Derrida's fusing "the search for the originary with the nostalgia for presence."[39]

After 1982, Caputo continued sending such "messages"—ostensibly always in defense of Heidegger's hermeneutics, but we would be wrong to think of him as no more than a spokesman of Heidegger. For as Caputo went on publishing, his views were gradually changing, although he himself did not necessarily see it happening.

One peripheral remark, as we draw nearer to the end of this book: I trust that careful readers will not fail to notice how words, names, and ideas from the previous chapters continue cropping up ever more frequently as we move on. Of course, any analysis of sufficient scope will experience the same phenomenon, as multiplication of connections becomes inevitable. But it is worth bearing in mind that such interweaving of concepts, itself part of the internal structure of an event, makes new interpretive events possible.

In addition to the mission, *mittere*, as well as freedom and the abyss—all referring back to the previous chapters—many of the "messages" that Caputo sent out during the three years following the publication of "Hermeneutics as the Recovery of Man" will also have a ring of familiarity. I shall briefly discuss articles from 1983 and 1984, respectively, and then conclude this section by looking at two of Caputo's texts published in 1985.

In "The Thought of Being and the Conversation of Mankind: The Case of Heidegger and Rorty," published in 1983,[40] Caputo again stood against a colleague of international fame, this time Richard Rorty, and he once again felt compelled to include a disclaimer:

> I am, I hope, worlds removed from arguing that Rorty has not "understood" Heidegger, which is in my view the first and last refuge of the Heideggerian epigones who think that to understand Heidegger is to talk as Heidegger talks, to write as Heidegger writes and to read Heidegger on one's knees—*die knieende Philosophie*.[41]

Indeed, watching out for the emerging patterns might be one more useful way to make sense of events. Concerning Caputo, it would seem that while he was himself still a Heideggerian, he had a rather low opinion of most other disciples of the "magician of Messkirch." Already something was brewing inside *Jack*, something that troubled him, but he could not yet put his finger on exactly what.

The thrust of the article under discussion is also akin to the previous piece: Caputo confesses that his "own sympathies are with Heidegger," and he accuses Rorty of taking up "only the deconstructive side of Heidegger" while remaining "quite hostile to Heidegger's project of retrieval," which is why he ends up empty-handed, with nothing better than "Derrida's play of signs."[42] Rorty, according to Caputo of 1983, is "not interested in the real matter to be thought in so far as Heidegger is concerned, [. . .] he is instead much closer to Derrida, who has adopted the deconstructive phase of Heidegger's thought, declaring the end of philosophy, but who rejects the 'task of thought,' the 'recollective' phase of Heidegger's thought."[43]

In contrast to Caputo's later works, where religion without religion dictates the tone, some of the things he had to say to Rorty sounded—what's the best way to describe it?—surprisingly balanced. I am sure that today Caputo would dismiss his early works as unprovocative and pious, the latter especially being as much an anathema to him now as was metaphysics then. But believe it or not, Caputo in his early forties was a traditionalist. By way of illustration, Caputo wondered if Rorty took Heidegger and, especially, Kierkegaard seriously enough when he heard "only language-games and social practice"[44] in their texts, but turned a deaf ear to anything that was "genuinely incommensurable" in their thought:

> Is there not a trace of "reductionism" in holding that thinkers like Heidegger and Kierkegaard are providing us with "alternate descriptions" of ourselves? Did Kierkegaard take himself to be giving an "alternate description" of becoming a Christian? Is this anything more than a reductionistic translation?[45]

On Caputo's reading, Rorty encourages us to "keep alternate descriptions alive, to prevent freezing-over of culture";[46] hermeneutics à la Rorty means the open-endedness of discourse, "a resolve not to close off innovative redescriptions of ourselves which are fresh and interesting";[47] and "the alpha and the omega of Rorty's hermeneutics is to be done with the tradition."[48] But if Rorty "considers Heidegger's life-long attempt to hear what is said there [in the tradition] as his final illusion,"[49] then it is also true, argues Caputo (like a true defender of the force of gravity), that Rorty's "language games have no ontological weight";[50] they are "weightless creatures and his hermeneutics [is] a mechanics of weightlessness."[51]

Rorty's problem is that his postmodern sensibilities do not allow him to fight *for* anything; the best he can do is to fight *against* things, specifically against metaphysics. Now, we do not need to be reminded that with regard to metaphysics, Caputo stands on Rorty's side. It needs to be overcome. But it worries him that

> Rorty's critique of Western ontology is not positively motivated. He denies metaphysics in order to make room for a plurality of languages. He wants to curb the pretensions of reason, whether in the form of naturalism or idealism, not like Kant, because of what he believes, but because of what he does not believe, viz., that it is ever possible to have more than a more or less successful language game. He does not want to overcome the history of ontology because of something more essential, but because he wants nothing to do with anything more or less essential . . .[52]

In 1983, conversely, Caputo believed—together with Heidegger, Kierkegaard, and, for that matter, Gadamer—that genuine hermeneutics does, in fact, have a positive task, let us say a mission. It is a "call, or better a recall, back to the human setting of our lives [and] to an understanding of ourselves in which we can recognize ourselves."[53] That is why hermeneutics cannot dispense with the tradition, on the contrary, the "hermeneutic task is to reestablish contact with that to which we already belong."[54]

> The hermeneutic situation means that we are always caught up in the historical sweep, thrown, factical, historical. Our language is handed over to us by the tradition. We are delivered over to a tradition and

> hermeneutics is the way to find what that tradition says to us here and now. Hermeneutics thus means listening to the voice of the tradition and to the voice of the things themselves as they speak to us in the tradition. It is hearing hitherto neglected possibilities, hitherto unspoken words which have been all along sounding.[55]

To sum up, everything that Rorty (and later Caputo) wanted from hermeneutics was to keep the discourse open-ended, whereas Heidegger (and early Caputo) had no respect for hermeneutics except as "our openness to the messages of the gods,"[56] and as a readiness to pass beyond deconstruction and reach the shores of something primordial. For "what I find in Rorty, and in Derrida, too," concluded Caputo,

> is that the deconstructive moment, the moment of critique, has been detached from its original matrix, discharged from the service of hermeneutic retrieval, and put on the loose to lead a life of its own. And a deconstruction of that sort can only come to grief.[57]

Only grief—that was, on Caputo's part, one rather grim prophecy, though at that time indeed little more than an opinionated prediction. For if Caputo was ever going to be proven right, then so too would be a great many parents where I come from. Much to our dismay, they used to warn us in the midst of our merriest games that grief usually followed after too much laughter. So too Caputo, in those early days, was able to hear only exuberant laughter—not grief at all, but the boisterous tones of a Dionysian dance above the abyss—when he examined Derrida.

In an article entitled "'Supposing Truth to Be a Woman . . .': Heidegger, Nietzsche, Derrida," Caputo followed Derrida's and Heidegger's reading of Nietzsche and also discussed Derrida's reading of Heidegger. Even more so now than before, Caputo seemed ready to give Derrida credit for his excellence as a commentator. Applauding what he regarded as "an important improvement on Derrida's earlier renderings of Heidegger,"[58] Caputo actually thought that Derrida now offered "a sound analysis of Heidegger" and even "put Heidegger's point quite nicely."[59] As a matter of fact, a growing sense of admiration for Derrida would soon become a trend in Caputo's works. Nevertheless, in 1984 Caputo still believed that Heidegger was right and Derrida wrong; or rather that Derrida, for all his brilliance, nevertheless fell short of appreciating retrieval as the proper motivation behind the call to overcome metaphysics.

Why, indeed, should we wish to get over metaphysics? Because it is mistaken? That would be a philosophically artless, to say nothing of also being decidedly metaphysical, position to defend. No, the effort should be aimed against what metaphysics has been secretly trying to achieve, namely, to cover up something that is simultaneously primordial and disturbing about the human condition. That being the case, a mere deconstruction of the ontological tradition that is not followed by the positive movement of retrieval misses the entire point, which Caputo articulated already in the previously discussed article: "The great continental thinkers of the last two centuries have been anti-metaphysical, not out of a negative urge to raze, but because they saw in metaphysics a flight from that which it should have been its first order of business to affirm."[60] On this account, at least, Caputo would not count Rorty among such thinkers, nor for that matter would he have thought differently about Derrida:

> Speaking from a Heideggerian perspective I should say that Derrida and Heidegger both want to subvert the authority of the metaphysical tradition; that Derrida does so by a Dionysian dance which throws it into confusion. But from a Heideggerian point of view this remains inadequate, still streaked with the traces of subjectivity and willfulness. For there is required a passage through this storm to its quiet eye, into the stillness of *Gelassenheit* in which the mystery holds sway. Derrida's Dionysian strategies serve a purpose; but left to themselves they cut us off entirely from the things themselves, delivering us over to a surfeit of fictions and willful constructions.[61]

Take note of the highly evocative use to which Caputo puts the metaphorics of the storm: "If Derrida exults in the Dionysian storm, Heidegger has entered its eye where all is still," elucidated Caputo. "Derrida's exuberance is a long way removed from Heidegger's solemn, even devout reverence towards the things themselves, his *Gelassenheit* towards the Mystery which withdraws."[62] In moments like these, I cannot help but wonder what Caputo's theology would look like had he never moved beyond Heidegger. How would it be different if the openness to the mystery had not been replaced by the sense of lostness? Everything hangs on one's interpretation of the abyss. In any case, we have to admire the poetic quality of Caputo's language, words he wrote the same year when he allegedly found his own voice. And still against Derrida, who was most instrumental in loosening Caputo's tongue, Caputo concluded his 1984 article contending that

> the task of thinking must rather be to stay with the elemental power in words, which is something more than the storm of dissemination, not indeed in order to awaken the morning after to the blinding light of a Platonic sun, but rather in order to meditate the blue-black

> depths of a quiet sea, illumined only by an infrequent star, and in this silent mystery to understand that we do not belong to ourselves.[63]

The next piece that we are going to discuss was actually a book chapter. It appeared in print in 1985 under the title "From the Primordiality of Absence to the Absence of Primordiality: Heidegger's Critique of Derrida," and as such it did not really bring forward new ideas. For the volume on *Hermeneutics and Deconstruction*, Caputo had been asked "to take up the matter of Derrida from the standpoint of Heidegger,"[64] a task he did not accept "without a certain hesitation" owing to his admiration for Derrida's productive attitude toward Heidegger.[65] On top of that, Caputo was not unappreciative of what Heidegger and Derrida had in common, "above all a great destructive unrest, an enormous energy for breaking through the commonplace and the familiar, the received interpretations, the common wisdom,"[66] and he praised Derrida for his "superlative critique of Husserl which any Heideggerian could embrace, were it not for the direction"[67] in which it was taken by him.

Then again, Derrida's conclusion about what the failure of presence really meant, namely, "the death of primordial experience,"[68] proved to Caputo once again that "this deconstruction needs itself to be deconstructed,"[69] and he took it upon himself to "try to make Derrida say what he does not want to say, to make him own up to something transcendent, to direct the bite of his critique of Husserl into his own hide."[70] For all his declared admiration for Derrida, those nine pages were to deliver Caputo's hitherto sharpest critique of his future friend:

> There is a wildness to Derrida's play, a Dionysian frenzy. Derrida's "thought of the trace" lacks the piety of thinking, for it is no longer in the service of anything. Like a Kierkegaardian aestheticism it refuses to be bound by anything but wants only to enjoy the play of differences. Like the "rotation method" described by Kierkegaard it wants to avoid at all costs being bound, to deny all genuine "contact" and "experience," in order to savor indefinite substitution and interchangeability. For it fears that anything else is the metaphysics of presence. Here the piety of thought is overturned by a wild play of supplements. The nostalgia for presence is countered, not by a readiness for anxiety and an openness to the mystery, but by the wholesale refusal of the matter for thought.[71]

These words, I believe, Caputo later came to regret the most. It was this passage that he would in due time wish never to have written, for it was here that Caputo came closest to nicknaming Derrida "Jacques the Seducer"—the postmodern counterpart to the protagonist of Kierkegaard's *Seducer's Diary*. It goes without saying that branding Derrida as an irresponsible aesthete was no trivial matter—quite the contrary. As we shall see, Caputo will mock mercilessly anyone and everyone insinuating the very same thing (talk about bad conscience). But in any case, we can fairly say that this was the sort of climax that heralds far-reaching changes, and they were already under way. If in 1985 it was still Heidegger, whom Caputo regarded as a spell-breaker—"Heidegger has broken the spell of the metaphysics of presence in order to hearken to the mystery within things . . ."[72]—the time was coming when Derrida would liberate Caputo from the spell cast by Heidegger.

In fact, the day when Caputo would part with his German teacher and once again look for friends in Paris was considerably closer than the last text might lead us to believe. The seeds of the estrangement had already been planted in "Heidegger's Critique of Derrida." There, Caputo singled out the concept of *Gelassenheit* as the point of "the most extreme divergence of Derrida from Heidegger."[73] "From the standpoint of Heidegger," Caputo argued, this divergence marked the "essential fault of Derrida."[74] Because *Gelassenheit* had no place in Derrida's vocabulary, Caputo believed his critique of metaphysics to be pointless: "If in Derrida the ruses of metaphysics are exposed for what they are, nothing is thereby served or preserved."[75]

Fair enough, but how exactly do I imagine that this could be turned against Heidegger? The answer is: by dint of the very same "extreme divergence" and the absence of anything that would be "served or preserved." What good, we heard Caputo asking, is Derrida's dexterity in overcoming metaphysics, if he remains blind to the mystery? However, he would later wonder, what good is Heidegger's openness to the mystery, his *Gelassenheit*, if he remains blind to ethics—the "other" dexterity, the art of doing the right thing? Maybe Derrida failed to move beyond his deconstruction and Caputo would not let him get away with that. But we also know from chapter 6, where we first encountered the concept of *Gelassenheit*, that just a couple of years down the road Caputo would be equally baffled by Heidegger's own failure to recognize the obvious ethical implications of his thinking. And just as he had tried before with Derrida, Caputo would pledge to stretch Heidegger's thought in the direction where Heidegger himself did not wish to go, so that *Gelassenheit* might again be understood in its ethical context.

Even though it was published in the same year, 1985, the last article from Caputo's pre-Derridean period that I want you to look at does already hint at Caputo's creeping doubts concerning Heidegger. Its title "Three Transgressions: Nietzsche, Heidegger, Derrida" tells us whom

Caputo discussed in the article, although it is somewhat misleading as to the number of transgressions.

"Nietzsche, Heidegger and Derrida: these are not merely the names of three authors, but of three matters for thought, of three ways beyond metaphysics, three transgressions,"[76] declares Caputo; they are all "ultimately united by an experience of the abyss,"[77] and they all "require a certain courage for anxiety, a readiness for the abyss, a capacity to face up to the groundless which does not attempt to arrest the play and bring it to a halt."[78] But because, on Caputo's reading, "Derrida is closer to Nietzsche than to Heidegger," he suggests that "perhaps we have to do here with two, and not three, ways beyond metaphysics,"[79] and indeed throughout the rest of the article he continues talking about two transgressions only.

It is certainly not my aim here to squabble over numbers. The important thing is that on his personal crusade against metaphysics Caputo distinguished between two possible alliances, but we would be only half-right if we assumed that he joined forces with Heidegger. The surprise factor resides in my near certainty that we all *would* assume it. For, according to Caputo,

> the difference between the two transgressions can be put in terms of different metaphorics. In the one case, a metaphorics of dance and celebration, of Dionysian play, prevails; in the other, a metaphorics of quiet calm, meditative stillness, silence and mystery, of what I would call a metaphorics of "depth" rather than of dance and dissemination.[80]

After all excoriation of Derrida that we have witnessed thus far, Caputo's preference would indeed seem nothing but obvious. Why, of course he would have chosen to keep calm? He had learned to appreciate silence years ago back in the monastery and, as I suggested in the chapter on Caputo's two loves, the allure of Heidegger was in making it possible for Caputo to explore new horizons without coercing him to lose sight of the shore. Caputo would sooner meditate in the region of stillness, though surrounded by the devil of the storm raging all around, but his ship gently rocked by the deep blue sea than, picking up dance on the deck and, with the blessing of Dionysus, laughing the devil in the eye. Surely Caputo would have picked Heidegger.

Yes, he would. But, mind you, this was 1985. Ronald Reagan got reelected, ushering in, as Caputo portrayed it later, a "conservative and even reactionary period in American politics, under which God's poor have been left even further behind while the wealthiest enjoy unprecedented prosperity."[81] Caputo was "no Reagan Democrat!"[82] Not ten miles away from Villanova, where Caputo taught at that time, Philadelphia police bombed a row house occupied by a black liberation group, killing eleven people, including five children, mainly by allegedly preventing firefighters from putting out the fire. Caputo's hometown became "the city that bombed its own people." No less than thirty terrorist attacks tormented innocents the world around, with the Air India Flight 182 explosion being the deadliest case of terrorism in all previous history. No year before, nor for that matter any after, saw as many aviation disasters as 1985. Hundreds of thousands of Ethiopians were either dying or already dead on account of the famine, while their government maintained the largest army south of the Sahara. In Antarctica, British scientists discovered the ozone hole; in New Zealand, French agents bombed the flagship of the Greenpeace fleet. And "then the Earth shook and quaked . . . ," killing more than ten thousand in Mexico City, ". . . and the foundations of the mountains were trembling," burying under mud and volcanic debris twenty-five thousand in Colombia.[83] As Hurricane Gloria approached the East Coast, there were all indications it would become the storm of the century. In a word, not only was this a very bad year to meditate inside the storm's quiet eye, 1985 was a bad year for meditation, tout court. And because Caputo had not been in his cell since he had left the monastery (Mandela still was, and that fateful year decided to stay there), he saw it all. Something had to be done for all those orphans and widows—if not as one of the Brothers of the Christian Schools, then as a philosophy professor. Except that here, alas, Heidegger offered no answers. In fact, he had not even asked himself questions like this. Nietzsche and Derrida had, on the other hand, and that was the grim reality Caputo saw as well:

> The Nietzschean-Derridean strategy, the appropriation of Nietzsche in contemporary French philosophy, is a fruitful philosophy of protest and disruption, which is carried out in the name of liberation or emancipation. It has an ethico-political cutting edge which is entirely missing from Heidegger's more meditative work. This is not to say that it has nothing to do with *Gelassenheit*, with letting-be, but rather that it is an emancipatory application of *Gelassenheit*, a strategy of disruption aimed at a concrete letting-be which lets others be.[84]

How long had Caputo been bothered by this remains a question. However, as fate would have it, it was he, together with Maria Alter, who had translated Heidegger's infamous 1966 interview "Only a God Can Save Us."[85] Nine years later in the article that we are discussing (the interview was published only in 1976, after Heidegger's death), Caputo wrote:

> One has only to read the *Der Spiegel* interview with Heidegger in 1966 to see the sense of helplessness which besets Heidegger when it comes to the question of the political order. The Nietzschean-Derridean strategy of critique and deconstruction gives an ethico-political edge to Heidegger's project of the destruction of the history of metaphysics, an edge which Heidegger himself never provided.[86]

These last words, I would say, marked the beginning of the end of Caputo's fascination with Heidegger. By the time he reached the end of the article, Caputo no longer insisted on choosing between the two strategies. Instead, he thought they should be kept together in some kind of a mutual check.

> On my accounting, then, the work of dissemination and deconstruction is always preparatory for thought. The work of disrupting hegemony always prepares the way for the mystery which holds sway. But the essential thing in the path of thought is the path itself, remaining underway, resisting the illusion that one has attained the master-name, that one has mastery at all, recognizing that the highest name, *lethe*, is not a master-name, but a sign pointing to that which withdraws behind every name. And that is why "thinking" remains continually exposed to Derrida's deconstructive critique, to the Nietzschean critique of fictions. It must resist being enamored of its own discourse. Dissemination and thought belong together in endless, negative dialectic. For dissemination is preparatory for thought—which is itself always essentially preparatory.[87]

Whence my previous assertion that to presume Caputo's continued association with Heidegger would be only partially correct. Besides, such conjecture would itself betray another biased view, to wit that out of all three transgressors, Heidegger alone had not lost his bearings and therefore could, at least in principle, lead Caputo back home. Developing the line of thought leading from Heidegger back to Aquinas might have been an arduous task, and Caputo did not deceive himself imagining that his conclusions would be accepted by every Thomist.[88] Still, the success of the endeavor was conceivable. Could he, on the other hand, have written a hypothetical *Nietzsche and Aquinas*, or *Derrida and Aquinas*, or perchance some *Mystical Element in Dionysian Thought*? If he could, he missed the opportunity; the latter in particular sounds like a killer title and now I will claim the copyright. But pranks aside, let us not forget that Caputo had two homes, not one. Instead of summoning up Saint Thomas, was it unthinkable that Nietzsche or Derrida would lend force to Caputo's love for Kierkegaard?

The answer to this question will become clear in the passages that follow. Just one last telltale sign of impending transformation, however, before we move on: While easy to pass over unnoticed, Caputo made a remark in the "Three Transgressions" about Heidegger's solemnity, which I find significant:

> Heidegger, it would seem, has been incised by the tip of Nietzsche's sword/pen/style. He has taken Nietzsche straightforwardly, humorlessly, unaware that Nietzsche believes in nothing, that Nietzsche lets the force of his own theory of fictions recoil onto himself, so that there is no will and hence no will to power.[89]

Heidegger misunderstood Nietzsche, Caputo seems to suggest, because he could not get a joke. Derrida, on the other hand, "assisted in the task of liberating Nietzsche from the Heideggerian critique."[90] So maybe Derrida was also going to be more fun to read—and Heidegger equally at a loss about the irony of Kierkegaard.

* * *

Caputo's first, or rather most lasting, impressions of Derrida were that he was a skilled lecturer—"I attended a summer conference in Italy years ago in which he led some very illuminating seminars on *Glas*"[91]—and a very kind man:

> Then I remember giving a paper "on" him, as he sat in the audience listening, at a conference in Chicago twenty years ago, which was published under the title *Deconstruction and Philosophy*. I remember being quite terrified about giving that paper. I was afraid he would say I had everything wrong, and then what would I do? Fortunately, he was very gracious with me then, as he always is.[92]

The year was still 1985, the conference was hosted by Loyola University, but the title Caputo mistakenly assigned to his own paper was actually the theme of the event and the title of the resulting proceedings published two years later. The paper itself was included in the proceedings as "The Economy of Signs in Husserl and Derrida: From Uselessness to Full Employment." We should not be surprised anymore to find here Caputo saluting Derrida for giving "the critique of metaphysics—hitherto understood only in terms of *Gelassenheit*—a socio-political cutting edge, pointing it in the direction of a politics of liberation."[93] Apparently, Derrida himself was not entirely happy with Caputo's formulation and he said so during the discussion. Nevertheless, as Caputo understood it,

> Derrida resisted this suggestion only to the extent that it implied optimism, utopianism, some kind of metaphysics of the future in which all will be free. I do not mean anything of the sort by liberation, but only a kind of local strategy to be put into place wherever possible.[94]

The latter is also a sign of a nascent strand in the DNA of Caputo's theology, its preference for the local, daily, immanent—even as the mystery itself recedes. If, two years before Chicago, Caputo worried about a certain "depth structure" being "drowned out by the conversation of mankind,"[95] then two years after Chicago he would talk about "the ethics of dissemination [that] operates only in a community and in the ongoing conversation of mankind,"[96] conceding that he would now rewrite some of his "The Thought of Being and the Conversation of Mankind: The Case of Heidegger and Rorty"; for this conversation is, after all, an excellent model for his ethics.[97] And when he later wrote *Against Ethics*, Caputo confessed that "having been abandoned by Being (*Seinsverlassenheit*), I have attached myself to proper names, to everything that Being quits, to everything Being leaves behind," for "my attention has turned—this is my *Kehre*—to beings with proper names, with dates and places."[98]

It was, indeed, Caputo's *Kehre*, and therefore also a turning point in the adventure of weak theology. But we need to stay in the 1980s for a little longer to appreciate the course of events that brought the transformation about.

Luckily, 1984 did not turn out to be the year when "thought criminals" were persecuted, not in the manner of Orwell's Thought Police anyway. Not yet! Derrida, who in his youth had never spent a night away from El Biar, wrote and traveled, and he wrote more and traveled more widely than ever:

> 1984, the year of the stone [*calcul*], is, however, the year in which I traveled and wrote the most in my life, although I hardly dare admit it: in barely a few months there was Yale, New York, Berkeley, Irvine, Cornell, Oxford (Ohio), Tokyo, Frankfurt, Toronto, Bologna, Urbino, Rome, Seattle, Lisbon, *Memoires: for Paul de Man*—who had just died, in December '83, and who therefore never again came to meet me at JFK with Hillis, as he always had, *Psyché* (the lecture), "No Apocalypse, Not Now," *Ulysse Gramophone*, *Schibboleth*, reading of *Droit de regards* [Right of Inspection], the text for Lyotard's *Les Immatériaux*, etc.[99]

Derrida had already made a name for himself and he had been to America a few times, most notably in 1966, when he was invited by René Girard to participate in a Johns Hopkins University colloquium, where he also met Paul de Man. But as his 1984 itinerary seems to suggest, he only began to really register on the other side of the Atlantic in the eighties. "Not too long ago one coped with 'The Availability of Wittgenstein.' Little did we anticipate how soon we would have to cope with another elusive invader from the Continent," wrote Robert Cumming in 1981. "And while American philosophers may be 'exasperated' at what they suspect Derrida is getting away with, not all of them are quite sure what it *is*," he added.[100]

Now, because they were both fervent readers of Heidegger, Caputo engaged Derrida's texts a few times in the early 1980s—as, of course, we already know. For the most part cool, calm, and collected, perhaps sometimes even slightly self-effacing, Caputo treated Derrida with respect even when he strongly disagreed with him. This was an "all quiet on the western front" in comparison with what attacks against Derrida were on the way. Then came 1987, when *The Simpsons* appeared for the first time and all the year's digits were different for the last time, before now (I shall leave it to numerologists to divine what awaits us in 2013); the year when Derrida would have considered himself lucky if he only got involved in one affair (Paul de Man, the Nazi), rather than two (Heidegger, the Nazi), or even three (an "affair" about an "affair").[101] The "academic Ingsoc" was on cloud nine: Deconstruction had, at long last, gone over the party line, for it was finally clear to everyone that Derrida, the Jew, was in fact a defender of Nazis.

I discuss the Paul de Man affair more extensively in the epilogue, so I will simply suggest here that at least some of the trouble that Derrida got himself into was caused by his reluctance to give up on a friend. He insisted on responsibility as the essence of friendship and he also attached himself to proper names; one only needs to look at the contents of *The Work of Mourning* to see what I mean. At any rate, both Caputo and Derrida seemed to be troubled by the fact that, as Caputo expressed it later, "proper names have always been too much—or too little?—for philosophy."[102] On top of that, or precisely because of that, Caputo sensed that "something has gone wrong in the debate over Derrida, that this is not the usual sort of disagreement that philosophers have among themselves."[103] One must wonder how Derrida—"the adolescent who basically only liked reading writers quick to tears" that he once used to be, "that child whom the grown-ups amused themselves by making cry for nothing"[104]—endured the vicious attacks inwardly. In public, however, Derrida defended himself as he could, even in newspapers. Despite him hating to do so; despite the fact that in an interview published by *Digraphe* as early as 1976, when the most "difficult" questions he might have faced would be those related to his intricate writing style, Derrida wondered whether evading impossible questions would be ill-judged: "So running away is a bad thing? And why is that? Does one have to be noble and brave?"[105]

Much of what I have written here is, needless to say, my own subjective interpretation of what happened. The facts are, of course, verifiable. But the way I present them, in what order and with what significance I endow them, is subject to the same set of limitations as any other hermeneutic project. Since this cannot be otherwise, I have learned to take it as an advantage. And so, while fully aware that I may fall into the trap of psychologism, I wish to suggest that behind Caputo's *Kehre*, his turn to proper names, was a sense of compassion.

> The name "Derrida" has become a red flag at the mere sight of which many philosophers today charge. And the charges come from many directions. The Anglo-Americans were sure all along that continental philosophy was bound to come to grief in just such an excess of non-sense which makes no apologies for, indeed which celebrates, its very non-sensicality. [. . .] But the Derrida affair is not simply one more round of Anglo-American/continentalist hostilities. For not a few shots have been fired in Derrida's direction by those who remain faithful to the "classical" continental tradition . . .[106]

With these words Caputo began his 1987 article entitled "Derrida, a Kind of Philosopher: A Discussion of Recent Literature." Let us pass over the memory, albeit fresh, of how Caputo himself predicted that Derrida's deconstruction could only come to grief; let us instead pay attention to Caputo's gesture whereby he drew an analogy between Derrida and Kierkegaard. For calling Derrida "a kind of philosopher" was, in fact, a deliberate allusion to *Kierkegaard: A Kind of Poet* by Louis Mackey,[107] or for that matter a reference to how Kierkegaard perceived himself. A remarkable shift from the previous talk about an aesthete.

Be that as it may, Caputo noticed how "something appears to snap when it comes to Derrida, something that sets tempers flaring," not least because "he appears to say a good many outrageous things, and there is no short supply of outrageous things said about him."[108] And under such circumstances—"in the midst of this brouhaha"—Caputo seemed to be thankful that "several sensitive Derrida readers have appeared on the scene to lend Derrida a hand by lending him a more favorable ear."[109] Specifically, Caputo referred to monographs by Rodolphe Gasché, Irene E. Harvey, and John Llewelyn, all three published in 1986.[110] I will skip over his assessment of these books, except for one diverting moment.

Caputo predicted that Gasché's work would do more "to set the record straight" than the other two. Not an unusual gesture for a reviewer, but interesting when coming from Caputo, who ended up himself being one of the most influential advocates of Derrida in America, but more or less by going against the example set by Gasché. *The Tain of the Mirror*, indeed, earned Gasché his fame as a rigorous reader of Derrida (and Heidegger, de Man, Bataille, et al.). So, in a sense, Caputo had been right. Of the three books that he reviewed, however, Gasché's was probably the most boring and certainly the most technical. "A tour de force of technical argumentation,"[111] Caputo wrote, "long and difficult" but "technical and precise," giving Derrida the "sober and sobering rendering which is at present so badly needed."[112] Llewelyn's *Derrida on the Threshold of Sense*, on the other hand, displayed a "flippant and playful style" that, according to Caputo, was "more in the spirit of Derrida." Caputo worried that this "may well undermine his attempt to speak to readers of Wittgenstein, Quine and Goodman. No such objection can made to Gasché."[113] Hence it is somewhat surprising that, under the influence of Derrida, Caputo himself chose the "flippant and playful style" over the sober academic argumentation. Whatever he thought back then, humor and irony were going to become increasingly prominent in his subsequent writings.

Aside from this anecdote about Caputo's stylistic development, and more to the point, "Derrida, a Kind of Philosopher" is an earnest call to stand up for Derrida:

> The task that faces serious readers and expositors of Derrida's thought is both clear and urgent—if you pardon the apocalyptic tone. It has to do with Derrida's "good name" which has been considerably blemished by serious misunderstandings of what he is up to. It has to do with laying to rest the unsavory images of nihilism and irrationalism which his work provokes. [. . .] The task then, here and now, beginning where we are, is for more clear-headed renderings of Derrida which, by demonstrating the power and subtlety of his analyses, and their continuity with Husserl and Heidegger, will raise the level of the debate a notch or two.[114]

A sense of compassion, therefore. Or it could be solidarity, if you like, maybe mutual support, sympathy—it does not really matter all that much how we call it. The point is that beginning with this article, Caputo once and for all stopped criticizing, even stopped critiquing Derrida. And at least to some degree, his motivation had to do with Derrida's "good name." At any rate, Caputo now spoke for, rather than simply about, Derrida.

Then finally the following year, in 1988, came the real turnabout with Caputo's publication of two articles: "Demythologizing Heidegger: 'Alētheia' and the History of Being" and "Beyond Aestheticism: Derrida's

Responsible Anarchy in Continental Philosophy and the Question of Ethics." A farewell and a hello, although I will discuss them in a reverse order.

"Beyond Aestheticism" does exactly what it says. The article marks a new phase in Caputo's reading of Derrida, whom he no longer regards as a Kierkegaardian aesthete, for Caputo now believes that "there is an 'ethico-religious' quality to the way deconstruction overcomes aestheticism."[115] Setting the stage for the subsequent counterargument, Caputo pointed out how "deconstruction is sometimes accused of being a version of aestheticism," practicing "its own version of the rotation method and aesthetic repetition," ushering in not only hermeneutic nihilism, which "may be confined to the academy and the reading of old books," but ultimately also in "ethical and political nihilism [which] is dangerous, for that may spill over into the streets."[116] "One of the things that the aestheticist reading likes to stick to Derrida," Caputo wrote, is that

> he does not believe in anything, that deconstruction is not moved by the call of anything, that it has no responsibility, no vocation. Hermeneutics, on the other hand (Gadamer is one of these critics), is just as pleased as it can be with itself for being open to the other, and it constantly pats itself on the back for heeding the call of Being.[117]

Of course, not so long before then Caputo had himself contributed to this image of Derrida and his work. He remembered this, conceding that he must include an earlier piece of his own in this ill-begotten critique, namely, his "Hermeneutics as the Recovery of Man," and simultaneously suggesting that he got things right in *Radical Hermeneutics*.[118] He either forgot, or chose not to, mention his other critical pieces, presumably on account of the more pressing, "clear and urgent task" that had to do "with Derrida's good name." Instead of repeating and analyzing, albeit in an apologetic endnote, everything that he had written about Derrida before, Caputo must have felt that the article space would be put to a much better use by settling conclusively whether

> deconstruction is bound to anything, whether there is any room in it for the prized terms of hermeneutics and indeed of Western morals generally: call, answerability, responsibility. Does deconstruction experience any obligation, or have a sense of responsibility, or experience a call? In short, does deconstruction have a vocation?[119]

In order to answer these questions, Caputo turned his attention to "The Principle of Reason: The University in the Eyes of Its Pupils."[120] I am imagining him picking up this 1983 essay by Derrida for the first time; it was obviously written in reference to Heidegger's *The Principle of Reason* that had so profoundly influenced Caputo's early thought. The sense of curiosity. The sense of argumentative purpose that we typically feel when choosing a text to read. Had Caputo any inkling of what he was going to discover? That this rather unassuming virtual dialogue between Derrida and Heidegger would set him on a path that he was going to follow even three decades later? Now, analyzing Caputo's text in detail would lead me too far off the track, but Caputo basically noticed that Derrida argued for

> another kind of responding and responsibility, one which, by putting the principle itself, the *arche* into question, wants to be *responsible for* the university and the first principle of all thinking. It is possible to answer *for* the principle of sufficient reason, to question its prestige and to wonder whether it has not gone too far. To do that is to answer the call not by obeying it but by questioning it.[121]

A different kind of responsibility, to be sure; but Caputo was nevertheless able to conclude that "the notion of responsibility, of responsive-ness, goes right to the heart of the deconstructive project," so much so, in fact, that "a sense of responsibility is pretty much what deconstruction is."[122] It is "set in motion by the rights of the different," heeding not "the mainstream call of Being, presence, and the same" but "the call of the other."[123] Deconstruction, according to Caputo, practices a more radical *Gelassenheit* than the hermeneutics of Gadamer and Ricoeur, because it makes space for the other rather than assimilating the other to the same.[124] Therefore "hermeneutics has picked the wrong fight when it criticizes deconstruction on this point of responsibility, and it comes off looking a lot like Judge Wilhelm"[125]—a big critic of the aesthete in Kierkegaard's *Either/Or*.

References to "Judge Wilhelm" and "the aesthete" characters should not surprise us in the context of the debate about whether deconstruction is but a version of aestheticism. However, one quickly notices that Kierkegaard was no longer "conspicuous by his near-absence," as had been the case during the years when Caputo worked on Heidegger. The Kierkegaardian thread had never entirely vanished from Caputo's texts, to be sure, but with "Beyond Aestheticism" allusions to Kierkegaard began to multiply. I believe Derrida was partly responsible for this surge, for in his version of "The Principle of Reason" he did not comment only on Heidegger, but also spoke about the other kind of responsibility as the

> chance for an event about which one does not know whether or not, presenting itself *within* the university, it belongs to the history of the

university. It may also be brief and paradoxical, it may tear up time, like the instant invoked by Kierkegaard, one of those thinkers who are foreign, even hostile to the university, who give us more to think about, with respect to the essence of the university, than academic reflections themselves.[126]

There was a certain irony in the alleged aesthete's reference to Kierkegaard in support of his own views. He believed that Kierkegaard was on his side.[127] And for Caputo, I think, there must have been a tantalizing force of discovery radiating from Derrida's remarks like this one. He repeated the previous quotation verbatim in "Beyond Aestheticism." He also believed that by being "excluded by the university," Kierkegaard "was emancipated from its protocol, freed of its good manners, and able really to write." This, in Caputo's opinion, "was something that Professor Heidegger never saw when he himself wrote about Kierkegaard." Thus Heidegger failed to understand that "the critique of *homo metaphysicus* is inextricable from a critique of *homo academicus*."[128] Finally with respect to Derrida, Caputo decided that he "occupies a space on the Kierkegaardian map which corresponds structurally to the religious rather than to the aesthetic,"[129] and that his "knack for disturbing the academic peace locates him closer to Socrates than to the aesthete on the Kierkegaardian map, a notch or two higher on the 'stages of existence.'"[130]

Incidentally, "a notch or two" appears to be Caputo's favorite turn of phrase. But while, as we have seen, in 1987 he wanted to *raise* the level of the debate about Derrida a notch or two,[131] and in 1988 he placed Derrida a notch or two *higher* on the stages of existence, that same year he also set out "to bring Heidegger's reading of the early Greek epoch *down* a notch or two," and he did so out of concern for "the matter of thought."[132] Caputo attempted this in "Demythologizing Heidegger: 'Alētheia' and the History of Being," yet another article that was later to be followed by a book of the same name (this time for real, although without the subtitle).

"Heidegger could never resist a good story," Caputo wrote in the opening line of the article under discussion. "He could never resist giving what he had discovered about *alētheia* and the oblivion of Being a narrative form."[133] If truth be told, on that account I also feel like a Heideggerian. Fortunately for me and my book, Caputo did not deny the importance of narratives: "There is always room for a good story," he wrote. "We do our best teaching and learning in stories."[134] He did, however, point out the potential dangers inherent in some stories, namely, those privileging a particular era or origin. It could be also said that "Demythologizing Heidegger" represents Caputo's denouncement of any kind of nostalgia for a lost paradise—it, too, is a work of responsible *an-archy*. But even though the article signaled Caputo's parting of the ways with Heidegger, being a farewell and even an adieu, it was by no means a "go to hell!" Caputo, in other words, did not mean to break the myth *of* Heidegger, as in "Heidegger is praised too highly, and we should all wise up about him, for he sided with Nazis." Nor does it seem like Caputo was in any acute sense aware of being under the spell of the Schwarzwaldian wizard: "Nobody has ever said that Heidegger was not a great teacher."[135] Of course, here Caputo was wrong, because Karl Jaspers in his letter to the denazification committee had for all intents and purposes said exactly that:

> Heidegger's manner of thinking, which to me seems in its essence unfree, dictatorial, and incapable of communication would today in its *pedagogical* effects be *disastrous*. [. . .] As long as in his case an authentic rebirth does not come to pass, one that would be evident in his work, *such a teacher cannot in my opinion be placed before the youth of today*, which, from a spiritual standpoint, is almost defenseless. The youth must first reach a point where they can think for themselves.[136]

If we can rely on Caputo's reminiscences—as, indeed, for the most part we must—then his real shift away from Heidegger coincided "with the writing of 'Heidegger's Scandal'[137] for the Margolis and Rockmore collection" published four years later in 1992.[138] Back (or rather now) in 1988, Caputo simply meant to say that Heidegger's great thinking about truth would be even greater without the accompanying myth:

> I want to argue in the present pages that Heidegger's best insights are obscured by his penchant for heroic tales and privileged epochs, for first dawns and new beginnings. What Heidegger has to say about the history of Being must be understood in critical, not heroic terms. It is necessary to delimit the mythos—the story—in the history of Being, in order to get at what *alētheia* means.[139]

What heroic tales and privileged epochs? Caputo refers to Heidegger's attempt to trace the historical development, or rather degeneration, from *alētheia* (truth as unconcealment) to *orthotes* (truth as correctness of assertions). Heidegger claims that the former was still experienced by the early Greeks but got covered up by the grand metaphysicians Plato and Aristotle. The memory of the original experience, when the early Greeks were still able to let things shine on their own—this is what Heidegger meant by *Gelassenheit*—was "steadily diminished over the centuries, until it finally devolved into the present crisis,"[140] the total objectification of the world in our technological age.

A truly great story, Caputo thought: "Heidegger is exceptionally good at making the early Greek texts dance. He can bring them alive, and he has a feel for them which few can match."[141] Moreover, Caputo even seemed to suggest the myth itself was essential for Heidegger:

> The narratival impulse is not without a purpose. Heidegger could not have done without his stories. The promise of the "destruction of the history of ontology" gave *Being and Time* a punch which no mere "existentialist" treatise could have mustered up. His fabulous account of the early Greeks and of the lightning flash that lit up the early Greek countryside was a large part of the power of the later Heidegger, and I have my doubts as to whether the later Heidegger would have made half the impact he did, had he not spun such a magnificent yarn. After all, not all stories are of equal merit and power. Great stories have power and impact. They have a "moral," make a point, impress upon us an otherwise lost lesson, and vividly embody a purely *sachlich* point.[142]

Despite that, Caputo wanted to free Heidegger's philosophy from this myth, hence finally some justification for the article's title "Demythologizing Heidegger." A somewhat perplexing move, after admitting that Heidegger could not have done without it. I will return to this puzzle before long, but first we need to understand why Caputo thought that "Heidegger's view is strengthened, not weakened, if it is disentangled from this story [. . .] if it is understood that his essential thought is not dependent upon really swallowing such a tall tale."[143] The answer lies in the last two words: Because he believed that this "was rather a tall story too, and easy to debunk."

> One would not be inclined to sing such anthems to the Greeks if one were writing a history of power—of women, say, or of slaves. The Greek world was built around a set of exclusionary and hierarchical power relations which placed male over female, free man over slave, Greek over non-Greek, of which the divided line provides the metaphysics, and the Pythagorean table of opposites the "early Greek experience." Do women and slaves also share in the clearing? Do the slaves who hauled the stones for the temple also participate in "setting the truth into the work"? How are the excluded present in the open? Heidegger would have had very different results if his perspective were the history of power instead of the poetics of truth.[144]

The world of the early Greeks, in other words, was not so perfect as to seriously believe that, in comparison with those golden days, everything in today's West is but a fall from the original greatness. Heidegger, according to Caputo, "very conveniently forgets a long list of the very forgettable things about the early Greek world."[145] And not only that. He also forgets that one can listen to others and "meditatively muse over many texts—from the scriptures, to the writings of the eastern thinkers, to medieval mystics—and [. . .] find in them a deeper structure."[146] Finally, Caputo also argued that "there is as much radiant splendor of the being in its Being, as much rising up into unconcealment, in Cézanne as there is in Anaximander, and it makes no sense, on Heidegger's own terms, to rank-order them."[147] "Therefore," concluded Caputo,

> let us treat this account of the early Greeks as a good story, not a sheer fabrication, because it exploits certain things about the pre-technical world, but which at the same time is not tied to some historical, epochal correlate. [. . .] Let us take it for what it is, a philosophical myth. [. . .] Nothing is accomplished if Heidegger's history of Being is taken to be anything more than a good story with a good punch line. Otherwise we are stranded in a nostalgic longing for a lost world and a longing hope for a new dawn, trapped between the two beginnings, too late for the gods and too early for Being, feeling bad that we no longer speak Greek and afraid of being in bad faith if we buy a computer.[148]

* * *

As much as Caputo's wanderings "between Heidegger and Derrida" are captivating in their own right, I now need to pause for a moment and make a few observations about how what we have seen relates to weak theology. The last two articles heralded a profound change in Caputo's thinking—his intellectual *Kehre*—which was either caused *by*, or itself caused the revision *of*, Caputo's academic alliances. Due to the paradoxical nature of exemplarity, we shall never know for sure, which is why I keep insisting that *The Adventure of Weak Theology* is also *only* a story, but either way these developments could not remain unreflected in what later came to be a theology of the event.

A good case in point is the "powers that be"—according to Caputo an "excellent English expression which shows very nicely the ethical spin which Derrida has put on his critique of the metaphysics of presence."[149] One can find these words in "Beyond Aestheticism," but this expression that Caputo had never used before suddenly pops up everywhere in this period: "What Derrida has done above everything else, in my mind, is to expose the primal and unsettling contingency which lies not far beneath the surface of our creations," Caputo argued in "The Economy of Signs in Husserl and Derrida," the 1985 Chicago conference article. "He interrogates entrenched authority, the established powers that be, which pretend to be, which pretend to be present."[150] *Radical Hermeneutics* published in 1987 is literally full of references to the powers that be. Thus Derrida was said to be "good at disrupting the claims of the powers that be, at disputing their authority, at confounding their claims and putting them into play," while Heidegger, according to Caputo, "never saw the ethico-political cutting edge of the delimitation of metaphysics. He was never a good Socrates."[151] Later in the book, and here the connection with the future weak theology becomes most apparent, Caputo talked about faith that "makes its way in the dark," which is why to "invoke a grace from on high is just one more familiar way of bailing out on the flux just when we are needed the most."[152]

> Now it is just then when religion starts to think in terms of a gift of grace given only to a chosen people that religion begins to degenerate into a factional power and a force of oppression. [. . .] Then religion sits down to the table with the powers that be, just when it ought otherwise to have been committed to their disruption.[153]

The powers that be took on new importance in Caputo's work. Nearly two decades before his first explicitly theological monograph, it already figured side by side with religion. And in *The Weakness of God* this very expression, which had once pulled Caputo closer to Derrida, is as common as butterflies and reserved for the sworn enemies of the kingdom:

> One gets nowhere in the kingdom of God by gaining the favor of the powers that be (*dynatoi*). The idea behind the kingdom, its an-archic *arche*, is to take the side of everyone who is out of power, the *asthena*, which from the point of view of worldly advancement is a recipe for disaster. In the kingdom, the powers that be are regularly denounced as vipers and white-washed tombs whose fathers have killed the prophets, rather like the sort of thing we find in *Kierkegaard's Attack Upon Christendom*.[154]

Another important element traceable back to "Beyond Aestheticism" is, of course, the connection Caputo began to perceive between deconstruction, ethics, and religion. I say "of course" because we have already heard Caputo say so, but also and especially because nothing shaped weak theology more than this. To be sure, Caputo could not have quite foreseen it back in 1988. At that time, he merely thought that

> the religious backdrop of the ethics of the other, while no more than a backdrop for Derrida personally, is more than a little interesting to us, who have taken upon ourselves to answer the charge of aestheticism which is thrown up against deconstruction. For it completes the Kierkegaardian analogy: the overcoming of aestheticism in deconstruction has not only an ethical, but even a religious "dimension" to it.[155]

Then again, the Kierkegaardian connection, so to say, was not the only thing Caputo had on mind. For he also remarked that "the interesting thing about Jesus" was "that he does not seem to attach an ethical quality to sameness but to difference, which is the light deconstruction throws on him." "The whole idea behind what he called the 'kingdom of God,'" argued Caputo, "was mixing with the different, not preserving the purity of the same."[156]

Finally, as far as I can tell it was there, in "Beyond Aestheticism," where Caputo for the first time spoke about "scandalizing the faithful" by suggesting affinity between deconstruction and religion.[157] Association with Derrida, it would seem, awakened in the former Brother Paul a taste for scandal. At any rate, "this link between Paul and Derrida," Caputo wrote later in *The Weakness of God*, "between deconstruction and First Corinthians, a scandal to the faithful and a stumbling block to the deconstructors, is a central point in this study . . ."[158]

Apropos "Demythologizing Heidegger," Caputo wrote that it was

> like all demythologizing, an attempt to avoid idolatry. It separates out the contingent and mutable structures which metaphysics stretches across the abyss and it does so precisely in order to shelter what withdraws and to preserve it in the mystery of its play.[159]

The quasi-religious vocabulary in the preceding quotation is easily discernible, but I do not mean to suggest that at the hour of his departure from Heidegger, Caputo came up with theological uses for idolatry or demythologization. The fact that he did not invent these words, however, makes things even more interesting. Demythologization became part of the theological parlance thanks to Rudolf Bultmann, himself a close friend of Heidegger, and it represents arguably one of the most distinguishing features of the modernist approach to religion. Now, what I find especially intriguing is a certain structural similarity between, on the one hand, Caputo's demythologization of Heidegger and, on the other hand, his use of the concept of religion without religion and perhaps even his strategy of reducing the name of God and of the Scriptures to the event, as it is applied in *The Weakness of God*.

As an expression, demythologization appears to be off duty in Caputo's theological debut: I only run across three instances and not a single one of them directly related to what Caputo wanted to say. So either I am completely off the mark, or else some version of "the will to purity of religion" operates there under a different guise. To Keith Putt, who as a reader is no lesser an expert on Caputo than Caputo is on Derrida, the answer seems obvious:

> In many ways, Caputo's kingdom poetics of the impossible complements Rudolf Bultmann's hermeneutical strategy of demythologization, so much so that, given the definite parallels between their theologies, one might label Caputo's poetics something of a post-secular Neo-Bultmannianism.[160]

The Weakness of God, on Putt's reading, is a work of demythologization, albeit a postsecular version thereof. Kevin Hart, for his part, does not think Caputo's views are so much postsecular or postmodern, as they descend from

> the Enlightenment construction of Christianity as a religion—that is, a species of a presumed genus "religion"—which makes a program of "religion without religion" inevitable long before the syntax of "X without X" was used in modern thought.[161]

Hart believes that religion without religion means for Caputo "a religion that has erased its reliance on historical moments, such as the coming of a messiah in space and time, the institution of a church, mosque, or synagogue, or the confession of creeds."[162] A religion that has been freed from everything metaphysical, so that "what remains might be a religion guided by ethics or politics, by faith or by the holy . . ."[163]

Oh, "no no, not at all," protests Caputo: "Alas, for such a one as me to be mistaken as casting my lot with a Kantian-Levinasian reduction of religion to morals! This life is not fair."[164] Nor does he agree with Hart's suggestion that he wishes to bring back Kant.

> I do not think of this "pure" faith or "religion without religion" as a faith that somebody believes, or a religion that somebody can inhabit, or a position that somebody takes, or as a proposition that somebody can propose. I am not an advocate of religious abstractionism or an abstractionist religion. I take this pure *foi* as a ghost, a specter, that

> haunts us in the sorts of concrete positions—philosophical, political, and religious—that we do take, the displacing place (*khôra*) in which they are situated.[165]

Caputo denies vehemently that he would wish to "replace religion in the concrete with a formal abstract religion without religion," or to replace it with ethics. "I would consider that an unfortunate impression for me to make upon my readers."[166]

Fair enough. If nothing else, this is a singularly complex issue and we ought to be attentive to what Caputo says about his own work. On the other hand, he should not complain too much about making an unfortunate impression upon his readers, for it would have been difficult to read *The Prayers and Tears of Jacques Derrida: Religion Without Religion* in any other way. In a paragraph entitled "Religion within the Limits of Reason Alone (Almost)," Caputo spoke about Derrida's intention to

> mime and mimic the Enlightenment's desire for a universal, transnational, neo-international, purely rational religion, by proposing a certain desertification of religion, but without entirely deserting it and without excluding faith.[167]

This was Derrida's answer to contemporary religious violence, fanaticism, and fundamentalism, and Caputo gives us no reason to believe that he was only presenting Derrida's views, without thereby endorsing them. Nor was this the only thing Caputo/Derrida wrote to explain the inevitable confusion and justify Hart's critique. Derrida does not hesitate to call his abstraction a universal religion, Caputo writes, "a religion that can be thought within reason alone, not a local or a national religion but a religion for all and everywhere, a place for the displaced";[168] in Derrida's desert "grows the desert flower of a religion which is 'older' than any known religion";[169] "two historical names are like the traces of invisible tracks left in the desert: the *messianic* and *khôra*."[170] Regarding these, continues Caputo, Derrida's religion, understood "as a universal messianicity despoiled of all messianism, as a faith without dogma advancing in the risk of absolute night, is the foundation of the law, the law of the law";[171] whereas "*khôra* is the stuff of a new tolerance, not of familiar Christian or Enlightenment tolerance, which are disguised ways of keeping the 'same' in place."[172] On top of this all, Caputo dedicates a separate block quote to Derrida saying that

> The chance of this desert in the desert (as of that which *resembles to a fault*, but without reducing itself to, that *via negativa* which

> makes its way from a Graeco-Judaeo-Christian tradition) is that in uprooting the tradition that bears it, in atheologizing it, this abstraction, without denying faith, liberates a universal rationality and the political democracy that cannot be dissociated from it.[173]

"This religion returns, again and again," concludes Caputo, "as postmodern faith and hope, as postmodern reason and universality, the heart of a justice and a democracy to come in a heartless world."[174]

If Caputo after all these words still in all honesty wonders *pourquoi pas*, why on the issue of religion without religion his readers did not understand him correctly, then the readers must themselves wonder how on earth can he wonder. As a matter of fact, one would be hard-pressed to put forward a more demythologized version of religion than this. My readers, on the other hand, may just as well wonder whether the foregoing overview of the ideas expressed in *The Prayers and Tears* is at all relevant to the present discussion. To recall, I set out to examine connections, if there are any, between the 1988 *Demythologizing Heidegger* and the present weak theology, whereas Caputo's book about Derrida predates *The Weakness of God* by about a decade and is, indeed, mainly about Derrida. I concede, although I still hold fast to my methodology whereby I consider everything that has come to pass as relevant. This is all part of one big adventure of weak theology. Should I, however, give one example of Caputo's more recent and more reserved views on these matters, an example that does, in fact, come from *The Weakness of God*, it could be this one:

> A theology of the event is in part a second-order act that maintains a certain ironic distance from strong theologies, which in a certain sense are the only theologies that "exist," that are found in concrete historical communities. I love the strong theologies that I know the way I love great novels, but I maintain an ironic distance from them occasioned not only by the fact that they are invariably in league with power but also by my conviction that the event that is astir in the name of God cannot be contained by the historical contingency of the names I have inherited in my tradition.[175]

Strong theologies, according to Caputo, are just good stories. But does this not remind you of Caputo's evaluation of Heidegger's myth of the early Greeks? Here, then, is the question—or a few related questions—that I have all along meant to pose, though not answer: Could perhaps these "demythologizations" separated by two decades be in any way homologous? And if they are, what does it say about weak theology? This is not simply a matter of pinpointing our exact whereabouts along the journey; why Caputo's years between Heidegger and Derrida are so important as to warrant such a lengthy tale (or, for that matter, why I might wish I had never begun telling it, when to bring it to an end I seem to struggle in vain like Sisyphus). That too, but insofar as this analogy is tenable, we may also notice something peculiar about Caputo's reductions, his demythologization of theology. A disjunction, perhaps, or in any case an oddity, that is much more noticeable in *Demythologizing Heidegger*.

Hart said Caputo considered religion without religion by way of two questions: "Is the positivity of revealed religion needed by the faith? If not, can the figure of responsibility replace it?"[176] Concerning Heidegger, he could have asked: "Is Heidegger's tale about the early Greeks necessary for his thought? If not, shall we be better off without it?" We know Caputo's answer to the second pair: "Nothing is accomplished if Heidegger's history of Being is taken to be anything more than a good story with a good punch line." In fact, Caputo believed Heidegger's best insights were obscured by this myth, therefore dispensing with it altogether would not harm anyone. Nothing would be lost if Heidegger lost this myth. Except, of course (and I promised to come back to this), Caputo understood that Heidegger could not have done without this story. Should we therefore conclude, coerced by the brute force of syllogism, that nothing of Heidegger's thought on *alētheia* would be lost because there would be no Heidegger's thought on *alētheia*? Can we "separate out contingent and mutable structures" without actually killing the mystery? Demythologizing Heidegger, Caputo said, "sets the play of withdrawal deeper than the contingent configurations in which it issues."[177] I said I would be careful not to venture answers, but I do wonder if "deeper" does not end up being a little too deep.

Then, finally, I also keep thinking about what might get lost when religion is stripped of religion. Or perhaps let me restate the problem, as I already discussed my reservations about this concept in the previous chapter: Does a poetics at the heart of weak theology run a risk of missing something important? Assuming that my analogy holds. In Caputo's poetics "the sacred texts are treated, not as the Divine Revelation that definitively props up the authority of some confessional faith or ecclesiastical office, nor as the record of some extraordinary empirical event from long ago."[178] "A poetics is true the way a novel is true," explains Caputo, "even if it is classified by the librarians as a fiction."[179] Caputo's poetic discourse arises from a double reduction of the Name and of the Word of God into the event of the call. The call is the deep truth, like Heidegger's *alētheia*, while particular traditions with their scriptures and theologies are just good stories with good punch lines. And sure enough, Caputo also understands that "you see the weak force that stirs within the name of God only when someone casts it in the form of a narrative, tells mad stories and perplexing parables about it, which is what Jesus did when he called for the kingdom of God."[180] We could not have done without these stories, but could we perhaps now do without them? Caputo does not suggest so, to be sure. For, as he says, "poetics is a discourse with a heart, supplying the heart of a heartless world."[181] Then again, so did Derrida's religionless religion that "returns, again and again as postmodern faith and hope, as postmodern reason and universality, the heart of a justice and a democracy to come in a heartless world."[182] We should not make too much of this coincidence; all authors have their favorite locutions.

* * *

In the winter semester 1942–1943 Heidegger gave a lecture course on Parmenides and Heraclitus. This was not merely an exercise in the history of philosophy, however. Heidegger also addressed contemporary issues that troubled him, namely, the question of technology and, more specifically in this course, the fate of writing after the introduction of the typewriter. "The typewriter veils the essence of writing and of the script,"[183] Heidegger complained; it is "one of the main reasons for the increasing destruction of the word. The latter no longer comes and goes by means of the writing hand, the properly acting hand, but by means of the mechanical forces it releases."[184] Even more alarming was the ubiquity of the typewriter. One could no longer simply ignore it, Heidegger seemed to think, except at the risk of irritating whoever was to read the text:

> In the time of the first dominance of the typewriter, a letter written on this machine still stood for a breach of good manners. Today a hand-written letter is an antiquated and undesired thing; it disturbs speed reading. Mechanical writing deprives the hand of its rank in the realm of the written word and degrades the word to a means of communication. In addition, mechanical writing provides this "advantage," that it conceals the handwriting and thereby the character. The typewriter makes everyone look the same.[185]

This was decades before computers superseded typewriters as the writers' tool of choice, but Caputo was undoubtedly correct assuming that Heidegger would have been equally unimpressed by the benefits of the PC.

Writing was an altogether different matter in "Die Hütte" in Todtnauberg: "On the steep slope of a wide mountain valley in the southern Black Forest, at an elevation of 1,150 meters, there stands a small ski hut" with a view of the farmhouses scattered below and "the meadows and pasture lands [leading] to the woods with its dark fir-trees, old and towering" above.[186] "This is my work-world," Heidegger wrote back in 1934.[187] And

> on a deep winter's night when a wild, pounding snowstorm rages around the cabin and veils and covers everything, that is the perfect time for philosophy. Then its questions must become simple and essential. Working through each thought can only be tough and rigorous. The struggle to mold something into language is like the resistance of the towering firs against the storm.[188]

Magical, meditative, even mystical. Through his commitment to the hut, where he "thought and wrote for over five decades, often alone, claiming an emotional and intellectual intimacy with the building, its surroundings, and its seasons,"[189] Heidegger was a living testimony to the profound connection between the thought and its place in space and time. It matters where we write. For his teaching duties and research, Heidegger often had to descend down to Freiburg, but then, like Nietzsche's Zarathustra, he always returned to his mountain:

> As soon as I go back up there, even in the first few hours of being at the cabin, the whole world of previous questions forces itself upon me in the very form in which I left it. I simply am transported into the work's own kind of rhythm, and in a fundamental sense I am not at all in command of its hidden law.[190]

It was an enchanted place—"Die Hütte" draws pilgrims to this day; long after Heidegger was gone, even Derrida visited once.[191] But while Heidegger lived there, no clickety-clacks, zips, and bings of the typewriter disturbed the silence inside the snow-covered hut. The storm's quiet eye.

Also in the winter of 1942–1943, hundreds of thousands of Heidegger's compatriots were dying in the "wild, pounding snowstorm rages" around Stalingrad, falling like cut down fir trees. It truly does matter where we write. Caputo wrote in Philadelphia some 1,138 (that would make George Lucas happy) meters closer to the ground, which is why he thought Heidegger's tale was rather tall and the mystical element in his thought, after all, rather mythical. So he wrote a letter to Heidegger, for he "just could not stand this stuff any longer" and, "*mirabile dictu*, I actually got a response—but, will you believe, it was typewritten!! I should have seen then that the whole thing had to be demythologized!"[192]

It also matters when we write. For my part I am sentimental about those good old typewriters that made writing feel like working, when one had to "struggle to mold something into language," because there was no drag-and-drop and there was no delete. In fact, not so long ago I bought a typewriter in a Belgian secondhand store, and I also make my computer sound like a typewriter. Caputo, as we have seen, would have satisfied himself with not "being in bad faith" when he bought a computer. But, in the end, he might have gone too far:

> I confess to having lost all contact with the First Beginning and everything Originary. I have given up hope of catching a glimpse of the last god's passing by in this end-time when the first gods have flown. I do not expect to be on hand for the Other Beginning, which can be granted if and only if one can maintain communications with the First Beginning. I have in short been abandoned, become a part of and a party to the very *Seinsverlassenheit* against which Heidegger has at length warned us all. Though I wait daily by my phone, though I keep my ear close to the ground, I cannot, for the life of me, hear the call of Being. I have been forsaken. (I think that Being has discovered I am American and that I use a computer. I suspect an informer.)[193]

The last passage comes from *Against Ethics*, published in 1993 together with its companion volume, *Demythologizing Heidegger* (the book).[194] "In these works," as Michael Zimmerman noted five years later, "one hears a prophetic voice speaking now with a French deconstructive accent, now with an American liberal accent. This liberal-prophetic voice had not been prominent in Caputo's earlier works on Heidegger and mysticism."[195] Indeed, by 1993 Caputo's shift from Heidegger to Derrida had been completed and as Heidegger went under in Caputo's eyes, Derrida's influence increased.

Unsurprisingly, these developments are easily discernible against the backdrop of Caputo's fondness for Kierkegaard. We have seen how in 1982 Caputo argued that "the relationship of Heidegger to Kierkegaard is much more intimate than either Heidegger himself or his commentators have been prepared to admit." In 1987, Caputo no longer saw the problem as that of mere readiness. Heidegger "not only understates his dependence on Kierkegaard, he misstates it," Caputo wrote in *Radical Hermeneutics*, he borrows Kierkegaard's theory of repetition without acknowledgment.[196] Then in 1993, when writing about Heidegger's *Kehre*, Caputo seemed to suggest that "the darkest days of Heidegger's life and work, [his] hellish endorsement of National Socialism and his ardent efforts to Nazify the German university" followed after Kierkegaard (as well as Luther, Pascal, Augustine, and Aristotle) "faded into the background."[197] Finally in 2003, Caputo said it bluntly: "[Al]though Heidegger stole some of his best lines in *Being and Time* from Kierkegaard, he never saw what Kierkegaard was doing."[198]

And the main reason behind this blindness, according to Caputo, was the "the utter humorlessness of Heidegger, the utter absence of laughter."[199] Something that Caputo actually complained about already as early as in *Radical Hermeneutics*:

> Though Heidegger is the great thinker of our time and even though the present work is in his debt on nearly every page, he remains vis-à-vis Kierkegaard in the acutely embarrassing situation of someone who does not get a joke. Worse still, who does not even know that the speaker is joking at all while everyone else is holding their sides. He missed the laughter in Kierkegaard and the woman/truth in Nietzsche, too, as Derrida shows. (Almost!)[200]

At this point my account of Caputo's Heideggerian period comes to an end. As Zimmerman remarked a few years later, "*Demythologizing Heidegger* is an act of intellectual patricide that separates Caputo from the father figure whom he both loves and hates."[201] Incidentally, this puts Caputo's recent critique of Martin Hägglund—"I understand the need to kill the father, but one ought at least to make some sense when asked for the motive for the murder"[202]—into a new perspective. We have, in any case, heard enough about why Caputo became a "kind of Heideggerian apostate."[203] That said, I cannot wrap this chapter up without a few more paragraphs about Derrida.

* * *

> I must note it right here, on the morning of 22 August 1979, 10 A.M., while typing this page for the present publication, the telephone rings. The American operator asks me if I accept a *"collect call"* from Martin (she says Martine or martini) Heidegger. I heard, as one often does in these situations which are very familiar to me, often having to call "collect" myself, voices that I thought I recognized on the other end of the intercontinental line, listening to me and watching my reaction. What will he do with the ghost or Geist of Martin? I cannot summarize here all the chemistry of the calculation that very quickly made me refuse (*"It's a joke, I do not accept"*) after having had the name of Martini Heidegger repeated several times . . .[204]

Derrida typed. He even knew someone who would plug in the electric typewriter "so as to receive the order to write: the slight whirring sound reminds him, like an unconscious, that he has to get his money's worth."[205] To Derrida, too, work meant typing—so what, that he would be forever haunted by the spirit of Martini? Derrida and Heidegger, in other words, were as different as chalk and cheese (as a German professor is different from a Frenchman). As a matter of fact, Derrida had the misfortune of being called a computer virus.[206] By *Der Spiegel*, by dint of irony of a blind event. *Nicht einmal ein Gott kann uns jetzt retten*. For, "in the weak and colorless theology whose cause I am promoting," Caputo wrote much later in *The Weakness of God*, "it is profane magic, thaumaturgy, to think of God as an omnipotent onto-power who could [. . .] put an end to [. . .] computer spam . . ."[207] But despite all of the differences, like Heidegger before him, Derrida also spoke the languages of Caputo's youth.

Although Caputo praised Derrida's responsible anarchy, in 1988 he did not (yet) want his readers to conclude that Derrida was a friend whom he felt called upon to defend.[208] Whatever closeness *Beyond Aestheticism* might have intimated, we were to only think about it as strictly academic. Always verifiable by a citation, if need be. At the same time, however, Caputo resolved to pass over the "wildness" and a "Dionysian frenzy" of Derrida's play. Undeterred by the "Seducer's" denial of "all genuine contact and experience," he now looked for the point of contact with Derrida and, almost too wonderful to tell, he found it in Meister Eckhart: Eckhart's "emancipatory words put the *powers that be* on the spot and tended to break open the rigid hierarchy and exclusionary order of the political system," opined Caputo; "in Eckhart everything turns on *Gelassenheit* [. . .] which includes everything which liberates and sets free."[209] "That is why I find in Meister Eckhart a great medieval deconstructive practice . . ."[210] In short, fourteen years after "Heidegger and Eckhart,"[211] Caputo wrote "Derrida and Eckhart."[212] But this way was shut right from the start. Intrigued by such suggestions as he was, Derrida protested against the assimilation of deconstruction with negative theology. Not that Caputo tried to point in that direction, but his reference to Eckhart certainly did, and he knew it. Besides, Eckhart was not one of Caputo's two first loves. Kierkegaard was. And with respect to the latter, Derrida had more to offer than Caputo had ever been able to find in Heidegger.

It is highly unlikely that Caputo would have known this at the time, but the young Derrida had also been split between the two incompatible philosophers:

> [W]hen I was 13, I read Nietzsche for the first time, and though I didn't understand him completely, he made a big impression on me. The diary I kept then was filled with quotations from Nietzsche and Rousseau, who was my other god at the time. Nietzsche objected violently to Rousseau, but I loved them both and wondered, how can I reconcile them both in me?[213]

Already this would have been interesting, but in 2001 Derrida also confessed:

> [B]asically the sense of desire and commitment I had when I read Rousseau, Nietzsche or Gide as a very young man is still with me. But it is Kierkegaard to whom I have been most faithful and who interests me most: absolute existence, the meaning he gives to the word subjectivity, the resistance of existence to the concept or the system—this is something I attach great importance to and feel very deeply, something I am always ready to stand up for.[214]

Kierkegaard, for that matter, was himself divided, albeit in a different way: "I am a two-faced Janus: with one face I laugh, with the other I cry . . ."[215] Then again Derrida, referring to his most autobiographical book *Circumfession*, said it was both a tragic and an ironic text: "I am constantly laughing in a way that is tragic throughout this text. At the same time, this mixture of tragedy, laughter, and irony is something which Jack manages to capture in a very lucid way."[216] John "Jack" Caputo, in a 2007 interview published under the title "The Power of the Powerless," said Kierkegaard had helped him to understand Derrida and he had learned from both: "What I try to cultivate, what I have learned from both Derrida and Kierkegaard, is this power of laughing through your tears, which distinguishes both from Heidegger. As Johannes Climacus says, humor serves as the incognito of the religious."[217]

Caputo's age of discovery, in other words, did not end when he gave up on Heidegger. Pieces of the puzzle continued to snap into place:

Once, when we were together in a conference in Italy that I used to go to in the eighties, Derrida was there lecturing on undecidability. That was when I first heard him say that undecidability is not the opposite of a decision, it is the condition of possibility of a decision. When I said to him, "That's *Fear and Trembling*!" Derrida said, "Of course it is!" And that was where *Against Ethics* came from. I decided then and there to present a Derridean reconstruction of *Fear and Trembling* (just as *Radical Hermeneutics* was a kind of reconstruction of *Repetition*!).[218]

Against Ethics, Caputo recalls, appeared at the same time as *Donner la mort*, Derrida's own analysis of *Fear and Trembling*.[219] "I thought I was seeing a ghost, like a spectral appearance of father Abraham himself," Caputo wrote elsewhere.[220] If truth be told, Derrida did seem to do this more often to Caputo:

> I will never forget the "surprise," the salutary shock of sitting on a plane one day, soaring off to another conference, reading *Circonfession* for the first time, coming to the words "my religion about which nobody understands anything," with the result, he says, that

> he has been "read less and less well over almost twenty years." That, I promised myself, then and there, some thirty thousand feet above the earth, up among the angels, *s'il y en a*, is the first paragraph of a new book that I therewith resolved to write. I will write a book about Derrida's religion and it will scandalize everyone, or so I hope and pray. (I had just written *Against Ethics* and was in search of new materials for scandal.)[221]

The book Caputo decided to write was, of course, *The Prayers and Tears of Jacques Derrida*, while the preceding quotation comes from *A Passion for the Impossible: John D. Caputo in Focus*, specifically from a chapter entitled "A Game of Jacks." There would be much more to say about Caputo *and* Derrida, enough indeed to also fill a book, but I want to conclude this part of the story here, with Caputo's play on names.

"You had no way to know this, of course," Caputo told Emmet Cole—who had just asked him which of the two, Jack or John, was his proper name—"but that is a very deep question for me, touching upon my whole destiny (if I have one!). Everything is at stake in this question."[222] "It was a popular custom among Algerian Jews in the 1930s to name their children after American movie stars," Caputo explained, "and 'Jacques' was named after Jackie Coogan, a child star who had appeared with Charlie Chaplin."[223] Caputo was himself nicknamed Jackie, as we saw in chapter 4. So "when I found out that his name was Jackie," Caputo said on another occasion, "it was just this absolutely felicitous thing, like a grace. [. . .] He's a kind of very distant soul mate for me, and because of him, because of this other, I write in my own name."[224] "And," Caputo confessed to Cole, "one of my most bitter-sweet moments was when, shortly before his death, Jacques signed his last letter to me 'Jackie.'"[225]

Jackie. "Forget about Jacques the Seducer and try 'Reb Rida' or perhaps 'Rabbi Augustinus Judaeus.'"[226] Derrida, *the new Kierkegaard*.

* * *

It truly matters where one writes and when. Throughout his career, I want to suggest, Caputo wrote in two very different places. At first, he wrote in the enchanted forests, not unlike those of Heidegger.

> In Heidegger the tropes turn[ed] on home and homecoming [. . .] and mystery . . .[227]

This "world was enchanted, aglow and radiant, a world of magic, of insight and depth and beauty, inhabited by men who could regularly find God in a sunflower."[228] But it was not meant to last, not for Caputo.

He met up with Derrida, "a merciless demystifier," and "then things began to change and the forest, Schwarzwaldian and otherwise, began to get disenchanted."[229]

> . . . but in Derrida everything is different because everything is turned toward the immigrant, the exile, excluded, homeless, dispossessed, those deprived of fatherland and mother tongue, the disjointed and uprooted—in short, the prophetic.[230]

We have so many competing and incommensurable sacred names, Caputo argued in *Against Ethics*, that no one can agree. "But we see daily the faces of Evil, and we often know their names, the proper names of the victims of unholy forces. That is the only simulacrum of the sacred we have left, the one *mysterium tremendum* in this world where we have not only disenchanted the forest but deforested it too."[231] This, then, was the second place where Caputo wrote: the disenchanted deforested forest, that is, the desert.

At the turn of the millennium, Caputo regarded *Against Ethics* as his "most personal statement to date." For better or for worse, he said,

> *Against Ethics* is where I stand (or fail to stand), what has become of me, today. I have more and more been taken by the thought of the anonymous, of the impersonal horizon by which we are everywhere surrounded, by the ring of impersonality that closes in all around us. I wonder now if what I once called the divine, the dark night and bottomless abyss of the Godhead, is not simply the anonymity of a nameless night, a darkness pure and simple, rather the veil of a deeper, more divine dimension. I wonder if we do not all speak a lost language, a language that will have been lost when once the earth drops back into the sun and turns to ash. It is in this light, or lack of light, that I try to think through the experience of "obligation," as a light that burns gently in this nocturnal abyss, meekly protesting the endless and encompassing void.[232]

Where one writes and when.

10

Dancing in the Void

They think to enrich themselves by enlarging their vocabulary. And no doubt I might easily add a new word to mine; for instance, one that meant to me 'October sun,' as contrasted with the sun at other times. But I cannot see what I would gain by coining this new word. Quite otherwise, it seems to me that by doing so I would lose the expression of that interdependence linking up in my mind October, October's fruit and its cool winds, with that word 'sun,' which, having spent its force, no longer speeds the ripening. [. . .] On the other hand, I increase your powers if I train you in exercises which enable you, while always using the same range of words, to weave divers nets with them, apt to snare any kind of prey. As when you knot a cord, you may dispose your knots in such a way that it can serve for catching foxes, or else for setting your sails so that the wind is trapped in them. And the inflexions of my verbs, the interlockings of my clauses, the cadence of my periods, the placing of my complements, the echoes and recalls—these are figures of the dance that I would have you dance, and, when you have completed it, you will have conveyed to others what you set out to transmit, and grasped in your book what you set out to grasp. All awareness begins with the acquiring of a style . . .

—Antoine Saint-Exupéry, *The Wisdom of the Sands*

If I were forced to live in the exile, I think I would want to do it with style. I would want to have a volume of pure poetry with me, Saint-Exupéry's *Citadelle*, when stranded on a desert island.

This morning I, too, pruned my rose trees . . .

as well as that hilarious trilogy in five parts, *The Hitchhiker's Guide to the Galaxy* by Adams—to which we will return:

> "I think," said Ford in a tone of voice which Arthur by now recognized as one which presaged something utterly unintelligible, "that there's an SEP over there . . ."

To weep and to howl with laughter, to laugh through my tears. Far from home, in order not to go mad—"indeed 'tis often thus, by reason of men's memories, that you pray to God"[1]—I would wish to preserve the ability to dance, albeit dance in the void, which would probably be . . . mad. "Ah, but they have already heard all of this," a small, still voice says in my head. True. There is hardly anything new I shall offer in this chapter, except collecting breadcrumbs and looking at things from a slightly different angle. For there is still something I must say, even for my own sake, about Caputo's style.

In the final three chapters of *Radical Hermeneutics* Caputo found his own voice. "I tried to take a colder, more deconstructed look at things," he says, "to face up to the difficulty of life without the support of metaphysical foundations or of the consolations of religion."[2] By all means, this is an old story for us by now, as is laughing through one's tears, be it Kierkegaard's, Derrida's, or Caputo's. But do you not find it interesting that Caputo's "colder, more deconstructed look" somehow took the form of a significantly more creative, literary writing? Why is it that only when he left the enchanted world of his youth, after magic—"I do not think Derrida is just a new spell!"[3]—Caputo began to write in a way that he had never done before? That only then Caputo as a writer became—well, enchanting?

A couple of images come to mind, that of Saint-Ex after he crashed in the Sahara for the first time, for instance:

> Sitting on the dune, I laid out beside me my gun and my five cartridge clips. For the first time since I was born it seemed to me that my life was my own and that I was responsible for it. Bear in mind that only two nights before I had been dining in a restaurant in Toulouse . . .[4]

and that of living with the flies, as Breyten Breytenbach, himself a famous émigré, has put it:

> Then comes exile, the break, the destitution, the initiation, the maiming which—I think—gives access to a deeper sight, provides a path into consciousness through the imitation of thinking. Now you can never again entirely relax the belly muscles. You learn, if you're lucky, the chameleon art of adaptation, and how to modulate your laughter. You learn to use your lips properly. Henceforth you are at home nowhere, and by that token everywhere. You learn to live with

> the flies, and how to slide from death into dream. You learn about creation—because you must compensate—and thus transformation and metamorphosis, although you also come to realize that everything is since all time.[5]

So perhaps this is it. Away from home, responsibility for one's self becomes critical, leading to a deep awareness, and awareness comes with a style. Also, remember Nietzsche? How under a hundred swords of Damocles one learns to dance, attaining freedom of movement? And a slide from death into dream

> of a dance between Kierkegaard and Derrida, two great comic masters, and Meister Eckhart, a master of *Leben und Lesen* the tradition says—but I would add of *Lachen*, too, of life, the letter, and laughter, a certain mystical laughter . . .[6]

did Caputo really say mystical?—and then, finally, the most unexpected turn, as we also hear him say: "Kierkegaard of the aesthetic literature is the model for the way that I write—which is, again, another difference between me and Derrida."[7] Could it be that the disenchanted Caputo turned into an aesthete now?

One thing is certain: Caputo knows how to say "October sun" without the help of technobabble, or how to weave a net to catch "this foxy fellow Felix." Caputo's texts dance, but it is a dance above the abyss, a dance in the exile, for:

> We are all siblings of the same dark night, disturbed by the same demons, haunted by the same specters. That is our discomforting comfort, our disturbing consolation, the faith of an infidel. The work in which I am currently engaged is to develop a certain more sober, more post-mystical, deconstructionist notion of religion, which is a faith without doctrine, a God without Being, a community that cannot say "we." This is, to be sure, to come back to where I started, to take up the questions of my earlier years, albeit with the full realization that one can never go home again.[8]

Now, what kind of a literary dance is this? What genre or style? Demons, specters, and infidels—clearly Caputo does not abide by the strict rules of academic writing. What we hear is his peculiar mode of expression, a fact that has been pointed out in this book more often than I care to account for. But what does this mean? What exactly is Caputo's voice anyway? And, more to the point, would a literary-critical analysis of Caputo's texts help us understand what he is getting at?

Conversely, would our lack of sensitivity for Caputo's literary techniques mean that we have read him "less and less well" for over thirty years?

Cleo McNelly Kearns, for one, believes that "an informed awareness of rhetoric and diction, genre, tone, and narrative persona" is indeed important if we are to understand Caputo properly. She points to Nietzsche, who "long ago argued, the formation of literary taste, old fashioned as that enterprise may sound, does have a bearing on philosophy and may even have something to contribute to its discourse."[9] Hence, in her contribution to *A Passion for the Impossible*, really a *Festschrift* in honor of Caputo, she said:

> I want therefore to talk here about the poetics of Caputo's work, and to place it less in a philosophical than in a literary context. For Caputo has taken great pleasure in developing a unique literary persona and style in his writing, and in shaping to his own textual purposes a wide range of genres from parody to polemic, from irony to lyric, from pastiche to revelation, and the results are not only pleasurable but profitable to observe.[10]

And Caputo did not fail to appreciate Kearns's reading:

> I am deeply indebted indeed to Cleo McNelly Kearns for a particularly striking analysis. She says that her gloss on *Prayers and Tears* represents an "ancillary discourse rather than a direct engagement" because it is focused not on the logic or argument but rather the poetics of *Prayers and Tears*. If so, that raises an interesting point. It is as incisive and illuminating to me as any response to my texts that concentrates on the arguments and stays steadfastly with my point, my logic, my argument. When the philosophers and theologians who read *Prayers and Tears* or *Against Ethics* read past the poetics—the style, the tone, the irony—in order to get to the standpoint, I often find myself remonstrating with them about misconstruing my stand.[11]

Further proof that at least a rudimentary awareness of what Caputo is "doing"—the *what* or *how* of his voice—is, therefore, hardly necessary. I shall return to Kearns's literary analysis in the epilogue, where I try to shed light on *my own* voice. Here I would like to draw attention to Caputo's literary tactic, which Kearns does not discuss in detail, but which might have been as useful a "net for catching foxes" as it was a treacherous web in which Caputo himself got caught. I am talking here about Caputo's voice in the sense in which he himself understands it: "Derrida loosened my tongue, that is to say, he gave me the nerve to write like Kierkegaard."[12] Although this statement is often interpreted, not least by Caputo himself, as meaning "to write with humor like Kierkegaard," in reality it also meant that Caputo began to use a very Kierkegaardian strategy of pseudonyms. Now, this does not mean that Caputo would publish his works under a pen name, like Kierkegaard often did (and never got a tenure), but he did include texts by "pseudonymous authors" in *Against Ethics* and then again in *The Weakness of God*. This is something that Kierkegaard not only did as well—he made the ploy famous!

As is often the case, a brief exposition of how Kierkegaard and Caputo respectively introduced their strategies will tell us more than pages of scholarly explanation.

* * *

Kierkegaard begins (almost) his first major work *Either/Or*—itself allegedly written, or I should say edited, by a certain Victor Eremita—with the latter's account of how seven years ago he spotted in a secondhand shop a writing desk that immediately attracted his attention. "It was not a modern piece of work, had been used considerably, and yet it captivated me."[13] Eremita would pass by the shop every day and, although he "had no use for this piece of furniture," he eventually bought it.

> The writing desk was set up in my apartment, and just as in the first phase of my infatuation I had my pleasure in gazing at it from the street, so now I walked by it here at home. Gradually I learned to know its numerous features, its many drawers and compartments, and in every respect I was happy with my desk. But it was not to remain that way.[14]

"In the summer of 1836," Eremita explains, he was to "make a little journey to the country for a week." He was to meet with the coachman at five o'clock in the morning, but for whatever reason he overslept. Thus it happened that at six-thirty the "coachman was already blowing his horn" and Eremita was running around, getting dressed, and just as he came downstairs, he remembered that he may not have enough money in his pocketbook. So he ran upstairs again and, as he recalls: "I opened the desk to pull out the money drawer and take what happened to be at hand. But the drawer would not budge. Every expedient was futile. It was a most calamitous situation."[15] The story goes on:

> The blood rushed to my head; I was furious. Just as Xerxes had the sea whipped, so I decided to take dreadful revenge. A hatchet was

> fetched. I gave the desk a terrible blow with it. Whether in my rage I aimed wrong or the drawer was just as stubborn as I, the result was not what was intended. The drawer was shut, and the drawer stayed shut. But something else happened. Whether my blow struck precisely this spot or the vibration through the entire structure of the desk was the occasion, I do not know, but this I do know—a secret door that I had never noticed before sprung open. This door closed off a compartment that I obviously had not discovered. Here, to my great amazement, I found a mass of papers, the papers that constitute the contents of the present publication.[16]

"It takes a stroke of luck to make such discoveries," Eremita reflected, and as soon as he reached the countryside and found some spare time, he went out to the woods to have privacy and began to look through what he had found:

> A quick look at the discovered papers readily showed me that they formed two groups, with a marked external difference as well. The one was written on a kind of letter-vellum, in quarto, with a rather wide margin. The handwriting was legible, sometimes even a bit meticulous, in one place slovenly. The other was written on full sheets of beehive paper with ruled columns such as legal documents and the like are written on. The handwriting was distinct, somewhat drawn out, uniform and even; it seemed to be that of a businessman.[17]

But, as Eremita quickly noticed, the groups of documents in the pile seemed mismatched also regarding their content, and he thought it

> necessary to find a more concise expression to characterize the two authors. With that in mind, I have gone through the papers very carefully but have found nothing or practically nothing. As far as the first author, the esthete, is concerned, there is no information at all about him. As far as the other, the letter writer, is concerned, we learn that his name is William and that he has been a judge, but the court is not stipulated.[18]

We have, needless to say, already made the acquaintance of both the esthete and the judge William (aesthete and Wilhelm, in Caputo's spelling) and we should not forget about the seducer, for as Eremita informed his readers, "the last of A[esthete]'s papers [was] a narrative titled 'The Seducer's Diary.'"[19] This piece of text apparently caused the editor of *Either/Or* further difficulties, because in it A also did "not declare himself the author but only the editor."[20] But the dilemmas that Eremita faced with regard to the seducer apparently went beyond the questions of proper editing. He almost seemed to be haunted by him:

> It seemed to me as if the seducer himself paced my floor like a shadow, as if he glanced at the papers, as if he fixed his demonic eyes on me, and said, "Well, well, so you want to publish my papers! You know that is irresponsible of you; you will indeed arouse anxiety in the darling girls. But, of course, in recompense you will make me and my kind innocuous. There you are mistaken, for I merely change the method, and so my situation is all the more advantageous . . ."[21]

Be that as it may, Eremita ordered the papers as he saw fit, he gave them titles,[22] occasionally changed a comment in the margin into a footnote,[23] and after five years of waiting and trying in vain to trace down the authors, and after coming up with the title for the volume—one which indicated the admittedly unlikely possibility that these diverse texts, in fact, represented the views of the same person "who in his lifetime had experienced both movements or had reflected upon both movements"[24]—he decided to publish them.

* * *

Caputo also spoke of a stroke of luck in connection with what, in his case, was a deed of a secret benefactor rather than his own chancy discovery. "I had reached just this point in my work when I was visited by a remarkable piece of good luck," he wrote in chapter 7 of *Against Ethics.*[25] He recalls how he was searching in his "personal library," as well as in "all the best libraries in the area," when a "happy event" happened:

> I received in the mail, anonymously and wholly unsolicited, a parcel, for which I signed only with some suspicion. The package, thin and neatly wrapped in brown paper, contained several typescripts which bore a disproportionately long and very odd title:
>
> SEVERAL LYRICAL-PHILOSOPHICAL DISCOURSES ON VARIOUS JEWGREEK PARABLES AND PARADIGMS WITH CONSTANT REFERENCE TO OBLIGATION
>
> Johanna de Silentio, Editor[26]

I shall more or less pass over the shock this had caused to Caputo—"I cannot describe the effect upon me of seeing the name 'Johanna de Silentio' looking back at me from this page. The experience was utterly uncanny. It was as if I were seeing a ghost, as if someone had come back from the dead . . ."[27] For after the initial surprise wore off, Caputo also resolved to study the papers in greater detail:

> Upon further examination I discovered that there were eight typescripts in all, each of a modest length and neatly printed out. Each typescript bore an unusual title and an equally unusual signature—like "Felix Sineculpa" or "Magdalena de la Cruz,"[28]

and just like Eremita before him, Caputo also considered the possibility that these were perhaps all works of a single author:

> On one point, however, I confess failure: whether all of these authors are the same as the editor, Johanna de Silentio, or the same as one another but different from Johanna de Silentio, or whether each name is the name of a different author, as is *prima facie* suggested, I have to this day been unable to determine.[29]

"This little mailing proved to be a breakthrough that greatly facilitated my work,"[30] Caputo tells his readers, so he could not let the opportunity to use them pass. But the documents also needed some editing:

> The typescripts, as you might imagine, were wholly devoid of documentation, and so the principal obligation visited upon me by their arrival was, like a good editorial clerk, to supply them with a scholarly supplement. [. . .] So I passed many hours searching my library for the omitted references. I supplied the missing footnotes, and I added to each discourse a short commentary, all this with the aim of making these sometimes whimsical texts presentable to a sober philosophical public.[31]

A tedious job, no doubt about that, but Caputo did it in a growing conviction that he had, in fact, been "singled out by the authors as their anthologizer,"[32] although as for their true identity he remained as ignorant as Eremita: "These authors are quite unknown to me, I who do not know who I myself am."[33] "One would need to be a Dupin or a Persian detective."[34] But like Eremita before him, after doing everything that he, as an editor, considered necessary, Caputo eventually published the papers in his book.

* * *

Now, of particular interest to us is one more parallel between Eremita's and Caputo's accounts of their felicitous discoveries. For, among the documents that Caputo had received, there were also two written by someone whom we could think of as Eremita's seducer. He signed himself as Felix Sineculpa, and he seemed to haunt Caputo no less than his counterpart from *Either/Or*. I will have to skip over his "joyously innocent" parables; let me just say that they present a very Nietzschean vision of the world, of the simultaneously innocent and indifferent Universe in which "Auschwitz is not a fact but a perspective."[35] A universe in which

> the disaster is just another constellation of nature, one not to the liking of the victim. It is an event of certain forces whose stars are marked for oblivion and extinction. But the perishing of one star is a matter of cold indifference to the galaxies as a whole. What does it matter to the great cosmos if this little globe is overrun by death and disease? Is not the disease of one organism simply the life of something else, of the microorganism or the parasite, one that we do not like?[36]

"Then the universe draws still another breath"—where did we hear this?—"continuing its cosmic dance across endless skies, unmindful of what has transpired off in some remote corner. The laments of the lamb, never very audible to the cosmic ear, disappear without a trace."[37]

As I said, Caputo was deeply affected by Sineculpa's words. "This little treatise has caused me many a sleepless night and I do not wish to pause over its disturbing story any longer than I am obliged," Caputo wrote in the commentary, and continued:

> This man Felix formulates my worst fears, puts into words the midnight thoughts I do not permit myself to think. I would like to have avoided the responsibility of commenting on it at all, were that possible. It is a coldhearted account and this Felix fellow, this fearsome, menacing figure, is no one I wish to meet soon.[38]

Conceding that he had previously also subscribed to the more merciless version of Nietzsche's doctrine of will to power, after reading Felix, Caputo was not so sure—"I am having my doubts about that now."[39] But as much as he might have hated to admit it, Caputo understood that "Felix—the joyful one—is a poet of a dangerous wisdom, the wisdom that, for the forces, there is no Evil,"[40] and that this

> cold wisdom of Felix, his tragic knowledge, hovers constantly in the background of the other discourses, disturbing not only my sleep but the sleep of the other authors as well, of that I am sure (if I can be sure of anything about these authors about whom I know nothing). That no doubt is why it has been placed first—whether by the editor

> Johanna de Silentio or by some hidden hand serving as an anonymous editor. The spectre of Felix's *fröhliche Wissenschaft* haunts the other authors and gives them no rest.[41]

As a matter of fact, the editor of the papers that Caputo received by mail put the second text by Sineculpa at the end of the pile. Observing this, Caputo concluded that "as their first and last voice, the terrifying laughter of Felix can always be heard in the background of the other discourses, disturbing their moving tributes to obligation."[42] The intent of the mysterious editor, Caputo believed, was to

> make the merciless standpoint of Felix the frame within which the lyrical-philosophical discourses on obligation are set. The voice of Felix is their setting, indeed I would say the spectre by which the other authors are continuously menaced. Felix haunts the other authors like a ghost. That is the best word. He haunts them and makes their words tremble. His cold vision is the fear and the trembling they confront. He robs their poetics of its power, breaks its hold on them and us. This fear and trembling is even more ominous than that of Abraham.[43]

Thus, Caputo wrote in his commentary on Sineculpa's second piece, the "radical honesty of Felix"[44] is a "dose of cold truthfulness,"[45] one that turns obligation into

> a perspective, a point of view that stands or falls on its own. The poetics of obligation is a function of a *hermeneia* of a radical sort, a grappling with an abyss, a kind of wrestling with shadows, in which it is resolved that suffering matters, but it does not arise from a deliverance from on high. Nothing comes from on high. We have no access to something Infinite, Categorical, Good, or Evil. We are divested of all categorical assurances, of all transcendent deep grounds that invite capitalization. We live our lives in the lowercase.[46]

* * *

It is easy to see, I think, how by these words Caputo brought upon himself the criticism of other religious philosophers of religion (yes, the duplicity is intended). I shall briefly mention here two of them, James K. A. Smith and Merold Westphal.

At the end of his contribution to *Religion With/out Religion: The Prayers and Tears of John D. Caputo*, Smith argued that Caputo should, on his own terms, "revise a distinction that has run through his work from *Radical Hermeneutics* to the present," namely, "his distinction between what he describes as the (Kierkegaardian) 'religious' and (Nietzschean) 'tragic' responses to suffering."[47] Such, at least, would be the requirement of the undecidability between the two that Caputo had himself professed. "But it seems," continued Smith while referring to *Radical Hermeneutics*, that

> ironically, Caputo privileges the Nietzschean by describing the religious response as a "construal," a hermeneusis based on faith which "has looked down the dark well of suffering and found there a loving power which takes the side of suffering."[48]

Indeed, in the same book and chapter, to which Smith pointed, Caputo also explains that by the "'eyes of faith,' we do not mean that a special light shines on the believer which is withheld from the rest of us but rather that the believer has a certain facility to construe the darkness, to grope in the dark."[49] Faith, it would seem, only comes second after the dark. The laughter of Felix is heard everywhere.

Another instance that Smith pointed out in support of his critique did, in fact, appear in *Against Ethics*:

> Faith is a matter of a radical hermeneutic, an art of construing shadows, in the midst of what is happening. Faith is neither magic nor an infused knowledge that lifts one above the flux or above the limits of mortality. Faith, on my view, is above all the *hermeneia* that Someone looks back at us from the abyss, that the spell of anonymity is broken by a Someone who stands with those who suffer, which is why the Exodus and the Crucifixion are central religious symbols. Faith, does not, however, extinguish the abyss but constitutes a certain reading of the abyss, a hermeneutics of the abyss.[50]

So for Caputo "faith is only a construal which is enveloped and haunted by undecidability," concludes Smith, and "Abraham is haunted by Zarathustra's laughter. The construal of the religious response is simply a faithful way to cope with the cold reality of the flux by construing it as something warm."[51] But what happened to the undecidability, wonders Smith: "Is not his characterization of the flux as 'cold' already a privileging of Nietzsche?"[52] And again, "though Abraham certainly hears the echo of Zarathustra's laughter, I wonder if Zarathustra ever lies awake at night wondering if Abraham is right."[53] Smith's critique of Caputo, in other words, boils down to the latter's apparent decision "to put the burden of proof upon the religious response, which must answer to Nietzsche."[54]

A couple of years later Merold Westphal voiced similar concerns regarding Caputo's privileging of the tragic view, only in a more severe manner, I would say. This was his contribution to *A Passion for the Impossible*, the same volume Kearns published in, and Westphal made his point quite bluntly. Highlighting Caputo's stance on obligations, as expressed in *Against Ethics*, "obligation does not mean answering the call of Being, or of the History of Being, or of the History of Spirit, or the Voice of God,"[55] or "obligations are strictly local events, sublunary affairs, between us. They are matters of flesh and blood, without cosmic import or support."[56] Westphal could not help but wonder:

> How does he know all this?
>
> There are times when he remembers that he doesn't (e.g., AE, pp. 28, 31, 33, 85) and adopts an agnostic stance. Far more frequent throughout the text are passages with a decidedly dogmatic metaphysical ring to them like those just cited, serenely confident, epistemologically speaking, that Nietzsche was right (in a rather non-Nietzschean sense of "right"). If we ask the real Caputo to stand up, however, I believe we get neither a dogmatist nor a skeptic but a believer. A Nietzschean believer, to be sure, not a Kierkegaardian believer. Kierkegaard acknowledges that we have no Knowledge that would settle the ultimate questions; faith occurs in the context of objective uncertainty. But when it comes to the question whether "the cosmos yawns" in response to our moral outrage or "has [a] heart on which to record our complaint," he believes the latter just as clearly as Nietzsche believes the former. Caputo sides with Nietzsche.[57]

We shall recall how in one of the previous chapters Caputo confessed that, as far as he was concerned, Kierkegaard had disappointed him; to say the least, on the point of the possibility of the tragic, indifferent Universe, Nietzsche has silenced de Silentio. According to Westphal, Caputo does not "seem to be allergic to 'any overarching principle' as such," but "what Caputo is allergic to, in his Nietzschean mode, is any claim that the ultimate cosmic power is good."[58]

It would be equally easy to show how the last remark cannot possibly apply to Caputo's later, theological view of the Universe infused with the weak power of the call and, especially, the promise resounding from the first chapters of Genesis; in Caputo's words: "Good, good, good, good, good—very good. Yes, I said, yes, yes. That's the word. That's the world."[59] But at the time when either of the aforementioned critical appraisals were published, there was yet no *Weakness of God* and in any case Caputo felt that he had to defend himself against what, in his eyes, was a misunderstanding. Smith and Westphal, though friends, misinterpreted him because they failed to appreciate Felix Sineculpa as a dramatic persona with whose views Caputo had nothing to do at all. After all, he had only published what he had found in his mailbox. A literary mishap, therefore, a net to catch foxes ensnaring the careless hunter.

There was a precedent, to be sure. Kierkegaard had also got himself into a lot of trouble by his, for some incomprehensible, penchant for pseudonyms. Many were utterly baffled. In a historical introduction to *Either/Or*, the editors (Howard and Edna Hong) recalled how "on the flyleaf of a copy of *Either/Or*, I, Kierkegaard wrote: 'Some think that *Either/Or* is a collection of loose papers I had lying in my desk. Bravo!—As a matter of fact, it was the reverse.'"[60] Years later, at the end of his *Concluding Unscientific Postscript to the Philosophical Crumbs*, Kierkegaard made things clear:

> As a matter of form, and for the sake of order, I hereby acknowledge, what it can hardly be of real interest to anyone to know, that I am, as people say, the author of *Either/Or* (Victor Eremita), Copenhagen, February 1843 . . .[61]

That said, Kierkegaard also felt that the precise character of his authorship needed to be further qualified. "What is written is indeed therefore mine," he wrote,

> but only so far as I have put the life-view of the creating, poetically actualized individuality into his mouth in audible lines, for my relation is even more remote than that of a poet, who *creates* characters and yet in the preface is *himself* the *author*. For I am impersonally, or personally, in the second person, a *souffleur* who has poetically produced the authors, whose *prefaces* in turn are their production, yes, as are their *names*. So in the pseudonymous books there is not a single word by myself. I have no opinion about them except as third party, no knowledge of their meaning except as reader, not the remotest private relation to them, that being impossible in a doubly reflected communication.[62]

Caputo, in his 2007 monograph *How to Read Kierkegaard*, pays close attention to the preceding passage. As he says, the few pages containing this passage (written in Kierkegaard's own name) "became the source of endless debates in the literature."[63] For Kierkegaard also wrote, he "wished and prayed," that "if it should occur to anyone to want to quote a particular remark from the books, he will do me the favour of citing the name of the respective pseudonymous author, not my own"[64]—a wish that went largely ignored by his readers. In fact, according to Caputo,

> Kierkegaard's fame rests on the fact that his most famous readers, like Heidegger, simply ignored his wishes. The closest Heidegger came to honouring Kierkegaard's request was in not citing Kierkegaard at all. His *Being and Time* (1927), arguably the single most important work of continental European philosophy written in the twentieth century, rests on a shameless 'ransacking' (Poole) or appropriation of the main insights of the pseudonyms, with a few parsimonious footnotes that largely brush off Kierkegaard as a minor player.[65]

Lest we forget about the great divorce between Heidegger and Caputo discussed in the previous chapter. Nevertheless, Caputo criticized on this point—not plagiarism but refusal to take Kierkegaard's wishes seriously—also Albert Camus and Jean-Paul Sartre and, not least of all, also theologians like Karl Barth. "It mattered not a whit to Heidegger, Camus or Sartre that the breakthrough category of 'existence' was made in the name of the pseudonym Climacus, who protested that he is not 'a devil of a fellow in philosophy' out to 'create a new trend.'"[66] As for the theologians, what mattered to them, according to Caputo, "was the very Christian faith that the philosophers had so massively and adroitly neutralized in these books."[67] Thus

> readers of Kierkegaard face an 'Either/Or': Either Kierkegaard the theologian or Kierkegaard the philosopher. Either way, it seems, Kierkegaard would regret it. For either way, one is ignoring Kierkegaard's request to leave him out of the picture.[68]

If, on the other hand, Caputo regretted anything, it was that he, too, became associated with Felix Sineculpa—essentially only a literary persona. "Westphal mistakes the *status* I assign to Nietzsche and to his poetic stand-in, Felix Sineculpa, who is a *dramatis persona* for Zarathustra, who is in turn a *dramatis persona* for Nietzsche (I suppose),"[69] Caputo said in response to the previous criticism:

> So when Merold Westphal decides that I *prefer* Nietzsche to Kierkegaard, that though I mostly hold an agnostic position, I occasionally let my Nietzschean *belief* slip out, which means I prefer the innocence of becoming to the me *me voici* of Abraham, he has, I think, been beguiled by this foxy fellow Felix.[70]

Whence, by the way, my hitherto cryptic references to foxes. At any rate, Caputo says it explicitly that for him "the very appearance of 'Felix' (and the other pseudonyms) is a Kierkegaardian ploy,"[71] and that he, like Kierkegaard with his personae, has "not the least first-person relation to Felix; I am no more identified with him than Shakespeare is with Richard III."[72]

Answering to the concerns raised by Smith proved a bit more difficult. This was mainly because Smith had based his critique also on *Radical Hermeneutics*, where there was no mention either of Felix, or of any other pseudonymous author. Hence, Caputo concedes:

> For this question I am very grateful, and I must respond yes, yes. To the extent to which my formulations have exposed themselves to this objection, to the extent to which I have drifted in that direction, this distinction needs reworking. For on the terms of any genuinely radical hermeneutic, everything is an interpretation, and it is always a question of knowing how to sort among the better and the worse interpretations. Both the tragic and the religious are opposing faiths, opposing evangelical words, of which Augustine and Nietzsche are the bearers or the apostles.[73]

When questioned by Keith Putt on the same matter, he repeats that when he had spoken in such a way as to privilege Nietzsche's view of things, it was a mistake:[74]

> Putt: You know that some of your critics, in reading the last section of *Radical Hermeneutics* and especially the last chapter of *Against Ethics*, accuse you of just that, of privileging the abyss.
>
> Caputo: I think to some extent I may have. That has been pointed out to me and I think that it was a mistake on my part. All I want to say is that there is something irreducible about that view, and that interpretation is always made in the face of it. So if we have an interpretation of life as religious, or ethical, or whatever interpretation we may have, it must always be "haunted" by this more disturbing perspective. I have sometimes portrayed this perspective as not an interpretation at all, but as simply there, an uninterpreted fact of the matter, a kind of raw fact, whereas—the objection goes—it too is another interpretation. Now I think that is a valid criticism of *Radical Hermeneutics* and *Against Ethics*.[75]

Putt, a kind reader of Caputo as he has always been, threw Caputo a line, asking whether "the Kierkegaardian character of *Against Ethics* mitigates that criticism a bit"—to which, of course, Caputo responded in the affirmative, admitting that he had never seen that he was getting himself into trouble until his critics pointed it out.[76] And that he never meant to say "that Felix has the first and last word, that his word is final, but that his word is irreducible and a permanent specter."[77]

* * *

I also believe that the Kierkegaardian character of Caputo's works—whether those discussed presently, or any other since Caputo has started using his own voice—needs to be taken into account, lest we risk misunderstanding Caputo's intentions. For my part, I would be scared to dream about writing fiction if I were to be associated with every character that I create. Thus I confirm what I suggested in the beginning of this chapter: Sensitivity to the literary forms is, indeed, indispensable, even if texts under consideration are works of philosophy.

But nothing is ever simple (just as clichés, like this one, are not *ipso facto* devoid of truth). Prescinding from the issue of our inherently short memory (as discussed in chapters 8 and 10)—if Felix did not have the first and last word, he certainly was the first and last voice—certain difficulty, or better ambiguity, remains even regarding how to read the pseudonymous texts. Caputo knows this. He, for example, thinks that Roger Poole, in his *Kierkegaard's Indirect Communication*, goes too far when he suggests that nothing said by the pseudonyms should be taken to be Kierkegaard's own view.[78]

> As Joel Rasmussen recently pointed out, Kierkegaard said that he took no position on what the pseudonyms were saying 'except as a reader' but there is nothing to prevent a reader from agreeing with what he reads. Any fair-minded reading of the whole corpus, of the journals and the books signed in his own name, indicates that Kierkegaard held many of the views expressed by the pseudonyms, some of which are to be found verbatim in his journals.[79]

In Caputo's case a similar point can be made, not least because he *did* sign his books in his own name; because, as Smith pointed out, the views expressed by Felix Sineculpa resonated elsewhere in Caputo's works; and finally also, and especially, because the views for which Caputo was criticized were, in fact, the views contained in *his* commentaries on Felix.

* * *

I would say "beyond" these technicalities, except that what I really mean is precisely "because" of them, my final point is in a way similar to what Caputo said about Kierkegaard—"Of course, in some ways his pseudonymity was an ill-conceived strategy which drew more attention to him personally by stirring up a controversy that would otherwise not have taken place"[80]—only perhaps a bit more general.

The desert king could not see what could be gained by coining a new word where 'October sun' radiated with the power that carried with itself, all at once, the fragrance of ripe fruit, the chill of winds, and the sun that would no longer warm you up. I, too, love the literary ways of expression, which is why the king gets so much space in this work. Much can be gained by *not* coining new words—or in our case *new styles*, new technical language of our philosophy or theology. "Kierkegaard invented a new philosophical discourse," Caputo says, "one that he himself treated with ironic distance and unmistakable humour by feeding his best lines to humourists."[81] That, I believe, was not really an invention, only a very important rediscovery. I need not repeat that on the matter of style I am on Kierkegaard's and Caputo's side. But neither should I forget, we should not forget, that they also both got themselves in trouble.

That is one thing the desert king is silent about, that not gaining anything is not the same as not losing anything. Sometimes experience brought about by text may exist at the cost of clarity, maybe sometimes the best thing is to coin a new word, or to be academically proper, or simply not to be too crazy. So I keep coming back to this: What do we gain and what do we thereby lose?

11
The Advent of Weak Theology

I confess I have a weakness for theology.

Against the sound advice of my attorneys, my investment counselors, and my confessor, and after holding out for as long as possible against my inner *daimon*, I have finally succumbed to the siren call of this name. I do not know how to avoid speaking of theology. So be it. I am prepared to face the consequences. *Hier stehe ich.*

Whatever may be the fortunes of the word *theology* at present, and even if I have tended in the past to avoid it, I cannot deny that what I am doing here is theological. Almost. The word *theology* has always been for me a double bind, a promise of my youth that I could never quite make, yet never quite break. I have never been able to resist theology even as I have never had the immodesty to presume that I could get as far as theology. I have tended to defer the flow of this desire and send it rushing down other channels, letting it sail under foreign flags. I am wounded by theology, unhinged and uprooted by the blow it has delivered to my heart. Theology is my weakness, the way one has a weakness for sex or money, what I secretly desire, or maybe not so secretly, even as it desires everything of me. Still, with all due deference, like Johannes Climacus speaking of being a Christian, I would say that on my best days I am working at becoming theological.

—John D. Caputo, *The Weakness of God*

So this is it. Here we are, at the end of the odyssey. "Caputo comes out of the closet as a theologian in this work," wrote Catherine Keller in her blurb for *The Weakness of God*. Her felicitous figure of speech caught on among Caputo's readers; it even took on a life of its own. Thus, for example, Christopher Ben Simpson in his *Religion, Metaphysics, and the Postmodern: William Desmond and John D. Caputo* suggested: "Desmond might need to 'come out of the closet' as a theologian as well—to be able to give a more robust accounting [. . .] of the indeed necessary relation between, not only philosophy and religion, but philosophy and theology."[1] Caputo did exactly that, and apparently himself also liked the "closet" metaphor:

> [I]n *The Weakness of God*, I decided to cave in—or to come out of the closet. I decided maybe I could get away with calling myself a theologian if I put it not in the form of an audacious claim but in the form of a confession.[2]

This "coming out" had not been entirely painless (is it ever?). Two years before *The Weakness of God*, Caputo left Villanova University, where he had taught for thirty-six years, and took a position at Syracuse University. Shortly after that Emmet Cole talked to him, and he had the audacity to suggest that Caputo is, "of course, well-known as a theologian . . ."[3] Don't do that! Don't commit the faux pas of breaking it to the terrified fellow that the chiffonier is gone. "But he hasn't got anything on. The Emperor is naked!" How embarrassing. Okay, now I am laying it on thick. Still and all, Cole took his words back: "Apologies. Although you are unknown as a theologian . . ."[4] And because this was a friendly discussion—after all, Cole addressed Caputo as "John Jack"—Caputo took no umbrage, he was only being cautious:

> . . . let us say a philosophical theologian, or a philosopher of religion. I was trained in philosophy and spent my whole life in the philosophy department at Villanova University. I confess that I have recently gotten religion, that is, I have moved to the religion department at Syracuse University, where I have been given the opportunity to spend the last phase of my teaching career peddling my wares among people who actually know a thing or two about religion. It is like a philosopher of science who moves to a physics department. When I speak about religion there I feel like a fellow in one of those old cowboy movies who raises his hat on a stick to see if someone is going to shoot at it. [. . .] given enough precautions, we could say that this is indeed just what it is. I have a new book entitled *The Weakness of God* that will be out sometime in 2005. This will be my most theological statement, philosophical-theological, that is, and here I speak of something I call a "sacred anarchy."[5]

As it happened, the book came out only in April 2006. In the meantime, Caputo began to appreciate his precarious position at Syracuse: "It's a good thing I retired from Villanova just as I was getting so heretical!"[6] But this is all history. For with Caputo, a theologian out of the closet, we are at the close. No more Either/Or: either Caputo the theologian or Caputo the philosopher. *Hier stehe ich*, Caputo said, as did

Martin Luther at the Diet of Worms. *Ich kann nicht anders.* Here stand I. I can do no other.

And so it is *hier*, at the end of the journey, that I shall also *stand* aside. We are at the close.

Appraisals were written, accolades rained down. The AAR honored *The Weakness of God* with its 2007 Award for Excellence in Religion: Constructive-Reflective Studies. "After over four decades of reinvigorating English language Continental philosophy of religion, John D. Caputo has boldly offered a volume in constructive theology," wrote Peter Goodwin Heltzel in his review. "In many post-structural circles 'God' has come on hard times, but Caputo sets out in this massive volume to save the name of God from its cultured despisers."[8] Heltzel also predicted that the book would spark off many interesting discussions.

> Caputo's "God without Sovereignty" will find sympathy among a growing group of theologians in a number of different pockets, including the "suffering God" theologians (e.g., Jürgen Moltmann), analytic philosophers doing kenotic theology (e.g., C. Stephens Evans), non-dogmatic theologians (e.g., Jeffrey W. Robbins), and evangelical open theists (e.g., Clark Pinnock); however, his constructive doctrine of God will meet resistance in other quarters. Fundamentalist and neo-evangelicals will be disconcerted by his call for "radical uncertainty"; Eastern Orthodox will be appalled by his rejection of Byzantine metaphysics; the Radical Orthodox will see weakness as another expression of postmodern nihilism; and the Holy See, symbolized in Caputo's texts by the ubiquitous Inquisitor, will see Caputo's rejection of arche as a rejection of the authority of the church. However, these critical responses are sure to engender a set of important theological debates, exactly where they should center—on the doctrine of God.[8]

Aside from the closet quip, Keller said Caputo's book was "irrepressible." While Caputo's view of God as a weak force "flies in the face of orthodox theology," she argued, "it also poses a provocative version of theology in a radical and postmodern mode."[10]

Incidentally, Keller had been implicated in Caputo's feat. "I am in a special way, however, following the lead taken in theologian Catherine Keller's *Face of the Deep*," he wrote in the chapter entitled "The Beautiful Risk of Creation." "I am engaging in a kind of partnership with her groundbreaking work on a new theology of creation, with which, as will become plain, the present chapter is very much a creative dialogue."[10]

Keith Putt, for his part, thought *The Weakness of God* might make some people cringe:

> Those who practice the "axiomatics of indignation" against any expression of post-modernism, deconstruction, or radical hermeneutics may well scoff at the claim that Caputo's theology of the event should be considered an authentic exercise in both doxology and doctrine. After all, are the above approaches not merely aliases for conventional relativism—no objective knowledge, no discernible linguistic meaning, no critical criteria for truth? Is Derrida not a self-avowed atheist who insists that language has seceded from any union with reality, leaving meaning at the manipulative mercy of a plurality of coequal interpretations? If all of this is so, then any attempt to talk about God or to interpret the Hebrew and Christian scriptures under such influences must be either droll academic futility at best or malignant profanation of the sacred at worst. Undoubtedly, the grand inquisitors of orthodoxy find it incredulous that Caputo should be taken seriously when he writes about God, or Christ, or the Spirit, or the Church . . .[11]

Putt, for that matter, had himself a couple of suggestions for improvement. Nevertheless, he insisted that

> anyone who would exercise a willful suspension of disbelief and actually read *The Weakness of God* must affirm that Caputo is not skipping playfully around vandalizing the Bible, ripping its texts to shreds; on the contrary, he writes on his knees, praying for wisdom, listening for the comforting and convicting call of what he loves most, that Other who may well be named God, or Christ, or Love, while simultaneously remaining unnamable.[12]

"And actually read" Caputo . . . Once upon a time Caputo, said he hoped that "the defenders of the Good and the True, those who have appointed themselves to make the world safe from deconstruction," would "find other means to display their love of virtue" and "leave the interpretation of Derrida's texts to those who actually read them."[13] All was well, out of the closet, when one had such readers.

Listening to the last sentence, it strikes me how sarcastic it sounds. It is not meant like that. I could, of course, change it or remove it altogether, but the "all is well" part reminds me that I want to draw this story to a close, as in "they lived happily ever after . . ."

But we have just begun. Am I seriously going to cut off just when the weak theology proper finally arrived? Well, yes and no.

Yes, I do intend to conclude. As I am sure any author will understand, there comes a point where you must end the work or else it will end you. Besides, as Margaret Atwood said:

> So much for endings. Beginnings are always more fun. True connoisseurs, however, are known to favor the stretch in between, since it's the hardest to do anything with. That's about all that can be said for plots, which anyway are just one thing after another, a what and a what and a what.[14]

But then there is also no. No, we have not just begun. Weak theology has not just arrived. On this point Putt remarked that

> faithful readers of Caputo have known for years that most of his works betray a genuine sensitivity to the religious and the theological to the extent that, if his theological identity has been in a closet, the door has always remained open.[15]

Once upon a time, Caputo said that "deconstruction, no less than Derrida, did not drop from the sky, and it cannot lift itself like an *aigle* on Hegelian wings above historical particularities. Derrida has brought his Jewish prayer shawl out of the closet."[16] So it was with Caputo's theology, and we have been through the plot. The plot, remember, was my main point. Finally, I shall also throw this quote into the bargain:

> Up to now, it has been mostly out of modesty that I myself declined the compliment of being called a theologian, the way Johannes Climacus declined to be called a Christian. I feel like I've never gotten as far as theology, I've never had the nerve to say that what I do is theology.[17]

In other words, Caputo's reluctance to call himself a theologian did not mean that what he did was not theological, or at least that it had no implications for theology.

Nevertheless, I too must come clean now. My main reason for quitting at this point is precisely the opposite, namely, that the story is *not* over (and I am perhaps guilty of dancing too much). Although Caputo retired in 2011, he continues to publish and so the adventure of weak theology continues. Frankly, I would rather have this book out before Caputo's *The Insistence of God: A Theology of Perhaps* appears. At the time being, the Indiana University Press website reads:

> *The Insistence of God* presents the provocative idea that God does not exist, God insists, while God's existence is a human responsibility, which may or may not happen. For John D. Caputo, God's existence is haunted by "perhaps," which does not signify indecisiveness

> but an openness to risk, to the unforeseeable. Perhaps constitutes a theology of what is to come and what we cannot see coming. Responding to current critics of continental philosophy, Caputo explores the materiality of perhaps and the promise of the world. He shows how perhaps can become a new theology of the gaps God opens.[18]

The additional workload is not my point here. Rather, I close because in an important sense weak theology is still to come, hence its "advent" in the title of this chapter. *Hier stehe ich. Ich kann nicht anders*—it was not in *The Weakness of God* that Caputo first spoke these words. When, for example, in 2001 James Olthuis talked about "a creational matrix already primed toward the good,"[19] Caputo replied:

> But I think my dear friend Jim Olthuis wants to stack the deck in favor of the good, to make of *khora/différance* something justice-friendly [. . .] like a madly benevolent casino operator who has loaded all the dice and stacked all the decks in favor of the customers! *Haec dies!* If he wants us to take the test of *khora*, he also wants to rig the results. [. . .] He wants me and Derrida to renounce *khora* and all her (non)works. But alas, *hier stehe ich, ich kann nicht anders.*[20]

Now, Caputo may disagree, but I still think that his "Good, good, good, good, good—very good. Yes, I said, yes, yes. That's the word. That's the world"[21] could, in fact, be interpreted as confirming Olthuis's point. As a matter of fact, I am sure he would disagree. But even that is largely irrelevant. What *is* relevant at this point is the fact that, as we heard Putt say before, Caputo's "life and thought are not exempt from existential motility."[22] That is to say, Caputo can, for example in order to achieve greater dramatic effect, repeat *Hier stehe ich. Ich kann nicht anders*—but ultimately, and with all due respect, it will amount to nothing more than a certain "Luther's fallacy."

Save for the dedication, the first words of *The Weakness of God* were the last words of Derrida:

> My friends, I thank you for coming. I thank you for the good fortune of your friendship. Do not cry: smile as I would smile at you. I bless you. I love you. I am smiling at you, wherever I am.[23]

As we were looking ahead toward the advent of weak theology, Caputo turned us around toward what had already come to pass. It must be always so, this is the repetition forward. This is the salutary invocation of ghosts.

In, as far as I know, the most recent published interview to date—if I may thus trick myself into *actually* coming to an end—entitled "Education as Event: A Conversation with John D. Caputo," the interviewer, T. Wilson Dickinson, brings up the ghost of young Brother Paul. How did the formation in the novitiate of the Brothers of the Christian Schools influence Caputo's work? "Now you have exposed my allergy to the word 'formation' and why I prefer to speak of 'transformability' to signify an alternate order of practices,"[24] Caputo answers, and he continues:

> My novitiate life was, if I may say so, a very "formative" experience for me, quite literally, especially since we were still steeped in the culture of the pre-Vatican II church. What will interest you to learn is that, in a religious order, the time spent preparing for entering the active ministry is called "formation" and the novitiate is called a "house of formation." And they mean it! We might think of this as a Nietzschean camel stage or alternately, as you indicate, a very Foucauldian space and time. [. . .] This is quite like a military boot camp, as your reference to Foucault on the "barracks" indicates, and it works best with eighteen year olds. [. . .] Of course, the idea, the "form," is the *imitatio Christi*. They want to engender someone Christ-like, not produce a robot but it is a massive disciplinary operation, which reaches down into the bones, "forming" "habits" that last a lifetime.[25]

An utterly unappealing conception, in other words. Nevertheless, although Caputo says he "shed no tears over abandoning the old disciplinary system and its ascetic ideal,"[26] we now also hear him saying something new:

> [T]he loss of these orders will mean the loss of the religious passion that drives the members of these orders to run schools and shelters and clinics in neighborhoods from which the rest of us keep a safe distance. It is these people above all else who serve *ta me onta*. That is also where celibacy (voluntary not mandatory!) has a role to play.[27]

To me, this is indeed a repetition forward. A restatement of *Hier stehe ich*. As is Caputo's confession—"I once was sure I had a religious vocation in the strict or narrow sense"[28]—followed by:

> But I have come to see that I had, that we all have, or should have, a religious vocation in the terms that I have been discussing, which means being visited by the grace of the event, in any of several orders . . .[29]

I read on as Caputo pointed out, me suspecting nothing, that there is a

> conflict between our vocation, our religious vocation, and the disciplinary system, the distribution of micro-power across the bodies who make up the university, the administered society of the university. On the one hand, I am writing from my heart, writing something because my life is at stake, because I am confounded by the mysteries of my existence, and on the other hand, I need another publication for tenure. I am doing both of these things at the same time. Is that possible? It seems not. I am not sure.[30]

I thought, this must have been how Caputo felt when his *Against Ethics* appeared at the same time as Derrida's *Donner la mort*. I also thought I was seeing a ghost. All that I have written in this work about the style, about the way I wish to write, and why—all of this had been written long before Caputo gave this interview. "Do you think there is a desire for bodies without flesh that is often operative in academic writing," Dickinson asks further, as if I was not already haunted enough, "which demands complete authorial control, and pursues the ideal of clarity (of making the fleshy matter of our language transparent for the sake of communicating meaning)?"[31] And again, Caputo repeats his old story about how he found his voice, he expands on it, but there is also a repetition forward. He still thinks that it is "dangerous, especially for young professors, to assume a position of non-knowing,"[32] but now he also wonders:

> Am I to be "accused" for what sometimes sounds like preaching—or congratulated? Should I, like Kierkegaard separate works of edification from the other works? I write in such a way that the objective and the edifying are mutually contaminated by the other. Each has its own danger, but I think that it is the one without the other that is most dangerous.[33]

I am presently thinking about the last words of the previous chapter. Yet, nothing of this should make me feel proud, only profoundly grateful, and very, very finite. *I* am, *this work* is, at the close. While the adventure of weak theology continues.

How could it be otherwise? At the heart of every adventure, there is an *advent*. That also means a promise, like the promise of Caputo's youth that he "could never quite make, yet never quite break" at the heart of *The Weakness of God*. Now, to the extent that a theology of event is itself a carrier of an event, it is unforeseeable, and it is precisely for that reason that for me the story ends here. I am, in other words, practicing here a version of *Gelassenheit*, letting the story be, as in opening myself for surprise. But not without a certain horizon of expectations. Personally, I shall be watching the developments in Caputo's thinking related to science and technology closely. This is an area of interest that I seem to share with Caputo, though I could not have known this when I first started reading him years ago. That is just one more reason for gratitude. I cannot go into this, not now. Nor can I leave without a teaser:

> The current transformations taking place in info-technology are deeply confounding. What we can be sure of is that everything we think about birth and death, about sickness and health, about materiality and carnality, sexuality and gender, will be affected, and maybe even totally transformed or even "overcome." We are approaching a technological "event" which, interestingly, has been dubbed the "singularity," using a word (inadvertently of course) that has a special prestige in continental philosophy, to describe a radical technological transformation that will render debates like the current one between *zoé* and *bios* obsolete and parochial. Here would be the ultimate body without flesh, pure deathless agents, achieved not by the "resurrection of the body" but by information technology; theology, angelology is realized by technology. But is this truly an "event?"[34]

* * *

Caputo's life and thought are not exempt from existential motility. Nor is weak theology in any way a finished or fixed project. *Hier stehe ich. Ich kann nicht anders. Gott helfe mir. Amen.*

And also: *Maranatha*!

12
Kingdom (In Place of a Conclusion)

> Loneliness is bred of a mind that has grown earthbound. For the spirit has its homeland, which is the realm of the meaning of things. Thus is it with the temple, when it bespeaks the meaning of the stones. Only in this boundless empyrean can the mind take wing. Not in things-in-themselves does it rejoice, but only in the visage which it reads behind them and which binds them into oneness. Grant me but this, O Lord: that I may learn to read.
>
> —Antoine de Saint-Exupéry, *The Wisdom of the Sands*

To the extent that Caputo's theology of the event is an ongoing project, offering a *conclusive* evaluation of its merits at this point would be somewhat untimely. There is still a lot to hope for and hopefully there is still a lot to come. Indeed, as the adventure continues, we could even say that weak theology is up to a point like the kingdom of God: already here but not quite yet. It exists—Caputo would probably say *insists*—stretched between its own past and future.

Now, as for the future of weak theology, it is not only open-ended but also uncertain, subject to the same kind of undecidability as ultimately any human endeavor. Throughout this book I pointed out that Caputo's theology of the event has itself an eventful character, because it harbors an event of which it is only one particular incarnation. There also lies the reason for its contingency, for as Caputo himself wrote:

> There are no guarantees about the course that events follow. An event is not an inner essence, like a Hegelian *Wesen*, the essential being of a thing that is unfolding more or less inevitably in time, but it is the endless possibilities of linking of which the name is capable. Events set off a chain or series of substitutions, not a process of essentialization or essential unfolding. Accordingly, an event can result in a disintegrating destabilization and a diminished

> recontextualization just as well as it can create an opening to the future. Nothing guarantees the success of the event. Its links are not assured of asymptotic progress toward some goal. Every promise is also a threat, and the event to come can be either for better or for worse.[1]

Is the future of Caputo's weak theology a promise or a threat? One cannot tell for sure, but one can hope and pray. That, I believe, is why Caputo ends *The Weakness of God* with a prayer. The very last words of the book are those that he most associates with Derrida: *Viens, oui, oui.*[2] Come, yes, yes. *Thy Kingdom Come.* Come, the future is open. And because I mean to keep it open, *The Adventure of Weak Theology* follows the example of Caputo's *Radical Hermeneutics* and does not end with a proper conclusion:

> The book is an illusion. It pretends to have a definite beginning and a distinct conclusion and to show the way from the one to the other. It claims to be able to steer its way through the flux, which is why Heidegger preferred to speak of detours, dead ends, and forest trails. This book has aimed at de-limiting such pretensions. And so it can claim here only to end, not to conclude. We do not aim at a conclusion but an opening. We do not seek a closure but an opening up.[3]

Conclusion "Not Without" Conclusion

That said, it is also true that after completing his manuscripts, Caputo did not lock them up in his drawer. He did not wait until he could finally say that his lifework was done and he wished to add nothing more. No, the manuscripts were published and therefore physically complete, front to back, real books that marked definite periods in Caputo's thought.

A certain closure, or let us say structural completeness, is visible even in *The Weakness of God*. The most easily discernible, if not the most compelling, example is the symmetry already hinted at in the previous chapter: The book does not only end with the words of Derrida. As a matter of fact, except for the dedication the first words in *The Weakness of God* are Derrida's final words read by his son at his graveside. Stylistically, therefore, the book presents itself to a reader as complete. Theoretically, Caputo offers conclusions in the interim.

For my part I set this work in motion by quoting Saint-Exupéry, beseeching his companionship and assistance on what was surely going to be "the ordeal of a journey through the desert." It was. But even if at first the journey seemed "hopelessly impracticable," it was not endless in the end. Thus before long, *The Adventure of Weak Theology* as a book will also reach its final point where we shall again hear the words of Saint-Ex. However, although the adventure itself continues, I do not wish to put the work on hold. If I cannot offer a conclusive evaluation of Caputo's theology, I nevertheless want to take some time to summarize the basic points, to also provide conclusions in the interim.

Let me first say a few words about the book itself. After that, I will move on to evaluate—by way of bringing all my scattered points of critique together—where Caputo's theology of the event stands as of now.

Structure, Scope, and Perspective

The most conspicuous features of this book are the highly personal style and the alternating historical and theoretical chapters. The entire epilogue is dedicated to the question of style, while my reasons for writing both history and theory, and then even letting one bleed into another, were explained in chapters 1, 2, and 8. At this point, just a few remarks concerning 1) how I came up with the division of chapters and their titles, 2) what *The Adventure of Weak Theology* covers and what it does not, and 3) what my perspective is as a scholar, rather than merely an author, on the ideas expressed in the work.

1) The logic of history, if indeed there is any logic to it, is the logic of sense (see chapter 8). The way I divided Caputo's story, and therefore also the history of his weak theology—Caputo's monastery life, fascination by Heidegger, transition from Heidegger to Derrida, and finally the way out of the closet—could be contested as arbitrary. That I must admit, because *The Adventure of Weak Theology* reflects merely how *I* made *sense* of the story. Consequently, the series, although theoretical in nature, also follow the logic preset by my historical chapters. There is a chapter exploring the concept of a call directly preceding Caputo's novitiate. Yet the call, more precisely the hermeneutics of the call, is the best definition of Caputo's theology one can give. The next theoretical chapter talks about transgression. This is after Caputo left the formation, but it also refers to his struggles to transgress the boundaries imposed by reason. The chapters on freedom come after we have already seen Caputo as a young and successful academic philosopher, but they also point to a directionless freedom in the desert of religion without religion. "Dance" refers to Caputo's style after he found his voice, but it is also a metaphor for writing in general, whereas "void" speaks about the omnipresent abyss in Caputo's thought. Finally, this chapter discusses Caputo's project as a theology of the kingdom of God, but it is also eschatological, pointing toward what, in weak theology, is (hopefully) still to come.

2) As indicated in a note at the beginning of chapter 4, all the biographical facts in this work come exclusively from what John D. Caputo revealed about himself on various occasions throughout his existing work and interviews. The same is for the most part true about Caputo's ideas. It is, in other words, Caputo who through my reading of his texts tells readers of *The Adventure of Weak Theology* what (he thinks) has happened and how he views these events. Had this work been intended as a straightforward biography, much wider context would have had to be taken into consideration, archives consulted, interviews made. I try to explain in the epilogue why *The Adventure of Weak Theology*, rather than being a mere biography and even less a cold analysis, is a reflection on an imaginary talk while sitting in a "rocking chair by the fire" and how it has affected my theological method.

3) This strategy was first of all a matter of choice when I faced the question of how I can write at all. Nevertheless, I do believe it is defensible despite the fact, or precisely because of the fact, that it has become somewhat rare in academic texts. A couple of remarks on this account, while, as I said, the rest will be explained in the epilogue.

First of all, misunderstandings are common when one uses strong rhetorics. There is always a risk of overemphasizing the point to the detriment of the point itself.

Caputo, for example, sounds so passionate about the unwillingness of theology to "present itself and understand itself except as sovereign theology, imperial theology" that his next remark, namely, that "not all Christian theology is this imperialistic, not all theology succumbs to the hybris of *extra ecclesiam nullus salus est*, and not all theology is Neoplatonism *redivivus*,"[4] might easily get overlooked.

Of course, it is possible that Caputo is simply trying to stay on the safe side—a not all-too-serious self-correction, so to say. Even so, we have to allow for the possibility that the former claim, the one about imperial theology, is in fact overemphasized beyond Caputo's real intentions.

As for my corrective for the rhetorics of *The Adventure of Weak Theology*, I would now like to say that the attitude of friendship does not mean that I hold all the views held by Caputo. I would be dishonest to claim that I have nothing in common with them, but this book is, I hope, only a first step in my own intellectual journey.

The Lostness of Weak Theology

What about my critique of Caputo's weak theology, then? Throughout this work I have operated under the seemingly trivial assumption that every journey is, in principle, characterized by its point of origin—what

I call "home"—and by its direction—the "whereto." Since I presented it as a journey, it follows that I also regard Caputo's theology as a well-defined vector. The problem is that Caputo, for reasons related to his own worldview, thinks differently. Let us, for instance, consider again Caputo's prayer that concludes *The Weakness of God*.

Derrida's *viens, oui, oui* are indeed the book's last words. Nevertheless, there is more to be found there than just the eschatological expectation of a theology to come. Caputo does not only pray "for theology to come true," he also prays "to an unknown God" (see my chapter 9) asking not to be lost, while admitting that lost he already is:

> I am praying not to be lost, praying because I am already lost, praying not to get any more lost than I already am, praying that my prayer does not make things worse. I am trying to think while praying, to pray while thinking, praying like mad—for theology, for theology's truth, for the event. The event for me is not an object but a matter for prayer. But I must make a confession. My central (if decentering) idea, my one contribution to human welfare, the one thing I want engraved on my headstone, is and has always been the modest proposal that if the truth be told, we none of us—neither believers nor nonbelievers, neither believers in this nor believers in that—know who we are. We are always kept in the dark. That unguarded confession is the culmination of a lifetime of study and writing, of a life spent earnestly seeking the light, not to mention a considerable amount of money spent on books, travel to learned conferences, and drinks in conference hotel bars. Indeed, I can barely say *I* confess.[5]

Caputo makes no secret about the sense of lostness at the heart of his weak theology. This lostness calls for prayer, so as not to get any more lost. But it is also clear, even if somewhat surprising—why then pray?—that he regards it as a virtue, rather than shortcoming, of his theology.

This is why I am somewhat skeptical about the true nature of Caputo's professed openness to the flux. His talk about lostness appeals to me on the level of experience, to be sure, but it seems to be in conflict with many other things that Caputo has to say. Indeed, he writes a whole lot of things that sound like confidence rather than doubts. Virtually all his texts betray a strong sense of orientation, rather than destinerrance, and they do so to an extent that cannot always be explained away by the traps of his own rhetorics.

Every time, just to give one example, when Caputo speaks about strong versus weak theology, not only does he present it as a clear-cut binary pair, which in itself is suspicious to say the least, but he is also very sure about which group he belongs to and therefore also who his "enemy" is. In everyday life this is, of course, quite normal. That is how we get to places, by choosing one direction over another. The difficulty arises when somebody insists on maintaining ironic distance vis-à-vis every tradition, then closes that distance anyway through a secret allegiance with one of the parties but continues talking like nothing has happened.

I do not insist that the latter is *exactly* Caputo's case. If his weak theology maintains such secret allegiance, if it belongs to a particular home and heads in a well-defined direction, Caputo does not necessarily need to perceive it so. He likes to mention "that mediocre fellow Climacus warns us against, a half-hearted lover who keeps his fingers crossed behind his back even as he takes the marriage vows."[6] Well, Caputo seems to show his fingers crossed upfront, claiming that he is lost, even as he hides his certainties behind his back, so that even he cannot see them.

This tension is worth pondering over, and I think it ultimately points toward that one question that Caputo says he is always asking himself: "Is it possible to inhabit a construction, understanding that it's a construction? Can you inhabit a tradition with ironic distance?"[7] I brought it up at the end of chapter 5.

My own question, after we have followed the journey of weak theology, is whether Caputo's aforementioned ambiguity does in fact suggest that inhabiting a tradition with ironic distance is impossible. I dare not go as far as saying a clear yes or no. It does, however, appear to be the case that inhabiting a construction with an understanding that it is a construction does not make a whole lot of real difference after all. For whatever it is that he believes, Caputo always acts like a true believer in the end, and perhaps we all do.

Either/Or

The issue at hand could also be restated as follows: Either Caputo is serious about lostness, or more generally about undecidability, or else he makes his picks *and* then presents them as hard truths, but he cannot have it both ways. The problem with weak theology, as it stands now, is that Caputo seems to be trying to do precisely that.

I argued in chapter 8 that this is weak theology's greatest risk, namely, that instead of being true to its own weak point of view it will become too dogmatic about its weakness, too convinced, for example, of its logic of doing without strong claims—as is already the case with the concept of religion without religion. Conversely, I also suggested that weak theology, if it is to be true to its own principles, cannot put limits on the nature of the event it purports to interpret.

The concept of religion without religion has been the main target of my critique of Caputo's version of weak theology in this work. In what follows, I shall first summarize the main points of this critique. Then I will expand on it by a few references indicating where Caputo's home of choice might be.

The Unbearable Lightness of Ironic Distance

When in chapter 9 I developed my own critique of the concept of religion without religion, I for the most part let Bark and the desert king do the heavy lifting. One of them exemplified, while the other meditated on, what I understand as the truth of home.

Where I now express my doubts about the possibility of inhabiting a tradition with ironic distance, the king, for example, reminisced about his father's palace and, in particularly strong prose, reflected on the fate of people who in the name of freedom tore down the walls of their cathedral and ended up in a marketplace.

The king's answer paraphrased? Before long, these people would start dreaming about a new home, a new tradition, because nobody can remain homeless for too long without thereby losing the vision of oneself. Bark illustrated the less mythical version of this truth in Agadir.

Caputo, of course, said on several occasions that he did not actually think anybody could *live* outside of concrete traditions, or that anybody could *live* in a pure messianic time. He just never showed his readers how they were supposed to reconcile this particular category of self-correctives with all the other statements in favor of religion without religion. All we ever got was, indeed, the unanswered question about the possibility of inhabiting a tradition with ironic distance—the possibility akin to, even in Caputo's own words, that of square circles.[8]

In any case, I maintained in chapter 9 that a "cost analysis" of Caputo's project was necessary if weak theology was to have any future. It became clear that what Caputo offers is "a certain version of the freedom of the children of God" for the price of praying only to an unknown God. Hence, without religion, after all.

Three practical problems in particular were brought to the fore. I argued that since religion without religion lacks a concrete sense of orientation, it results in a sterile dreaming. What this means is that such an abstract religiosity is about as effective in achieving its goals as the concept of *democracy to come* is useful for governing a state. Perhaps great to keep all excesses at bay, but otherwise absolutely unusable in real life.

Next, I claimed that insofar as Caputo's thinking precludes any concrete sense of mission, he cuts himself off from an important strand of cultural dreaming. There can be no saints in the "Church without religion." The fact that all known cultures have their heroes indicates that the concept of religion without religion has never been lived.

But these are just good stories, like the myth of the early Greeks brought to us by Heidegger, we heard Caputo say in chapter 10. Heidegger could do without his myth, in fact such demythologization strengthened his point, right? I am not sure it did. More importantly, my third point of critique had to do with the very particular understanding of what these "just good stories" are.

At that point, I was mostly interested in what such reductionism does to Caputo's understanding of his own journey. But the "just good stories" view is, in fact, characteristic of a specific tradition—a telltale sign that Caputo, after all, may indeed be less lost than he is prepared to admit.

Is Caputo a Kantian?

Several authors have argued over the last two decades or so that Caputo's true allegiance lies with the Enlightenment, specifically with the ideas about religion expressed by Immanuel Kant. In chapter 10 I briefly presented one such critique by Kevin Hart, together with some remarks about Caputo's demythologization by Keith Putt. Hart's article, which I quoted before, entitled "Without," is quite recent (2010), but Putt voiced similar concerns about Caputo's work already back in 1997 in "The Im/Possibility of a Passionate God."[9] Hence the problem apparently lasts. As an example of Putt's version of the critique, he writes:

> Caputo's Christian deconstruction is, indeed, a postmodern *tour de force*, a powerful, quasi-Kantian interpretation of Jesus as an ethical archetype; however, one can also argue (using Derridean language) that it is a *Tour de Babel*, not a deconstruction of modernity but merely another construction or translation of modernity, the confusion (Babel) of an Enlightenment imagination with the Aramaic imagination. Unfortunately, Caputo's "postmodern" Christology still bears a striking resemblance to modernist paradigms developing out of nineteenth-century quests for the "historical" Jesus. One could say that Caputo has abandoned his "post" and returned to the same types of modernist criticisms of the biblical narratives that one would expect to find in a David Hume, a David Strauss, or a Rudolf Bultmann. Like them, Caputo continues to adhere to a

> presuppositional structure that preempts any possibility of empirical manifestations of divine action within the flux of history and that rejects as incoherent any claim to the supernatural that does not fit with the expectations of scientifically institutionalized reason. Although he criticizes the metaphysical polarity of the "Jesus of history" and the "Christ of faith," he actually operates within that polarity, specifically as it comes to expression in the historico-critical theology of John Dominic Crossan.[10]

Putt finds it difficult to understand how Caputo can require "that reason be loosened up a bit, that exceptions be respected, and that alterity be welcomed with a rousing *Viens!* and *at the same time* "surreptitiously genuflect before its throne with reference to what may be 'rationally' presupposed as historically possible."[11]

Now, I do not intend to multiply quotations or to follow this argument in any greater detail at this point. In short, I think that both Putt and Hart have raised an issue that Caputo, I think, has not yet sufficiently answered. In particular, I appreciate Putt's argument whereby the historico-critical method preferred by Caputo

> must also be another interpretation, another construal caught in the flux of undecidability. It cannot be exempt from the flux and firmly fixed upon hard truths. If undecidability means that the future cannot be programmed within the milieu of the present, that totalization can never be achieved, and that the invention of the alterity to come must be an open passion for the impossible, so, too, the same dynamic must be at work with reference to the past. Undecidability must also mean that what has occurred must maintain a certain non-closure, that past events cannot be programmed within the milieu of the present.[12]

Hence again my previously expressed skepticism about Caputo's lostness. He does indeed seem to choose where undecidability applies and where it does not. Or where binary oppositions betray dangerous metaphysics and where they are just fine.

Incidentally, it is almost ironic that at some point in *The Prayers and Tears of Jacques Derrida* Caputo says that he regards "the binary opposition between the spirit of love and the dead letter of the law to be largely Christian propaganda meant to deface Judaism, particularly in the politics and polemics between Jew and Christian in the latter part of the first century."[13] Could Caputo withstand a similar argument about the political loading of his own binary opposition between weak and strong theologies? I seriously doubt that he could.

Caputo's "Somebody Else's Problem"

Why is Caputo's indebtedness to the Enlightenment way of thinking about religion a problem and what can be done about it? It is a problem precisely because the "presuppositional structures" involved in such view lead, on Caputo's part, to a certain structural blindness.

As I already mentioned, it is quite possible that Caputo does not even perceive his secret allegiance. He does, after all, continue holding on to the idea about being lost—and that even after the critical evaluations like the ones by Hart and Putt.

Similarly, there are questionable ideas and/or omissions in his weak theology that seem evident to many of his readers, but Caputo appears oblivious to them. For all intents and purposes, it is as if he regarded them automatically as an SEP. I very much love this concept and I did bring it up without any further explanation in chapter 11, so I'll let Douglas Adams address this loose end:

> "Something's on your mind, isn't it?" said Arthur.
>
> "I think," said Ford in a tone of voice which Arthur by now recognized as one which presaged something utterly unintelligible, "that there's an SEP over there."
>
> He pointed. Curiously enough, the direction he pointed in was not the one in which he was looking. Arthur looked in the one direction, which was towards the sight-screens, and in the other which was at the field of play. He nodded, he shrugged. He shrugged again.
>
> "A what?" he said. "An SEP." "An S . . . ?" ". . . EP."
>
> "And what's that?" "Somebody Else's Problem."
>
> "Ah, good," said Arthur and relaxed. He had no idea what all that was about, but at least it seemed to be over. It wasn't.
>
> "Over there," said Ford, again pointing at the sight-screens and looking at the pitch.
>
> "Where?" said Arthur.
>
> "There!" said Ford.
>
> "I see," said Arthur, who didn't.
>
> "You do?" said Ford.
>
> "What?" said Arthur.
>
> "Can you see," said Ford patiently, "the SEP?"
>
> "I thought you said that was somebody else's problem."
>
> "That's right."
>
> Arthur nodded slowly, carefully and with an air of immense stupidity.
>
> "And I want to know," said Ford, "if you can see it."
>
> "You do?"

"Yes."

"What," said Arthur, "does it look like?"

"Well, how should I know, you fool?" shouted Ford. "If you can see it, you tell me."

Arthur experienced that dull throbbing sensation just behind the temples which was a hallmark of so many of his conversations with Ford. His brain lurked like a frightened puppy in its kennel. Ford took him by the arm.

"An SEP," he said, "is something that we can't see, or don't see, or our brain doesn't let us see, because we think that it's somebody else's problem. That's what SEP means. Somebody Else's Problem. The brain just edits it out, it's like a blind spot. If you look at it directly you won't see it unless you know precisely what it is. Your only hope is to catch it by surprise out of the corner of your eye."

"Ah," said Arthur, "then that's why . . ."

"Yes," said Ford, who knew what Arthur was going to say.

". . . you've been jumping up and . . ."

"Yes."

". . . down, and blinking . . ."

"Yes."

". . . and . . ."

"I think you've got the message."

"I can see it," said Arthur, "it's a spaceship."[14]

Now, to answer the question what can be done to further the case of weak theology, I suggest that our task as theologians and friends of Caputo is to be his Arthurs. That is to say, to keep weak theology open for the possibilities that he does not see. It is, at the very least, a good start and, as we saw in chapter 6, Caputo once did try to do the same with the thought of Heidegger.

The Absent Trinity

One such blind spot in Caputo, certainly in *The Weakness of God*, is the Trinity. The discrepancy, in Caputo's theology, between the omnipresence of the kingdom and the total absence of the Trinity has been noticed by a number of Caputo's readers. As an example, I can mention Heltzel, who remarked:

> The conspicuous lack of reference to the Trinity throughout the volume exposes a Unitarian tendency in Caputo's doctrine of God. This is a serious weakness in his proposal because he is not able to access the growing body of Trinitarian resources to discuss these problems.[15]

Theologically speaking, this is a serious issue, indeed, although if we can agree with Hart, no Christian theologian finds it easy to keep the kingdom of God and the Trinity together. According to Hart, "the principal motifs of Christianity are the Kingdom and the Trinity, and the main difficulty that Christianity has faced, still faces, and will continue to face, is how to relate them."[16] "To speak about either the Kingdom or the Trinity," Hart continues, "is to be involved in the relations between experience and revelation, scripture and theology, history and truth,"[17] and he points out

> the incommensurability of talk about the Kingdom and the Trinity. That there are specific and highly detailed dogmas about the Trinity that are binding on all Catholics is well known. Yet there is no dogma of the Kingdom: one can read Henry Denzinger's *Enchiridion Symbolorum* from beginning to end without encountering a reference to it. The preaching of the Kingdom strikes us from the first as resisting reduction to propositions; it concerns something that is "already but not yet," and the parables about it are notoriously hard to harmonize.[18]

If Hart is correct, then Caputo's reluctance to talk about the Trinity is at least understandable, which nevertheless does not mean excusable. Caputo would need different models for understanding revelation, history, truth, and so on.

Putt's critique also applies quite nicely in this regard. For as long as Caputo holds on to the religious views typical for the Enlightenment, he will continue avoiding the talk about the Trinity just as he avoids talking about magic. The incarnation, for that matter, will remain for Caputo something "too palpable."[19]

However, Caputo could and perhaps on his own reasoning should see things differently. For example, I have described Caputo's story in this book through the prism of Kierkegaard, and for a good reason. But Putt rightly points out that Caputo, as a good Kierkegaardian,

> should not be disturbed by the idea that one encounters God mediated through a historical individual instead of through universal truths. Caputo must reject the traditional ontotheological interpretation that attempts to universalize Christ through a Hellenistic understanding of logos. As a good Derridean, he cannot traffic in such logocentrism; however, the Johannine narrative of Jesus as logos subverts Greek metaphysics and presents Christ as heterological, as another, different kind of logos that enters the aleatorics of the flux, suffers for and with every other other, and confronts the possibility of the

impossible through the meontics of death and resurrection. Although Caputo limits his Christian deconstruction to the Synoptic Yeshua, his hermeneutic of the kingdom does seem to open the im/possibility of just such a Johannine logos Christology.[20]

Bringing Caputo into the Kingdom of God

If in these concluding pages I have quoted Keith Putt more often than anyone else, I have done so primarily because he is, so to say, one of my "points." By this I mean that over the years I have come to think of him as the model case of Caputo's reader with the potential to both correct weak theology and to move it further.

I can only assume that this is due to his different cultural background, or his intellectual journey, but Putt has the vision of "Arthur," unencumbered by the presuppositions that impair Caputo's sight. It was he, for example, who brought to Caputo's attention how the Kantian triad (What can we know? What ought we to do? What can we hope for?), which guided Caputo through the final three chapters of *Radical Hermeneutics* and thus through everything else that he has written ever since, gradually transformed into the Pauline triad of faith, hope, and love:

> Although there is no denying the Kantian provenance for the three guiding topics, when one examines the rubrics under which Caputo has prosecuted them during the last ten years, one may discover another possible source for his postmodern radical hermeneutics of religion. For him, epistemology eventually becomes the question of faith, ethics becomes the question of love, and hope becomes the question of a certain teleological openness to the unprogrammable future. If one reverses the order of the second and third topics, one discovers a familiar trinity—faith, hope, and love—and one is, thereby, confronted with the possibility that Caputo's philosophy of religion is not only Kantian but also Pauline, specifically bearing the marks of St. Paul's taxonomy of Christian virtues found in I Corinthians 13.[21]

Now, if we are to take Caputo's word on this, he says he "did not see it coming"—which is my point here—but that "what Keith Putt says is completely true."[22]

Of course, I do not mean to suggest that all that Caputo's weak theology needs to be healed of its presuppositions is that some friendly theologian redescribes Caputo as orthodox against his own expectations. However, a willingness to read Caputo carefully, with an open heart, and yes, sometimes against or beyond Caputo himself, is in my opinion a necessary step on the way toward a better weak theology. Caputo certainly did not shy away from reading Heidegger beyond Heidegger and even Derrida beyond Derrida.

Not so long ago, Keith Putt again attempted just such a reading. I am referring now to his article entitled "Reconciling Pure Forgiveness and Reconciliation: Bringing John Caputo into the Kingdom of God."[23] He offers no groundbreaking strategy. He simply offers Caputo a kind of openness that I have just talked about and that I expound in detail in the epilogue. One may call it a friendly methodological benefit of the doubt:

> As usual, however, any critique of Caputo must remain prudent and not presume that he maintains a strict consistency throughout his thought. His mind is not that "little"! Typically, he invites dissent more for the reductive propensities in his interpretations than for any unrestricted rejection. Such is the case with my negative evaluation of his undervaluing of reconciliation.[24]

This is my first point and it is also related to what I meant when I said in several places throughout this book that Caputo's theology was more than one. Nevertheless, and here comes my second and final point, in his discussion of Caputo's kingdom theology Putt also writes:

> I contend that he must mitigate his somewhat obstinate depreciation of the value of reconciliation in order to have his theology of the weak force of the event adequately reflect the biblical texts that he intentionally privileges. In other words, Caputo cannot tenaciously hold to his "absolute" non-economy of pure forgiveness and do justice to either Jesus' or Paul's interpretation of divine grace.[25]

What exactly is at stake in this discussion is actually less important to me at this point than Putt's willingness to name Caputo's obstinacy where such an attitude does indeed seem to prevent Caputo from moving further.

The future of Caputo's weak theology, if there will be any, is in the hands of readers who are willing to take Caputo seriously, but not always too seriously. In other words, for a theology of the event to bear fruits, we must be able to regard it with what Caputo calls the "ironic distance." And so I pray with Saint-Ex: Grant me but this, O Lord: that I may learn to read.

Epilogue: How?

There was an old gardener who liked to speak to me about his friend. Before life separated them, for many, many years the two had lived like brothers, drinking the evening tea together, observing the same feast days, each repairing to the other when he needed counsel or wished to confide his troubles to a friendly ear. Yet true it was that they spoke rarely to each other; far oftener one would see them, after the day's work was done, walking together and, without uttering a word, gazing at the flowers and gardens, trees and sky. But when one of them bent down, and shaking his head, touched a plant, the other, too, would bend and, seeing the traces of caterpillars on the leaves, would likewise shake his head. And both showed equal delight when they came on flowers in full and perfect bloom.

It befell on a certain day that a great merchant hired one of them and bade him accompany, for some few weeks, his caravan. But forays of predatory nomads, wars between great empires, storms and shipwrecks, deaths and disasters, divers mischances and the need to earn his living tossed the man to and fro, like a cask buffeted by the waves, until from garden to garden, he was carried away to a far country, on the very margent of the world.

Years went by and, after half a lifetime's silence, my gardener received a letter from his friend. God alone knows how many years that letter had been awandering; what ships and caravans, horsemen and diligences had sped it on its devious ways, with the tenacity of the myriad waves of the sea, before it reached his garden. So that morning he was beaming with delight and, wishing others to share in it, he begged me read the letter, as one begs a friend to read a poem. And watched my face, so as to see the emotion it quickened in me.

True, there were but a few words, for the two gardeners were, as befitted them, handier with the spade than with the pen. Indeed all I read was: This morning I pruned my rose trees. Then, meditating

> on those essential things which, methought, cannot be expressed in words, I slowly nodded my head, as they, too, would have done.
>
> But now a change befell my gardener: his peace of mind was gone. You might have heard him sedulously enquiring as to distances, sea routes, couriers, caravans and the wars in progress on the desert's face. Then three years later, as chance would have it, I had occasion to dispatch envoys to the edge of the world. So I sent for my gardener. "Now you can write to your friend."
>
> —Antoine de Saint-Exupéry, *The Wisdom of the Sands*

How did I want to write this work? Or perhaps more appropriately at this point: *How else?* Is it really impossible to draft an account of weak theology that would be free of personal clutter and unencumbered by this purportedly literary style?

Of course not. It is quite possible, to be sure, but one can also outline the theory of relativity while remaining completely silent about physics, or discuss it with friends by a bonfire without so much as a single reference to the cluttering mathematics. And I do not mean to come across as being sarcastic now. I am not. On the contrary, one would wish that keeping things simple was the norm rather than a rare gift in the academic world. For Saint-Exupéry, simplicity was a sign of perfection "finally attained not when there is no longer anything to add, but when there is no longer anything to take away."[1] Simplicity equals elegance, in literature just as well as in science.

But it is equally true—true for the very same reason—that writing economically is anything but simple. The task is particularly daunting when the "clutter" really seems to be of the essence. Einstein honestly could not do without his equations, but the man was a genius. He managed so well that by today $E=mc^2$ no longer counts as mathematics; it is more like a magical formula. Maybe it helped that he did not yet possess that long desired doctorate, when he first jotted it down.

About such magic I can dream, I can write more in order to learn how to write less, but it is unlikely that I will ever find the way to keep my texts free from the personal clutter. Make an effort to keep it discreet? The greater the effort the better! Avoid unnecessary repetitions? Yes, at least out of respect for my readers' stomachs! Whenever possible, that is, but not now. For as I said, I have some loose ends to tie up. Perhaps most obviously, I need to explain what I meant when I wrote that one of the motivations behind *The Adventure of Weak Theology* was that I really liked the author of *The Weakness of God*.

On the surface the answer is quite straightforward: I referred to a certain affinity that I feel with Caputo. Never mind that this rapport is for all intents and purposes unilateral: We only had a face to face conversation once and never exchanged as much as a single email, so why should he, after decades of teaching and meeting all sorts of people, remember a fleeting encounter with one student from abroad? Networking has never been my strong suit, but this is, of course, not my point. It is perfectly possible to feel close with somebody even if meeting with that person is inconceivable. I dare say there is a lot more to Caputo's liking for Kierkegaard than can be accounted for by the penmanship of, say, Johannes de Silentio, Constantin Constantius, or Johannes Climacus; even as the one writer I truly regret not being able to chat with, in real time, is Saint-Exupéry. I thus share with Caputo the same sense of a loss; our heroes are dead and yet so much alive in everything that we write that it is almost painful. I would even say we also share Kierkegaard, but that would be presumptuous—I did not read him secretly after the lights went out in my monastery cell, as Caputo jokes he did.[2] I did, however, on numerous occasions forget to turn the lights off in my seminary room, when I was reading Saint-Exupéry's *Citadelle*. That Caputo is not a monk today, and I am not a priest, is the result of our common inability to trade intellectual curiosity for obedience. Not because of our habit to read secretly after hours, to be sure, but because we both wanted to study while the principals insisted that the last word should be theirs.[3] I said I had a chance to meet with Professor Caputo once. I picked him up from the train station when he arrived in Leuven, and later that evening we had dinner together, in the course of which he asked me about my plans after I have finished studies. I told him I wanted to write but write independently, that is to say, outside of academia. Then I asked back. He said he would do the same, if he could decide again. Of course I like him. His haunted and somewhat lost soul hovering by Abraham's faith above the abyss; his almost childlike love for life, which he refers to as his upbeat voice;[4] his heterodox provocations, which suddenly take on a new meaning when he talks to you over the dinner table about the charity activities in his parish—even as those, who know him well enough to quote from his unpublished manuscripts, "warrant that Caputo does know what he loves when he loves his God," that "he loves a Hebraic God of passion, a God of tears and compassion, who suffer[s] with his suffering people, who [is] moved by their sighs and lamentations, [and] who [is] angered by their meanness of mind . . .";[5] his youthful soul inside a mature man joking about his "present sorry state"[6] and perhaps wondering—as yet another joke goes—what the hell has happened . . .

* * *

Caputo, for his part, liked Derrida, that is a well-known fact. A little less widely circulated truth is that it took Caputo several years to grow fond of Derrida. In the early 1980s, Caputo thought of Derrida as an unquestionably brilliant commentator of Husserl,[7] and a refreshingly unconventional reader of Heidegger, "far remove[d] from the epigonism and bad repetitions of the Heidegger literati who talk like Heidegger talks, who repeat what Heidegger says, and who regard every criticism of Heidegger as a misunderstanding."[8] At the same time, however, Caputo felt "troubled" by this new "Derrida's Franco-Heideggerian alliance."[9] What he missed in Derrida (and for that matter, Richard Rorty) was "the voice which calls us back to ourselves, which bids us to say what we already know."[10] While ready to admit that Derrida's reading "strategies serve a purpose," Caputo worried, like so many others before and after him, that "left to themselves they cut us off entirely from the things themselves, delivering us over to a surfeit of fictions and willful constructions."[11] To Caputo, Derrida appeared as a kind of "Jacques the Seducer"—a Kierkegaardian aesthete who never got as far as understanding "the anxiety of Job and Abraham"[12]—and at one point Caputo even pledged "to try to make Derrida say what he does not want to say, to make him own up to something transcendent, to direct the bite of his critique of Husserl into his own hide."[13]

These last words date back to 1985, the same year when Caputo attended a conference at Loyola University of Chicago where he presented a paper on Derrida. It was not really a critical paper; what is more, in it Caputo acknowledged that Derrida "gives the critique of metaphysics—hitherto understood only in terms of *Gelassenheit*—a socio-political cutting edge, pointing it in the direction of a politics of liberation,"[14] something that Caputo increasingly missed in Heidegger. Nevertheless, he was "quite terrified" because Derrida "sat in the audience listening" and Caputo worried that he would chide him for getting it all wrong.[15] Anxiety was unnecessary, however, for Derrida proved very gracious[16] and, before long, Caputo began to display the same kind of chivalry.

Two years after the Chicago conference, Caputo mused over the annoyance Derrida seemed to face everywhere, his name serving as a "red flag at the mere sight of which many philosophers today charge,"[17] and he seemed quite pleased that "in the midst of this brouhaha several sensitive Derrida readers have appeared on the scene to lend Derrida a hand by lending him a more favorable ear."[18] He was of the opinion that "the time has come to show with some patience that Derrida is engaged in a critical project which is deeply in accord with the critique of metaphysics which has marked continental philosophy throughout this century."[19]

Now the critique of metaphysics was also Caputo's professional interest but, as we have seen, beneath the surface lurked another, much more powerful, passion—the one for religion. Perhaps I am reading too much into those events, but it seems to me as if Caputo, consciously or not, tried to "read himself" into Derrida. To appropriate, nay, to discover Derrida for what was always dearest to him. Because, despite what Caputo had called for, he did not seem to care all too much about explaining how Derrida was in line with the big philosophical project of the century; instead, he began experimenting with the idea that "there is a religious element on the backburners of [Derrida's] deconstruction."[20] And as if out of solidarity with an incessantly vilified Derrida, he went about it "in a way calculated to scandalize."[21]

At the same time, Caputo pulled a one-eighty with respect to portraying Derrida as an aesthete who advocates an engagement "in an endless free play of variant readings which are indulged in for the sheer pleasure they give but without regard for truth,"[22] while confessing, albeit only in an endnote, that he too had been guilty of such "ill-begotten critique,"[23] so perhaps he had indeed got him all wrong after all. One of Caputo's utterances from this period, from the very same article in fact, I find particularly mesmerizing: "Lest anyone think that Derrida must be a friend of mine whom I feel called upon to defend, I can, with the best manners of the university, cite a text."[24] I am repeating myself here, given that much of this history is the subject matter of chapter 10, but I simply cannot resist the temptation: No friend of mine, I'll cite a text—four years *after* Caputo found his own voice thanks to Derrida . . .

Be that as it may, within a year or so Caputo was on a plane "soaring off to another conference, reading *Circonfession* [Derrida's recent autobiographical book] for the first time,"[25] in which

> God help us, this is what he actually said—Derrida confessed that he was a man of prayer, that he prayed all the time, and that if we understood this about him we would understand everything, and that failure to understand this had caused him to be misread again and again. I was 37,000 feet above the earth when I first read this but I signaled the stewardess to let me off the plane immediately, a parachute would do, so that I could get to my computer.[26]

Derrida's unexpected confession startled the bejesus out of Caputo, a theologian hiding in the closet; he could not remember the correct altitude when explaining why he so much wanted to get to his computer: "Flying thirty thousand feet above the ground, I decided to write about Derrida's religion without religion . . ."[27] He was "up among the angels, *s'il y en a*."[28] "Maybe also," Caputo thought

> if I can fit this in, I will speak about my religion. I can slip my religion in, in pockets, like the windows in *Glas*, in little asides, *apartés*, like commercial, "words from our sponsor," or what my hero Johannes Climacus called "edifying divertissements." His religion and mine, intertwined in a kind of unscientific double helix, all along trying to keep them straight.[29]

Caputo wrote the book, once again hoping to "scandalize everyone"[30]—well, everyone except Derrida. Nearly a decade after dreaming for the first time about teaming up deconstruction with religion, Caputo sent the yet unpublished manuscript of *The Prayers and Tears of Jacques Derrida: Religion Without Religion* to Derrida because he was "concerned about 'coopting' him for religion, about domesticating deconstruction, and worried about whether [he] was respecting the difference between deconstruction and religion."[31] And yet again, Caputo's worries proved unnecessary, because Derrida "liked the manuscript a lot" and he even said that Caputo "read him the way he 'loves to be read.'"[32] An additional three years down the line, Derrida gave an interview in which he expressed how very precious it was for him to be read by someone that he benefited from reading in his own turn, because in reading Caputo he was not simply looking at the reflection of his own text.[33] Caputo, in turn, spoke about vertigo:

> I have so often written about Derrida, stretched out his texts on the analytic table and dissected them, that I am unprepared for the dizzying effects of the reversal, of the inverted world produced by Derrida discussing my texts. I never thought he would look back, talk back, get up off the table and analyze back, agree and disagree, as Mark Dooley has made him do. No one has prepared me for this, or warned me that this could happen, now in *my* fifty-ninth year. I meant to give him a gift—and I did not expect a return. I thought it was impossible. Still, if it were impossible, I should have known.[34]

My fifty-ninth year? That, I believe, was not only a reference to Derrida's "Circonfession/Circumfession," which was subtitled "Fifty-Nine Periods and Periphrases Written in a Sort of Internal Margin, Between Geoffrey Bennington's Book and Work in Preparation (January 1989–April 1990),"[35] but also the acknowledgment, on Caputo's part, of the transience of time, of history, of his story with Derrida.

Indeed, Caputo liked Derrida. "He's a kind of very distant soul mate for me," he said twenty years after he wrote his first (critical) article about Derrida, "and because of him, because of this other, I write in my own name."[36] "I feel I instinctively know what he's getting at when I read him—that I have the same kind of impulse."[37]

* * *

Derrida, on the other hand, is said to have been very likable. "Derrida spoke with me recently in his modest office at Irvine," wrote an *LA Weekly* reporter Kristine McKenna in 2002. "Given the fearlessness and ambition of his work, he's surprisingly approachable in person, and his ideas seem considerably less daunting in conversation than they do on the page. He's a very charming man."[38] Caputo felt the same: "One of the things that impresses me about Derrida, that impresses everyone who gets to know him, is that he is an extraordinarily decent man, kind and appreciative of the work that others are doing, and disarmingly modest about his own importance."[39] "As a speaker, he never failed to be extremely generous with his questioners and their difficulties reading and listening to him. In the event, he made the difficult seem nearly transparent in his effort to show how language does and undoes itself in our very making of meaning," remembered Fran Bartkowski after Derrida's death.[40] "He responded to my letters and questions with handwritten pages that I will always cherish. He encouraged my work with the wisdom of a dedicated teacher,"[41] wrote Marko Zlomislić in a response to one of the first of Derrida's biographies, while expressing his "hope that someone will attempt to write about the man and his life rather than his works . . ."[42] Those who met him in person were drawn to Derrida, even to the point where Martin McQuillan "often thought that in the case of Derrida he did not choose his friends but on the contrary he was chosen by them."[43]

There is no denying, however, that controversies were also part of Derrida's career. Caputo, as we have seen, decried attacks on Derrida even before he actually thought of him as a friend. Incidentally—or was it, really, only a coincidence?—Caputo called for lending Derrida a helping hand just as Derrida was waging a war of words on behalf of his defenseless friend Paul de Man. Did compassion multiply there, consciously or not? And if it did, if compassion led to more compassion, if it spread even among professors, especially among professors, where would we be, what would happen to science, what would become of truth? This is the sense I am getting at, only not just yet.

Derrida, to repeat, had to put up with much misunderstanding and he certainly was not entirely blameless in this respect. If, for example, the media perceived Derrida as a notoriously difficult, even an "abstruse" theorist,[44] if in the eyes of many he was a kind of "judge who neither feared God nor respected any human being," he himself grew increasingly irritated by journalists:

> For me it would be an intolerable obscenity to reject a difficult formulation, a fold, a paradox, yet another contradiction, because it is not going to be understood, or because such and such journalist who does not understand it, who can not get even the title of the book, and thinks that the reader or viewer will not understand either, and that therefore management won't like it or his career will suffer as a result. You might as well ask me to bow and scrape, or to die of stupidity.[45]

Said Derrida two months before his death. Simultaneously likable and stubborn (I for my part would say likably stubborn), possessed of a "peculiar combination of battle-ready obstinacy and amiability," as David Mikics observed, a trait he thought "characterized both Derrida and de Man, drawing the two friends together."[46]

The war I alluded to a moment ago was also for the most part fought in the media. While I will not delve too deeply into the matter, here is basically what happened:[47] Less than four years after Paul de Man's death a young Belgian researcher, Ortwin de Graef (currently a professor at KU Leuven), discovered a number of newspaper articles written by de Man between 1941 and 1942 at a time when Belgium was occupied by the Germans. The newspapers, the French-language *Le Soir* and the Flemish-language *Het Vlaamsche Land*, were under Nazi control and therefore collaborationist and expressly anti-Semitic. Although only in his early twenties, Paul de Man already had his own literary column to which he contributed, in toto, around 150 articles, some of them quite clearly ideological. The discovery, especially of the piece entitled "The Jews in Contemporary Literature,"[48] caused a media outcry, particularly in the United States where de Man had been a prominent professor after the war. "For some," summed up Martin McQuillan,

> it was unthinkable that a leading member of the Yale School of deconstruction had been associated with the collaborationist press in occupied Europe; for others it proved what they had always suspected about the political credentials of deconstruction. It is clear that many who rushed into print to denounce de Man as a Nazi had not read the articles and had made up their minds about them before they were ever published. The logic ran: de Man wrote for *Le Soir* during the war therefore he must be a Nazi, therefore the whole of deconstruction is Nazism.[49]

Indeed, right from the start the "Paul de Man affair" served as the battleground for the ongoing culture wars. For the attackers, this campaign meant far more than a denouncement of de Man's juvenile faux pas; they aimed at the "theory." McQuillan relates how after Geoffrey Hartman, a Yale colleague of de Man, wrote a defense of de Man's later work and character,[50] the journalist Jacob Neusner replied in *The Jewish Advocate*:

> Hartman uses every trick of the trade to shift attention from a fact he wishes would go away: that his teacher, colleague, and friend hated Jews and was a Nazi [. . .] To deconstructionism, things are what you say they are. So up is down and black is white and east is west and somehow this disreputable and disgusting Nazi, de Man, has been turned into a man of conscience, no less.[51]

From the opposing camp, Joseph Hillis Miller, then Derrida's colleague at the University of California, Irvine, pointed out in the *Times Literary Supplement* that the

> strongest motivation for the irresponsible errors and insinuations in these newspaper articles is clear enough. The real target is not de Man himself. He is dead, beyond the reach of attack. The real aim is to discredit that form of interpretation called 'deconstruction,' to obliterate it, as far as possible, from the curriculum, to dissuade students of literature, philosophy, and culture from reading de Man's work or that of his associates, to put a stop to the 'influence' of 'deconstruction.' Beyond that, as the article in *Newsweek* and a later one in the *Wall Street Journal* attacking the English Department at Duke University made clear, the target is literary theory or critical theory generally, for example the so-called 'new historicists,' or feminist theorists, or students of popular culture, or practitioners of so-called 'cultural criticism.' The rapid widening of the targets of hostility has been a conspicuous fact.[52]

"This time, finding as always its foothold in aggressivity, simplism has produced the most unbelievably stupid statements,"[53] Derrida wrote in response to what was going on. "I will have neither the room nor the patience nor the cruelty to cite them all. I merely recall that they often appear in university campus newspapers and are generally passed along to the journalists by professors."[54]

These words appeared in the article entitled "Like the Sound of the Sea Deep within a Shell: Paul de Man's War," which was first published in the spring 1988 issue of *Critical Inquiry*. Derrida wrote it on the invitation of the journal's editors, from whom he had received a telephone call some four months after he had first heard about de Man's wartime articles and in next to no time after the *New York Times* reported that "Yale Scholar Wrote for Pro-Nazi Newspaper."[55] They wanted him to be the first to speak: "it has to be you, we thought that it was up to you to do this before anyone else."[56]

Interestingly, as for the attacks leveled against deconstruction, Derrida felt relatively little need to argue—in fact, he seemed almost amused:

> Some might smile with disabused indulgence at the highly transparent gesticulations of those who leap at the chance to exploit without delay an opportunity they think is propitious: at last, still without reading the texts, to take some cheap revenge on a "theory" that is all the more threatening to institutions and individuals because, visibly, they do not understand anything about it. One may also wonder, with the same smiling indulgence: but, after all, what does deconstruction (in the singular) have to do with what was written in 1940–42 by a very young man in a Belgian newspaper? Is it not ridiculous and dishonest to extend to a "theory," that has itself been simplified and homogenized, as well as to all those who are interested in it and develop it, the trial one would like to conduct of a man for texts written in Belgian newspapers forty-five years ago and that moreover, once again, one has not really read? Yes, this deserves perhaps hardly more than a smile and most often I manage to shrug it off.[57]

On that particular occasion, however, Derrida did not simply pass over such a vilification of deconstruction in a disillusioned silence. He did stand up for the theory—a "theory" in quotation marks. But, as I already suggested, nothing written in defense of deconstruction came even close, both in extent and intensity, to what Derrida wrote, not without some prior hesitation, on behalf of Paul de Man. Not without some hesitation, I should perhaps say anxiety, because for Derrida this war was personal: "Why me, who knew nothing about the dark time spent between 1940–42 by the Paul de Man I later read, knew, admired, loved?"[58]

Liked? Loved! How could any theory—even the theory of which Derrida was credited as the founder—compete for words with love? What could possibly matter more than the friendship *at* pain?

"Since that morning in 1966 when I met him at a breakfast table in Baltimore," professed Derrida at de Man's funeral, "nothing has ever come between us, not even a hint of disagreement. It was like the golden rule of an alliance, no doubt that of a trusting and unlimited friendship . . ."[59] Already then, four years before all the media hell broke loose, for Derrida everything was "painful, so painful."[60] And then he read the *Le Soir* articles and his first feelings were "of a wound, a stupor, and a sadness" that he wished "neither to dissimulate nor exhibit."[61] When Derrida reflected on the past at a time when everything was already happening, he reconciled himself with the fact that he could not have known what "ordeal the future held in store for my bereaved friendship, for that promise that friendship always is—a promise and a grief which are never over."[62]

> Yet, what was I saying about this nonknowledge? That it is the very thing that makes of the promise to the other a true promise, the only true promise, if there is any, an excessive and unconditional promise, an impossible promise. One can never promise in a halfway fashion, one always has to promise too much, more than one can fulfill. I could not know that one day, the experience of such a wound would have to include responding for Paul de Man.[63]

He could not have known because they never talked about what had happened during the war. Derrida knew that de Man had been "through some difficult times" but, as he told the group of de Man scholars at a conference held in October 1987 at the University of Alabama in Tuscaloosa, he had "never felt indiscreet enough to ask him about what had happened then."[64] Derrida would not ask and, as he also said during the conference, he had never read or heard anything from de Man that left the least suspicion in his memory "as to any persistence of, let us say—how to name it?—a certain ideology."[65] The discovery of de Man's wartime articles, therefore, struck Derrida as a bolt from the blue.

Soon, however, Derrida became conscious of other feelings besides those of "of a wound, a stupor, and a sadness." While he did not want to play down the "unpardonable violence and confusion" of what de Man had written—"What could possibly attenuate the fault? And whatever may be the reasons or the complications of a text, whatever may be going on in the mind of its author, how can one deny that the effect of these conclusions went in the sense and the direction of the worst?"[66]—while Derrida admitted that those texts had to be condemned, there was also something else:

> Rethinking about all of this in an obsessional way and with much [. . .] worry, consternation, the feeling that wins out over all the others in my bereaved friendship, bereaved once again, is, I have to say, first of all a feeling of immense compassion [. . .] This man must have lived a real agony and I believe that what he wrote later,

> what he taught, what he lived through in the United States obviously carry the traces of this suffering. I want to say that whatever may be [. . .] the wound that these texts are for me, they have changed nothing in my friendship and admiration for Paul de Man.[67]

Sad, hard truth *and* compassion, therefore. But also a meticulous, even cold[68] analysis *and* a story: "I have never known how to tell a story"[69]—with these words Derrida began his lecture series on Paul de Man, which he gave at the University of California, Irvine, in 1984 and which were later published under the title *Memoires: For Paul de Man*. "How could I then have imagined that it would be from the friend, from him alone, singularly from him, that would one day come the obligation to tell a story?"[70]—Derrida later wrote, for a large part of "Like the Sound of the Sea Deep within a Shell" was precisely that, a story.

Hard truth, cold analysis—cold truth? Compassion, story—even a "courage to answer injustice with justice?"[71] Which of these should we choose in the face of the cold truth? Which of these shall we, who are haunted by the specter of great cosmic stupidity, find more bearable? Theory or narrative? Can we choose? Do we have to choose? Or is the answer perhaps simpler, more straightforward, that we really need to choose responsibility?

Derrida for one thought so: "However obscure this may remain, we have to register it: we still have responsibilities toward him, and they are more alive than ever, even as he is dead."[72] Responsibility toward his friend, responsibility beyond but not without theory, that was the ultimate driving force behind Derrida's defense of Paul de Man. And it was a force of such magnitude that it bedazzled even some journalists. James Atlas from the *New York Times* wrote about thus far "the most persuasive defense of [Derrida's] good friend, an astonishing 30,000-word cry of pain," in which, "parsing de Man's *Le Soir* contributions virtually line by line, Derrida worried the issues with agonizing thoroughness," and "reiterated with hypnotic vigor [that] de Man's suppression of his past was the central fact of his life, its determining element: 'Paul de Man's war [was] the one that this man must have lived and endured in himself. He was this war.'"[73] About the revised edition of *Memoires*, in which the defense was reprinted, the *Choice* reviewer wrote that this "warm, personal, and at times touching account of the de Man/Derrida intellectual friendship and the existential experience of a friend's death shows a very human side to a thinker whose humanity has been questioned by the critics."[74]

Of course, inasmuch as "Like the Sound of the Sea Deep within a Shell" was a shot fired during the war, a powerful salvo, it was not appreciated in the opposing camp. In fact (although for a different reason), not even Derrida himself was entirely at peace with everything that he had written. Ten years later, he recalled how that was the only time in his life when he used the word "unforgivable" (unpardonable). "I am not sure I forgive myself for having written this word. But I did write it," Derrida said in an interview with Michal Ben-Naftali.[75] Also, he was aware that he might be misread:

> Having just reread my text, I imagine that for some it will seem I have tried, when all is said and done and despite all the protests or precautions, to protect, save, justify what does not deserve to be saved. I ask these readers, if they still have some concern for justice and rigor, to take the time to reread, as closely as possible.[76]

That fear actually came true, for as Benoît Peeters points out in the most recent biography of Derrida, it was precisely "from around 1987" that Derrida "was successively depicted as an anti-democratic nihilist and an adept of two Nazi theorists—Carl Schmitt and Martin Heidegger—whose work he had investigated," as well as "accused of being a Nazi, after making a clumsy attempt to defend his friend De Man."[77]

* * *

So much for Derrida's involvement in the Paul de Man affair. A rather depressing story, even for someone who had absolutely nothing to do with that unfortunate campaign. If I still went through the unpleasantry of researching and retelling it, I did so in view of the attitudes and elements of style manifested by Derrida. The tale of Caputo's growing appreciation of Derrida, on the other hand, I found quite heartwarming. The story and the tale, however, display similar traits. Those traits, Caputo's and Derrida's modalities of expression—what they said, how and why—were of interest to me as "proximate paradigms" for what I have been trying to achieve in this work. To elucidate this point, however, I now must return to where we began.

One of the reasons why I wrote about weak theology, I confessed, was because of a certain sympathy I feel toward Caputo. I put so much effort into describing his work because I like him, I feel close to him. Now, that was a sincere but admittedly rather nonstandard way to justify writing this book. That being so, my most immediate and perceptible motivation was to show that to at least a couple of important authors referenced in this work a certain pathos was not entirely anathema. I wanted to demonstrate that I am not the only one among scholars who can get carried away by passion and affectivity, even to the point of being melodramatic.

"But naturally," someone might argue, "and what do you imagine that you are proving by calling upon Caputo and Derrida? Yes indeed, those two do not seem to know how to keep within bounds. What else is new? Birds of a feather flock together, but surely you do not think that the mere existence of such complicity constitutes a sufficient excuse for their, not to mention yours, stylistic excesses? Hardly so. Not in any greater degree, to say the least, than it also bears witness to the self-referential indulgence prevalent in that postmodern gang . . ."

Perhaps. Another way to look at this, to be sure, also counts as a proverb—great minds think alike—but never mind. I cannot amuse anyone with such comical presumptuousness when I am, in fact, laboring to put into words even the sheer basics: How is this book written and why? By what scholarly means do I propose to justify my frequent departures from scholarly manners? By showing that others, even well-established scholars, did so too? Was I not warned not to follow in their footsteps, not before establishing myself first?

The truth is that if this should be my only argument, if *ei quoque* was my sole defense, then indeed I would merely prove myself a copycat. Parroting others, of course, can pass itself off as a method, and not always an inferior one. But it was not my method. While presenting and following my authors, I had no wish to become a mindless epigone. I would have rather risked getting off track than shy away from exploring. This adventurous attitude might have actually backfired on me, for at the end of the day I have some doubts whether the ideals that I had set for myself constitute any method at all. The problem I have in this regard, why I have found the question of methodology intimidating, is that having a method implies knowing in advance how I want to do things, whereas the honest truth is that, for the most part, I only knew with certainty how I did not want to do them. This is why I found it easier to get the present section going indirectly, that is to say, not by answering the question *how?* but rather by musing over *how else?*

Then again, "crookedly all good things approach their goal, like cats they arch their backs,"[78] another great mind who could not quite fit into academia said, leaving me at once at ease and ill at ease. An indirect approach, to say the least, can prove quite valuable. Certain situations even require it; sometimes there are no viable alternatives, like there is no substitute for negative theology. Few doubt, for example, that Karl Barth's famous *Nein!* was a methodologically valid position, although it is also true that he had more than enough to say as for the *Ja!*—while I have not. Perhaps in time I will be able to formulate clearly and in a composed manner my views on how to free theological thinking from its academic confinement so as to revive an informed theological discussion in the public sphere. For this has been my principal concern throughout this study and the true "excuse" for my stylistic excesses. Working out a strategy that would respond to the signs of the times, however, requires experience and, indeed, a lot of time. So as I said, at this point I feel prepared to offer little more than an explanation of the structure and style of *The Adventure of Weak Theology* in terms of the pitfalls that I wished to avoid. That is to say, to account for *how not?* rather than for *how?*

And yet, to borrow a felicitous turn of phrase from Caputo, I do not think that my tentative method, this indirect and sometimes convoluted approach, represents a "sorry spinelessness."[79] Rather, I am tendering here a work in progress: neither more nor less than an attempt at finding a way to write theology differently. Yes, even in defiance of the standards, but for what I genuinely believed to be good reasons. Understood thusly, this very labor—for I will, in actual fact, venture some sketchy opinions—this very labor *is the spine* of my book and I am quite forthrightly putting it forward for evaluation. Rather than apologizing, or trying to fend off potential criticism by bringing it upon myself, I invite readers to pay attention to the methodological struggle that marks this work. I hope they will not turn a deaf ear to the voice while focusing only on the substance. Who knows, it could be that the voice *is* the substance, the most important thing I have to say.

Let me now, therefore, talk more specifically about how it was that I wished to write and/or wished not to write. And once again, the question is why I said that this book was motivated by my sympathy toward Caputo. Was I trying to make a case for pathos and affectivity? Well yes and no, for things just are not that simple.

First of all, despite appearances to the contrary, I would not be able to convince even Derrida, and we saw how passionately he wrote when things were tough. On a theoretical level, however, Derrida told Tom Keenan that he was trying not to give in to pathos, "not too much." "But when I do give in to it," continued Derrida, "I try to make it such that the pathos is not too easily translatable into terms of subjective affectivity."[80]

How then? Without pathos and affectivity—and failing miserably at that? I would be quite a fool, but no, I am not that simple either. Perhaps the closest answer came again from Derrida, when he admitted that he was not trying to avoid pathos in any case and at any price.[81] He did not think it would make much sense, because pathos

> is something that is before the subject, that is before what we call affectivity in the usual sense. And yet there is suffering . . . there is suffering. Nor do I really believe in the possibility of a language that

> is absolutely apathetic, neutral. I do not believe it exists. There are ways of controlling the pathos, of making it as discreet as possible, almost neutralized, but this creates yet another pathos.[82]

Thus neither with pathos, nor without pathos. If, on the one hand, this sounds like an impossible contradiction—which it is, in a sense—on the other hand it also illustrates the difficulties involved in writing so that the wolf be full and the sheep unharmed. I wanted to write *not without* pathos, not to avoid it at any price. Rather, the point was to avoid slipping into the kind of "academic writing" that, according to Jacoby, "developed into unreadable communiques sweetened by thanks to colleagues and superiors,"[83] those thanks confined within the preface or the acknowledgments. Why, after all, should one not express gratitude wherever it feels right? What exactly makes such personal references incompatible with the main body of an academic text?

Nevertheless, it must be obvious by now that I am making a big thing of what would have likely been served much better by keeping it discreet. True, I did not really need to insist on this point. I wonder now—and this may come as a surprise—I wonder what, if anything at all, would have changed, had I maintained a certain sobriety and simply refrained from talking about whom I like and why? One thing would have been different, to be sure: I would have spared myself the trouble of explaining the melodrama away. But seriously, how does *that* make sense? Why distort the image only to later try to put it straight again?

That is, indeed, the right question to ask, for whatever its shortcomings, the tentative method at work in *The Adventure of Weak Theology* is anything but a weepy supplication, a somewhat naïve petition to let me repeat freely (and pretty much ad nauseam) how much I sympathize with my author. So why say it in the first place? And after it has been said once, why draw attention to it by repeating it over and over, when maybe otherwise nobody would have cared? What held me back from neutralizing (almost) the unnecessary pathos?

Nothing did, but the theatrics was intentional. As I announced at the end of the previous section, my objective was to set the stage for the concluding discussion about the sense of the work at hand and I thought a little bit of suspense would be helpful. I meant to establish the distance, to manifest and perhaps even overstate the rift that exists between, on the one hand, cold analysis—the proper academic style—and, on the other hand, whatever went by the name of pathos. There is passion and suffering, there is compassion and also sympathy. And then there are the dispassionate rules of scholarly writing. This very modernistic division has disturbed me for a long time, and to the extent that the question whether or not it was okay to claim that my book was motivated by the sympathy toward Caputo was not an unrelated one,

I think it served the purpose well. That said, from the perspective of the content of *The Adventure of Weak Theology* it really did not matter all that much. I neither felt the need to, nor did I actually expose such feelings anywhere else down the line.

No, at heart this labyrinthine method of mine is far more than a poorly argued case for the permissibility of a particular turn of phrase. This is a call, albeit a minor one, for a revolution; an indictment against the ubiquity, even in humanities and especially in humanities, of the cold analysis divested of all signs of humanness. Sweet thanks to colleagues and superiors held captive in one spot predetermined for the maximum impact, for an entire academic economy is built around the recognition of patronage and wars are occasionally fought over bylines. Cold analysis against a backdrop of pitiless competition of theories, depicting Derrida as a Nazi and driving Caputo to a prophetic self-delusion of scandalizing everyone. Oh he would wish, but who really cares? Away with such literature! At heart, my labyrinthine method is an act of defiance against such loss, in academic writing, of heart, of art, of hearth—which is to say, of home. For I am under the obligation to make sense and there is no sense outside home.

A few observations about a particular revolution that took place some two centuries ago might help explain my point. I am not referring to the French Revolution, which completely altered the course of European politics, but to the one that followed a few years later and forever changed Western classical music—the premiere of Ludwig van Beethoven's Symphony No. 3 in April 1805. Beethoven did, in fact, originally dedicate his *Eroica* symphony to Napoleon Bonaparte, whom he admired as the flag-bearer of the revolution and the promoter of the ideals of *liberté, égalité, fraternité* in Europe, but he then had a change of heart after Napoleon had proclaimed himself an emperor. The analogy I wish to draw here, however, has less to do with the political background of the *Eroica*, although it was by no means unimportant, and more to do with how and why Beethoven broke away from the established musical tradition.

It is important that we understand that music, like any form of art, has objective and subjective components, for want of a less dualistic way of describing it. Equally significant, at least with regard to the present argument, is the absence of clear boundaries between various kinds of art. What does this mean? First of all, as a form of communication, music presupposes the existence of shared language, which is in turn characterized by objective rules—musical forms. Contrary to popular stereotypes, orchestral music is no less accessible than any other language, after one gets the hang of it. Nor is the language of music simply arbitrary. Instead, it participates in the cultural paradigm of the day and it evolves with that paradigm. In what order such changes come about is, of course, an entire issue in itself and a fitting example of the paradox of exemplarity: Does music, and art in general, merely reflect the metamorphoses of culture, or does it initiate them? Whatever the answer to this unanswerable question may be, it has to do with the second, subjective component of orchestral music. For, if virtuosity designates the composer's mastery of the form, then genius means the ability to use that form to convey the experience, to bear witness to the joys and sorrows of the lifeworld—or, when the form proves inadequate, the guts to reinvent it. Musical forms do not change of their own accord. Like languages, or genres in literature, they are stretched and altered by the living individuals to fit their needs of expression. Finally, since art reflects various aspects of what is, in fact, an undivided organic experience—"what is it like to be alive here and now"—different kinds of art can and often do blend together. Of particular interest for us will be the combination of music and drama, but not as it is embodied in opera, where the libretto and musical score together constitute a single performance, nor as it is found in so-called program music, where the audience's familiarity with the narrative is either taken for granted, or the narrative is given in the form of program notes, but there is no actual singing involved. These are good examples, but orchestral music can also function as drama in the absence of explicit internal or external narratives. Music can tell stories of its own. Among the classical musical forms, the sonata form was particularly suited for this purpose and it is this form that is most relevant for our discussion, not only in view of its connection to Beethoven's revolution, but also because the proposed analogy with my methodological considerations will benefit most greatly from an example that entails drama without drama.

So what exactly did Beethoven change? As Maynard Solomon points out, "the startling and unprecedented characteristics of the *Eroica*" were made possible precisely because Beethoven had realized what the flexible framework of the sonata form allowed him to pull off.[84] The structure of the sonata form—introduction, exposition of the two contrasting themes, development, recapitulation, and coda—indeed resembles the basic outline of a narrative, and Beethoven certainly was not the first to recognize these parallels.[85] Yet, even such giants of the Classical period as Joseph Haydn and Wolfgang Amadeus Mozart, although by no means oblivious to this analogy, never exploited the sonata form to the extent that Beethoven did. "Their psychological outlook and the requirements of the forms of patronage under which they worked," argues Solomon, "apparently did not predispose Haydn and Mozart (not to speak of their lesser contemporaries) to fully develop those possibilities."[86] Both Haydn and Mozart were too constricted by the expectations and niceties of their own times: Music was supposed to be light, accessible, melodic, strictly symmetrical. So when either of them composed in the sonata form, the result was inevitably limited to a very particular kind of musical drama:

> [T]he sonata cycles of Mozart and Haydn were musical analogues of the comedy of manners—rational, unsentimental, objective, witty, satirical treatments of the conventions, customs and mores of society. In the comedy of manners, disruptions of the social fabric are momentary; the loss of love or status is provisional and temporary; undercurrents of sadness and melancholy are almost invariably dissolved in a reaffirmation of social norms and in a return to sanity and wholeness. As Einstein observed, the symphonies of Haydn and Mozart "always remained within the social frame"; and in their sonata-form works they "limited themselves to the attainment of noble mirth, to a purification of the feelings." Hence, however well it mirrored the rich variety of emotional states and strivings of its composers, its patrons, its audience, and the larger collectivity of which these were parts, the high-Classic style failed to map several inescapable and fundamental features of the emotional landscape in so tumultuous an era. In particular, it rarely plumbed either the heroic or the tragic levels of experience.[87]

Beethoven, on the other hand, would have probably given anything to be spared of his all too personal knowledge of the meaning of heroism and tragedy. At the time of the completion of the *Eroica*, he had been progressively losing his hearing for the past eight years; two years prior to that, Beethoven had even contemplated suicide but decided to "take fate by the throat" and continue composing. His third symphony reflects this struggle, which makes it different, indeed revolutionary. For in order to speak of hope, Beethoven also needed to speak of loss:

> Beethoven took music beyond what we may describe as the pleasure principle of Viennese Classicism; he permitted aggressive and disintegrative forces to enter musical form: he placed the tragic experience at the core of his heroic style. He now introduced elements into instrumental music that had previously been neglected or unwelcome. A unique characteristic of the Eroica Symphony—and of its heroic successors—is the incorporation into musical form of death, destructiveness, anxiety, and aggression, as terrors to be transcended within the work of art itself. And it will be this intrusion of hostile energy, raising the possibility of loss, that will also make affirmations worthwhile.[88]

Just like faith only makes sense against a backdrop of the abyss. The latter must be taken seriously to make the former worthwhile. In any case, I like Beethoven—"a dusk of eternal loss and eternal, wild hope lies over his music"[89]—but I doubt anybody will give a damn by now.

More likely, I think, the question would be what has Athens to do with Jerusalem and science with . . . well, art? What has it not? "If you take a long enough look," wrote Caputo in response to what Tertullian really meant by his question,

> beyond the debates that divide philosophy and theology, over the walls that they have built to keep each other out or beyond the wars to subordinate one to another, you find a common sense of awe, a common gasp of surprise or astonishment, like looking out at the endless sprawl of stars across the evening sky or upon the waves of a midnight sea.[90]

Besides offering an example of doing science artistically, this quote reaffirms, albeit in a different context, the basis for my analogy, because science also shares with art the common sense of awe. Ultimately, no human activity stands in total isolation from the others. "And that," somebody may argue again, "is as true as it is unhelpful. For did not differentiation bring us only good? Did it not, to say the least, liberate science from superstition?" That may be, although I wonder what else was thus science "liberated" from. Still, insofar as the benefits of defining scientific methodology in contradistinction to the *modi operandi* of arts cannot be denied, I indeed prefer to use as my example the sonata form, even if *The Adventure of Weak Theology* is in fact an opera. To make the most of the analogy at hand, I would say that the sonata form is my ideal, the opera is the reality, and the tension between the two is the driving force behind the search for my method. It is easy to see, if you put disbelief on hold, how the sonata form also parallels the general structure of an academic text: introduction followed by the statement of a hypothesis and of the competing ideas, the development of the argument, summary of the findings and a conclusion. Scholarly writing, on this account, should be perfectly capable of telling a story of its own, without the need for an external narrative and maybe—who knows, it is an ideal—even without the "contamination" by the forms of expression that are regarded as foreign to science. At any rate, there is a proven potential in the academic form and I would like to emphasize that it was never my ambition to break completely free from it but to extend it so that it fits my needs of expression. Here, again, I agree with Derrida who thought that

> for the risk to be worth the trouble, so to speak, and for it to be really something risky or risking, one must take this risk with all possible insurance [. . .] One has to be sure that the risk is taken. And to be sure that the risk is taken, one has to negotiate with the assurances. And thus speak in the mode of philosophy, of demonstration, of logic,

> of critique so as to arrive at the point where that is no longer possible, so as to see where that is no longer possible. What I am calling here assurance or insurance are all the codes, the values, the norms [. . .] that regulate philosophical discourse: the philosophical institution, the values of coherence, truth, demonstration, and so forth.[91]

Derrida, in other words, did not want to do away with the standards of academic discourse, just as Beethoven did not mean to completely disregard the Classical tradition. Even if he, in actual fact, inaugurated a new, Romantic period, he did so by means of utilizing the full potential of the most important Classical form.

That said, a willingness and the ability to take risks was crucial for both of them. We saw the forces that triggered Beethoven's revolution, why Beethoven chose to risk being misunderstood, as he indeed often was. Fate—his own and that of Europe—drove him to the point where composing honest music in line with the general expectations was no longer possible. As for Derrida, I find it quite gratifying that he should also use a quasi-musical terminology when talking about the "very complicated pleasure" of doing philosophy, and that in order to get this pleasure

> one must, at a given moment, stand at the edge of catastrophe or of the risk of loss. Otherwise, one is only applying a surefire program. So, one must take risks. That's what experience is. I use this word in a very grave sense. There would be no experience otherwise, without risk.[92]

There would be no experience without risk. Yet without experience, ultimately, there would be no invention either. We would remain forever stuck in the moment when we ceased risking new approaches. For Derrida, "to experience is to advance by navigating, to walk by traversing [. . .] a limit or a border."[93] It has just dawned on me, eureka, I have found—night precedes these cries. Dark night of an adventurer adrift on a ship in the open sea, having already sailed beyond the point of no return: "¡Tierra! ¡Tierra!" resounded from the crow's nest atop *Pinta*, where even the toughest sailors got easily sick, not from the salons of the learned men in Lisbon or Seville.

Now, if the audacity to do things otherwise is an essential ingredient in the process of invention, then one cannot but wonder why, in contemporary academia, the safety of the well-trodden paths seems preferred over the spirit of adventure. Why is it, to push my musical analogy even further, that we get at best Haydns and Mozarts, but so very few Beethovens? And one last time, by "at best" I do not mean to play down the influence of the phenomenally talented but conservative authors, nor do I wish to indiscriminately canonize all rebels. I hope I have been clear on that, for I cannot imagine that anyone would seriously think that I wish to criticize Mozart. It also goes without saying that the learned men in Lisbon and Seville were, in fact, right—while somebody described Columbus, quite wittily, as the father of modern government, "He didn't know where he was going when he started, he didn't know where he was when he got there, and he did it all on borrowed money." Truth be told, I feel this far more often than I like, whence also my acknowledgment of the importance of guidelines. But the point is that the rules of proper academic writing do not really need any more backing than they already get. So please permit me to change the register for a while; it would be a shame if I kept on timidly excusing myself and retreating all the time, like a "type of little girl and *noli me tangere*."[94] For there is also "at worst" at work in the academic world certain scholarly beliefs and practices, which deserve the exact opposite of endorsement.

Let us not for a moment think that ours are not tumultuous times and therefore we need no Beethovens to explore novel ways of expression; that since the culture wars are over, we can dispense with Derridas and their works of agonizing passion; that with nearly all brilliant lunatics gone anyway, we can now embark on the path of consolidation, retire the apologists, and replace them by bookkeepers, for hopefully in the foreseeable future we shall have little need for Caputos and their skills in mocking the narrow-minded; in time of peace, you see, narrow-mindedness is superseded by specialization and focus.

Or perhaps yes, let us, for the sake of argument, believe all of that and then some more: Why not regard the expansion of the universities and the unprecedented proliferation of scholarly publishing as the conclusive evidence that, at long last, we are doing things right? And that, in the interest of the well-being of science, this is the way to carry on—composedly and methodically, avoiding excesses of expression and, especially, staying within the bounds of discipline. For if we all manage to be reasonable and if we stick to our own businesses, as the principle of differentiation requires, everybody should be fine. Academic *live and let live*, stay cool, there are enough funding resources for everyone. Live and let live turned into *noli me tangere* indeed, or into *nemo me impune lacessit*, reserved for the uninvited transgressors, like those unruly scientists who steal jobs from poets, philosophers who have the nerve to pass judgment on theology, not to mention theologians who seem inclined to appropriate shamelessly everything from Nietzsche to string theory. Let us, in the interest of science, prune away such dilettantism and we shall all have perfectly uncontaminated methods that will give us the most perfectly . . . sterile results.

I am now needlessly dramatizing, to be sure. We do not really need to imagine anything of the sort, because all of this has already been happening. The sorry predicament of the burgeoning (or bourgeois?) academia—and this is ever so much truer for humanities, since they seldom need to prove their value by pointing to some practical applications—can be described by the chain of transformations whereby differentiation led to insularization, which resulted in an increasing self-referentiality and eventually irrelevance. *Noli me tangere?* Fine, let everyone have a monopoly on their expertise with their own methods and modes of expression. Let mathematicians count, but only count, and as for theologians, who obviously cannot count, let them pray or do whatever they are doing best, for we do not really know what they are doing and, frankly, we could not care less. As long as mathematicians are free to count in whatever way they like without fear of inquisition and they, in turn, refrain from making silly comments about the peculiar way that theologians count, say, the Trinity—all is fine, finally fine. Except that there is a heavy price to pay for the emancipatory benefits of differentiation: What happened to thinking—the capacity to find new connections where they are not obvious—when interdisciplinarity itself must be encouraged? And let us not be mistaken about this: Far from being yet another of our glorious new discoveries, the contemporary emphasis on the cooperation between the disciplines represents only a late realization that sometime in the past we threw the baby out with the bathwater. With academia expanding like the Universe after the Big Bang, distances between the individual islands of knowledge also continue to grow until they reach such magnitudes that mutual communication becomes close to impossible.

Why is this a problem and how is it related to my methodological considerations? It is a problem because, with no communication between the various areas of research, the way we see the world becomes increasingly fragmentary and the stereotype of a mad scientist lost in his incomprehensible formulations becomes a reality. Without communication, external checks and balances are missing, too—that is what the self-referentiality of a discipline means—and, ultimately, there is no reality check either. Things being as they are, it is perfectly possible to do research just for the sake of doing it; one can publish dozens of articles without saying anything meaningful about life or the world. Indeed, sometimes it seems as if the fragmentary academic universe was under no obligation to make any sense at all.

When, for example, was the last time that somebody wondered what on earth is happening? Was it in 1968, the year of revolt (how appropriate), when Lewis Mumford attacked the "encroaching academezation of culture"? Jacoby relates how Mumford came across a new scholarly edition of his favorite writer, Ralph Waldo Emerson, published by Harvard University Press:

> Mumford was appalled. Teams of academics had transmuted Emerson's fluid prose into sludge. In the name of accuracy, the good professors had flagged every inconsequential divergence between various manuscripts and published editions. They used twenty different diacritical marks, which became part of the printed text, that "spit, and sputter at the reader, not only to indicate cancellations, insertions or variants, but also unrecovered matter, unrecovered cancelled matter, accidentally mulitilated [*sic*] manuscript, even erasures." For Mumford, the academic enterprise had gone amuck. "Thus these 'Journals' have now performed current American scholarship's ultimate homage to a writer of genius: they have made him unreadable."[95]

Even more revealing is the story of Edmund Wilson who, following the example of Mumford, also looked at some scholarly editions sponsored by the Modern Language Association (MLA), and what he found—"a vast scholarly libido channeled into textual annotations mangling America's authors"—did not amuse him at all:[96]

> Thirty-five scholars were busy going through variant texts of Mark Twain; eighteen of them were "reading Tom Sawyer backward," in order to ascertain without being diverted from this drudgery by attention to the story or style, how many times "Aunt Polly" is printed as "aunty Polly." While universities lavished funds and research on unreadable scholarly editions, often of unimportant books or authors, cheap usable editions of essential American writings hardly existed. For Wilson this all demonstrated that the academic enterprise had become a bloated boondoggle.[97]

The best part of this anecdote, however, is the response of the insulted MLA entitled *Professional Standards and American Editions: A Response to Edmund Wilson*.[98] The gist of their counterattack, as Jacoby tells us, was that "Wilson and his supporters represented obsolete amateurism in the age of high-performance professionals."[99] Wilson's attack

> derives in part from the alarm of amateurs at seeing rigorous professional standards applied to a subject in which they have a vested interest. Here, at least, the issue is not in doubt. As the American world has come to full maturity since the second World

> War, a similar animus has shown itself and been discredited in field after field from botany to folklore. In the long run professional standards always prevail.[100]

Oh people just got to love us, the self-important professionals. Incidentally, although I have to admit that I found reading Russell Jacoby's *The Last Intellectuals* most exhilarating and I quote him a lot, he is by no means the only author I came across who troubles himself about what is happening in contemporary academic culture. Josef Joffe, for example, discusses how

> given the exponential expansion of academia and hence the competitive quest for differentiation and specialization, more and more is asked about less and less in ever more arcane ways. Professionalization is the watchword, and this has led Stanley Hoffmann, Harvard's doyen of international relations, to muse: "Today, I would not get tenure."[101]

Consider also the academic "poetry" of Elisabeth Roudinesco, a French historian and a good friend of Derrida's. All we are entitled to do today, she worries, "is to take stock and draw up assessments, as though the distance that every intellectual enterprise requires amounted to no more than a vast ledger full of entries for things and people—or rather people who have become things."[102] And then she comes up with:

> Whom do you prefer; who are the puniest figures, the greatest ones, the most mediocre, the biggest charlatans, the most criminal? Classify, rank, calculate, measure, put a price on, normalize: this is the absolute nadir of contemporary interrogation, endlessly imposing itself in the name of a bogus modernity that undermines every form of critical intelligence grounded in the analysis of the complexity of things and persons.[103]

The absolute nadir of contemporary interrogation, which I called—admittedly somewhat at variance with Roudinesco—a cold, inhuman analysis. The point is the same, however: people who have become things to us. Add to this Roudinesco's talk about the "gap between the academicism that is returning in force to official schooling and the massive demand for 'living' teaching outside the universities,"[104] a demand we no longer seem able to meet, because we are, not entirely unlike Haydn and Mozart, too restricted by the expectations of our scholarly environment. And in the midst of all of that, "a melancholic

Easterner" writing a book. I had to call for a revolution, I had to attempt it myself, if I were to make any sense at all.

But how? By reversing the differentiation and by completely disregarding the rules of my own discipline? No one can achieve the former and the latter is far beyond my league; when all is said and done, I do not fancy myself a rebel. How then? By permitting aggressive and disintegrative forces to enter my text? No, at least not intentionally. *The Adventure of Weak Theology* is neither heroic nor tragic; but if it is unconventional at all, it is because I allowed for the interruption of an unbiased analysis by the forces of sympathy and compassion. I did not mean to criticize Caputo, not even to merely critique his work; rather, I wanted a "link of affinity, suffering, and hope, a still discreet, almost secret link,"[105] to run through my work, to borrow Derrida's words from *Specters of Marx* about the "New International." Speaking of which, to finally bring all the threads together, Derrida also confessed:

> I know that I myself can personally be very sensitive to the emotion attached to revolutionary pathos. This does not prevent me from also trying to scrutinize at the same time. But it sometimes happens that I experience moments of classic left-wing pathos—never of right-wing pathos. This is true: I am unable to have moments of right-wing pathos. Moments of a classic left-wing pathos that cohabit with a cold analysis, this is my history. I am still, as they say, viscerally left-wing. Thus, when I hear—even today when it has gone out of fashion—when I hear the International, I may sing along and tears come to my eyes.[106]

Stated in yet another, but by now familiar way, I meant for this book to be permeated by the sense of responsibility toward Caputo, in the same way that Derrida's "Like the Sound of the Sea Deep within a Shell" never failed to be responsible toward Paul de Man. I also never got around to citing any of the critics of Derrida's passionate apologia. Well, now is the time, after we have heard some music:

> The central theme of the prologue [of "Like the Sound of the Sea Deep within a Shell"] is the notion of responsibility, as well it might be, given the subject. Accordingly, those first seven pages swamp the reader with the word "responsibility" to the point where they could be described as "variations on the theme." Inundation, alas, is not elucidation, and all closer references to the notion remain impenetrably elliptic: Derrida possesses the unique art of combining extreme ellipsis with extreme verbosity. In fact these "variations"

> are more musical than analytic: "responsibility" comes close to being a Wagnerian leitmotiv. Like a characteristic melody, the word winds through the text in a constant sequence of appearances and temporary disappearances, ever expected, always ready to reemerge. Although there is no clear-cut line of argument, there does seem to be a general direction of development.[107]

Wolfgang Holdheim clearly did not like what he read, but he got Derrida right. Derrida's 1988 text, and for that matter Derrida's work in general, was indeed all about responsibility—albeit responsibility rethought. And since one reaps what one has sown, Derrida received the same gift from Caputo in *Prayers and Tears*. This book, conceived as it was "up among the angels" and the "hole from which Caputo never reemerged," also happens to bear marks of comedy. Not that of manners, however, as was the case with Haydn and Mozart, but, as Cleo McNelly Kearns observed *pace* Steve Helmling, an *esoteric comedy*. I said as much in this regard in chapter 11, so for now suffice it to say that this is a genre often deployed "when a writer is caught between a subject matter in some sense sublime and an audience whose expectations run to the other extreme."[108] A perfect tool, in other words, to keep the hazards of academese at bay. Kearns also employs a quasi-musical terminology when she argues that

> [t]here is pleasure in hearing in counterpoint his [Caputo's] open, humorous, democratic voice and the European elegance, the aristocratic high-handedness, the witty elaborations of Derrida's. Nor is this counterpoint merely instrumental. Caputo's plain style testifies to the willingness of the writer to sacrifice dignity, decorum and respectability, to forfeit his place among the knights of good conscience, in the name of something he wishes to present, much against the spirit of his times, as of higher value than these. As Helmling remarks, one may be a fool for ideas as well as a fool for love. We might add that one may be a fool for style as well, running the risks of mistranslation in order to serve another's unique voice, unique persona, unique mode of being.[109]

Whose "another's unique voice"? The songs of the suffering Europe, which would have never been heard, had Beethoven not "taken fate by the throat" and broken from the niceties of the Viennese tradition? The prayers and tears of Jacques Derrida, his religion "about which nobody understands anything," and before Caputo few really tried to understand? The "at once Kierkegaardian and Philadelphian, melancholy and upbeat, religious and aesthetic" voice of John D. Caputo?

In *The Adventure of Weak Theology*, my own voice perhaps? Even if that meant, at times, sacrificing scholarly decorum and respectability, for there are things of higher value than a cold "Viennese" (remember Wittgenstein?) analysis? "Too many definitions, too much caution," Jacoby warns us, "kill thought," which is why, he thinks, "modern analytic philosophy, laboring for decades to establish sound conceptual methods, has only established its inability to think."[110] Funny that it should be philosophers from precisely that quarter that criticized Derrida and Caputo most earnestly . . .

Beyond cold analysis, Derrida called for responsibility, which, in the case of his responsibility toward Paul de Man, took the form of a story. This book, too, has the structure of a narrative. It is also haunted by the consciousness of my storytelling ineptitude and it is motivated by the same realization that, over and beyond cold analysis, we are called to responsibility. For, as Saint-Exupéry remarked, "to be a [hu] man is, precisely, to be responsible. It is to feel shame at the sight of what seems to be unmerited misery. It is to take pride in a victory won by one's comrades. It is to feel, when setting one's stone, that one is contributing to the building of the world."[111] What point would there be in becoming a great scholar, if in the process I was to suffer the loss of heart? What sense would a thorough theological analysis of Caputo's project make, if I but for a moment lost sight of the simple truth that weak theology is a history of the quest that cost Caputo his life?

Insofar as a scholarly, cold analysis forgets that we are all in the same boat, all partakers in the same search for whatever sense there is to find—whether we agree with one another, or not—it only contributes to the increasingly senseless body of academic writing in the increasingly meaningless world. I could, indeed, read Caputo backward and count how many times, for example, he contradicts himself—were it not for the fact that I take pride in Caputo's lifework. I am proud that a fellow theologian tried to think the way he did.

Now, if by sidestepping a serious and methodical critique of Caputo's theology I have forfeited my place among the serious academics and will henceforth be counted for no more than a "high-class journalist,"[112] then so be it. But before the curtain falls, I would like to say that for some time I saw myself on the verge of a discovery. I believed I had something deceptively simple, yet quite unique to say. Unfortunately, it turns out that I do not, unless speaking for the first time, as far as I can say, about the "old gomer Universe" also counts. That silly grammatical idiosyncrasy, however, was not what I had in mind; and I still cannot decide whether being cheated out of my particular contribution to academic thinking—*that even, and especially, on the level of method, responsibility toward theorists matters at least as much as their theories themselves*—is something that I should regret or celebrate.

I was going to say: "Look, I would rather sit in a rocking chair by the fire sipping on a glass of twelve-year-old Redbreast, listening and only listening to Caputo's tale about what he has lost and found, than to be challenged to a *disputatio* and attempt to wipe the floor with him in public, all in the name of some truth. And I still think that as a scholar . . ." I was going to say that, even though Caputo must have held the very same belief all along. He had been writing like Derrida's friend for decades and yes, I was aware of that, but in my not-so-youthful arrogance I thought I would formalize qua method what he seemed to have done instinctively. So when I then stumbled across Kearns's article, I thought: "Exactly, yes, yes! This is what I have been thinking, I must make sure to quote her"—only to realize a moment later: "Darn! There goes my 'unique' point . . ."

In her analysis of Caputo's *Prayers and Tears*, Kearns pointed out how the book represents "an instantiation of what *Against Ethics* defines as a poetics of obligation, obligation in this case to the other, not perhaps so *tout autre* after all, [but to the other] that is Jacques Derrida."[113] Similarly, I described *Prayers and Tears* as Caputo's work of responsibility toward Derrida. The similarity between the positions taken by Kearns and myself clearly depends on regarding Caputo's "obligation" and Derrida's "responsibility" as merely two sides of the same dynamics, which was so wonderfully explained by Levinas. This is a defendable view, in my opinion, but I cannot delve into it just now. It is Caputo's own take on obligation that I cannot skip here (more in chapter 9) because, apropos my tentative method, that's where the money is.

"By obligation," explains Caputo in *Against Ethics*, "I do not mean anything profound":

> Like Johannes de Silentio, whom I have taken as a certain mentor, I have no such "prodigious head" for profundity. It is all I can do to get through the days and nights of everydayness; the superficial world is already more than I can handle. Obligation does not mean answering the call of Being, or of the History of Being, or of the History of Spirit, or of the Voice of God. I have, I repeat, lost all communications from On High. My satellite has been knocked out. I have in mind instead a very earthbound signal, a superficial-horizontal communication between one human being and another, a certain line of force that runs along the surface upon which you and I stand: the obligation I have to you (and you to me, but this is different) and the both of "us" to "others."[114]

Let us not be deceived, however. If Caputo appears to downplay what he has to say about obligation, we can rest assured that he is, in fact, relating something of the utmost importance. Laughing through tears—"laughing in order not to be overcome with tears"[115]—Caputo also calls his theology weak: this is all a Kierkegaardian ploy. So by obligation, he may not mean anything profound, but he draws our attention to the fact that obligations happen. Obligations, according to Caputo, wield the power of facts; obligation is as much a fact as any other fact, very much like the empirical facts of science.[116] And it is a fact that "serious science" cannot drive away:

> Obligations rebound after every philosophical debate, after every academic conference, just shortly after the invited plenary speaker has collected his check and is headed for the airport. Prescriptives are a fact of factical life, of linguistic, social, political, institutional, personal, family life, of any sphere of life.[117]

Hence Derrida's obligation (or responsibility) to de Man after the conference in Tuscaloosa, or Caputo's obligation to Derrida after, say, the Cambridge affair. Neither of the two imagined that their science should stand above their obligations to fellow humans. They dismissed the rigid dichotomy between science and obligation (or between cold analysis and pathos) as one more modernistic myth, at least in practice if not always explicitly in theory. After all, does not the question "What ought we to do?" have its origin on the same planet floating "in some remote corner of the universe, flickering in the light of the countless solar systems," where "clever animals" at "the most arrogant and most mendacious minute in the history of the world" invented knowing?[118] "Substitute 'obligation' for 'knowing' in this passage," Caputo tells us, "and you will see what I mean by impiety and by the disaster."[119] Caputo's fascination with Nietzsche's tale of a little star surfaced in chapter 11, but for now note that obligation finds itself in company with knowledge when viewed against the backdrop of an abyss. It would seem that, for Caputo, the abyss is "the great leveler" that puts everything on an equal footing: "'knowledge,' 'obligation,' 'justice'—these are so many obsolete inventions of the little animals," fictions that we invent

> to make it through the day and to persuade ourselves of our meaning and significance. Until at last, weary of its peculiar little local experiment, the cosmos draws another and moves on. Then we disappear without a trace.[120]

But does this really represent the totality of Caputo's perspective on life? Not quite so. The father of weak theology respects Nietzsche for his guts to face up to the abyss, and he thinks highly of Nietzsche's refusal to make things easier for ourselves. That, in fact, is the credo of radical hermeneutics: Thou shalt not cover up the difficulty of life! Nevertheless, Caputo does not subscribe to Nietzsche's vision of the world tout court. The main point of contention, aside from the answer (if he actually has one) to the final question raised by the clever animals—"What can we hope for?"—lies with obligation. Stripped of its pretense to profundity, obligation offers something that neither Nietzsche nor for that matter highbrow science ever will. In the midst of a disaster, constantly tugging at our sleeves and calling upon us for a response,[121] it lets us put our foot in the door of a home away from home. How so? Because, on Caputo's rendering

> the discourse on obligation is a treatise on proper names, on the affirmation of "someone," something more or less proper, personal, over and beyond or within the cosmic hum.[122]

Obligation does not result in mere naming, but in the answer to the very concrete other. Here we are far removed from Roudinesco's "ledger full of entries for people who have become things." To be sure, naming has become our scientific "style" of choice, but the consequences are dire: "In vain is the whole of 'world literature' piled up around modern man for his solace," complained Nietzsche,

> in vain is he placed amongst all the artistic styles and artists of all times, so that he may give them names—as Adam gave names to the beasts; despite all this, he remains eternally hungry, a 'critic' without desire or energy, Alexandrian man who is basically a librarian and proof-reader, sacrificing his sight miserably to book-dust and errors.[123]

Such is the risk of cold analysis and an all-too-likely fate of many a decent scholar, whereas

> obligations shatter the silence of anonymity with proper names, if only temporarily, shooting proper names into the night-dark sky like darts of light, like shooting stars, fleeting moments of illumination. We send up small, tiny, limited little infinities into the night, as if there were something Infinite that contracts the vastness of the sky, as if there were an Infinity that shrinks the seas and dwarfs the mountaintops, that makes all of nature bow down.[124]

Stroke after stroke, image after image, Caputo paints the picture of a little star adrift in the vastness of the indifferent Universe, a planet that is only our home insofar as we have each other: "When a proper name is used, when a proper name happens, it is like a voice crying in the void, like a prophet crying in a cosmic wilderness";[125] indeed, "proper names are our temporary triumphs, and passing protests against the anonymity of *il y a*, against the transciency [what a marvelous typo] of *es gibt*, against the namelessness that surrounds us."[126] Obligations and proper names belong together, because

> to follow the way of obligation means to be stirred by the appeals, to answer the calls of lowly proper names, of what is laid low. The right response to what is laid low is not the invocation of a sacred name but offering relief, lending a hand. Without why. Because. Because flesh is flesh, because flesh calls to flesh, because to promote flourishing and joy, in particular that of the least among us, of the *me onta*, is its own form of life . . .[127]

Nothing profound, only "facts as it were"[128]—yet profoundly moving facts and, concerning Caputo's texts about Derrida, also strikingly true. And *that* is the whole point. That is what Cleo McNelly Kearns named:

> There is, however, a moment of truth, a kind of realized eschatology in this text [*Prayers and Tears*], though not the one we perhaps expected. Rather, it is a moment more fraternal than numinous, more earthly than sublime. For [. . .] Caputo directs his affirmation to his friend and colleague, Jacques Derrida himself, to whom he offers the gift of a saving faith in the other's work which marks a singular act of solidarity. "*Me voici*," Caputo says to that friend: "*viens, viens, oui, amen*, I am here praying and crying with you."[129]

Derrida recognizes this gift. "Another reason why I am so grateful for [Caputo's] writings," he said in an interview with Mark Dooley, "is because when he reads my texts, which is especially the case throughout *Prayers and Tears*, he is the first one, and so far the only one, to bring the most philosophical and theoretical of my writings together with those which are most autobiographical."[130] If, as somebody said, my proper name is the most important word to me, Derrida is grateful for that word being spoken; in science especially, it is wonderful to be more than just a text. Is this, on Caputo's part, nothing more than humanism?—Kearns asks. "Is this fellow-being all that Caputo 'loves' when he 'loves his God'? Yes, I think so. Unless, of course, by a strange chance, this other, this 'you,' is the *tout autre* after all."[131] Unless, of course, this other, this you, *is* the truth, the only one that truly makes sense—I would add.

In *Prayers and Tears* Caputo, according to Kearns, recognizes Derrida's religious hunger:

> Here he expresses a poetic obligation toward that hunger, clothing and supplementing Derrida's thought in an answering work at once original and dedicated to another's point of view. If a certain theological indeterminacy haunts this supplement, that indeterminacy marks a genuinely open space, one into which others, in their turn, may inscribe other and different marks. May these further inscriptions be as generous as those that have inspired them.[132]

My hope is that *The Adventure of Weak Theology* will be just such an inscription, a generous work of a fellow human in the same cold Universe. For that is ultimately *How?* I meant to write it.

* * *

> "Now you can write to your friend." Whereat my rose trees suffered a little, and in the vegetable garden, too, the caterpillars held high festival. For now he took to spending whole days in his room, jotting down phrases, crossing them out, starting again, sticking out his tongue the while, like a schoolboy poring over his lesson-book. He knew he had something most important to say, and somehow he must transport himself, lock, stock and barrel, as it were, to his absent friend. For he had to build a bridge over the sundering gulf and, communing with the friend who was his other self, across Space and Time, make known to him his love. Thus a day came when, blushing, he came to me and showed his answer, hoping to glimpse on my face a reflection of the joy that would light up that of its recipient, and to test on me the power of his message. And when I read it, I saw these words, written in a careful yet unskilled hand—earnest as a prayer coming from the heart, yet how simple and how humble!—This morning I, too, pruned my rose trees. . . . And could he indeed have imparted to his friend news more important than this, standing as it did for that for which, supremely, he was bartering his life, like those old women who wear their eyes out over their needlework in the making of some altarcloth for their God? And, having read, I fell silent, musing on that essential thing which I was beginning to perceive more clearly; for it was Thou, O Lord, whom they were honoring, fusing their lives together within Thee, above and beyond their rose trees, though they knew it not.[133]

Afterword: An Ear for My Voice

"[T]his book is, I hope, only a first step in my own intellectual journey" (186). In these few words Štefan Štofaník sums up the bittersweet task before me and any reader of this beautiful book. His hope, and the hope of everyone who knew him, was dashed by the cruelty of misfortune. His first step, an engaging, promising, and creative study, was to be his last, leaving the rest of us to wonder what the next step would have been, and the one after that.

How

If Štefan wanted to be a writer, he already was. He had already become restless with the protocols of the university and sought to reach a wider audience, to weave the arcane deliberations of the academy into the wider fabric of the world. Part of his interest in my work, for which I am very grateful, was that he heard a bit of the same restlessness in me, but he also heard, with some chagrin, the caution I regularly expressed to my graduate students. Do not start out writing like that, and in particular do not start out writing like me, at least not the way I began to write from *Radical Hermeneutics* on, which appeared when I was forty-seven years old and a tenured full professor. My own early work, like the early work of the philosophers whom I admired, conformed perfectly with the protocols and good manners of the university, before which one has first to prove oneself. This was not a clever long-term strategy I had adopted, not part of a cunning attempt to keep a more impudent spirit safely under wraps until the time to strike was at hand. Not a bit. It never entered my head to do otherwise, to do anything other than make myself commensurate with the university—not until Jacques Derrida loosened my tongue.

But Štefan would have none of that. If the university would not tolerate his personal, passionate, and poetic spirit, then so much the worse for the university! He would march to the beat of his own inner drummer and lead the life of an author. Whence the unorthodox form of this book, which is laced with autobiographical reflections, asides to the reader that suspend the authorial voice, the unexpected pairing of the academic theology with Antoine de Saint-Exupéry's works, all of which is centered around the narratival-genetic-biographical approach Štefan takes to my work, meaning both to me, personally, and to the "adventure"—the advent of the event—of weak theology, with or without me.

The result for me is uncanny. We had only occasional personal contact. I met him only once, when I lectured in Leuven in March 2008. But he was a bit shy and we did not get a chance to speak at length and there were only a few emails in April 2013 when he sent me his recently defended dissertation. Still, he has read my work with extraordinary care and he has done so with a very acute ear for my authorial voice, this person whom I impersonate when I write, this persona I inhabit in my books. I am not sure if this fellow who appears in print is the real me or a put-on, the one who I really am or the one I want to be. Either way, he only emerges, or emerges best of all, when I write, and Štefan had a pitch-perfect ear for that voice. He didn't miss anything. He caught it every time it was important. He picked out sentences that I remember writing, remember thinking to myself, I hope they notice this sentence, I hope they can hear everything I am putting into it. I cannot say it any better than this. This is everything I have to say, inscribe it on my tombstone, make it the lead quote in my obit. This is it; this is what I am trying to say. I hope someone hears it. Štefan always did.

He understood the indissociability of *what* I was saying from the *how*. Those are the very Kierkegaardian terms—and Štefan had an unfailing ear for my Kierkegaardianism—referring to the distinction between the objective thinker and the subjective thinker, between the truth that can be fitted into concepts, propositions, and arguments, and the truth for which, as the young Kierkegaard would put it, we would be willing to live or die. This is the difference between the technical problems of philosophy and theology and the unfathomable mystery of our lives. Štefan understood that the "objective content," the *what*, was imbedded in the *how*, that I am *doing* what I am *saying*. And "what" is that? What am I doing? I am confessing, circumfessing, praying, weeping, dreaming, *in literis*, in writing, in public, for myself and for others to read and appropriate for themselves. Confessing or circumfessing *what*? That we do not know who we are, that we are all a little lost, and not just little, and so *that*—that non-knowing, that radical apophasis, the passion of that non-knowing—*is* who and what we are. *Quaestio mihi magna factus sum*, Augustine said, as Kierkegaard and Heidegger and Derrida listen attentively, pen in hand, and I in their wake. Štefan grasped that. He saw that, from *Radical Hermeneutics* on, my work had a performative character, that the message had melted into the medium.

Štefan had an unnerving insight into and an acute ear for the fellow I become when I write. He had congeniality, a connaturality for it, but this was not the result of an intuition that dropped out of the sky into his lap. It was the fruit of a careful, assiduous academic study of my texts, and of reading with scrupulous attention the several interviews I have given over the years in which I disclosed some personal details that motivate my work. When I say assiduous, I am not paying him a routine compliment. He had even put most of my works into digital form and would search for the frequency with which a given term appeared. I read with some embarrassment that, at the time of the writing of this dissertation, and based upon the work he was able to digitalize, he had counted some 1.3 million words! Surely, I thought, I must have been capable of putting things more succinctly than that! It made me feel like one of those graduate students you meet in a conference hotel bar whom you deeply regret having asked about the topic of their dissertation! He sorted out little but deeply significant things—my early interests in Jacques Maritain and Pierre Rousselot, even in mathematical logic, and he remembered things I wanted everyone to forget, like the fact that my first reading of Derrida left me with a very negative impression of deconstruction. He found everything, including things that present readers of mine would find incongruous, even amusing.

Above all, it was positively eerie for me to see "Brother Paul" appear in print and to hear the things that Štefan overheard Brother Paul thinking to himself, or so Brother Paul and I thought. I was so impressed with this that, about a year after he sent me his dissertation, when I was writing *Hoping Against Hope*,[1] I stole Brother Paul (back) from him and used him in the first chapter of that book. Upon reading the manuscript of this book, my editor at Fortress Press immediately demanded more! So I revised the book, dropping extended discussions of the theology from the first version of that book in order to make room for the little dialogue I had constructed between Jackie, Brother Paul, John D., and the other Jackie (Derrida). Štefan heard the game of Jacks that was going on in my head and he grasped perfectly that and how "Brother Paul" was also a party to this game. And mind you, we had very little personal contact.

What

Štefan grasped that my entire discourse is a performative. He saw that I am *both* speaking *about* a kind of lost, disoriented, let us say, impossible prayer, and, at the same time, *also praying* this impossible prayer, hence his acute sensitivity to my style. But he also thought that I was, for that very reason, caught in a performative contradiction—a highly well-respected form of academic argumentation, I cannot resist pointing out! Štefan was just enough of a traditionalist, just enough of a theologian in the classical sense, that he balked at this:

You can't pray to an unknown God, Štefan objects to me (187, 189).

Of course, you can't, I would respond. So what?

It's impossible, a contradiction, he says.

Of course, it is, I respond. So what? That impossibility is why it is the only kind of prayer that is really possible. Only a prayer that is exposed, vulnerable, uncertain, on the edge of despair (which, as an edge, is also on the edge of hope) is worthy of the name. Only a prayer that is completely uncertain as to whether there is anyone to whom to pray or to any expectation that prayer will be answered, only a prayer that has to pray to be able to pray—that, I am saying, praying, weeping, is the only prayer worthy of the name.

St. Paul expressly mocks such a prayer to an unknown God, Štefan objects.

But I say there's little chance that Paul ever uttered those words, which are most likely a concoction of Luke's.

That's modernist historical-critical method, he complains.

And I say, so what? Postmodern is not antimodern; it passes through the modern and comes out the other side! The modernist critique of religion is not the end of theology but the beginning of another religion and another theology.

That's modernist demythologizing, he says.

So what? Every demythologizing is a step in the construction of a new and more salutary *re*mythologizing, or as I would rather put it, a new theo-poetizing of the theologians to come.

Štefan had his doubts about religion without religion. He thought it made for a dubious religion. But religion without religion is not a religion; it is a structure that inhabits existing religions. It does not "exist"; it "insists" itself into any existing tradition and keeps it up at night. It is not a new postmodern rival in the field of contemporary religious movements looking for converts but a hauntological structure that disturbs the concrete historical religious traditions by reminding them of their deconstructibility. There is no clear-cut binary opposition between strong and weak theology, as Štefan maintains (191), because a weak theology is only to be found *in* the strong theologies, which it inhabits from within like a ghost.[2] Weak theology is not an ahistorical rationalist a priori, which would be very strong indeed, but a vulnerability, an exposure of the deep historicity of religious "beliefs," a reminder of the historical contingency of their origins and the symbolic character of their "beliefs." The simplest example of this is found in the fact that what, inside the religious community, is called a "gift of faith" is, from a cooler, more distant point of view, an accident of birth. "Beliefs" are what get inside our head by reason of the time and place in which we are born—whether into an Irish Catholic family in Boston or somewhere deep in the middle of Islam makes all the difference. So I am not recommending life in an arid desert, as Štefan thinks. I am just saying that when we make ourselves at home in a confessional tradition, we need to remember that the house is haunted, that the home is *unheimlich*.

Above all else, a deconstruction is an *affirmation* of something *un*deconstructible, a *viens, oui, oui*. The deconstruction of concrete historical "beliefs" is made in the name of a deeper *faith*—in the future, in the coming of what we cannot see coming, of the "event." But the event is not only a call for the future, it is also a *recall* of what we have inherited, of our legacy, which is why every call for something to-come—like democracy or justice, or hospitality or forgiveness—is a call for the coming of what is already here, having been inherited or handed down to us by the tradition. Our legacy is a set of *promises* and deconstruction that arises from the fact that these promises are always already *unkept*. The affirmation of the future in deconstruction is an act of fidelity—of faith and hope and love—to these promises. That is why it is always an act of *mourning* the death and violence that have frustrated these promises in the past while resolving to *make these promises come true* in the future. So what we dream is not, as Štefan argues, an empty, sterile dream, devoid of orientation, cut off from a concrete culture that is dismissed offhand (106). It is exactly the opposite. We dream of the promises that have been made to us by our legacy, handed over by our tradition, which is why I will never give up the word "hermeneutics." The forgiveness-to-come and hospitality-to-come come to us from the biblical tradition and deconstruction is the call to make them come true in a future we cannot see coming.

The best way I have found lately to express this point of view is to go back to Hegel's notion of a *Vorstellung*, which is repeated in Tillich's notion of a "symbol."[3] Weak theology is not Kant's ahistorical a priori; it is inspired not by Kant but by Hegel's radically historical thinking—*sans* the *savoir absolu*, of course, and *sans* the Absolute Spirit, which has been weakened into a specter. The concrete religious traditions are so many indispensable ways to give concrete cultural expression to a deeper faith, to a deeper desire for an open-ended future, every determinate desire igniting a desire beyond desire, not for this or that, but for I know not what, for a future I cannot see coming. *Inquietum est cor nostrum.* They are symbolic figurations of the event. Without them, there is no event; but fidelity to the event cannot be confined to them. This desire or affirmation of the event would be impossible without the confessional traditions—it would have no meaning, content, or significance—but it is also impossible to contain or restrict this desire *to* them. The confessional traditions contain something that they cannot contain. They desire something that exceeds desire, with a desire beyond desire.

To be sure, Štefan did not have the benefit of my more recent work in which I have responded more explicitly to these criticisms.[4] That being said, one criticism I would make of Štefan's work is that, after having brilliantly traced the genealogy of weak theology, once he got there, he never really worked out, step by step, exactly what it is. He never really worked his way through the way that weak theology works. My hope is that, had he done so, he would not have been content with these criticisms. Of course, he might very well have said this is just Caputo's SEP (192) all over again, a sign of his closet dogmatism. If I sound dogmatic about my deconstruction of dogmatism, too strong in my advocacy of weak theology, I must apologize. That is not my intention or my view. It is, I think, a rhetorical impression I might leave, an optical illusion created in my texts by my passion. But this passion is what Derrida calls the passion of non-knowing, not for absolute knowledge. The idea behind radical hermeneutics is that interpretations go all the way down. That does not mean anything goes, but it does mean that some interpretations are better than others. So what I have to offer is meant as my best construal, better than the alternatives by my lights.

"Stroke after stroke, image after image," Štefan writes, "Caputo paints the picture of a little star adrift in the vastness of the indifferent Universe, a planet that is only our home insofar as we have each other: 'When a proper name is used, when a proper name happens, it is like a voice crying in the void, like a prophet crying in a cosmic wilderness'" (228). That is not a dogmatic pronouncement that I make based on inside metaphysical information I have acquired that life is a tale told by an idiot. It is a specter, a hauntological possibility that does not defeat life but represents a condition of possibility for our faith in life, our faith beyond belief in the promise in the world.

I can only conclude these remarks by thanking Joeri Schrijvers and Lieven Boeve for making this precious work available to us in print, and—speaking of hauntology—for giving me the opportunity to engage its haunting insights into my personal journey and the wider adventures of weak theology, of which there is, as Štefan kept saying, more than one.

—John D. Caputo
Thomas J. Watson Professor of Religion Emeritus,
Syracuse University;
David R. Cook Professor of Philosophy Emeritus,
Villanova University

Notes

Preface

1. Alexander Bloom, *Prodigal Sons: The New York Intellectuals and Their World* (New York and Oxford: Oxford University Press, 1986), vii.

2. Neil M. Agnew and Sandra W. Pyke, Science Game: Introduction to Research in the Behavioral Sciences (Englewood Cliffs: Prentice Hall, 1969), 146.

Editor's Introduction

1. John D. Caputo, *Hoping Against Hope: Confessions of a Postmodern Pilgrim* (Minneapolis: Fortress Press, 2015), 165, "The part that really interests me is the unanswerability, the endless, irrepressible flow of self-interrogating life. That bears testimony to the *driving force*, the *élan*, the underlying faith and hope which along with love are the very stuff of religion . . ."

2. Caputo, *Hoping Against Hope*, 165.

Introduction

1. Robert P. Kirshner, "Exploding Stars and the Expanding Universe (The 1990 Grubb Parsons Lecture)," *Quarterly Journal of the Royal Astronomical Society* 32, no. 3 (1991): 233–244; 240.

2. Keith Putt, "Faith, Hope, and Love: Radical Hermeneutics as a Pauline Philosophy of Religion," in *A Passion for the Impossible: John D. Caputo in Focus*, ed. Mark Dooley, SUNY series in Theology and Continental Thought (Albany: State University of New York Press, 2003), 238.

3. Putt, "Faith, Hope, and Love: Radical Hermeneutics as a Pauline Philosophy of Religion."

4. John D. Caputo and Keith Putt, "What Do I Love When I Love My God? An Interview with John D. Caputo," in *Religion With/out Religion: The Prayers and Tears of John D. Caputo*, ed. James H. Olthuis (London and New York: Routledge, 2001), 150.

5. John D. Caputo and Gianni Vattimo, "The Power of the Powerless: Dialogue with John D. Caputo," in *After the Death of God*, ed. Jeffrey W. Robbins (New York: Columbia University Press, 2007), 114.

6. John D. Caputo, "Abyssus Abyssum Invocat: A Response to Kearney," in *A Passion for the Impossible: John D. Caputo in Focus*, ed. Mark Dooley, SUNY series in Theology and Continental Thought (Albany: State University of New York Press, 2003), 125.

7. Caputo, "Abyssus Abyssum Invocat: A Response to Kearney."

8. Michael E. Zimmerman, "John D. Caputo: A Postmodern, Prophetic, Liberal American in Paris," *Continental Philosophy Review* 31, no. 2 (1998): 195–214; 195.

9. Zimmerman, "John D. Caputo: A Postmodern, Prophetic, Liberal American in Paris," 213.

10. John D. Caputo, "Of Mystics, Magi, and Deconstructionists," in *Portraits of American Continental Philosophers*, ed. James R. Watson (Bloomington and Indianapolis: Indiana University Press, 1999), 25.

11. Caputo and Vattimo, "The Power of the Powerless: Dialogue with John D. Caputo," 135.

12. Caputo and Vattimo, "The Power of the Powerless: Dialogue with John D. Caputo."

13. Ian Leask, ed., "From Radical Hermeneutics to the Weakness of God: John D. Caputo in Dialogue with Mark Dooley," *Philosophy Today* 51, no. 2 (2007): 216–226; 216.

14. Caputo and Vattimo, "The Power of the Powerless: Dialogue with John D. Caputo," 138.

15. Caputo and Vattimo, "The Power of the Powerless: Dialogue with John D. Caputo."

16. Caputo and Vattimo, "The Power of the Powerless: Dialogue with John D. Caputo."

17. Georges Dottin, *La langue Gauloise: grammaire, textes et glossaire* (Paris: C. Klincksieck, 1920), 277.

18. Caputo and Putt, "What Do I Love When I Love My God? An Interview with John D. Caputo," 150.

19. John D. Caputo, *The Weakness of God: A Theology of the Event*, Indiana Series in the Philosophy of Religion (Bloomington: Indiana University Press, 2006), 1.

20. Leask, "From Radical Hermeneutics to the Weakness of God: John D. Caputo in Dialogue with Mark Dooley," 217.

21. Leask, "From Radical Hermeneutics to the Weakness of God: John D. Caputo in Dialogue with Mark Dooley."

22. Caputo, *The Weakness of God*, 7.

23. Caputo, *The Weakness of God*, 41.

24. Caputo, *The Weakness of God*, 113.

25. Caputo, *The Weakness of God*, 114–115.

26. Caputo, *The Weakness of God*, 113.

27. John D. Caputo, "Living by Love: A Quasi-Apostolic Carte Postale on Love in Itself, If There Is Such a Thing," in *Transforming Philosophy and Religion: Love's Wisdom*, ed. Norman Wirzba and Bruce Ellis Benson (Bloomington: Indiana University Press, 2008), 110.

28. Caputo, "Living by Love: A Quasi-Apostolic Carte Postale on Love in Itself, If There Is Such a Thing."

29. Štefan Štofaník, "Introduction to the Thinking of John Caputo: Religion Without Religion Is the Way Out of Religion," in *Between Philosophy and Theology: Contemporary Interpretations of Christianity*, ed. Lieven Boeve and Christophe Brabant (Farnham: Ashgate, 2010), 22.

30. John D. Caputo, "The Insistence and Existence of God: A Response to DeRoo," in *Cross and Khôra: Deconstruction and Christianity in the Work of John D. Caputo*, ed. Marko Zlomislić and Neal DeRoo (Eugene: Wipf and Stock, 2010), 319.

31. John D. Caputo, "The Return of Anti-Religion: From Radical Atheism to Radical Theology," *Journal for Cultural and Religious Theory* 11, no. 2 (2011): 32–125; 38.

32. Caputo, "The Return of Anti-Religion: From Radical Atheism to Radical Theology," 42.

33. Caputo, "The Return of Anti-Religion: From Radical Atheism to Radical Theology," 39–42.

34. Emmanuel Levinas, *Totality and Infinity: An Essay on Exteriority*, trans. Alphonso Lingis (The Hague: Martinus Nijhoff, 1979), 160.

35. Friedrich Nietzsche, *Daybreak: Thoughts on the Prejudices of Morality*, ed. Maudemarie Clark and Brian Leiter, trans. R. J. Hollingdale, Cambridge Texts in the History of Philosophy (Cambridge: Cambridge University Press, 1997), 80.

36. Friedrich Nietzsche, *Beyond Good and Evil: Prelude to a Philosophy of the Future*, ed. Rolf-Peter Horstmann and Judith Norman, trans. Judith Norman, Cambridge Texts in the History of Philosophy (Cambridge: Cambridge University Press, 2002), 67.

37. Caputo, "Abyssus Abyssum Invocat: A Response to Kearney," 123.

38. Antoine Saint-Exupéry, *The Wisdom of the Sands* (Citadelle), trans. Stuart Gilbert (London: Hollis & Carter, 1952), 129.

39. John D. Caputo, "God and Anonymity: Prolegomena to an Ankhoral Religion," in *A Passion for the Impossible: John D. Caputo in Focus*, ed. Mark Dooley, SUNY Series in Theology and Continental Thought (Albany: State University of New York Press, 2003), 6.

40. Caputo, "God and Anonymity: Prolegomena to an Ankhoral Religion," 4.

41. Caputo, "Of Mystics, Magi, and Deconstructionists," 29.

42. Caputo, "God and Anonymity: Prolegomena to an Ankhoral Religion," 16.

43. John D. Caputo, *Radical Hermeneutics: Repetition, Deconstruction, and the Hermeneutic Project* (Bloomington: Indiana University Press, 1987), 281.

44. Caputo, "God and Anonymity: Prolegomena to an Ankhoral Religion," 4.

45. Caputo, *The Weakness of God*, 299.

46. "Being" and "other" are actually more frequent, but not always used as nouns.

47. Sean M Carroll, *From Eternity to Here: The Quest for the Ultimate Theory of Time* (New York: Dutton, 2010).

48. Caputo, "The Return of Anti-Religion: From Radical Atheism to Radical Theology," 59.

49. "It's a Spanish village to me" is a Slovak idiom roughly translating as "It's all Greek to me . . ." in US English. Or alternatively as "double Dutch." (How appropriate!)

50. Jefferson Hane Weaver, Lloyd Motz, and Dale McAdoo, *The World of Physics: A Small Library of the Literature of Physics from Antiquity to the Present* (New York: Simon and Schuster, 1987), 63.

51. Francis Crick, *What Mad Pursuit: A Personal View of Scientific Discovery*, Alfred P. Sloan Foundation Series (New York: Basic Books, 1988), 35.

52. Caputo and Putt, "What Do I Love When I Love My God? An Interview with John D. Caputo," 157.

53. Douglas Adams, *The Ultimate Hitchhiker's Guide to the Galaxy* (New York: Del Rey, Ballantine Books, 2002), xiii.

54. Adams, *The Ultimate Hitchhiker's Guide to the Galaxy*, vii.

55. Nicholas Birch, "7,000 Years Older than Stonehenge: The Site That Stunned Archaeologists," *The Guardian* (April 23, 2008).

56. David Gelernter, "Study Talmud," in *How Things Are: A Science Tool-Kit for the Mind*, ed. John Brockman and Katinka Matson (New York: W. Morrow, 1995), 213.

57. Martin Cohen, *Philosophical Tales: Being an Alternative History Revealing the Characters, the Plots, and the Hidden Scenes That Make Up the True Story of Philosophy*, illus. Raul Gonzales (Malden: Blackwell, 2008), 250.

58. James H. Olthuis, ed., *Religion With/out Religion: The Prayers and Tears of John D. Caputo* (London and New York: Routledge, 2001).

59. Caputo and Putt, "What Do I Love When I Love My God? An Interview with John D. Caputo."

60. Caputo and Putt, "What Do I Love When I Love My God? An Interview with John D. Caputo," 154.

61. John D. Caputo and Carl Raschke, "Loosening Philosophy's Tongue: A Conversation with Jack Caputo," *Journal for Cultural and Religious Theory* 3, no. 2 (2002): www.jcrt.org/archives/03.2/caputo_raschke.shtml.

62. Caputo and Raschke, "Loosening Philosophy's Tongue: A Conversation with Jack Caputo."

Chapter 1. Adventure

1. John D. Caputo, "The Sense of God: A Theology of the Event with Special Reference to Christianity," in *Between Philosophy and Theology: Contemporary Interpretations of Christianity*, ed. Lieven Boeve and Christophe Brabant (Farnham: Ashgate, 2010), 27. This essay was a lecture first delivered at KU Leuven on March 19, 2008.

2. Caputo, "The Sense of God: A Theology of the Event with Special Reference to Christianity," 27.

3. Caputo, "The Sense of God: A Theology of the Event with Special Reference to Christianity."

4. Caputo, "The Sense of God: A Theology of the Event with Special Reference to Christianity," 27.

5. Caputo, "The Sense of God: A Theology of the Event with Special Reference to Christianity," 27.

6. Saint-Exupéry, *The Wisdom of the Sands*, 121.

7. Saint-Exupéry, *The Wisdom of the Sands*, 119.

8. Saint-Exupéry, *The Wisdom of the Sands*, 121–122.

9. William Desmond, *Is There a Sabbath for Thought? Between Religion and Philosophy* (New York: Fordham University Press, 2005), 11.

10. John D. Caputo, *Against Ethics: Contributions to a Poetics of Obligation with Constant Reference to Deconstruction*, Studies in Continental Thought (Bloomington: Indiana University Press, 1993), ix.

11. Caputo and Raschke, "Loosening Philosophy's Tongue: A Conversation with Jack Caputo."

12. Caputo, "The Sense of God: A Theology of the Event with Special Reference to Christianity," 27.

13. Caputo and Raschke, "Loosening Philosophy's Tongue: A Conversation with Jack Caputo."

14. Caputo and Raschke, "Loosening Philosophy's Tongue: A Conversation with Jack Caputo."

15. Caputo and Raschke, "Loosening Philosophy's Tongue: A Conversation with Jack Caputo."

16. Caputo and Raschke, "Loosening Philosophy's Tongue: A Conversation with Jack Caputo."

17. Caputo and Raschke, "Loosening Philosophy's Tongue: A Conversation with Jack Caputo."

Chapter 2. Call

1. Antoine de Saint-Exupéry, *Citadelle*, édition abrégée établie et préfacée par Michel Quesnel (Paris: Gallimard, 2000), 421: "seul véritable géomètre."

2. Saint-Exupéry, *Citadelle*, 200: "un homme qui rêve quelquefois de géométrie quand plus urgent ne le gouverne pas, tel que le sommeil, la faim ou l'amour."

3. Saint-Exupéry, *Citadelle*, "La vérité ne m'est point apparue."

4. Saint-Exupéry, *Citadelle*, "Mais il ne m'a pas été donné de découvrir autre chose que moi-même . . ."

5. Saint-Exupéry, *Citadelle*, "La nuit, parfois, dans l'insomnie, je m'étais rendu sous sa tente, m'étant pieusement déchaussé, et j'avais bu son thé et goûté le miel de sa sagesse."

6. Saint-Exupéry, *The Wisdom of the Sands*, 317.

7. Saint-Exupéry, *The Wisdom of the Sands*, 317–318.

8. Caputo, *The Weakness of God*, 301 n. 5.

9. James Williams, *Gilles Deleuze's Logic of Sense: A Critical Introduction and Guide* (Edinburgh: Edinburgh University Press, 2008), 15.

Chapter 3. Brother Paul

1. John D. Caputo, "A Game of Jacks: A Response to Derrida," in *A Passion for the Impossible: John D. Caputo in Focus*, ed. Mark Dooley, SUNY series in Theology and Continental Thought (Albany: State University of New York Press, 2003), 34.

2. Caputo, "A Game of Jacks: A Response to Derrida."

3. John D. Caputo and Emmet Cole, "Emmet Cole Interviews John D. Caputo," *The Modern World* (May 16, 2005): http://www.themodernword.com/features/interview_caputo.html (accessed December 6, 2010).

4. John D. Caputo, "Not in Tongues, but Tongue in Cheek: A Response to Kearns," in *A Passion for the Impossible: John D. Caputo in Focus*, ed. Mark Dooley, SUNY series in Theology and Continental Thought (Albany: State University of New York Press, 2003), 295.

5. John D. Caputo, "Holding on by Our Teeth: A Response to Putt," in *A Passion for the Impossible: John D. Caputo in Focus*, ed. Mark Dooley, SUNY series in Theology and Continental Thought (Albany: State University of New York Press, 2003), 251.

6. Caputo, "Holding on by Our Teeth: A Response to Putt."

7. Leask, "From Radical Hermeneutics to the Weakness of God: John D. Caputo in Dialogue with Mark Dooley," 225.

8. Caputo and Vattimo, "The Power of the Powerless: Dialogue with John D. Caputo," 138.

9. Caputo and Vattimo, "The Power of the Powerless: Dialogue with John D. Caputo," 137.

10. John D. Caputo, *Heidegger and Aquinas: An Essay on Overcoming Metaphysics* (New York: Fordham University Press, 1982), 46.

11. Caputo and Raschke, "Loosening Philosophy's Tongue: A Conversation with Jack Caputo."

12. John D. Caputo, "Confessions of a Postmodern Catholic: From Saint Thomas to Derrida," in *Faith and the Life of the Intellect*, ed. Curtis L Hancock and Brendan Sweetman (Washington, DC: Catholic University of America Press, 2003), 73.

13. Caputo, "Confessions of a Postmodern Catholic: From Saint Thomas to Derrida," 73.

14. John D. Caputo, "Kant's Refutation of the Cosmological Argument," *Journal of the American Academy of Religion* 42, no. 4 (1974): 686–691.

15. Caputo and Putt, "What Do I Love When I Love My God? An Interview with John D. Caputo," 153.

16. Caputo, *Heidegger and Aquinas*, 252–253.

17. Caputo, *Heidegger and Aquinas*, 253.

18. W. Norris Clarke, "Reflections on Caputo's Heidegger and Aquinas," in *A Passion for the Impossible: John D. Caputo in Focus*, ed. Mark Dooley, SUNY series in Theology and Continental Thought (Albany: State University of New York Press, 2003), 53.

19. Caputo and Putt, "What Do I Love When I Love My God? An Interview with John D. Caputo," 154.

20. One can find references to this "first question" in various places, for example in: Caputo, "Confessions of a Postmodern Catholic: From Saint Thomas to Derrida," 72.

21. Caputo and Vattimo, "The Power of the Powerless: Dialogue with John D. Caputo," 114.

22. Caputo, "Confessions of a Postmodern Catholic: From Saint Thomas to Derrida," 70.

23. Leask, "From Radical Hermeneutics to the Weakness of God: John D. Caputo in Dialogue with Mark Dooley," 225.

Chapter 4. Transgression

1. Blaise Pascal, *Pensées*, IV:277.

2. Saint-Exupéry, *Citadelle*, 199–201. My translation of: "Nous protestons, dirent-ils, au nom de la raison. Nous sommes les prêtres de la vérité. Tes lois sont lois d'un dieu moins sûr que n'est le nôtre. Tu as pour toi tes hommes d'armes, et ce poids de muscles nous peut écraser. Mais nous aurons raison contre toi, même dans les caves de tes geôles. [. . .] Tu dois nous prendre pour ministres, nous qui savons."

3. Saint-Exupéry, *Citadelle*, 204: "Prétentieux que vous êtes, leur dis-je, qui suivez la danse des ombres sur les murs avec l'illusion de connaître . . ."

4. Michel Foucault, *Discipline and Punish: The Birth of the Prison*, trans. Alan Sheridan (New York: Random House, 1995), 184.

5. John D. Caputo, ed. and comm., *Deconstruction in a Nutshell: A Conversation with Jacques Derrida*, Perspectives in Continental Philosophy Series (New York: Fordham University Press, 1997), 38. Caputo refers to Derrida, *Points . . . Interviews, 1974–1994*, 419–421.

6. *The Times* (London), May 9, 1992.

7. Caputo, *Deconstruction in a Nutshell*, 38.

8. Caputo, *Deconstruction in a Nutshell*, 39.

9. Caputo, *Deconstruction in a Nutshell*, 38.

10. Caputo, *Deconstruction in a Nutshell*, 39.

11. Caputo and Vattimo, "The Power of the Powerless: Dialogue with John D. Caputo," 141.

12. Caputo and Putt, "What Do I Love When I Love My God? An Interview with John D. Caputo," 151.

13. John D. Caputo, "The Weakness of God and the Iconic Logic of the Cross," in *Cross and Khôra: Deconstruction and Christianity in the Work of John D. Caputo*, ed. Marko Zlomislić and Neal DeRoo (Eugene: Wipf and Stock, 2010), 18.

14. Caputo and Vattimo, "The Power of the Powerless: Dialogue with John D. Caputo," 117.

15. Caputo and Vattimo, "The Power of the Powerless: Dialogue with John D. Caputo," 151.

16. Caputo and Vattimo, "The Power of the Powerless: Dialogue with John D. Caputo,"152.

17. John D. Caputo, *On Religion*, Thinking in Action Series (London and New York: Routledge, 2001), 108.

18. Caputo, *On Religion*, 107.

19. Saint-Exupéry, *Citadelle*, 204: "Prétentieux que vous êtes, leur dis-je, qui suivez la danse des ombres sur les murs avec l'illusion de connaître [. . .] ne venez pas auprès de moi, vous les esclaves, armés de votre marteau à clous, feindre d'avoir conçu et lancé le navire."

20. Saint-Exupéry, *Citadelle*, 203. My translation of: "Car la création est d'une autre essence que l'objet créé, s'évade des marques qu'elle laisse derrière elle, et ne se lit jamais dans aucun signe. Toujours ces marques, toujours ces traces et toujours ces signes tu les découvriras qui découlent les uns des autres. Car l'ombre de toute création sur le mur des réalités est logique pure. Mais cette découverte évidente n'empêchera point que tu sois stupide."

21. Caputo, "The Weakness of God and the Iconic Logic of the Cross," 16.

22. Caputo, "The Weakness of God and the Iconic Logic of the Cross," 18.

23. Caputo, "The Weakness of God and the Iconic Logic of the Cross," 16.

24. Caputo, "The Sense of God: A Theology of the Event with Special Reference to Christianity," 27.

25. Caputo, "The Sense of God: A Theology of the Event with Special Reference to Christianity," 27.

26. Caputo, "The Weakness of God and the Iconic Logic of the Cross," 17.

27. Caputo and Vattimo, "The Power of the Powerless: Dialogue with John D. Caputo," 155.

28. Caputo and Vattimo, "The Power of the Powerless: Dialogue with John D. Caputo," 155.

29. Caputo, "A Game of Jacks: A Response to Derrida," 47.

Chapter 5. Two Loves

1. For example, in Caputo and Vattimo, "The Power of the Powerless: Dialogue with John D. Caputo," 115.

2. Caputo, "Confessions of a Postmodern Catholic: From Saint Thomas to Derrida," 74.

3. I owe this succinct description to B. Keith Putt, arguably one of the most engaging commentators of Caputo's work. Cf. Putt, "Faith, Hope, and Love: Radical Hermeneutics as a Pauline Philosophy of Religion," 240.

4. Saint-Exupéry, *The Wisdom of the Sands*, 219–220.

5. Caputo, "Confessions of a Postmodern Catholic: From Saint Thomas to Derrida," 74.

6. Caputo, "Confessions of a Postmodern Catholic: From Saint Thomas to Derrida," 75.

7. Caputo, "Confessions of a Postmodern Catholic: From Saint Thomas to Derrida," 75.

8. Caputo, "Confessions of a Postmodern Catholic: From Saint Thomas to Derrida," 72.

9. Caputo, "Confessions of a Postmodern Catholic: From Saint Thomas to Derrida," 66–67.

10. Saint-Exupéry, *Citadelle*, 270. Paraphrase of: "Quand les vérités sont évidentes et absolument contradictoires, tu ne peux rien, sinon changer ton langage."

11. Caputo, "Confessions of a Postmodern Catholic: From Saint Thomas to Derrida," 73.

12. Caputo, "Confessions of a Postmodern Catholic: From Saint Thomas to Derrida," 73.

13. Caputo and Vattimo, "The Power of the Powerless: Dialogue with John D. Caputo," 135: "Heidegger casts a spell over people . . ."

14. Caputo, "Confessions of a Postmodern Catholic: From Saint Thomas to Derrida," 84.

15. Cf. Caputo and Vattimo, "The Power of the Powerless: Dialogue with John D. Caputo," 135. No extra five years mentioned here, but that is the figure we get after comparing "captive for fifteen years or more" with "I worked on Heidegger for twenty years."

16. Caputo and Vattimo, "The Power of the Powerless: Dialogue with John D. Caputo," 135.

17. Caputo and Vattimo, "The Power of the Powerless: Dialogue with John D. Caputo," 135.

18. Caputo, "Confessions of a Postmodern Catholic: From Saint Thomas to Derrida," 69–70.

19. John D. Caputo, "Philosophy and Prophetic Postmodernism: Toward a Catholic Postmodernity," *American Catholic Philosophical Quarterly* 74, no. 4 (2000): 549 567; 554.

20. Caputo, "Philosophy and Prophetic Postmodernism: Toward a Catholic Postmodernity," 555.

21. Caputo, "Philosophy and Prophetic Postmodernism: Toward a Catholic Postmodernity," 555.

22. Caputo, "Philosophy and Prophetic Postmodernism: Toward a Catholic Postmodernity."

23. Angelus Silesius, *Der Cherubinische Wandersmann*, Hrsg. U. Eingel. v. C. Waldemar (München: Goldmann, 1960), I, 289/66. Translation found in *The Book of Angelus Silesius*, with observations by the Ancient Zen Masters, translated, drawn and handwritten by Frederick Franck (New York: Knopf, 1976).

24. Jorge Luis Borges, *Seven Nights*, trans. Eliot Weinberger (New York: New Directions, 2009), 93.

25. Martin Heidegger, *The Principle of Reason*, trans. Reginald Lilly, Studies in Continental Thought (Bloomington: Indiana University Press, 1996), 36–37.

26. Heidegger, *The Principle of Reason*, 38.

27. Caputo, "Confessions of a Postmodern Catholic: From Saint Thomas to Derrida," 76.

28. Caputo, *Radical Hermeneutics*, 224.
29. Caputo, *Radical Hermeneutics*, 224.
30. Caputo, *Radical Hermeneutics*.
31. Caputo, *The Weakness of God*, 48.
32. Caputo, *The Weakness of God*, 48.
33. Caputo, *The Weakness of God*, 108.
34. Caputo, *The Weakness of God*, 19.
35. Caputo, *The Weakness of God*, 19.
36. Caputo, *The Weakness of God*, 171.
37. John D. Caputo, *The Mystical Element in Heidegger's Thought* (Athens: Ohio University Press, 1978), 66.
38. Caputo, *The Weakness of God*, 171.
39. Caputo, *Radical Hermeneutics*, 266.
40. Caputo, *Radical Hermeneutics*, 266–267.
41. Caputo, *Radical Hermeneutics*, 267.
42. Caputo, *Radical Hermeneutics*, 267.
43. Caputo, *The Weakness of God*, 172.
44. Caputo, *Radical Hermeneutics*, 265.
45. Caputo, *Radical Hermeneutics*, 288.
46. Caputo, *Radical Hermeneutics*, 265.
47. Caputo and Putt, "What Do I Love When I Love My God? An Interview with John D. Caputo," 154.
48. Grover A. Zinn, "Review of Maria Shrady 'Angelus Silesius: The Cherubic Wanderer,'" *Church History* 59, no. 03 (1990): 406–407.
49. Zinn, "Review of Maria Shrady 'Angelus Silesius: The Cherubic Wanderer,'" 406.
50. Caputo, *The Mystical Element in Heidegger's Thought*, 98.
51. For example: *The Mystical Element in Heidegger's Thought*, 97ff.
52. Caputo, "Confessions of a Postmodern Catholic: From Saint Thomas to Derrida," 76.
53. Clarke, "Reflections on Caputo's Heidegger and Aquinas," 55.
54. Clarke, "Reflections on Caputo's Heidegger and Aquinas," 55.
55. Caputo, "Confessions of a Postmodern Catholic: From Saint Thomas to Derrida," 78.
56. Caputo, "Confessions of a Postmodern Catholic: From Saint Thomas to Derrida."
57. Caputo and Vattimo, "The Power of the Powerless: Dialogue with John D. Caputo," 115.
58. Caputo and Vattimo, "The Power of the Powerless: Dialogue with John D. Caputo," 115.
59. Caputo and Vattimo, "The Power of the Powerless: Dialogue with John D. Caputo," 116.
60. John D. Caputo, "Returning Mystical Theology to the Trace: A Response to Carlson," in *Cross and Khôra: Deconstruction and Christianity in the Work of John D. Caputo*, ed. Marko Zlomislić and Neal DeRoo (Eugene: Wipf and Stock, 2010), 165.
61. Caputo, *The Mystical Element in Heidegger's Thought*, 253.
62. Thomas A. Carlson, "Negative Theology and Deconstructive Ethics: Caputo's Reading of the Mystical," in *Cross and Khôra: Deconstruction and Christianity in the Work of John D. Caputo*, ed. Marko Zlomislić and Neal DeRoo (Eugene: Wipf and Stock, 2010), 154–155.
63. Caputo, *The Mystical Element in Heidegger's Thought*, 251.

64. Carlson, "Negative Theology and Deconstructive Ethics: Caputo's Reading of the Mystical," 155.

65. Caputo and Putt, "What Do I Love When I Love My God? An Interview with John D. Caputo," 177.

66. Caputo, "Returning Mystical Theology to the Trace: A Response to Carlson," 165.

Chapter 6. Freedom

1. For the following background information on Aéropostale, on Saint-Exupéry's duties in Cape Juby, as well as his involvement in the rescue of Bark, I am primarily indebted to Stacy Schiff's unforgettable biography of Saint-Exupéry. Cf. Stacy Schiff, *Saint-Exupéry: A Biography*, A Holt Paperback (New York: Henry Holt and Company, 2006), 3–30.

2. Schiff, *Saint-Exupéry*, 5.

3. Schiff, *Saint-Exupéry*, 7–8.

4. Schiff, *Saint-Exupéry*, 29.

5. Schiff, *Saint-Exupéry*, 12.

6. Antoine de Saint-Exupéry, *Wind, Sand and Stars*, published as part of the Airman's Odyssey trilogy, trans. Lewis Galantiere (Orlando: Harcourt, 1984), 97.

7. Saint-Exupéry, *Wind, Sand and Stars*, 98.

8. Saint-Exupéry, *Wind, Sand and Stars*, 96.

9. Saint-Exupéry, *Wind, Sand and Stars*, 96.

10. Saint-Exupéry, *Wind, Sand and Stars*.

11. Saint-Exupéry, *Wind, Sand and Stars*.

12. Saint-Exupéry, *Wind, Sand and Stars*, 100.

13. Schiff, *Saint-Exupéry*, 17.

14. Schiff, *Saint-Exupéry*, 18.

15. Saint-Exupéry, *Wind, Sand and Stars*, 95.

16. Saint-Exupéry, *Wind, Sand and Stars*, 101.

17. Saint-Exupéry, *Wind, Sand and Stars*, 101.

18. Saint-Exupéry, *Wind, Sand and Stars*, 98.

19. Or a National Identification Number, for that matter, since names are obviously repeatable. The matter of discussion here is the difference between unique and generic identification and its relatedness to individual freedom. Whatever has been said about the im/possibility of proper names may well be true but is not immediately at issue here.

20. Caputo, *The Weakness of God*, 138.

21. John D. Caputo, "An American and a Liberal: John D. Caputo's Response to Michael Zimmerman," *Continental Philosophy Review* 31 (1998): 215–220; 216.

22. Caputo, "An American and a Liberal: John D. Caputo's Response to Michael Zimmerman," 216.

23. Caputo, *Radical Hermeneutics*, 254.

24. Caputo, *Radical Hermeneutics*, 254.

25. Caputo, *Radical Hermeneutics*, 255.

26. Caputo, "An American and a Liberal: John D. Caputo's Response to Michael Zimmerman," 216–217.

27. Caputo, "An American and a Liberal: John D. Caputo's Response to Michael Zimmerman," 217.

28. Caputo, *The Weakness of God*, 28. Caputo quotes this beautiful phrase from Amos in numerous places throughout his work.

Chapter 7. Interlude (More than One)

1. Jacques Derrida, *Acts of Religion*, ed. Gil Anidjar (London and New York: Routledge, 2002), 7.

2. Caputo, "What Do I Love When I Love My God? Deconstruction and Radical Orthodoxy," 309.

3. Caputo, "What Do I Love When I Love My God? Deconstruction and Radical Orthodoxy," 309.

4. Jacques Derrida, "Circumfession: Fifty-Nine Periods and Periphrases Written in a Sort of Internal Margin, Between Geoffrey Bennington's Book and Work in Preparation (January 1989–April 1990)," in *Jacques Derrida*, trans. Geoffrey Bennington (Chicago and London: University of Chicago Press, 1993), 155.

5. Caputo, "The Possibility of the Impossible: A Response to Kearney," 143.

6. John D. Caputo, "Achieving the Impossible—Rorty's Religion: A Response to Dooley," in *A Passion for the Impossible: John D. Caputo in Focus*, ed. Mark Dooley, SUNY series in Theology and Continental Thought (Albany: State University of New York Press, 2003), 279.

7. Caputo, "An American and a Liberal: John D. Caputo's Response to Michael Zimmerman," 217.

8. Caputo, "Achieving the Impossible—Rorty's Religion: A Response to Dooley," 8.

9. Caputo and Vattimo, *After the Death of God*, 27.

10. Caputo, *The Weakness of God*, 3.

11. Caputo, "The Possibility of the Impossible: A Response to Kearney," 18.

12. Milan Kundera, *The Unbearable Lightness of Being*, trans. Michael Henry Heim (New York: Harper Perennial, 1999), 3.

13. Kundera, *The Unbearable Lightness of Being*, 4.

14. Williams, *Gilles Deleuze's Logic of Sense*, 144.

15. John Ayto, *Word Origins: The Secret Histories of English Words from A to Z* (London: A & C Black, 2005), 416.

16. Jorge Luis Borges, "Pierre Menard, Author of *Don Quixote*," in Cervantes's *Don Quixote*, ed. Harold Bloom, Bloom's Modern Critical Interpretations (New York: Infobase, 2001), 108.

17. Borges, "Pierre Menard, Author of *Don Quixote*," 109.

18. Borges, "Pierre Menard, Author of *Don Quixote*," 107.

19. Borges, "Pierre Menard, Author of *Don Quixote*," 110.

20. Borges, "Pierre Menard, Author of *Don Quixote*," 110–111.

21. Borges, "Pierre Menard, Author of *Don Quixote*," 110.

22. Caputo, "The Possibility of the Impossible: A Response to Kearney," 58.

23. Ayto, *Word Origins*, 150.

24. Zimmerman, "John D. Caputo: A Postmodern, Prophetic, Liberal American in Paris," 195.

25. Caputo, "An American and a Liberal: John D. Caputo's Response to Michael Zimmerman," 215.

26. Caputo, "An American and a Liberal: John D. Caputo's Response to Michael Zimmerman," 215.

27. Caputo, "Achieving the Impossible—Rorty's Religion: A Response to Dooley," 297.

28. While I have no intention for this little story of "Caputo's deconstructor" to be taken for more than what it actually is—indeed, a quasi-fiction to illustrate my point—the statistical figures of Caputo's usage of the words

"never" and "always" are nevertheless not a joke. They are based on my own digital analysis (concordance) of approximately 1.13 million words of Caputo, his articles, interviews, and books from across his very fruitful career. Not all Caputo's writings are included, though, as I do not have them all digitalized. Hence, the figures are only approximate but, I believe, still statistically sound.

29. Caputo, "Abyssus Abyssum Invocat: A Response to Kearney," 123.

30. Caputo, "Abyssus Abyssum Invocat: A Response to Kearney," 123.

Chapter 8. Freedom Again

1. For the account of Bark's day in Agadir, see Saint-Exupéry, *Wind, Sand and Stars*, 104–107.

2. Matthew 2:2.

3. Saint-Exupéry, *The Wisdom of the Sands*, 15.

4. Saint-Exupéry, *The Wisdom of the Sands*, 16.

5. Saint-Exupéry, *The Wisdom of the Sands*, 16–17.

6. Saint-Exupéry, *The Wisdom of the Sands*, 17.

7. Saint-Exupéry, *The Wisdom of the Sands*, 16.

8. Saint-Exupéry, *The Wisdom of the Sands*, 17–18.

9. Saint-Exupéry, *The Wisdom of the Sands*, 16.

10. Saint-Exupéry, *The Wisdom of the Sands*, 16.

11. Saint-Exupéry, *The Wisdom of the Sands*, 14.

12. Caputo, *Against Ethics*, 85.

13. Caputo, *The Weakness of God*, 114–115.

14. Caputo, *The Weakness of God*, 7.

15. Caputo, *The Weakness of God*, 296.

16. Caputo, *The Weakness of God*, 296.

17. Caputo, *The Weakness of God*, 296.

18. Caputo, *The Weakness of God*, 296.

19. Matthew 12:30.

20. Mark 9:40.

21. Caputo, *The Weakness of God*, 295ff.

22. Caputo, "Holding on by Our Teeth: A Response to Putt," 251.

23. Cf. Acts 17:16–34.

24. Caputo, *The Weakness of God*, 271.

25. Caputo, *The Weakness of God*, 5.

26. For example Caputo, "Achieving the Impossible—Rorty's Religion: A Response to Dooley," 35.

27. Caputo and Raschke, "Loosening Philosophy's Tongue: A Conversation with Jack Caputo."

28. Caputo, "The Return of Anti-Religion: From Radical Atheism to Radical Theology," 38.

29. Caputo, *The Weakness of God*, 59.

30. Lawrence Maxwell Krauss, *A Universe from Nothing: Why There Is Something Rather than Nothing* (New York: Free Press, 2012), chapter 10. Admittedly, Krauss would not like me borrowing his line, as his argument is decidedly atheistic.

31. Saint-Exupéry, *The Wisdom of the Sands*, 19.

32. Johann Wolfgang von Goethe, *West-Eastern Divan*, trans. Edward Dowden (London and Toronto: J. M. Dent & Sons Ltd., 1914), 74–75.

33. Nietzsche, *Beyond Good and Evil: Prelude to a Philosophy of the Future*, 77–79.

34. Caputo, *Against Ethics*, 85.

35. Nietzsche, *Beyond Good and Evil: Prelude to a Philosophy of the Future*, 78.

36. Friedrich Nietzsche, *On the Genealogy of Morals*, ed. Walter Kaufmann, trans. Walter Kaufmann and R. J. Hollingdale (New York: Random House, 1989), 57.

37. Nietzsche, *On the Genealogy of Morals*, 59–60.

38. John 3:8.

39. Levinas, *Totality and Infinity: An Essay on Exteriority*, 271.

40. See for example Jill Stauffer, "The Imperfect: Levinas, Nietzsche, and the Autonomous Subject," in *Nietzsche and Levinas: "After the Death of a Certain God,"* ed. Jill Stauffer and Bettina Bergo (New York: Columbia University Press, 2009).

41. Caputo, *Against Ethics*, 60.

42. Caputo, *Against Ethics*, 57.

43. Caputo, *Deconstruction in a Nutshell*, 73.

44. Caputo, *Deconstruction in a Nutshell*, 74.

45. Caputo, *Against Ethics*, 49.

46. Ayto, *Word Origins*, 348.

47. Helen Rowland, *A Guide to Men: Being Encore Reflections of a Bachelor Girl* (New York: Dodge Publishing Company, 1922), 19.

48. Caputo, *Against Ethics*, 48.

49. Caputo and Putt, "What Do I Love When I Love My God? An Interview with John D. Caputo," 155.

50. Friedrich Nietzsche, *Ecce Homo*, ed. and trans. Walter Kaufmann (New York: Random House, 1989), 276.

51. Søren Kierkegaard, *Fear and Trembling*, trans. Howard V. Hong and Edna H. Hong (Princeton: Princeton University Press, 1983), 15.

52. Caputo, *Against Ethics*, 16.

53. Caputo, *Against Ethics*, 15.

54. Kierkegaard, *Fear and Trembling*, 15.

55. Caputo, *Against Ethics*, 16.

56. Caputo, *Against Ethics*, 16.

57. Caputo, *Against Ethics*, 233.

58. Caputo, *Against Ethics*, 54.

59. Caputo, "Of Mystics, Magi, and Deconstructionists," 28.

60. Caputo, *The Weakness of God*, 160–161.

61. For example in Caputo, *The Weakness of God*, 206.

62. Caputo, *Against Ethics*, 59.

63. Caputo, *Against Ethics*, 263.

64. Caputo, *Against Ethics*, 30.

65. Caputo, *Against Ethics*, 233.

66. Nietzsche, *Beyond Good and Evil: Prelude to a Philosophy of the Future*, 77–79.

67. G. B. Madison, "On What It Means to Be Responsible: A Hermeneutical-Confucian Response to Caputo/Derrida," 294.

68. Madison, "On What It Means to Be Responsible: A Hermeneutical-Confucian Response to Caputo/Derrida," 294.

69. Caputo, *Against Ethics*, 60.

70. Leask, "From Radical Hermeneutics to the Weakness of God: John D. Caputo in Dialogue with Mark Dooley," 225.

71. Leask, "From Radical Hermeneutics to the Weakness of God: John D. Caputo in Dialogue with Mark Dooley," 225.

72. Caputo, *Against Ethics*, 20.

73. Caputo, "A Game of Jacks: A Response to Derrida," 35.

74. Caputo, *Against Ethics*, 65.

75. Leask, "From Radical Hermeneutics to the Weakness of God: John D. Caputo in Dialogue with Mark Dooley," 220.

76. Caputo and Vattimo, "The Power of the Powerless: Dialogue with John D. Caputo," 130.

77. Caputo, *Against Ethics*, 59.

78. John D. Caputo and Michael J. Scanlon, eds., *Transcendence and Beyond: A Postmodern Inquiry*, Indiana Series in the Philosophy of Religion (Bloomington: Indiana University Press, 2007), 219.

79. Friedrich Nietzsche, *The Will to Power*, ed. Walter Kaufmann, trans. Walter Kaufmann and R. J. Hollingdale (New York: Random House, 1968), 404, point 770.

Chapter 9. Between Heidegger and Derrida

1. 1:167–168; 1:173–176.

2. Bill Bryson, *A Short History of Nearly Everything* (New York: Broadway Books, 2003), 3–4.

3. "[I]f life is going to exist in a Universe of this size, then the one thing it cannot afford to have is a sense of proportion."

4. Schiff, Saint-Exupéry, 129.

5. Acts 9:16

6. Luke 24:32

7. Caputo and Raschke, "Loosening Philosophy's Tongue: A Conversation with Jack Caputo."

8. Caputo and Vattimo, "The Power of the Powerless: Dialogue with John D. Caputo," 121.

9. Putt, "Faith, Hope, and Love: Radical Hermeneutics as a Pauline Philosophy of Religion," 237.

10. Caputo, "Holding on by Our Teeth: A Response to Putt," 251.

11. John D. Caputo, "Hermeneutics as the Recovery of Man," *Man and World* 15 (1982): 343–367.

12. Caputo, "Hermeneutics as the Recovery of Man," 353.

13. Caputo, "Hermeneutics as the Recovery of Man," 343.

14. Caputo, *Radical Hermeneutics*, 6.

15. Caputo, *Radical Hermeneutics*, 184.

16. Caputo, *Radical Hermeneutics*.

17. Caputo, "Hermeneutics as the Recovery of Man," 362.

18. John D. Caputo, "From the Primordiality of Absence to the Absence of Primordiality: Heidegger's Critique of Derrida," in *Hermeneutics and Deconstruction*, ed. Hugh J. Silverman and Don Ihde (Albany: State University of New York Press, 1985), 191.

19. Caputo, "Hermeneutics as the Recovery of Man," 344.

20. Jacques Derrida, "The Ends of Man," Philosophy and Phenomenological Research 30, no. 1 (1969): 31–57.

21. Derrida, "The Ends of Man," 49.

22. Caputo, "Hermeneutics as the Recovery of Man," 343.

23. Caputo, "Hermeneutics as the Recovery of Man," 344.

24. Caputo, "Hermeneutics as the Recovery of Man," 343.
25. Caputo, "Hermeneutics as the Recovery of Man," 344.
26. Caputo, "Hermeneutics as the Recovery of Man," 354.
27. Caputo, "Hermeneutics as the Recovery of Man," 353.
28. Caputo, "Hermeneutics as the Recovery of Man," 362.
29. Robert Denoon Cumming, "The Odd Couple: Heidegger and Derrida," *The Review of Metaphysics* 34, no. 3 (1981): 487–521; 490.
30. Caputo, "Hermeneutics as the Recovery of Man," 363.
31. Caputo, "Hermeneutics as the Recovery of Man," 363.
32. Caputo, "Hermeneutics as the Recovery of Man," 358.
33. Caputo, "Hermeneutics as the Recovery of Man," 354–355.
34. Caputo, "Hermeneutics as the Recovery of Man," 362.
35. Caputo, "Hermeneutics as the Recovery of Man," 363.
36. Caputo, "Hermeneutics as the Recovery of Man," 363.
37. Caputo, "Hermeneutics as the Recovery of Man," 347.
38. Caputo, "Hermeneutics as the Recovery of Man," 363–364.
39. Caputo, "Hermeneutics as the Recovery of Man," 364.
40. John D. Caputo, "The Thought of Being and the Conversation of Mankind: The Case of Heidegger and Rorty," *The Review of Metaphysics* 36, no. 3 (1983): 661–685.
41. Caputo, "The Thought of Being and the Conversation of Mankind: The Case of Heidegger and Rorty," 662.
42. Caputo, "The Thought of Being and the Conversation of Mankind: The Case of Heidegger and Rorty," 662.
43. Caputo, "The Thought of Being and the Conversation of Mankind: The Case of Heidegger and Rorty," 676.
44. Caputo, "The Thought of Being and the Conversation of Mankind: The Case of Heidegger and Rorty," 680.
45. Caputo, "The Thought of Being and the Conversation of Mankind: The Case of Heidegger and Rorty," 681.
46. Caputo, "The Thought of Being and the Conversation of Mankind: The Case of Heidegger and Rorty," 673.
47. Caputo, "The Thought of Being and the Conversation of Mankind: The Case of Heidegger and Rorty,"678.
48. Caputo, "The Thought of Being and the Conversation of Mankind: The Case of Heidegger and Rorty," 680.
49. Caputo, "The Thought of Being and the Conversation of Mankind: The Case of Heidegger and Rorty," 680.
50. Caputo, "The Thought of Being and the Conversation of Mankind: The Case of Heidegger and Rorty," 679.
51. Caputo, "The Thought of Being and the Conversation of Mankind: The Case of Heidegger and Rorty," 679.
52. Caputo, "The Thought of Being and the Conversation of Mankind: The Case of Heidegger and Rorty,"677.
53. Caputo, "The Thought of Being and the Conversation of Mankind: The Case of Heidegger and Rorty," 684.
54. Caputo, "The Thought of Being and the Conversation of Mankind: The Case of Heidegger and Rorty," 678.
55. Caputo, "The Thought of Being and the Conversation of Mankind: The Case of Heidegger and Rorty," 679.
56. Caputo, "The Thought of Being and the Conversation of Mankind: The Case of Heidegger and Rorty," 678.

57. Caputo, "The Thought of Being and the Conversation of Mankind: The Case of Heidegger and Rorty," 684–685.

58. John D. Caputo, "'Supposing Truth to Be a Woman . . .': Heidegger, Nietzsche, Derrida," *Tulane Studies in Philosophy* 32 (1984): 15–21; 19.

59. Caputo, "'Supposing Truth to Be a Woman . . .': Heidegger, Nietzsche, Derrida," 19.

60. Caputo, "The Thought of Being and the Conversation of Mankind: The Case of Heidegger and Rorty," 684.

61. Caputo, "'Supposing Truth to Be a Woman . . .': Heidegger, Nietzsche, Derrida," 21.

62. Caputo, "'Supposing Truth to Be a Woman . . .': Heidegger, Nietzsche, Derrida," 20.

63. Caputo, "'Supposing Truth to Be a Woman . . .': Heidegger, Nietzsche, Derrida," 21.

64. Caputo, "From the Primordiality of Absence to the Absence of Primordiality: Heidegger's Critique of Derrida," 191.

65. Caputo, "From the Primordiality of Absence to the Absence of Primordiality: Heidegger's Critique of Derrida," 191.

66. Caputo, "From the Primordiality of Absence to the Absence of Primordiality: Heidegger's Critique of Derrida," 191–192.

67. Caputo, "From the Primordiality of Absence to the Absence of Primordiality: Heidegger's Critique of Derrida,"193.

68. Caputo, "From the Primordiality of Absence to the Absence of Primordiality: Heidegger's Critique of Derrida," 194.

69. Caputo, "From the Primordiality of Absence to the Absence of Primordiality: Heidegger's Critique of Derrida,"193.

70. Caputo, "From the Primordiality of Absence to the Absence of Primordiality: Heidegger's Critique of Derrida," 195.

71. Caputo, "From the Primordiality of Absence to the Absence of Primordiality: Heidegger's Critique of Derrida," 199.

72. Caputo, "From the Primordiality of Absence to the Absence of Primordiality: Heidegger's Critique of Derrida," 199–200.

73. Caputo, "From the Primordiality of Absence to the Absence of Primordiality: Heidegger's Critique of Derrida,"197.

74. Caputo, "From the Primordiality of Absence to the Absence of Primordiality: Heidegger's Critique of Derrida,"198.

75. Caputo, "From the Primordiality of Absence to the Absence of Primordiality: Heidegger's Critique of Derrida," 200.

76. John D. Caputo, "Three Transgressions: Nietzsche, Heidegger, Derrida," *Research in Phenomenology* 15 (1985): 61–78; 61.

77. Caputo, "Three Transgressions: Nietzsche, Heidegger, Derrida," 74.

78. Caputo, "Three Transgressions: Nietzsche, Heidegger, Derrida," 75.

79. Caputo, "Three Transgressions: Nietzsche, Heidegger, Derrida," 73.

80. Caputo, "Three Transgressions: Nietzsche, Heidegger, Derrida," 76.

81. Caputo, *On Religion*, 104.

82. Caputo, "Philosophy and Prophetic Postmodernism: Toward a Catholic Postmodernity," 554.

83. Psalm 18:7.

84. Caputo, "Three Transgressions: Nietzsche, Heidegger, Derrida," 75.

85. Martin Heidegger, "Only a God Can Save Us: *Der Spiegel*'s Interview with Martin Heidegger (September 23, 1966)," in *Philosophical and Political Writings*,

ed. Manfred Stassen, trans. Maria P. Alter and John D. Caputo, The German Library Series (London and New York: Continuum, 2003).

86. Caputo, "Three Transgressions: Nietzsche, Heidegger, Derrida," 75–76.

87. Caputo, "Three Transgressions: Nietzsche, Heidegger, Derrida," 76–77.

88. Caputo, *Heidegger and Aquinas*, 10.

89. Caputo, "Three Transgressions: Nietzsche, Heidegger, Derrida," 72.

90. Caputo, "Three Transgressions: Nietzsche, Heidegger, Derrida," 71.

91. Caputo and Raschke, "Loosening Philosophy's Tongue: A Conversation with Jack Caputo."

92. Raschke and Caputo, "Loosening Philosophy's Tongue: A Conversation with Jack Caputo."

93. John D. Caputo, "The Economy of Signs in Husserl and Derrida: From Uselessness to Full Employment," in *Deconstruction and Philosophy: The Texts of Jacques Derrida*, ed. John Sallis (Chicago: University of Chicago Press, 1987), 108.

94. John D. Caputo, "Derrida, a Kind of Philosopher: A Discussion of Recent Literature," *Research in Phenomenology* 17, no. 1 (1987): 245–259; 112 n. 10.

95. Caputo, "The Thought of Being and the Conversation of Mankind: The Case of Heidegger and Rorty," 682.

96. Caputo, *Radical Hermeneutics*, 263–264.

97. Caputo, *Radical Hermeneutics*, 312, point 12.

98. Caputo, *Against Ethics*, 69.

99. Jacques Derrida and Catherine Malabou, *Counterpath: Traveling with Jacques Derrida*, trans. David Wills, Cultural Memory in the Present series (Stanford: Stanford University Press, 2004), 209.

100. Cumming, "The Odd Couple: Heidegger and Derrida," 487.

101. See for example: Jacques Derrida and Peggy Kamuf, "The Work of Intellectuals and the Press," in *Points . . . Interviews, 1974–1994*, ed. Elisabeth Weber, trans. Peggy Kamuf (Stanford: Stanford University Press, 1995).

102. Caputo, *Against Ethics*, 72.

103. Caputo, "Derrida, a Kind of Philosopher: A Discussion of Recent Literature," 258.

104. Derrida, "Circumfession: Fifty-Nine Periods and Periphrases Written in a Sort of Internal Margin, Between Geoffrey Bennington's Book and Work in Preparation (January 1989–April 1990)," 118.

105. Jacques Derrida, "Between Brackets I," in *Points . . . Interviews, 1974–1994*, ed. Elisabeth Weber, trans. Peggy Kamuf (Stanford: Stanford University Press, 1995), 10.

106. Caputo, "Derrida, a Kind of Philosopher: A Discussion of Recent Literature," 245.

107. Louis Mackey, *Kierkegaard: A Kind of Poet* (Philadelphia, PA: University of Pennsylvania Press, 1971).

108. Caputo, "Derrida, a Kind of Philosopher: A Discussion of Recent Literature," 245–246.

109. Caputo, "Derrida, a Kind of Philosopher: A Discussion of Recent Literature," 246.

110. Rodolphe Gasché, *The Tain of the Mirror: Derrida and the Philosophy of Reflection* (Cambridge: Harvard University Press, 1986); Irene E. Harvey, *Derrida and the Economy of Différance* (Bloomington: Indiana University Press, 1986); John Llewelyn, *Derrida on the Threshold of Sense* (New York: St. Martin's Press, 1986).

111. Caputo, "Derrida, a Kind of Philosopher: A Discussion of Recent Literature," 249.

112. Caputo, "Derrida, a Kind of Philosopher: A Discussion of Recent Literature," 258.

113. Caputo, "Derrida, a Kind of Philosopher: A Discussion of Recent Literature," 249.

114. Caputo, "Derrida, a Kind of Philosopher: A Discussion of Recent Literature," 258.

115. John D. Caputo, "Beyond Aestheticism: Derrida's Responsible Anarchy in Continental Philosophy and the Question of Ethics," *Research in Phenomenology* 18 (1988): 59–73; 60.

116. Caputo, "Beyond Aestheticism: Derrida's Responsible Anarchy in Continental Philosophy and the Question of Ethics," 59.

117. Caputo, "Beyond Aestheticism: Derrida's Responsible Anarchy in Continental Philosophy and the Question of Ethics," 60.

118. Caputo, "Beyond Aestheticism: Derrida's Responsible Anarchy in Continental Philosophy and the Question of Ethics," 73, point 2.

119. Caputo, "Beyond Aestheticism: Derrida's Responsible Anarchy in Continental Philosophy and the Question of Ethics," 60.

120. Jacques Derrida, "The Principle of Reason: The University in the Eyes of Its Pupils," *Diacritics* 13, no. 3 (1983): 2–20.

121. Caputo, "Beyond Aestheticism: Derrida's Responsible Anarchy in Continental Philosophy and the Question of Ethics," 61–62.

122. Caputo, "Beyond Aestheticism: Derrida's Responsible Anarchy in Continental Philosophy and the Question of Ethics," 60.

123. Caputo, "Beyond Aestheticism: Derrida's Responsible Anarchy in Continental Philosophy and the Question of Ethics," 67.

124. Caputo, "Beyond Aestheticism: Derrida's Responsible Anarchy in Continental Philosophy and the Question of Ethics," 67–68.

125. Caputo, "Beyond Aestheticism: Derrida's Responsible Anarchy in Continental Philosophy and the Question of Ethics," 67.

126. Derrida, "The Principle of Reason: The University in the Eyes of Its Pupils," 19–20.

127. Caputo, "Beyond Aestheticism: Derrida's Responsible Anarchy in Continental Philosophy and the Question of Ethics," 64.

128. Caputo, "Beyond Aestheticism: Derrida's Responsible Anarchy in Continental Philosophy and the Question of Ethics," 66.

129. Caputo, "Beyond Aestheticism: Derrida's Responsible Anarchy in Continental Philosophy and the Question of Ethics," 65.

130. Caputo, "Beyond Aestheticism: Derrida's Responsible Anarchy in Continental Philosophy and the Question of Ethics," 60.

131. Caputo, "Derrida, a Kind of Philosopher: A Discussion of Recent Literature," 258.

132. John D. Caputo, "Demythologizing Heidegger: 'Alētheia' and the History of Being," *The Review of Metaphysics* 41, no. 3 (1988): 519–546; 539. My emphasis.

133. Caputo, "Demythologizing Heidegger: 'Alētheia' and the History of Being," 519.

134. Caputo, "Demythologizing Heidegger: 'Alētheia' and the History of Being," 536.

135. Caputo, "Demythologizing Heidegger: 'Alētheia' and the History of Being," 541.

136. Karl Jaspers, "Letter to the Freiburg University Denazification Committee (December 22, 1945)," in *The Heidegger Controversy: A Critical Reader*, ed. Richard Wolin, trans. Richard Wolin (Cambridge, MA, and London: MIT Press, 1993), 149. My emphasis.

137. John D. Caputo, "Heidegger's Scandal: Thinking and the Essence of the Victim," in *The Heidegger Case: On Philosophy and Politics*, ed. Tom Rockmore and Joseph Margolis (Philadelphia: Temple University Press, 1992).

138. John D. Caputo, *Demythologizing Heidegger*, Indiana University Series in the Philosophy of Religion (Bloomington: Indiana University Press, 1993), 1.

139. Caputo, "Demythologizing Heidegger: 'Alētheia' and the History of Being," 519.

140. Caputo, "Demythologizing Heidegger: 'Alētheia' and the History of Being," 535.

141. Caputo, "Demythologizing Heidegger: 'Alētheia' and the History of Being," 536.

142. Caputo, "Demythologizing Heidegger: 'Alētheia' and the History of Being," 541.

143. Caputo, "Demythologizing Heidegger: 'Alētheia' and the History of Being," 536.

144. Caputo, "Demythologizing Heidegger: 'Alētheia' and the History of Being," 536.

145. Caputo, "Demythologizing Heidegger: 'Alētheia' and the History of Being," 542.

146. Caputo, "Demythologizing Heidegger: 'Alētheia' and the History of Being," 536.

147. Caputo, "Demythologizing Heidegger: 'Alētheia' and the History of Being," 544.

148. Caputo, "Demythologizing Heidegger: 'Alētheia' and the History of Being," 544–545.

149. Caputo, "Beyond Aestheticism: Derrida's Responsible Anarchy in Continental Philosophy and the Question of Ethics," 60.

150. Caputo, "The Economy of Signs in Husserl and Derrida: From Uselessness to Full Employment," 108.

151. Caputo, *Radical Hermeneutics*, 192.

152. Caputo, *Radical Hermeneutics*, 281.

153. Caputo, *Radical Hermeneutics*, 282.

154. Caputo, *The Weakness of God*, 135.

155. Caputo, "Beyond Aestheticism: Derrida's Responsible Anarchy in Continental Philosophy and the Question of Ethics," 70.

156. Caputo, "Beyond Aestheticism: Derrida's Responsible Anarchy in Continental Philosophy and the Question of Ethics," 71.

157. Caputo, "Beyond Aestheticism: Derrida's Responsible Anarchy in Continental Philosophy and the Question of Ethics," 70.

158. Caputo, *The Weakness of God*, 26.

159. Caputo, "Demythologizing Heidegger: 'Alētheia' and the History of Being," 546.

160. B. Keith Putt, "Reconciling Pure Forgiveness and Reconciliation: Bringing John Caputo into the Kingdom of God," *Crosscurrents* 59, no. 4 (2009): 500–531; 505.

161. Kevin Hart, "Without," in *Cross and Khôra: Deconstruction and*

Christianity in the Work of John D. Caputo, ed. Marko Zlomislić and Neal DeRoo (Eugene: Wipf and Stock, 2010), 84.

162. Hart, "Without," 84.

163. Hart, "Without," 96.

164. John D. Caputo, "Only as Hauntology Is Religion Without Religion Possible: A Response to Hart," in *Cross and Khôra: Deconstruction and Christianity in the Work of John D. Caputo*, ed. Marko Zlomislić and Neal DeRoo (Eugene: Wipf and Stock, 2010), 116.

165. Caputo, "Only as Hauntology Is Religion Without Religion Possible: A Response to Hart," 114.

166. Caputo, "Only as Hauntology Is Religion Without Religion Possible: A Response to Hart," 116.

167. John D. Caputo, *The Prayers and Tears of Jacques Derrida: Religion Without Religion*, Indiana Series in the Philosophy of Religion (Bloomington: Indiana University Press, 1977), 154.

168. Caputo, *The Prayers and Tears of Jacques Derrida*, 155.

169. Caputo, *The Prayers and Tears of Jacques Derrida*, 155.

170. Caputo, *The Prayers and Tears of Jacques Derrida*, 155.

171. Caputo, *The Prayers and Tears of Jacques Derrida*, 155.

172. Caputo, *The Prayers and Tears of Jacques Derrida*, 156.

173. Caputo, *The Prayers and Tears of Jacques Derrida*, quoting Jacques Derrida, "Faith and Knowledge: The Two Sources of 'Religion' at the Limits of Reason Alone," in *Acts of Religion*, ed. Gil Anidjar (London and New York: Routledge, 2002), 57.

174. Caputo, *The Prayers and Tears of Jacques Derrida*, 156.

175. Caputo, *The Weakness of God*, 9.

176. Hart, "Without," 89.

177. Caputo, "Demythologizing Heidegger: 'Alētheia' and the History of Being," 546.

178. Caputo, *The Weakness of God*, 117.

179. Caputo, *The Weakness of God*, 118.

180. Caputo, *The Weakness of God*, 14.

181. Caputo, *The Weakness of God*, 104.

182. Caputo, *The Prayers and Tears of Jacques Derrida*, 156.

183. Martin Heidegger, *Parmenides*, trans. André Schuwer and Richard Rojcewicz (Bloomington and Indianapolis: Indiana University Press, 1992), 85.

184. Heidegger, *Parmenides*, 80–81.

185. Heidegger, *Parmenides*, 81.

186. Martin Heidegger, "Why Do I Stay in the Provinces? (1934)," in *Philosophical and Political Writings*, ed. Manfred Stassen, The German Library Series (London and New York: Continuum, 2003), 16.

187. Heidegger, "Why Do I Stay in the Provinces? (1934)," 16.

188. Heidegger, "Why Do I Stay in the Provinces? (1934)," 16.

189. Adam Sharr, *Heidegger's Hut*, photography by Digne Meller-Marcovicz (Cambridge, MA, and London: The MIT Press, 2006), 3.

190. Heidegger, "Why Do I Stay in the Provinces? (1934)," 17.

191. Derrida and Malabou, *Counterpath*, 267.

192. Caputo and Cole, "Emmet Cole Interviews John D. Caputo."

193. Caputo, *Against Ethics*, 2.

194. Caputo, *Against Ethics*, 249, point 11.

195. Zimmerman, "John D. Caputo: A Postmodern, Prophetic, Liberal American in Paris," 199.

196. Caputo, *Radical Hermeneutics*, 82.

197. Caputo, *Demythologizing Heidegger*, 175.

198. Caputo, "A Game of Jacks: A Response to Derrida," 38.

199. Caputo, "A Game of Jacks: A Response to Derrida," 38.

200. Caputo, *Radical Hermeneutics*, 292.

201. Zimmerman, "John D. Caputo: A Postmodern, Prophetic, Liberal American in Paris," 199.

202. Caputo, "The Return of Anti-Religion: From Radical Atheism to Radical Theology," 33.

203. Caputo and Cole, "Emmet Cole Interviews John D. Caputo."

204. Jacques Derrida, *The Postcard: From Socrates to Freud and Beyond*, trans. Alan Bass (Chicago and London: University of Chicago Press, 1987), 21.

205. Jacques Derrida, "Ja, or the Faux-bond II," in *Points . . . Interviews, 1974–1994*, ed. Elisabeth Weber, trans. Peggy Kamuf (Stanford: Stanford University Press, 1995), 35.

206. Jacques Derrida, "Honoris Causa: «This Is Also Extremely Funny»," in *Points . . . Interviews, 1974–1994*, ed. Elisabeth Weber, trans. Peggy Kamuf (Stanford: Stanford University Press, 1995), 406.

207. Caputo, *The Weakness of God*, 40.

208. Caputo, "Beyond Aestheticism: Derrida's Responsible Anarchy in Continental Philosophy and the Question of Ethics," 67.

209. John D. Caputo, "Mysticism and Transgression: Derrida and Meister Eckhart," in *Derrida and Deconstruction*, ed. Hugh J. Silverman (London: Routledge, 1989), 37. My emphasis.

210. Caputo, "Mysticism and Transgression: Derrida and Meister Eckhart," 31.

211. John D. Caputo, "Meister Eckhart and the Later Heidegger: The Mystical Element in Heidegger's Thought Part Two," *Journal of the History of Philosophy* 13, no. 1 (1975): 61–80.

212. Caputo, "Mysticism and Transgression: Derrida and Meister Eckhart."

213. Jacques Derrida and Kristine McKenna, "The Three Ages of Jacques Derrida: An Interview with the Father of Deconstructionism," *LA Weekly*, November 6, 2002.

214. Jacques Derrida, "'I Have a Taste for the Secret,'" in *A Taste for the Secret*, ed. Giacomo Donis and David Webb, trans. Giacomo Donis (Cambridge: Polity Press, 2001), 40.

215. Søren Kierkegaard, *Either/Or: Part 1*, ed. Howard V. Hong and Edna H. Hong, trans. Howard V. Hong and Edna H. Hong, Kierkegaard's Writings (Princeton: Princeton University Press, 1987), 482.

216. Mark Dooley and Jacques Derrida, "The Becoming Possible of the Impossible: An Interview with Jacques Derrida," in *A Passion for the Impossible: John D. Caputo in Focus*, ed. Mark Dooley, SUNY series in Theology and Continental Thought (Albany: State University of New York Press, 2003), 25.

217. Caputo and Vattimo, "The Power of the Powerless: Dialogue with John D. Caputo," 138.

218. Caputo and Vattimo, "The Power of the Powerless: Dialogue with John D. Caputo," 138–139.

219. John D. Caputo, "After Jacques Derrida Comes the Future," *Journal for Cultural and Religious Theory* 4, no. 2 (2003): 8.

220. Caputo, *The Prayers and Tears of Jacques Derrida*, 357, point 20.

221. Caputo, "A Game of Jacks: A Response to Derrida," 35.

222. Caputo and Cole, "Emmet Cole Interviews John D. Caputo."

223. Caputo and Cole, "Emmet Cole Interviews John D. Caputo."

224. Caputo and Vattimo, "The Power of the Powerless: Dialogue with John D. Caputo," 137.

225. Caputo and Cole, "Emmet Cole Interviews John D. Caputo."

226. John D. Caputo, "Either-Or, Undecidability, and Two Concepts of Irony: Kierkegaard and Derrida," in *The New Kierkegaard*, ed. Elsebet Jegstrup (Bloomington and Indianapolis: Indiana University Press, 2004), 15.

227. Caputo, "A Game of Jacks: A Response to Derrida," 37.

228. Caputo, "Of Mystics, Magi, and Deconstructionists," 25.

229. Caputo, "Of Mystics, Magi, and Deconstructionists," 28.

230. Caputo, "A Game of Jacks: A Response to Derrida," 37.

231. Caputo, *Against Ethics*, 34.

232. Caputo, "Of Mystics, Magi, and Deconstructionists," 29.

Chapter 10. Dancing in the Void

1. Saint-Exupéry, *The Wisdom of the Sands*, 148.

2. Caputo, "Of Mystics, Magi, and Deconstructionists," 28.

3. Caputo and Vattimo, "The Power of the Powerless: Dialogue with John D. Caputo," 136.

4. Saint-Exupéry, *Wind, Sand and Stars*, 78.

5. Breyten Breytenbach, "The Long March from Hearth to Heart," Social Research 58, no. 1 (1991): 69–83, 74.

6. Caputo, "A Game of Jacks: A Response to Derrida," 38.

7. Caputo and Vattimo, "The Power of the Powerless: Dialogue with John D. Caputo," 138.

8. Caputo, "Of Mystics, Magi, and Deconstructionists," 30.

9. Cleo McNelly Kearns, "The Prayers and Tears of Jacques Derrida: Esoteric Comedy and the Poetics of Obligation," in *A Passion for the Impossible: John D. Caputo in Focus*, ed. Mark Dooley, SUNY series in Theology and Continental Thought (Albany: State University of New York Press, 2003), 283.

10. Kearns, "The Prayers and Tears of Jacques Derrida: Esoteric Comedy and the Poetics of Obligation," 286.

11. Caputo, "Not in Tongues, but Tongue in Cheek: A Response to Kearns," 295.

12. Caputo and Raschke, "Loosening Philosophy's Tongue: A Conversation with Jack Caputo."

13. Kierkegaard, *Either/Or: Part 1*, 4.

14. Kierkegaard, *Either/Or: Part 1*, 5.

15. Kierkegaard, *Either/Or: Part 1*, 5.

16. Kierkegaard, *Either/Or: Part 1*, 6.

17. Kierkegaard, *Either/Or: Part 1*, 6–7.

18. Kierkegaard, *Either/Or: Part 1*, 7.

19. Kierkegaard, *Either/Or: Part 1*, 8.

20. Kierkegaard, *Either/Or: Part 1*, 8.

21. Kierkegaard, *Either/Or: Part 1*, 9.

22. Kierkegaard, *Either/Or: Part 1*, 10.

23. Kierkegaard, *Either/Or: Part 1*, 11.

24. Kierkegaard, *Either/Or: Part 1*, 13.

25. Caputo, *Against Ethics*, 129.

26. Caputo, *Against Ethics*, 129.

27. Caputo, *Against Ethics*, 129.
28. Caputo, *Against Ethics*, 130.
29. Caputo, *Against Ethics*, 129.
30. Caputo, *Against Ethics*, 131.
31. Caputo, *Against Ethics*, 131.
32. Caputo, *Against Ethics*, 131.
33. Caputo, *Against Ethics*, 132.
34. Caputo, *Against Ethics*, 133.
35. John D. Caputo and Mark Yount, eds., *Foucault and the Critique of Institutions*, Studies of the Greater Philadelphia Philosophy Consortium (University Park: Pennsylvania State University Press, 1993), 186.
36. Caputo, *Against Ethics*, 188.
37. Caputo, *Against Ethics*, 190.
38. Caputo, *Against Ethics*, 137.
39. Caputo, *Against Ethics*, 137.
40. Caputo, *Against Ethics*, 138.
41. Caputo, *Against Ethics*, 139.
42. Caputo, *Against Ethics*, 139.
43. Caputo, *Against Ethics*, 191.
44. Caputo, *Against Ethics*, 190.
45. Caputo, *Against Ethics*, 192.
46. Caputo, *Against Ethics*, 190.
47. James K. A. Smith, "Is Deconstruction an Augustinian Science? Augustine, Derrida, and Caputo on the Commitments of Philosophy," in *Religion With/out Religion: The Prayers and Tears of John D. Caputo*, ed. James H. Olthuis (London and New York: Routledge, 2001), 57.
48. Is Deconstruction an Augustinian Science? Augustine, Derrida, and Caputo on the Commitments of Philosophy," 58.
49. Caputo, *Radical Hermeneutics*, 279.
50. Caputo, *Against Ethics*, 245.
51. Smith, "Is Deconstruction an Augustinian Science? Augustine, Derrida, and Caputo on the Commitments of Philosophy," 58.
52. Smith, "Is Deconstruction an Augustinian Science? Augustine, Derrida, and Caputo on the Commitments of Philosophy," 58.
53. Smith, "Is Deconstruction an Augustinian Science? Augustine, Derrida, and Caputo on the Commitments of Philosophy," 58.
54. Smith, "Is Deconstruction an Augustinian Science? Augustine, Derrida, and Caputo on the Commitments of Philosophy," 58.
55. Caputo, *Against Ethics*, 5.
56. Caputo, *Against Ethics*, 227.
57. Merold Westphal, "Postmodernism and Ethics: The Case of Caputo," in *A Passion for the Impossible: John D. Caputo in Focus*, ed. Mark Dooley, SUNY series in Theology and Continental Thought (Albany: State University of New York Press, 2003), 159.
58. Westphal, "Postmodernism and Ethics: The Case of Caputo," 160.
59. Caputo, *The Weakness of God*, 67.
60. Kierkegaard, *Either/Or: Part 1*, xi.
61. Søren Kierkegaard, *Concluding Unscientific Postscript to the Philosophical Crumbs*, ed. and trans. Alastair Hannay, Cambridge Texts in the History of Philosophy (Cambridge: Cambridge University Press, 2009), 527.
62. Kierkegaard, *Concluding Unscientific Postscript to the Philosophical Crumbs*, 527–528.

63. John D. Caputo, *How to Read Kierkegaard* (London: Granta Books, 2007), 69.

64. Kierkegaard, *Concluding Unscientific Postscript to the Philosophical Crumbs*, 529.

65. Caputo, *How to Read Kierkegaard*, 69–70.

66. Caputo, *How to Read Kierkegaard*, 70.

67. Caputo, *How to Read Kierkegaard*, 71.

68. Caputo, *How to Read Kierkegaard*, 72.

69. John D. Caputo, "'O Felix Culpa,' This Foxy Fellow Felix: A Response to Westphal," in *A Passion for the Impossible: John D. Caputo in Focus*, ed. Mark Dooley, SUNY series in Theology and Continental Thought (Albany: State University of New York Press, 2003), 171–172.

70. Caputo, "'O Felix Culpa,' This Foxy Fellow Felix: A Response to Westphal," 172.

71. Caputo, "'O Felix Culpa,' This Foxy Fellow Felix: A Response to Westphal," 172.

72. Caputo, "'O Felix Culpa,' This Foxy Fellow Felix: A Response to Westphal," 172.

73. John D. Caputo, "Hoping in Hope, Hoping Against Hope: A Response," in *Religion With/out Religion: The Prayers and Tears of John D. Caputo*, ed. James H. Olthuis (London and New York: Routledge, 2001), 132–133.

74. Caputo and Putt, "What Do I Love When I Love My God? An Interview with John D. Caputo," 156.

75. Caputo and Putt, "What Do I Love When I Love My God? An Interview with John D. Caputo," 156.

76. Caputo and Putt, "What Do I Love When I Love My God? An Interview with John D. Caputo," 156.

77. Caputo and Putt, "What Do I Love When I Love My God? An Interview with John D. Caputo," 156.

78. Caputo, *How to Read Kierkegaard*, 72.

79. Caputo, *How to Read Kierkegaard*, 72–73.

80. Caputo, *How to Read Kierkegaard*, 75.

81. Caputo, *How to Read Kierkegaard*, 80.

Chapter 11. The Advent of Weak Theology

1. Christopher Ben Simpson, *Religion, Metaphysics, and the Postmodern: William Desmond and John D. Caputo* (Bloomington: Indiana University Press, 2009), 94.

2. Caputo and Vattimo, "The Power of the Powerless: Dialogue with John D. Caputo," 143.

3. Caputo and Cole, "Emmet Cole Interviews John D. Caputo."

4. Caputo and Cole, "Emmet Cole Interviews John D. Caputo."

5. Caputo and Cole, "Emmet Cole Interviews John D. Caputo."

6. Caputo and Vattimo, "The Power of the Powerless: Dialogue with John D. Caputo," 143.

7. Peter Goodwin Heltzel, "*The Weakness of God* (Review)," *Journal for Cultural and Religious Theory* 7, no. 2 (2006): 96–101; 96.

8. Heltzel, "*The Weakness of God* (Review)," 97–98.

9. Caputo, *The Weakness of God*, back cover.

10. Caputo, *The Weakness of God*, 57.

11. Putt, "Reconciling Pure Forgiveness and Reconciliation: Bringing John Caputo into the Kingdom of God," 501.

12. Putt, "Reconciling Pure Forgiveness and Reconciliation: Bringing John Caputo into the Kingdom of God," 501.

13. Caputo, *The Prayers and Tears of Jacques Derrida*, 211–212.

14. Margaret Atwood, "Happy Endings," in *The Contemporary American Short Story*, ed. Minh Bich Nguyen and Porter Shreve (New York: Pearson Longman, 2004), 20.

15. Putt, "Reconciling Pure Forgiveness and Reconciliation: Bringing John Caputo into the Kingdom of God," 500.

16. Caputo, *Deconstruction in a Nutshell*, 177.

17. Caputo and Vattimo, "The Power of the Powerless: Dialogue with John D. Caputo," 142.

18. John D. Caputo, The Insistence of God: A Theology of Perhaps (2013). See http://www.iupress.indiana.edu/product_info.php?cPath=6040_1152&products_id=806898.

19. James H. Olthuis, "The Test of Khôra: Grâce À Dieu," in *Religion With/out Religion: The Prayers and Tears of John D. Caputo*, ed. James H Olthuis (London and New York: Routledge, 2001), 117.

20. Caputo, "Hoping in Hope, Hoping Against Hope: A Response," 146.

21. Caputo, *The Weakness of God*, 67.

22. Putt, "Faith, Hope, and Love: Radical Hermeneutics as a Pauline Philosophy of Religion," 237.

23. Caputo, *The Weakness of God*, vii.

24. John D. Caputo and T. Wilson Dickinson, "Education as Event: A Conversation with John D. Caputo," *Journal for Cultural and Religious Theory* 12, no. 2 (2012): 25–46; 29.

25. Caputo and Dickinson, "Education as Event: A Conversation with John D. Caputo," 29.

26. Caputo and Dickinson, "Education as Event: A Conversation with John D. Caputo," 30.

27. Caputo and Dickinson, "Education as Event: A Conversation with John D. Caputo," 30.

28. Caputo and Dickinson, "Education as Event: A Conversation with John D. Caputo," 31.

29. Caputo and Dickinson, "Education as Event: A Conversation with John D. Caputo," 31.

30. Caputo and Dickinson, "Education as Event: A Conversation with John D. Caputo," 32.

31. Caputo and Dickinson, "Education as Event: A Conversation with John D. Caputo," 37.

32. Caputo and Dickinson, "Education as Event: A Conversation with John D. Caputo," 37.

33. Caputo and Dickinson, "Education as Event: A Conversation with John D. Caputo," 37.

34. Caputo and Dickinson, "Education as Event: A Conversation with John D. Caputo," 39–40.

Chapter 12. Kingdom (In Place of a Conclusion)

1. Caputo, *The Weakness of God*, 5.

2. Caputo, *The Weakness of God*, 299, and Caputo, *The Prayers and Tears of Jacques Derrida*, 69.

3. Caputo, *Radical Hermeneutics*, 293–294.

4. Caputo, "The Sense of God: A Theology of the Event with Special Reference to Christianity," 29.

5. Caputo, *The Weakness of God*, 283.

6. Caputo, "A Game of Jacks: A Response to Derrida," 47.

7. Caputo and Vattimo, "The Power of the Powerless: Dialogue with John D. Caputo," 155.

8. Caputo, "A Game of Jacks: A Response to Derrida," 47.

9. B. Keith Putt, "The Im/Possibility of a Passionate God: A Postconservative Mani(n)festation of Caputo's Kingdom Christology," *Perspectives in Religious Studies* 24 (1997): 447–468.

10. Putt, "The Im/Possibility of a Passionate God: A Postconservative Mani(n)festation of Caputo's Kingdom Christology," 457.

11. Putt, "The Im/Possibility of a Passionate God: A Postconservative Mani(n) festation of Caputo's Kingdom Christology," 465.

12. Putt, "The Im/Possibility of a Passionate God: A Postconservative Mani(n)festation of Caputo's Kingdom Christology," 466.

13. Caputo, *The Prayers and Tears of Jacques Derrida*, 226.

14. Adams, *The Ultimate Hitchhiker's Guide to the Galaxy*, 333.

15. Heltzel, "The Weakness of God (Review)," 98.

16. Kevin Hart, "The Kingdom and the Trinity," in *Religious Experience and the End of Metaphysics*, ed. Jeffrey Bloechl, Indiana Series in the Philosophy of Religion (Bloomington and Indianapolis: Indiana University Press, 2003), 153.

17. Hart, "The Kingdom and the Trinity," 153.

18. Hart, "The Kingdom and the Trinity," 154.

19. Caputo, *The Prayers and Tears of Jacques Derrida*, 243.

20. Putt, "The Im/Possibility of a Passionate God," 467.

21. Putt, "Faith, Hope, and Love," 238–239.

22. Caputo, "Holding on by Our Teeth: A Response to Putt," 251.

23. B. Keith Putt, "Reconciling Pure Forgiveness and Reconciliation: Bringing John Caputo into the Kingdom of God," *Crosscurrents* 59, no. 4 (2009): 500–531.

24. Putt, "Reconciling Pure Forgiveness and Reconciliation: Bringing John Caputo into the Kingdom of God," 520.

25. Putt, "Reconciling Pure Forgiveness and Reconciliation: Bringing John Caputo into the Kingdom of God," 520.

Epilogue: How?

1. Saint-Exupéry, *Wind, Sand and Stars*, 39.

2. Caputo and Raschke, "Loosening Philosophy's Tongue: A Conversation with Jack Caputo."

3. Leask, "From Radical Hermeneutics to the Weakness of God: John D. Caputo in Dialogue with Mark Dooley," 225.

4. Caputo, "Not in Tongues, but Tongue in Cheek: A Response to Kearns," 295.

5. Putt, "The Im/Possibility of a Passionate God: A Postconservative Mani(n) festation of Caputo's Kingdom Christology," 447–468. Putt refers to John D. Caputo, "Metanoetics: Elements of a Postmodern Christian Philosophy," unpublished manuscript, 3.

6. Caputo, "Returning Mystical Theology to the Trace: A Response to Carlson," 165.

7. Caputo, "Hermeneutics as the Recovery of Man," 362.

8. Caputo, "From the Primordiality of Absence to the Absence of Primordiality: Heidegger's Critique of Derrida," 191.

9. Caputo, "The Thought of Being and the Conversation of Mankind: The Case of Heidegger and Rorty," 684–685.

10. Caputo, "The Thought of Being and the Conversation of Mankind: The Case of Heidegger and Rorty," 685.

11. Caputo, "'Supposing Truth to Be a Woman . . .': Heidegger, Nietzsche, Derrida," 21.

12. Caputo, "Hermeneutics as the Recovery of Man," 363.

13. Caputo, "From the Primordiality of Absence to the Absence of Primordiality: Heidegger's Critique of Derrida," 195.

14. Caputo, "The Economy of Signs in Husserl and Derrida: From Uselessness to Full Employment," 108.

15. Caputo and Raschke, "Loosening Philosophy's Tongue: A Conversation with Jack Caputo."

16. Caputo and Raschke, "Loosening Philosophy's Tongue: A Conversation with Jack Caputo."

17. Caputo, "Derrida, a Kind of Philosopher: A Discussion of Recent Literature," 245.

18. Caputo, "Derrida, a Kind of Philosopher: A Discussion of Recent Literature," 246.

19. Caputo, "Derrida, a Kind of Philosopher: A Discussion of Recent Literature," 258.

20. Caputo, "Beyond Aestheticism: Derrida's Responsible Anarchy in Continental Philosophy and the Question of Ethics," 70.

21. Caputo, "Beyond Aestheticism: Derrida's Responsible Anarchy in Continental Philosophy and the Question of Ethics," 70.

22. Caputo, "Beyond Aestheticism: Derrida's Responsible Anarchy in Continental Philosophy and the Question of Ethics," 59.

23. Caputo, "Beyond Aestheticism: Derrida's Responsible Anarchy in Continental Philosophy and the Question of Ethics," 73 n. 2.

24. Caputo, "Beyond Aestheticism: Derrida's Responsible Anarchy in Continental Philosophy and the Question of Ethics," 67.

25. Caputo, "A Game of Jacks: A Response to Derrida," 35.

26. Caputo, "After Jacques Derrida Comes the Future," 9.

27. Caputo, "A Game of Jacks: A Response to Derrida," 45.

28. Caputo, "A Game of Jacks: A Response to Derrida," 35.

29. Caputo, "A Game of Jacks: A Response to Derrida," 35.

30. Caputo, "A Game of Jacks: A Response to Derrida," 35.

31. Caputo and Raschke, "Loosening Philosophy's Tongue: A Conversation with Jack Caputo."

32. Caputo and Raschke, "Loosening Philosophy's Tongue: A Conversation with Jack Caputo."

33. Dooley and Derrida, "The Becoming Possible of the Impossible: An Interview with Jacques Derrida," 22. The interview was recorded in Paris on January 15, 2000.

34. Caputo, "A Game of Jacks: A Response to Derrida," 34.

35. Derrida, "Circumfession: Fifty-Nine Periods and Periphrases Written in a Sort of Internal Margin, Between Geoffrey Bennington's Book and Work in Preparation (January 1989–April 1990)."

36. Caputo and Vattimo, "The Power of the Powerless: Dialogue with John D. Caputo," 137.

37. Caputo and Vattimo, "The Power of the Powerless: Dialogue with John D. Caputo," 136.

38. Derrida and McKenna, "The Three Ages of Jacques Derrida: An Interview with the Father of Deconstructionism."

39. Caputo and Raschke, "Loosening Philosophy's Tongue: A Conversation with Jack Caputo."

40. Fran Bartkowski, "Rereading Jacques Derrida: Afterwords 2005," *Differences: A Journal of Feminist Cultural Studies* 16, no. 3 (2006): 95–101; 97.

41. Marko Zlomislić, "Powell, Jason, Jacques Derrida: A Biography," *Kritike* 2, no. 1 (2008): 145–148; 148.

42. Zlomislić, "Powell, Jason, Jacques Derrida: A Biography," 148.

43. Martin McQuillan, "'Another Death' Jacques Derrida (1930–2004)," *Parallax* 11, no. 1 (2005): 79–87; 80.

44. Jonathan Kandell, "Jacques Derrida, Abstruse Theorist, Dies at 74," *New York Times*, October 10, 2004.

45. Jacques Derrida, "The Last Interview," *SV (Studio Visit)*, November 2004.

46. David Mikics, *Who Was Jacques Derrida? An Intellectual Biography* (New Haven and London: Yale University Press, 2009), 197.

47. For a good overview of the Paul de Man affair, cf. Martin McQuillan, Paul De Man, Routledge Critical Thinkers series (London and New York: Routledge, 2001), 97–11.

48. *Le Soir*, March 4, 1941.

49. McQuillan, *Paul De Man*, 98.

50. *The New Republic*, March 7, 1988.

51. *The Jewish Advocate*, March 31, 1988. Cited in McQuillan, *Paul De Man*, 98–99.

52. *Times Literary Supplement*, June 17–23, 1988, 676. Cited in J. Hillis Miller, *The J. Hillis Miller Reader*, ed. Julian Wolfreys (Stanford: Stanford University Press, 2005), 310.

53. Jacques Derrida, "Like the Sound of the Sea Deep within a Shell: Paul De Man's War," *Critical Inquiry* 14, no. 3 (1988): 590–652; 646.

54. Derrida, "Like the Sound of the Sea Deep Within a Shell: Paul De Man's War," 646 n. 49.

55. *New York Times*, December 1, 1987.

56. Derrida, "Like the Sound of the Sea Deep within a Shell: Paul De Man's War," 596.

57. Derrida, "Like the Sound of the Sea Deep within a Shell: Paul De Man's War," 646–647.

58. Derrida, "Like the Sound of the Sea Deep within a Shell: Paul De Man's War," 597.

59. Jacques Derrida, "In Memoriam: Of the Soul," in *The Work of Mourning*, ed. Pascale-Anne Brault and Michael Naas (Chicago and London: University of Chicago Press, 2001), 72–73.

60. Derrida, "In Memoriam: Of the Soul," 75.

61. Derrida, "Like the Sound of the Sea Deep within a Shell: Paul De Man's War," 600.

62. Derrida, "Like the Sound of the Sea Deep within a Shell: Paul De Man's War," 596.

63. Derrida, "Like the Sound of the Sea Deep within a Shell: Paul De Man's War," 596.

64. Derrida, "Like the Sound of the Sea Deep within a Shell: Paul De Man's War," 634.

65. Derrida, "Like the Sound of the Sea Deep within a Shell: Paul De Man's War," 634.

66. Derrida, "Like the Sound of the Sea Deep within a Shell: Paul De Man's War," 623.

67. Derrida, "Like the Sound of the Sea Deep within a Shell: Paul De Man's War," 636.

68. Derrida, "Like the Sound of the Sea Deep within a Shell: Paul De Man's War," 623.

69. Jacques Derrida, *Memoires: For Paul de Man*, trans. Cecile Lindsay, Jonathan Culler, Eduardo Cadava, and Peggy Kamuf, The Wellek Library Lectures at the University of California, Irvine (New York: Columbia University Press, 1989), 3.

70. Derrida, "Like the Sound of the Sea Deep within a Shell: Paul De Man's War," 595.

71. Derrida, "Like the Sound of the Sea Deep within a Shell: Paul De Man's War," 623.

72. Derrida, "Like the Sound of the Sea Deep within a Shell: Paul De Man's War," 593.

73. James Atlas, "The Case of Paul De Man," *New York Times*, August 28, 1988.

74. Back cover of Derrida, *Memoires: For Paul de Man*.

75. Jacques Derrida and Michal Ben-Naftali, "An Interview with Professor Jacques Derrida" (Jerusalem: SHOAH Resource Center, January 8, 1998), www.yadvashem.org, 16.

76. Derrida, "Like the Sound of the Sea Deep within a Shell: Paul De Man's War," 651.

77. Derrida by Benoît Peeters—review by Elisabeth Roudinesco, http://www.derridalabiographie.com/en/ (accessed May 14, 2012). Cf. Benoît Peeters, *Derrida: A Biography*, trans. Andrew Brown (London: Polity, 2012).

78. Friedrich Nietzsche, *Thus Spoke Zarathustra*, ed. Adrian Del Caro and Robert B. Pippin, trans. Adrian Del Caro, Cambridge Texts in the History of Philosophy (Cambridge: Cambridge University Press, 2006), 239.

79. Caputo, *The Weakness of God*, 301.

80. Jacques Derrida, Deborah Esch, and Tom Keenan, "Negotiations," in *Negotiations: Interventions and Interviews, 1971–2001*, trans. Elizabeth Rottenberg (Stanford: Stanford University Press, 2002), 37.

81. Derrida, Esch, and Keenan, "Negotiations."

82. Derrida, Esch, and Keenan, "Negotiations," 37–38.

83. Russell Jacoby, *The Last Intellectuals: American Culture in the Age of Academe*, second edition, with a new introduction by the author (New York: Basic Books, 2000), 16.

84. Maynard Solomon, *Beethoven* (New York: Schirmer Books, 1979), 192.

85. Solomon, *Beethoven*.

86. Solomon, *Beethoven*, 192.

87. Solomon, *Beethoven*, 193.

88. Solomon, *Beethoven*, 195.

89. Nietzsche, *Beyond Good and Evil: Prelude to a Philosophy of the Future*, 137, point 245.

90. John D. Caputo, *Philosophy and Theology*, Horizons in Theology (Nashville: Abingdon Press, 2006), 74.

91. Jacques Derrida and Didier Cahen, "There Is No One Narcissism

(Autobiographies)," in *Points . . . Interviews, 1974–1994*, ed. Elisabeth Weber, trans. Peggy Kamuf (Stanford: Stanford University Press, 1995), 198–199.

92. Derrida and Cahen, "There Is No One Narcissism (Autobiographies)," 198.

93. Jacques Derrida, "Passages—From Traumatism to Promise," in *Points . . . Interviews, 1974–1994*, ed. Elisabeth Weber, trans. Peggy Kamuf (Stanford: Stanford University Press, 1995), 373.

94. Nietzsche, *Beyond Good and Evil: Prelude to a Philosophy of the Future*, 137, point 246.

95. Jacoby, *The Last Intellectuals*, 192–193.

96. Jacoby, *The Last Intellectuals*, 194.

97. Jacoby, *The Last Intellectuals*, 194–195.

98. Gordon N. Ray, ed., *Professional Standards and American Editions: A Response to Edmund Wilson* (New York: Modern Language Association, 1969).

99. Jacoby, *The Last Intellectuals*, 195.

100. Ray, *Professional Standards and American Editions*, i, cited in Jacoby, *The Last Intellectuals*, 195.

101. Josef Joffe, "The Decline of the Public Intellectual and the Rise of the Pundit," in *The Public Intellectual: Between Philosophy and Politics*, ed. Arthur M. Melzer, Jerry Weinberger, and M. Richard Zinman (Lanham: Rowman & Littlefield, 2003), 114.

102. Elisabeth Roudinesco, *Philosophy in Turbulent Times: Canguilhem, Sartre, Foucault, Althusser, Deleuze, Derrida*, trans. William McCuaig (New York: Columbia University Press, 2008), ix.

103. Roudinesco, *Philosophy in Turbulent Times: Canguilhem, Sartre, Foucault, Althusser, Deleuze, Derrida*, ix.

104. Roudinesco, *Philosophy in Turbulent Times: Canguilhem, Sartre, Foucault, Althusser, Deleuze, Derrida*, x.

105. Jacques Derrida, *Specters of Marx: The State of the Debt, the Work of Mourning and the New International*, trans. Peggy Kamuf (New York and London: Routledge, 1994), 106.

106. Derrida, Esch, and Keenan, "Negotiations," 39.

107. W. Wolfgang Holdheim, "Jacques Derrida's Apologia," Critical Inquiry 15, no. 4 (1989): 784–796, 785.

108. Kearns, "The Prayers and Tears of Jacques Derrida: Esoteric Comedy and the Poetics of Obligation," 289.

109. Kearns, "The Prayers and Tears of Jacques Derrida: Esoteric Comedy and the Poetics of Obligation," 293.

110. Jacoby, *The Last Intellectuals*, xii.

111. Saint-Exupéry, *Wind, Sand and Stars*, 37.

112. Joffe, "The Decline of the Public Intellectual and the Rise of the Pundit," 114.

113. Kearns, "The Prayers and Tears of Jacques Derrida: Esoteric Comedy and the Poetics of Obligation," 293.

114. Caputo, *Against Ethics*, 5.

115. Caputo, "An American and a Liberal: John D. Caputo's Response to Michael Zimmerman," 216.

116. Caputo, *Against Ethics*, 25.

117. Caputo, *Against Ethics*, 25.

118. Friedrich Nietzsche, "On Truth and Lying in a Non-Moral Sense," in *The Birth of Tragedy and Other Writings*, ed. Raymond Geuss and Ronald

Speirs, trans. Ronald Speirs, Cambridge Texts in the History of Philosophy (Cambridge: Cambridge University Press, 1999), 141.

119. Caputo, *Against Ethics*, 17.

120. Caputo, *Against Ethics*, 17.

121. Caputo, *Against Ethics*, 6.

122. Caputo and Yount, *Foucault and the Critique of Institutions*, 245.

123. Friedrich Nietzsche, "The Birth of Tragedy," in *The Birth of Tragedy and Other Writings*, ed. Raymond Geuss and Ronald Speirs, trans. Ronald Speirs, Cambridge Texts in the History of Philosophy (Cambridge: Cambridge University Press, 1999), 88.

124. Caputo, *Against Ethics*, 246.

125. Caputo, *Against Ethics*, 226.

126. Caputo, *Against Ethics*, 246.

127. Caputo, *Against Ethics*, 237.

128. Caputo, *Against Ethics*, 246.

129. Kearns, "The Prayers and Tears of Jacques Derrida: Esoteric Comedy and the Poetics of Obligation," 294.

130. Dooley and Derrida, "The Becoming Possible of the Impossible: An Interview with Jacques Derrida," 22.

131. Kearns, "The Prayers and Tears of Jacques Derrida: Esoteric Comedy and the Poetics of Obligation," 294.

132. Kearns, "The Prayers and Tears of Jacques Derrida: Esoteric Comedy and the Poetics of Obligation," 294.

133. Saint-Exupéry, *The Wisdom of the Sands*, 347.

Afterword by John D. Caputo

1. John D. Caputo, *Hoping Against Hope: Confessions of a Postmodern Pilgrim* (Minneapolis: Fortress Press, 2015).

2. Weak theology already exists in the concrete traditions. We see this whenever a theologian is persecuted for speaking out on behalf of same-sex marriage, or for the rights of women to choose or, believe it or not (I am writing from the United States), in defense of the theory of evolution! In each case the truth of the event comes burning through the tradition—with the result that the theologians get burned by the powers that be.

3. John D. Caputo, *The Folly of God: A Theology of the Unconditional* (Salem: Polebridge Press, 2016).

4. John D. Caputo, "On Not Settling for an Abridged Edition of Postmodernism: Radical Hermeneutics as Radical Theology," in *Reexamining Deconstruction and Determinate Religion: Toward a Religion with Religion*, ed. J. Aaron Simmons and Stephen Minister (Pittsburgh: Duquesne University Press, 2012), 271–353. Here I respond to a set of critics who, armed with the arguments of Merold Westphal, make similar objections. I think it is less misleading to speak of religion "with/out" religion, both with and without, neither purely with or purely without, a locution possible in the Anglo-Saxon without, but not the Latin French *sans*. Here I follow James Olthuis in *Religion With/out Religion: The Prayers and Tears of John D. Caputo*, ed. James H. Olthuis (London and New York: Routledge, 2001). The "event" is never separable from the concrete historical traditions it inhabits and disturbs. That is also why in *The Insistence of God: A Theology of Perhaps* (Bloomington: Indiana University Press, 2013)—another work Štefan knew was coming but did not see—I developed at great length the "chiasmic" intertwining of

the event, the subject of what I called "radical theology," with the concrete confessional traditions. My version of theology—which, Štefan is right, is more than one—is entirely Christian, not in the sense that it is entirely orthodox, but in the sense that it is entirely a radicalization of the Christian tradition—which is its provenance. A radical theology is always a parasitology, inhabiting the host by which it is nourished. My radical theology is a radical Christianity whose ear is cocked to the insistence of the event harbored in what Jesus called the kingdom of God.

Bibliography

Adams, Douglas. *The Ultimate Hitchhiker's Guide to the Galaxy.* New York: Del Rey, Ballantine Books, 2002.

Agnew, Neil M., and Sandra W. Pyke. *Science Game: Introduction to Research in the Behavioral Sciences.* Englewood Cliffs: Prentice Hall, 1969.

Atlas, James. "The Case of Paul de Man." *New York Times.* August 28, 1988.

Ayto, John. *Word Origins: The Secret Histories of English Words from A to Z.* Second ed. London: A & C Black, 2005.

Bartkowski, Fran. "Rereading Jacques Derrida: Afterwords 2005." *Differences: A Journal of Feminist Cultural Studies* 16, no. 3 (2006): 95–101.

Birch, Nicholas. "7,000 Years Older than Stonehenge: The Site That Stunned Archaeologists." *The Guardian,* April 23, 2008.

Bloom, Alexander. *Prodigal Sons: The New York Intellectuals and Their World.* New York and Oxford: Oxford University Press, 1986.

Borges, Jorge Luis. "Pierre Menard, Author of *Don Quixote.*" In *Cervantes's Don Quixote,* edited by Harold Bloom, 105–112. Bloom's Modern Critical Interpretations. New York: Infobase, 2001.

———. *Seven Nights,* revised ed. Translated by Eliot Weinberger. New York: New Directions, 2009.

Breytenbach, Breyten. "The Long March from Hearth to Heart." *Social Research* 58, no. 1 (1991): 69–83.

Bryson, Bill. *A Short History of Nearly Everything.* New York: Broadway Books, 2003.

Caputo, John D. "Kant's Refutation of the Cosmological Argument." *Journal of the American Academy of Religion* 42, no. 4 (1974): 686–691.

———. "Meister Eckhart and the Later Heidegger: The Mystical Element in Heidegger's Thought Part Two." *Journal of the History of Philosophy* 13, no. 1 (1975): 61–80.

———. *The Mystical Element in Heidegger's Thought.* Athens: Ohio University Press, 1978.

———. *Heidegger and Aquinas: An Essay on Overcoming Metaphysics.* New York: Fordham University Press, 1982.

———. "Hermeneutics as the Recovery of Man." *Man and World* 15 (1982): 343–367.

———. "The Thought of Being and the Conversation of Mankind: The Case of Heidegger and Rorty." *The Review of Metaphysics* 36, no. 3 (1983): 661–685.

———. "'Supposing Truth to Be a Woman . . .': Heidegger, Nietzsche, Derrida." *Tulane Studies in Philosophy* 32 (1984): 15–21.

———. "Three Transgressions: Nietzsche, Heidegger, Derrida." *Research in Phenomenology* 15 (1985): 61–78.

———. "From the Primordiality of Absence to the Absence of Primordiality: Heidegger's Critique of Derrida." In *Hermeneutics and Deconstruction*, edited by Hugh J. Silverman and Don Ihde, 191–200. Albany: State University of New York Press, 1985.

———. "Heidegger and Derrida: Cold Hermeneutics." *Journal of the British Society for Phenomenology* 17 (1986): 252–274.

———. "The Economy of Signs in Husserl and Derrida: From Uselessness to Full Employment." In *Deconstruction and Philosophy: The Texts of Jacques Derrida*, edited by John Sallis, 99–113. Chicago: University of Chicago Press, 1987.

———. "Derrida, a Kind of Philosopher: A Discussion of Recent Literature." *Research in Phenomenology* 17, no. 1 (1987): 245–259.

———. *Radical Hermeneutics: Repetition, Deconstruction, and the Hermeneutic Project.* Bloomington: Indiana University Press, 1987.

———. "Beyond Aestheticism: Derrida's Responsible Anarchy in Continental Philosophy and the Question of Ethics." *Research in Phenomenology* 18 (1988): 59–73.

———. "Demythologizing Heidegger: 'Alētheia' and the History of Being." *The Review of Metaphysics* 41, no. 3 (1988): 519–546.

———. "Mysticism and Transgression: Derrida and Meister Eckhart." In *Derrida and Deconstruction*, edited by Hugh J. Silverman, 24–39. London: Routledge, 1989.

———. "Gadamer's Closet Essentialism: A Derridean Critique." In *Dialogue and Deconstruction: The Gadamer-Derrida Encounter*, edited by Diane P. Michelfelder and Richard E. Palmer, 258–264. Albany: State University of New York Press, 1989.

———. "Heidegger's Scandal: Thinking and the Essence of the Victim." In *The Heidegger Case: On Philosophy and Politics*, edited by Tom Rockmore and Joseph Margolis, 265–281. Philadelphia: Temple University Press, 1992.

———. *Demythologizing Heidegger.* Indiana University Series in the Philosophy of Religion. Bloomington: Indiana University Press, 1993.

———. *Against Ethics: Contributions to a Poetics of Obligation with Constant Reference to Deconstruction.* Studies in Continental Thought. Bloomington: Indiana University Press, 1993.

———. *The Prayers and Tears of Jacques Derrida: Religion Without Religion*. Indiana Series in the Philosophy of Religion. Bloomington: Indiana University Press, 1997.

———. *Deconstruction in a Nutshell: A Conversation with Jacques Derrida*. Perspectives in Continental Philosophy Series. New York: Fordham University Press, 1997.

———. "An American and a Liberal: John D. Caputo's Response to Michael Zimmerman." *Continental Philosophy Review* 31 (1998): 215–220.

———. "Of Mystics, Magi, and Deconstructionists." In *Portraits of American Continental Philosophers*, edited by James R. Watson, 25–34. Bloomington and Indianapolis: Indiana University Press, 1999.

———. "Philosophy and Prophetic Postmodernism: Toward a Catholic Postmodernity." *American Catholic Philosophical Quarterly* 74, no. 4 (2000): 549–567.

———. "Hoping in Hope, Hoping Against Hope: A Response." In *Religion With/out Religion: The Prayers and Tears of John D. Caputo*, edited by James H. Olthuis, 120–149. London and New York: Routledge, 2001.

———. *On Religion*. Thinking in Action Series. London and New York: Routledge, 2001.

———. "What Do I Love When I Love My God? Deconstruction and Radical Orthodoxy." In *Questioning God: Religion and Postmodernism*, edited by John D. Caputo, Mark Dooley, and Michael Scanlon, 291–317. Indiana Series in the Philosophy of Religion. Bloomington, IN: Indiana University Press, 2001.

———. "After Jacques Derrida Comes the Future." *Journal for Cultural and Religious Theory* 4, no. 2 (2003): http://www.jcrt.org/archives/04.2/ caputo.shtml.

———. "Abyssus Abyssum Invocat: A Response to Kearney." In *A Passion for the Impossible: John D. Caputo in Focus*, edited by Mark Dooley, 123–128. SUNY series in Theology and Continental Thought. Albany: State University of New York Press, 2003.

———. "Achieving the Impossible—Rorty's Religion: A Response to Dooley." In *A Passion for the Impossible: John D. Caputo in Focus*, edited by Mark Dooley, 229–236. SUNY series in Theology and Continental Thought. Albany: State University of New York Press, 2003.

———. "Confessions of a Postmodern Catholic: From Saint Thomas to Derrida." In *Faith and the Life of the Intellect*, edited by Curtis L. Hancock and Brendan Sweetman, 64–92. Washington, DC: Catholic University of America Press, 2003.

———. "A Game of Jacks: A Response to Derrida." In *A Passion for the Impossible: John D. Caputo in Focus*, edited by Mark Dooley, 34–50.

SUNY series in Theology and Continental Thought. Albany: State University of New York Press, 2003.

———. "God and Anonymity: Prolegomena to an Ankhoral Religion." In *A Passion for the Impossible: John D. Caputo in Focus*, edited by Mark Dooley, 1–20. SUNY series in Theology and Continental Thought. Albany: State University of New York Press, 2003.

———. "Holding on by Our Teeth: A Response to Putt." In *A Passion for the Impossible: John D. Caputo in Focus*, edited by Mark Dooley, 251–254. SUNY series in Theology and Continental Thought. Albany: State University of New York Press, 2003.

———. "Not in Tongues, but Tongue in Cheek: A Response to Kearns." In *A Passion for the Impossible: John D. Caputo in Focus*, edited by Mark Dooley, 251–254. SUNY series in Theology and Continental Thought. Albany: State University of New York Press, 2003.

———. "'O Felix Culpa,' This Foxy Fellow Felix: A Response to Westphal." In *A Passion for the Impossible: John D. Caputo in Focus*, edited by Mark Dooley, 171–174. SUNY series in Theology and Continental Thought. Albany: State University of New York Press, 2003.

———. "Either-Or, Undecidability, and Two Concepts of Irony: Kierkegaard and Derrida." In *The New Kierkegaard*, edited by Elsebet Jegstrup, 14–41. Bloomington and Indianapolis: Indiana University Press, 2004.

———. *Philosophy and Theology*. Horizons in Theology. Nashville: Abingdon Press, 2006.

———. *The Weakness of God: A Theology of the Event*. Indiana Series in the Philosophy of Religion. Bloomington: Indiana University Press, 2006.

———. *How to Read Kierkegaard*. London: Granta Books, 2007.

———. "Living by Love: A Quasi-Apostolic Carte Postale on Love in Itself, If There Is Such a Thing." In *Transforming Philosophy and Religion: Love's Wisdom*, edited by Norman Wirzba and Bruce Ellis Benson, 103–120. Bloomington: Indiana University Press, 2008.

———. "The Insistence and Existence of God: A Response to DeRoo." In *Cross and Khôra: Deconstruction and Christianity in the Work of John D. Caputo*, edited by Marko Zlomislić and Neal DeRoo, 318–326. Eugene: Wipf and Stock, 2010.

———. "Only as Hauntology Is Religion Without Religion Possible: A Response to Hart." In *Cross and Khôra: Deconstruction and Christianity in the Work of John D. Caputo*, edited by Marko Zlomislić and Neal DeRoo, 109–117. Eugene: Wipf and Stock, 2010.

———. "The Possibility of the Impossible: A Response to Kearney." In *Cross and Khôra: Deconstruction and Christianity in the Work of John D. Caputo*, edited by Marko Zlomislić and Neal DeRoo, 140–150. Eugene: Wipf and Stock, 2010.

———. "Returning Mystical Theology to the Trace: A Response to Carlson." In *Cross and Khôra: Deconstruction and Christianity in the Work of John D. Caputo*, edited by Marko Zlomislić and Neal DeRoo, 165–173.Eugene: Wipf and Stock, 2010.

———. "The Weakness of God and the Iconic Logic of the Cross." In *Cross and Khôra: Deconstruction and Christianity in the Work of John D. Caputo*, edited by Marko Zlomislić and Neal DeRoo, 15–36. Eugene: Wipf and Stock, 2010.

———. "The Sense of God: A Theology of the Event with Special Reference to Christianity," Lecture given at KU Leuven on March 19, 2008. In *Between Philosophy and Theology: Contemporary Interpretations of Christianity*, edited by Lieven Boeve and Christophe Brabant, 27–42. Farnham: Ashgate, 2010.

———. "The Return of Anti-Religion: From Radical Atheism to Radical Theology." *Journal for Cultural and Religious Theory* 11, no. 2 (2011): 32–125.

———. *The Insistence of God: A Theology of Perhaps.* Indiana Series in the Philosophy of Religion. Bloomington: Indiana University Press, 2013.

———. *Hoping Against Hope: Confessions of a Postmodern Pilgrim.* Minneapolis: Fortress Press, 2015.

Caputo, John D., and Emmet Cole. "Emmet Cole Interviews John D. Caputo." http://www.themodernword.com/features/interview_caputo.html. Accessed December 6, 2010.

Caputo, John D., and B. Keith Putt. "What Do I Love When I Love My God? An Interview with John D. Caputo." In *Religion With/out Religion: The Prayers and Tears of John D. Caputo*, edited by James H. Olthuis, 150–180. London and New York: Routledge, 2001.

Caputo, John D., and Carl Raschke. "Loosening Philosophy's Tongue: A Conversation with Jack Caputo." *Journal for Cultural and Religious Theory* 3, no. 2 (2002): www.jcrt.org/archives/03.2/caputo_raschke.shtml.

Caputo, John D., and Michael J Scanlon, eds. *Transcendence and Beyond: A Postmodern Inquiry.* Indiana Series in the Philosophy of Religion. Bloomington: Indiana University Press, 2007.

Caputo, John D., and Gianni Vattimo. *After the Death of God.* Edited by Jeffrey W. Robbins. New York: Columbia University Press, 2007.

———. "The Power of the Powerless: Dialogue with John D. Caputo." In *After the Death of God*, edited by Jeffrey W. Robbins, 114–162. New York: Columbia University Press, 2007.

Caputo, John D., and T. Wilson Dickinson. "Education as Event: A Conversation with John D. Caputo." *Journal for Cultural and Religious Theory* 12, no. 2 (2012): 25–46.

Caputo, John D., and Mark Yount, eds. *Foucault and the Critique of Institutions.* Studies of the Greater Philadelphia Philosophy

Consortium. University Park: Pennsylvania State University Press, 1993.

Carlson, Thomas A. "Negative Theology and Deconstructive Ethics: Caputo's Reading of the Mystical." In *Cross and Khôra: Deconstruction and Christianity in the Work of John D. Caputo*, edited by Marko Zlomislić and Neal DeRoo, 151–164. Eugene: Wipf and Stock, 2010.

Carroll, Sean M. *From Eternity to Here: The Quest for the Ultimate Theory of Time*. New York: Dutton, 2010.

Chargaff, Erwin. *Voices in the Labyrinth: Nature, Man, and Science*. New York: Seabury Press, 1977.

Clarke, W. Norris. "Reflections on Caputo's Heidegger and Aquinas." In *A Passion for the Impossible: John D. Caputo in Focus*, edited by Mark Dooley, 51–68. SUNY series in Theology and Continental Thought. Albany: State University of New York Press, 2003.

Cohen, Martin. *Philosophical Tales: Being an Alternative History Revealing the Characters, the Plots, and the Hidden Scenes That Make Up the True Story of Philosophy*. Illustrated by Raul Gonzales. Malden: Blackwell, 2008.

Crick, Francis. *What Mad Pursuit: A Personal View of Scientific Discovery*. Illustrated ed. Alfred P. Sloan Foundation series. New York: Basic Books, 1988.

Cumming, Robert Denoon. "The Odd Couple: Heidegger and Derrida." *The Review of Metaphysics* 34, no. 3 (1981): 487–521.

Derrida, Jacques. "The Ends of Man." *Philosophy and Phenomenological Research* 30, no. 1 (1969): 31–57.

———. "The Principle of Reason: The University in the Eyes of Its Pupils." *Diacritics* 13, no. 3 (1983): 2–20.

———. *The Postcard: From Socrates to Freud and Beyond*. Translated by Alan Bass. Chicago and London: University of Chicago Press, 1987.

———. "Like the Sound of the Sea Deep within a Shell: Paul De Man's War." *Critical Inquiry* 14, no. 3 (1988): 590–652.

———. *Memoires: For Paul de Man*. Revised ed. Translated by Cecile Lindsay, Jonathan Culler, Eduardo Cadava, and Peggy Kamuf. The Wellek Library Lectures at the University of California, Irvine. New York: Columbia University Press, 1989.

———. "Circumfession: Fifty-Nine Periods and Periphrases Written in a Sort of Internal Margin, Between Geoffrey Bennington's Book and Work in Preparation (January 1989–April 1990)." In *Jacques Derrida*. Translated by Geoffrey Bennington. Chicago and London: University of Chicago Press, 1993.

———. *Specters of Marx: The State of the Debt, the Work of Mourning and the New International*. Translated by Peggy Kamuf. New York and London: Routledge, 1994.

———. "Between Brackets I." In *Points . . . Interviews, 1974–1994*, edited by Elisabeth Weber, translated by Peggy Kamuf, 5–29. Stanford: Stanford University Press, 1995.

———. "Honoris Causa: «This Is Also Extremely Funny»." In *Points . . . Interviews, 1974–1994*, edited by Elisabeth Weber, translated by Peggy Kamuf, 399–421. Stanford: Stanford University Press, 1995.

———. "Ja, or the Faux-bond II." In *Points . . . Interviews, 1974–1994*, edited by Elisabeth Weber, translated by Peggy Kamuf, 30–77. Stanford: Stanford University Press, 1995.

———. "Passages—From Traumatism to Promise." In *Points . . . Interviews, 1974–1994*, edited by Elisabeth Weber, translated by Peggy Kamuf, 372–398. Stanford: Stanford University Press, 1995.

———. "'I Have a Taste for the Secret.'" In *A Taste for the Secret*, edited by Giacomo Donis and David Webb, translated by Giacomo Donis, 1–92. Cambridge: Polity Press, 2001.

———. "In Memoriam: Of the Soul." In *The Work of Mourning*, edited by Pascale-Anne Brault and Michael Naas, 9–76. Chicago and London: University of Chicago Press, 2001.

———. *Acts of Religion.* Edited by Gil Anidjar. London and New York: Routledge, 2002.

———. "Faith and Knowledge: The Two Sources of 'Religion' at the Limits of Reason Alone." In *Acts of Religion.* Edited by Gil Anidjar. London and New York: Routledge, 2002.

———. "The Last Interview." *SV (Studio Visit).* November 2004.

Derrida, Jacques, and Michal Ben-Naftali. "An Interview with Professor Jacques Derrida." January 8, 1998. Jerusalem: SHOAH Resource Center. www. yadvashem.org.

Derrida, Jacques, and Didier Cahen. "There Is No One Narcissism (Autobiographies)." In *Points . . . Interviews, 1974–1994*, edited by Elisabeth Weber, translated by Peggy Kamuf, 196–215. Stanford: Stanford University Press, 1995.

Derrida, Jacques, Deborah Esch, and Tom Keenan. "Negotiations." In *Negotiations: Interventions and Interviews, 1971–2001.* Translated by Elizabeth Rottenberg. Stanford: Stanford University Press, 2002.

Derrida, Jacques, and Peggy Kamuf. "The Work of Intellectuals and the Press." In *Points . . . Interviews, 1974–1994*, edited by Elisabeth Weber, translated by Peggy Kamuf, 422–456. Stanford: Stanford University Press, 1995.

Derrida, Jacques, and Catherine Malabou. *Counterpath: Traveling with Jacques Derrida.* Translated by David Wills. Cultural Memory in the Present Series. Stanford: Stanford University Press, 2004.

Derrida, Jacques, and Kristine McKenna. "The Three Ages of Jacques Derrida: An Interview with the Father of Deconstructionism." *LA Weekly.* November 6, 2002.

Desmond, William. *Is There a Sabbath for Thought? Between Religion and Philosophy.* New York: Fordham University Press, 2005.

Dobie, J. Frank. *A Texan in England.* New York: Little, Brown and Company, 1944.

Dooley, Mark, and Jacques Derrida. "The Becoming Possible of the Impossible: An Interview with Jacques Derrida." In *A Passion for the Impossible: John D. Caputo in Focus,* edited by Mark Dooley, 21–33. SUNY series in Theology and Continental Thought. Albany: State University of New York Press, 2003.

Dottin, Georges. *La langue Gauloise: grammaire, textes et glossaire.* Paris: C. Klincksieck, 1920.

Einstein, Albert. *The Collected Papers of Albert Einstein: The Early Years, 1879–1902.* English translation ed. Translated by Anna Beck. Princeton: Princeton University Press, 1987.

Foucault, Michel. *Discipline and Punish: The Birth of the Prison.* Second ed. Translated by Alan Sheridan. New York: Random House, 1995.

Gelernter, David. "Study Talmud." In *How Things Are: A Science Tool-Kit for the Mind,* edited by John Brockman and Katinka Matson, 211–219. New York: W. Morrow, 1995.

Godzieba, Anthony J. "Ontotheology to Excess: Imagining God Without Being." *Theological Studies* 56 (1995): 1–20.

———. "Prolegomena to a Catholic Theology of God Between Heidegger and Postmodernity." *The Heythrop Journal* 40 (1999): 319–339.

Goethe, Johann Wolfgang von. *West-Eastern Divan.* Translated by Edward Dowden. London and Toronto: J. M. Dent & Sons, 1914.

Hart, Kevin. "The Kingdom and the Trinity." In *Religious Experience and the End of Metaphysics,* edited by Jeffrey Bloechl, 153–173. Indiana Series in the Philosophy of Religion. Bloomington and Indianapolis: Indiana University Press, 2003.

———. "Without." In *Cross and Khôra: Deconstruction and Christianity in the Work of John D. Caputo,* edited by Marko Zlomislić and Neal DeRoo, 80–108. Eugene: Wipf and Stock, 2010.

Heidegger, Martin. *Parmenides.* Translated by André Schuwer and Richard Rojcewicz. Bloomington and Indianapolis: Indiana University Press, 1992.

———. *The Principle of Reason.* Translated by Reginald Lilly. Studies in Continental Thought. Bloomington, IN: Indiana University Press, 1996.

———"Only a God Can Save Us: *Der Spiegel*'s Interview with Martin Heidegger (September 23, 1966)." In *Philosophical and Political Writings,* edited by Manfred Stassen, translated by Maria P. Alter and John D. Caputo, 24–48. The German Library Series 76. London and New York: Continuum, 2003.

———. "Why Do I Stay in the Provinces? (1934)." In *Philosophical and Political Writings,* edited by Manfred Stassen, 16–18. The German Library Series 76. London and New York: Continuum, 2003.

Heltzel, Peter Goodwin. "The Weakness of God (Review)." *Journal for Cultural and Religious Theory* 7, no. 2 (2006): 96–101.

Holdheim, W. Wolfgang. "Jacques Derrida's Apologia." *Critical Inquiry* 15, no. 4 (1989): 784–796.

Jacoby, Russell. *The Last Intellectuals: American Culture in the Age of Academe.* Second edition with a new introduction by the author. New York: Basic Books, 2000.

Jaspers, Karl. "Letter to the Freiburg University Denazification Committee (December 22, 1945)." In *The Heidegger Controversy: A Critical Reader*, edited and translated by Richard Wolin, 144–151. Cambridge, MA, and London: MIT Press, 1993.

Joffe, Josef. "The Decline of the Public Intellectual and the Rise of the Pundit." In *The Public Intellectual: Between Philosophy and Politics*, edited by Arthur M. Melzer, Jerry Weinberger, and M. Richard Zinman, 109–129. Lanham: Rowman & Littlefield, 2003.

Kandell, Jonathan. "Jacques Derrida, Abstruse Theorist, Dies at 74." *New York Times.* October 10, 2004.

Kearns, Cleo McNelly. "The Prayers and Tears of Jacques Derrida: Esoteric Comedy and the Poetics of Obligation." In *A Passion for the Impossible: John D. Caputo in Focus*, edited by Mark Dooley, 283–294. SUNY series in Theology and Continental Thought. Albany: State University of New York Press, 2003.

Kierkegaard, Søren. *Fear and Trembling.* Translated by Howard V. Hong and Edna H. Hong. Princeton: Princeton University Press, 1983.

———. *Either/Or: Part 1.* Edited and translated by Howard V. Hong and Edna H. Hong. Kierkegaard's Writings 3. Princeton: Princeton University Press, 1987.

———. *Concluding Unscientific Postscript to the Philosophical Crumbs.* Edited and translated by Alastair Hannay. Cambridge Texts in the History of Philosophy. Cambridge: Cambridge University Press, 2009.

Kirshner, Robert P. "Exploding Stars and the Expanding Universe (The 1990 Grubb Parsons Lecture)." *Quarterly Journal of the Royal Astronomical Society* 32, no. 3 (1991): 233–244.

Krauss, Lawrence Maxwell. *A Universe from Nothing: Why There Is Something Rather than Nothing.* New York: Free Press, 2012.

Kundera, Milan. *The Unbearable Lightness of Being.* Translated by Michael Henry Heim. New York: Harper Perennial, 1999.

Leask, Ian, ed. "From Radical Hermeneutics to the Weakness of God: John D. Caputo in Dialogue with Mark Dooley." *Philosophy Today* 51, no. 2 (2007): 216–226.

Levinas, Emmanuel. *Totality and Infinity: An Essay on Exteriority.* 4th, revised, reprint ed. Translated by Alphonso Lingis. The Hague: Martinus Nijhoff, 1979.

Mackey, Louis. *Kierkegaard: A Kind of Poet.* Philadelphia: University of Pennsylvania Press, 1971.

Madison, G. B. "On What It Means to Be Responsible: A Hermeneutical-Confucian Response to Caputo/Derrida." In *Cross and Khôra: Deconstruction and Christianity in the Work of John D. Caputo*, edited by Marko Zlomislić and Neal DeRoo, 282–295. Eugene: Wipf and Stock, 2010.

McQuillan, Martin. "'Another Death' Jacques Derrida (1930-2004)." *Parallax* 11, no. 1 (2005): 79–87.

———. *Paul De Man*. Routledge Critical Thinkers series. London and New York: Routledge, 2001.

Mikics, David. *Who Was Jacques Derrida? An Intellectual Biography*. New Haven and London: Yale University Press, 2009.

Miller, J. Hillis. *The J. Hillis Miller Reader*. Edited by Julian Wolfreys. Stanford: Stanford University Press, 2005.

Nietzsche, Friedrich. *The Will to Power*. Edited by Walter Kaufmann. Translated by Walter Kaufmann and R. J. Hollingdale. New York: Random House, 1968.

———. *Ecce Homo*. Edited and translated by Walter Kaufmann. New York: Random House, 1989.

———. *On the Genealogy of Morals*. Edited by Walter Kaufmann. Translated by Walter Kaufmann and R. J. Hollingdale. New York: Random House, 1989.

———. *Daybreak: Thoughts on the Prejudices of Morality*. Edited by Maudemarie Clark and Brian Leiter. Translated by R. J. Hollingdale. Cambridge Texts in the History of Philosophy. Cambridge: Cambridge University Press, 1997.

———. "The Birth of Tragedy." In *The Birth of Tragedy and Other Writings*. Edited by Raymond Geuss and Ronald Speirs. Translated by Ronald Speirs. Cambridge Texts in the History of Philosophy. Cambridge: Cambridge University Press, 1999.

———. "On Truth and Lying in a Non-Moral Sense." In *The Birth of Tragedy and Other Writings*. Edited by Raymond Geuss and Ronald Speirs. Translated by Ronald Speirs. Cambridge Texts in the History of Philosophy. Cambridge: Cambridge University press, 1999.

———. *Beyond Good and Evil: Prelude to a Philosophy of the Future*. Edited by Rolf-Peter Horstmann and Judith Norman. Translated by Judith Norman. Cambridge Texts in the History of Philosophy. Cambridge: Cambridge University Press, 2002.

———. *Thus Spoke Zarathustra*. Edited by Adrian Del Caro and Robert B. Pippin. Translated by Adrian Del Caro. Cambridge Texts in the History of Philosophy. Cambridge: Cambridge University Press, 2006.

Olthuis, James H., ed. *Religion With/out Religion: The Prayers and Tears of John D. Caputo*. London and New York: Routledge, 2001.

———. "The Test of Khôra: Grâce À Dieu." In *Religion With/out Religion: The Prayers and Tears of John D. Caputo*, edited by James H. Olthuis, 110–119. London and New York: Routledge, 2001.

Peeters, Benoît. *Derrida: A Biography*. Translated by Andrew Brown. London: Polity, 2012.

Pieper, Josef. *The Silence of S. Thomas: Three Essays*. Translated by John Murray and Daniel O'Connor. New York: Pantheon, 1957.

Putt, B. Keith. "The Im/Possibility of a Passionate God: A Postconservative Mani(n)festation of Caputo's Kingdom Christology." *Perspectives in Religious Studies* 24 (1997): 447–468.

———. "Faith, Hope, and Love: Radical Hermeneutics as a Pauline Philosophy of Religion." In *A Passion for the Impossible: John D. Caputo in Focus*, edited by Mark Dooley, 237–250. SUNY series in Theology and Continental Thought. Albany: State University of New York Press, 2003.

———. "Reconciling Pure Forgiveness and Reconciliation: Bringing John Caputo into the Kingdom of God." *Crosscurrents* 59, no. 4 (2009): 500–531.

Ray, Gordon N., ed. *Professional Standards and American Editions: A Response to Edmund Wilson*. New York: Modern Language Association, 1969.

Roudinesco, Elisabeth. *Philosophy in Turbulent Times: Canguilhem, Sartre, Foucault, Althusser, Deleuze, Derrida*. Translated by William McCuaig. New York: Columbia University Press, 2008.

Rowland, Helen. *A Guide to Men: Being Encore Reflections of a Bachelor Girl*. New York: Dodge, 1922.

Saint-Exupéry, Antoine de. *The Wisdom of the Sands*. (Citadelle). Translated by Stuart Gilbert. London: Hollis & Carter, 1952.

———. *Wind, Sand and Stars*. Published as part of the Airman's Odyssey trilogy. Translated by Lewis Galantiere. Orlando: Harcourt, 1984.

———. *Citadelle*. Édition abrégée établie et préfacée par Michel Quesnel ed. Paris: Gallimard, 2000.

Schiff, Stacy. *Saint-Exupéry: A Biography*. A Holt Paperback. New York: Henry Holt and Company, 2006.

Sharr, Adam. *Heidegger's Hut*. Photography by Digne Meller-Marcovicz. Cambridge, MA, and London: MIT Press, 2006.

Simpson, Christopher Ben. *Religion, Metaphysics, and the Postmodern: William Desmond and John D. Caputo*. Bloomington: Indiana University Press, 2009.

Smith, James K. A. "Is Deconstruction an Augustinian Science? Augustine, Derrida, and Caputo on the Commitments of Philosophy." In *Religion With/out Religion: The Prayers and Tears of John D. Caputo*, edited by James H. Olthuis, 50–61. London and New York: Routledge, 2001.

Solomon, Maynard. *Beethoven*. Paperback ed. New York: Schirmer Books, 1979.

Stauffer, Jill. "The Imperfect: Levinas, Nietzsche, and the Autonomous Subject." In *Nietzsche and Levinas: "After the Death of a Certain God,"* edited by Jill Stauffer and Bettina Bergo, 33–47. New York: Columbia University Press, 2009.

Štofaník, Štefan. "Introduction to the Thinking of John Caputo: Religion Without Religion Is the Way Out of Religion." In *Between Philosophy and Theology: Contemporary Interpretations of Christianity*, edited by Lieven Boeve and Christophe Brabant, 19–26. Ashgate, 2010.

Weaver, Jefferson Hane, Lloyd Motz, and Dale McAdoo. *The World of Physics: A Small Library of the Literature of Physics from Antiquity to the Present.* New York: Simon and Schuster, 1987.

Westphal, Merold. "Postmodernism and Ethics: The Case of Caputo." In *A Passion for the Impossible: John D. Caputo in Focus*, edited by Mark Dooley, 153–170. SUNY series in Theology and Continental Thought. Albany: State University of New York Press, 2003.

Williams, James. *Gilles Deleuze's Logic of Sense: A Critical Introduction and Guide.* Edinburgh: Edinburgh University Press, 2008.

Zimmerman, Michael E. "John D. Caputo: A Postmodern, Prophetic, Liberal American in Paris." *Continental Philosophy Review* 31, no. 2 (1998): 195–214.

Zinn, Grover A. "Review of Maria Shrady 'Angelus Silesius: The Cherubic Wanderer.'" *Church History* 59, no. 03 (1990): 406–407.

Zlomislić, Marko. "Powell, Jason, Jacques Derrida: A Biography." *Kritike* 2, no. 1 (2008): 145–148.

Index

Abraham (Hebrew patriarch), 50, 77, 164, 199; anxiety of, 120, 200; Zarathustra and, 165, 168
abyss, 9–10, 86–88, 165, 215; freedom and, 119–21; Nietzsche on, 88, 102, 104, 169
Adams, Douglas, 12, 103, 114, 155–56, 192–93
aestheticism, 34, 134–35, 151; Derrida and, 75, 77–78, 120, 126, 135; Kierkegaard and, 77, 125, 135, 136; orthodoxy and, 46
aion, 31, 48, 81. *See also* time
alētheia (truth as unconcealment), 134–35, 137–38, 146
Alter, Maria, 128
Amos (biblical prophet), 74
anarchy, 73; responsible, 135, 138, 151; sacred, 99, 174
Anselm of Canterbury, Saint, 23
Aquinas, Thomas. *See* Thomas Aquinas, Saint
Aristotle, 138
atheism, 99; Derrida on, 75, 147, 176; Hägglund on, 8; Heidegger on, 54
Atlas, James, 208
Atwood, Margaret, 176–77
Augustine of Hippo, Saint, 105, 169; Aquinas and, 23; *Confessiones*, 22
autonomy, 73–74, 102. *See also* freedom

Barth, Karl, 168, 210
Bartkowski, Fran, 203
"basileology," 8
Bates, Marston, 11
Beethoven, Ludwig van, 213–15, 217, 218, 223
Benjamin, Walter, 7
Ben-Naftali, Michal, 209
Bennington, Geoffrey, 202
Bloom, Alexander, xiii
Boeve, Lieven, ix–xi, 13–14, 77, 237
Borges, Jorge Luis, 55, 82–84, 88
Braig, Carl, 34–35
Breytenbach, Breyten, 156–57
Brothers of the Christian Schools, 34, 38, 108, 128, 179
Brown, Dan, 25, 26
Bryson, Bill, 113
Bultmann, Rudolf, 142–43, 190

calling, 28–32, 100, 105, 107
Campbell, Joseph, 107, 109
Camus, Albert, 168
Canetti, Elias, 100
Caputo, John D., 2–5; afterword by, 231–37; early years of, 33–38; festschrift for, 158; literary voice of, 2–3, 156, 223–24; as novitiate, 33–38, 49, 98, 108–9, 179, 233; writing style of, 24–26, 34, 223
Caputo, John D., works of: *Against Ethics*, 86, 102–3, 109, 131, 152–53, 161–66, 169; *Heidegger and Aquinas*, 63, 116; *Hoping Against Hope*, xv, 233; *The Mystical Element in Heidegger's Thought*, 37, 58, 62–64, 116;

Caputo, John D., works of *(continued)*: *The Prayers and Tears of Jacques Derrida*, 11, 78, 144–45, 153, 191, 201–2; *Radical Hermeneutics*, 58, 117–18, 135, 150, 152, 233. *See also The Weakness of God*
Carlson, Thomas A., 64–65
Cervantes, Miguel de, 82–84, 88
Cézanne, Paul, 140
Clarke, W. Norris, 37, 63
Coelho, Paulo, 69, 93
Cole, Emmet, 153, 174
Columbus, Christopher, 217–18
Crick, Francis, 11
critical consciousness, 76–77
Crossan, John Dominic, 191
Cumming, Robert, 119, 132
Daurat, Didier, 68, 114
de Graef, Ortwin, 204
de Man, Paul, xviii, 131–32, 203–8, 222, 224
Deleuze, Gilles, 4; on events, 29, 30; Nietzsche and, 102, 103, 105; on time, 32, 81
Denzinger, Henry, 194
Derrida, Jacques, 75, 102–3, 150–54; aestheticism and, 75, 77–78, 120, 126, 135; Cambridge's honorary degree to, 42–43, 226; on de Man, 203–8; film about, 13; Heidegger and, 3–4, 52–53, 115–18, 124–27, 140, 145–46, 150–51, 200; *khora* of, 86–87, 95–96; Kierkegaard and, 75, 117, 133, 136–37, 152; Nazi Germany and, 132; Nietzsche and, 123, 127–30, 151–52; as "prophetic" thinker, 74; on religion without religion, 7, 75, 97, 202, 228; on revolutionary pathos, 222; Rousseau and, 151–52
Desmond, William, 23, 173
"destinerrance," 48, 64, 187
Dickinson, T. Wilson, 179, 180
Dooley, Mark, 3, 108–9, 228
Eckhart, Meister, 3, 35, 55, 86–88, 151; Aquinas and, 63, 65, 116; Heidegger and, 61–64, 86, 87; prayer of, 98
Einstein, Albert, 198, 215
Emerson, Ralph Waldo, 220
Enlightenment philosophy, 50, 51, 73–76, 101; modernity and, 36, 42; religion and, 143, 144, 190–92, 194
Evans, C. Stephens, 175

faith, 8–11, 141–47, 195, 215; confession of, 22; "gift" of, 235–37; Kierkegaard's leap of, 37, 75, 105, 166, 199; Maritain on, 49; postmodern, 147, 157; as radical hermeneutics, 165; reason and, 35, 50, 51, 54
Farias, Victor, 59
Foucault, Michel, 34, 42, 179
freedom, 67–74, 91–110; abyss and, 119–20; autonomy and, 73–74, 102; to be unfree, 73; from choice, 77; Levinas on, 101–2, 108; Nietzsche on, 101, 110; from religion, 106; responsibility and, 71–72, 102
fundamentalism, 44–45, 107, 144, 175

Gadamer, Hans-Georg, 122, 136
Gasché, Rodolphe, 133–34
Gelassenheit ("letting-be"), 59–65, 130, 136–38, 151, 181, 200; Derrida and, 126, 128; stillness of, 124
Gelernter, David, 13
genealogical method, 79
Gide, André, 152
Girard, René, 131
Göbekli Tepe (archaeological site), 12–13
Goethe, Johann Wolfgang von, 100

Hägglund, Martin, 8
Hart, Kevin, 143–44, 146, 190, 191, 194
Hartman, Geoffrey, 205
Harvey, Irene E., 133

Haydn, Joseph, 214–15, 217, 221, 223
Hegel, G. W. F., 42, 79, 177, 183, 236
Heidegger, Martin, 52–61, 209; abyss of, 86, 87; Aquinas and, 61–63, 116, 129; on being-in-the-world, 53; Braig and, 34–35; critique of modernity by, 54–56; demythologizing of, xvii, 142–43, 145–46; Derrida and, 3–4, 52–53, 115–18, 124–27, 140, 145–46, 200; Eckhart and, 61–64, 86, 87; humorlessness of, 150; Kierkegaard and, 105, 116–19, 149–50, 168; Nazi Germany and, 132, 138, 149; Nietzsche and, 123, 130; Rorty and, 121, 123; on Silesius, 55–58, 62; "system" of, xviii; Todtnauberg cabin of, 147–48; on typewriters, 147–48
Heidegger, Martin, works of: *Being and Time*, 118–19, 139, 149–50, 168; *The Principle of Reason*, 52, 56–58
Helmling, Steve, 223
Heltzel, Peter Goodwin, 175, 193
hermeneutics, 118, 122–23, 135. *See also* radical hermeneutics
heteronomism, 102, 108
Hitchhiker's Guide to the Galaxy (Adams), 12, 103, 114, 155–56, 192–93
Holdheim, Wolfgang, 223
Holocaust, 80–81
Homer, 93, 101
Hume, David, 190
Husserl, Edmund, 117–19, 134, 141, 200

impiety, 104
individualization, 72
irony, 47–48, 77–78, 98, 130, 188
irreverence, 79

Jacoby, Russell, 212, 220–21
James, William, 25, 83
Jaspers, Karl, 138
John of the Cross, Saint, 47

Kant, Immanuel, 51, 106, 190–91; Anselm and, 23; Aquinas and, 36; Hegel and, 36; Levinas and, 143
Kearns, Cleo McNelly, 34, 158, 223, 225, 228–29
Keenan, Tom, 211
Kehre ("turn"), 23–24, 131, 133, 140
Keller, Catherine, 173, 175
kenotic theology, 175
khora, 86–87, 95–96, 144, 178
Kierkegaard, Søren, 3–4, 14, 25, 104; aestheticism and, 77, 125, 135, 136; Aquinas and, 37, 49–52, 116; Caputo's discovery of, 34–35; Derrida and, 75, 117, 133, 136–37, 152; on existential repetition, 118–20; Hegel and, 42; Heidegger and, 105, 116–19, 149–50, 167; on humor, 152; irony of, 130; Nietzsche and, 104–6, 168; pseudonyms of, 167, 170, 199; Putt on, 194–95; reductionism and, 122
Kierkegaard, Søren, works of: *Concluding Unscientific Postscript to the Philosophical Crumbs*, 50, 167; *Either/Or*, 136, 159–71, 167, 168; *Fear and Trembling*, 152
kingdom of God, 142, 270n4; theology of the event and, 52, 56–57, 183–84; Trinity and, 194
Kirshner, Robert, 1
Krauss, Lawrence M., 99, 250n30
Kuhn, Thomas, 25
Kundera, Milan, 80–81

La Salle, Jean-Baptiste de, Saint, 34
Leibniz, Wilhelm Gottfried: principle of sufficient reason of, 56
Levinas, Emmanuel, 4, 9, 73, 86, 225; on freedom, 101–2, 108; Kant and, 143; as "prophetic" thinker, 74

Llewelyn, John, 133, 134
Lyotard, Jean-François, xvi, 131

Mackey, Louis, 133
Madison, Gary Brent, 106–7, 110
Maritain, Jacques, 3, 35, 49, 51–52, 233
Marlowe, Christopher, 112
McKenna, Kristine, 203
McQuillan, Martin, 203–5
melancholy, 34, 50, 215, 224; music and, 215; "Slavonic," x, xiv, 221–22
Melville, Herman, 2
messianism, 95, 107, 144
Metz, Johann Baptist, x
Milbank, John, 46
Miller, Joseph Hillis, 205
Moltmann, Jürgen, 175
Mozart, Wolfgang Amadeus, 214–15, 217–18, 221, 223
Mumford, Lewis, 219–20
music, 213–18, 221, 223
mysticism, 55–64; Aquinas and, 36–37; Maritain and, 49, 51

names, 71–73, 153, 167, 170, 227–28, 248n19
Neoplatonism, 186
Neusner, Jacob, 205
Nietzsche, Friedrich, xvi–xvii, 9–10, 165–66, 227; on the abyss, 88, 102, 104, 169; Deleuze and, 102, 103, 105; Derrida and, 123, 127–30, 151–52; on eternal return, 80, 81; on freedom, 101, 110; Heidegger and, 123, 130; Kierkegaard and, 104–6, 168; on slavery, 100; on will to power, 163
nostalgia, 88, 120

Occam, William of, 40
Olthuis, James H., works of, 178, 269n4; *Religion With/out Religion*, 14
"onto-theo-logic," 54, 63, 73
orthotes (truth as correct assertions), 138
Orwell, George, 131
Ott, Hugo, 59

Pascal, Blaise, 40–42
Paul, Saint (the apostle), 98, 105, 115, 195–96, 234
Paul of the Cross, Saint, 47
Pinnock, Clark, 175
Plato, 28–29, 41, 124–25, 138, 186
Plotinus, 63
Poole, Robert, 170
Putt, Keith, 2, 43, 116, 169, 175–77, 190–91
Pyke, Sandra, xiii

Quine, Willard Van Orman, 134
quotidianism, 61, 100, 105, 225

radical hermeneutics: faith as, 165; Nietzsche and, 169, 227; point of view in, 44
Radical Hermeneutics (Caputo), 58, 117–18, 135, 150, 152, 233
radical orthodoxy, 15, 44–47, 175
radical theology, 99, 269n4
Rasmussen, Joel, 170
Reagan, Ronald, 127
religion without religion, xviii, 95–96, 106, 189–90, 269n4; advantages of, 101; Derrida on, 7, 75, 97, 202, 225; faith and, 143–44; future of, 98–99
responsibility, 135, 138, 151; freedom and, 71–72, 102; obligation and, 225–28; Saint-Exupéry on, 224
Ricoeur, Paul, 136
Robbins, Jeffrey, 109, 175
Rorty, Richard, 25, 120, 124, 200; Heidegger and, 121, 123
Roudinesco, Elisabeth, 221, 227
Rousseau, Jean-Jacques, 151–52

Rousselot, Pierre, 3, 51–52, 233
Rowland, Helen, 103

Sagan, Carl, 89–90
Saint-Exupéry, Antoine de, x–xi, xv, 27–29, 114, 224; as airmail pilot, 67–68; on desire, 44–45; full name of, 68; on loneliness, 183; on mountain climbing, 21–22; on poetry, 21; on silence of God, 1, 9; on simplicity, 198
Saint-Exupéry, Antoine de, works of: *Citadelle*, 27–28, 39–45, 155, 199; *The Little Prince*, 5, 68; *Wind, Sand and Stars*, 67, 91–96, 101; *The Wisdom of the Sands*, 1, 29–30, 99–100, 155, 183, 197–98, 229
saints, xix, 10, 47
Sartre, Jean-Paul, 72, 168
Scheffler, Johannes. *See* Silesius, Angelus
Schiff, Stacy, 68, 70, 248n1
Schmidt, Klaus, 12
Schmitt, Carl, 209
Schrijvers, Joeri, xv–xx, 237
Seinsverlassenheit (abandoned by Being), 131, 149
Shakespeare, William, 112
Silentio, Johannes de, 104
Silesius, Angelus, 3, 35, 55–58, 61–62, 116
Simpson, Christopher Ben, 173
slavery, 67, 69–72, 100
Smith, James K. A., 164–65, 168, 169
Solomon, Maynard, 214
Sorge ("worry"), 5, 105, 109
Strauss, David, 190
strong theology, xvi, 145; at seminaries, xviii; weak theology versus, 7–8, 77, 97–98, 187–88
Swinburne, Richard, 36

Tauler, Johann, 62
Teresa of Calcutta, Saint, 10, 47
Tertullian, 216
theology: credibility of, 19–20, 46; critically conscious, 76–77; definition of, 7; of interruption, 77; of interruption, 77; jargon of, 24–26; kenotic, 175; radical, 99, 269n4; sovereign, 19; without theology, 7, 97
theology of the event, 20–24, 31, 76–77, 145, 176; contingency of, 183–84; fundamentalism and, 45; kingdom of God and, 52, 56–57, 183–84; point of view in, 44; recontexualizing of, 78
Thérèse of Lisieux, Saint, 47
Thomas Aquinas, Saint, 3; Augustine and, 23; Caputo's discovery of, 35–36; Eckhart and, 63, 65, 116; Heidegger and, 61–63, 116, 129; Kant and, 36; Kierkegaard and, 37, 49–52, 116; Maritain and, 49, 51–52; mystical experience of, 36–37; *Summa Theologica*, 22–23
Tillich, Paul, 236
time, 10–11, 48; boredom and, 100; Deleuze on, 31, 81
transgression, 39–48, 55, 88; directionless, 47
Trinity, 193–95, 219
Twain, Mark, 220
typewriters, 147–49

Vattimo, Gianni, 7

weak theology, xvii, 100–101, 173–81; definitions of, 6–7; elements of, 8; future of, 183; historians of, 78–79; lostness of, 186–88, 192; origin of, 6; orthodoxy versus, 46; poetics of, 146; promise of, 98; "secret" of, 76; strong theology versus, 7–8, 77, 97–98, 187–88
The Weakness of God (Caputo), xvii, 6, 141, 145, 173–81;

The Weakness of God (Caputo) (*continued*) concluding prayer in, 97–98, 184, 187; Deleuze and, 30; Heidegger and, 58; time in, 10–11
Westphal, Merold, 164, 166, 168, 269n4
whistle-blowers, 85
Williams, James, 32
Wilson, Edmund, 220–21
Wittgenstein, Ludwig, 79, 132, 134, 224

Zimmerman, Michael, 2–3, 149, 150
Zinn, Grover, 62
Zlomislić, Marko, 203

www.ingramcontent.com/pod-product-compliance
Lightning Source LLC
LaVergne TN
LVHW050149080826
844660LV00002B/127

* 9 7 8 1 4 3 8 4 7 1 9 5 2 *